The Pinkster King
•• and the ••
King of Kongo

The Pinkster King
•• and the ••
King of Kongo

THE FORGOTTEN HISTORY OF
AMERICA'S DUTCH-OWNED SLAVES

Jeroen Dewulf

University Press of Mississippi / Jackson

The manuscript for this book was the winner of the University of California, Berkeley Institute of International Studies Robert O. Collins Award in African Studies, the New Netherland Institute Hendricks Award, and the Clague and Carol Van Slyke Prize.

www.upress.state.ms.us

The University Press of Mississippi is a member of the Association of American University Presses.

First printing 2017
∞
Library of Congress Cataloging-in-Publication Data

Names: Dewulf, Jeroen, 1972– author.
Title: The Pinkster King and the King of Kongo : the forgotten history of America's Dutch-owned slaves / Jeroen Dewulf.
Description: Jackson : University Press of Mississippi, 2017. | Includes bibliographical references and index.
Identifiers: LCCN 2016019248| ISBN 9781496808813 (hardback) | ISBN 9781496808837 (epub institutional) | ISBN 9781496808844 (pdf single)
Subjects: LCSH: Pinkster (Festival) | Slavery—New York (State)—History. | Dutch—New York (State)—History. | African Americans—Social life and customs. | BISAC: SOCIAL SCIENCE / Ethnic Studies / African American Studies. | SOCIAL SCIENCE / Black Studies (Global). | SOCIAL SCIENCE / Slavery.
Classification: LCC E445.N56 D48 2017 | DDC 305.896/073—dc23 LC record available at https://lccn.loc.gov/2016019248

British Library Cataloging-in-Publication Data available

Contents

Acknowledgments

When I was appointed in 2007 as the successor to Johan Snapper as incumbent of the Queen Beatrix Chair in Dutch Studies at the University of California, Berkeley, there was much to look forward to. I would be leading one the most prestigious Dutch Studies programs outside of the Low Countries, joining a world-renowned research university, and moving to the golden San Francisco Bay Area. The one thing I regretted was that the expertise in Portuguese Studies I had acquired after several years of study and academic work in Portugal, Brazil, and Portuguese-speaking Africa seemed of little use to my new position. While my research at Berkeley focused first on World War II following my discovery of a unique collection of Dutch clandestine materials in the Bancroft Library, the creation of a new course in 2011 made me shift the focus of my research. This new course on New Netherland and the little-known Dutch chapter in American history was conceived as an American Cultures course. Since American Cultures courses must consider three major ethnic groups, preparations involved the study of the relationship between the early Dutch settlers in seventeenth-century Manhattan and the Native American populations as well as the enslaved Africans. The moment I looked at the first document mentioning the names of these Africans, I realized that the Lusophone world had reentered my life. I dedicate this book to Sebastião, Cecília, Manuel, Bárbara, Isabel, António, Fernando, Luís, Maria, and all other members of Manhattan's charter generation.

This book would not have been possible without the UC Berkeley American Cultures Innovation in Teaching Award in 2012, which gave me a chance to further explore the Luso-African identity of the first men and women who were brought as slaves to Manhattan and the impact this charter generation had on the development of the African American community in New York/New Jersey and its annual Pinkster celebrations. This research was also made possible through generous grants provided by the Andrew W. Mellon Foundation, the UC Berkeley Committee of Research, and the UC Berkeley Portuguese Studies Program. Equally important for my research was the financial support that came with the UC Berkeley Institute of International Studies Robert O. Collins Award in African Studies in 2012, the Hendricks Award of the New Netherland Institute in 2014, and the Clague and Carol Van Slyke Prize in 2015.

At my university, I would like to thank James H. Spohrer, Seth Meyer, and Julie Lynn van den Hout for their editing work. My gratitude also goes to Steve Mendoza and Claude Potts, librarians for the Dutch and Hispanic Collections at the UC Berkeley Main Library, and Elaine C. Tennant, for facilitating my use of the Engel Sluiter collection at the Bancroft Library. I would also like to thank my student research assistant Yichu Cao, who assisted me in collecting materials on Pinkster and spent many hours reading through historic newspapers in search for traces of the festival, and Flynn Walsh, for making the map on recorded Pinkster celebrations in Early America.

I am especially grateful to Jaap Jacobs for his comments on the sections in the manuscript dealing with New Netherland. In my entire academic career, I have never met a researcher who was as generous with advice and assistance as Jaap. Other researchers linked to the New Netherland Institute in Albany, Janny Venema, Charles Gehring, Dennis Maika, and Peter Christoph in particular, were also helpful to this project. I am thankful for the opportunity to use the New Netherland Research Center, located in the New York State Research Library, for my research on Pinkster.

I would also like to thank the input by researchers and assistants linked to the Núcleo de Apoio à Pesquisa Brasil-África at the University of São Paulo, in particular Marina de Mello e Souza and Márcio Vianna Filho. My gratitude also goes to Juliana Ribeiro for showing me materials belonging to black brotherhoods in São Paulo's Museu Afro-Brasil and to Toninho Macedo for sharing with me his knowledge on Afro-Brazilian performance culture. Hein Vanhee allowed me to touch fascinating artefacts relating to Kongo's Afro-Catholic heritage preserved at Belgium's Royal Museum for Central Africa, while José Augusto Nunes da Silva Horta and Gerhard Seibert, scholars at the University of Lisbon, provided useful comparative insights between what had occurred in the Kingdom of Kongo and other parts of Africa with a strong Portuguese influence. With the help of Leão Lopes and José Maria Semedo, I learned about the *tabancas* in the Cape Verde Islands. A visit to the Sojourner Truth Institute in Battle Creek, Michigan, brought me closer to the person with whom I initiate and close this manuscript. Portions of this book have been presented at various conferences. For constructive comments at these conferences I thank John M. Janzen, John Thornton, Linda Heywood, Cécile Fromont, Maureen Warner-Lewis, Dianne M. Stewart, Lisa Voigt, Koen Bostoen, David Geggus, Aldair Rodrigues, Glaura Lucas, Peter Mark, and Jelmer Vos.

My gratitude also goes to Wim Klooster for his comments on Dutch involvement in the transatlantic slave trade, to Lucas Ligtenberg on the Dutch language in America, to Luc Renders on Dutch materials about the Kingdom of Kongo, to Walter Prevenier, Cees Slegers, Stefaan Top, Jelle Haemers, Koenraad Brosens, Frank Willaert, Samuel Mareel, Arjan van Dixhoorn, Herman Pleij, Eddy Stols, and Armand Sermon on festive traditions in Dutch culture, to Cynthia McLeod, Michiel van Kempen, Han Jordaan, Bart Jacobs, and Luc Alofs on folkloric traditions in the Dutch-speaking Caribbean, Colin Wells, Ed Nizalowski, and Margaret Downs Hrabe for providing copies of rare materials about Pinkster, and to Adélio Fernando de Lima Pinto Abreu, Jorge Teixeira da Cunha, Constantino Hatende, Fr. Nuno da Silva Gonçalves, SJ, and Fr. Francisco van der Poel, OFM, for their advice on Catholic brotherhoods in the Lusophone world.

Portions of this book have appeared in the form of articles in academic journals: "Pinkster: An Atlantic Creole Festival in a Dutch-American Context," *Journal of American Folklore* 126, no. 501 (2013): 245–71; "Emulating a Portuguese Model: The Slave Policy of the West India Company and the Dutch Reformed Church in Dutch Brazil (1630–1654) and New Netherland (1614–1664) in Comparative Perspective," *Journal of Early American History* 4 (2014): 3–36 [© Koninklijke Brill NV, Leiden, 2014 | doi 10.1163/18770703-00401006]; "The Many Languages of American Literature: Interpreting Sojourner Truth's *Narrative* (1850) as Dutch-American Contact Literature," *Dutch Crossing* 38, no. 3 (2014): 220–34; "Black Brotherhoods in North America: Afro-Iberian and West-Central African Influences," *African Studies Quarterly* 15, no. 3 (June 2015): 19–38; "'A Strong Barbaric Accent': America's Dutch-Speaking Black Community from Seventeenth-Century New Netherland to Nineteenth-Century New York and New Jersey," *American Speech: A Quarterly of Linguistic Usage* 90, no. 2 (May 2015): 131–53 [http://dx.doi.org/10.1215/00031283-3130302]. I thank all publishers for their license to republish part of these contributions in revised form in this book.

The Pinkster King
•• and the ••
King of Kongo

Introduction

A remarkable passage in Sojourner Truth's *Narrative* (1850) expresses her wish to return to the slaveholder John Dumont from whom she had walked away only months before. Despite having been rescued by the Van Wagenen family, Truth—then called Isabel(la)—voices a sudden desire to go back to the same man who had beaten her, broken his promise to grant her freedom, and sold her son Peter. Her justification for looking "back into Egypt" is the approaching Pinkster festival, where everything looked "so pleasant."[1]

The almost irresistible allure for Truth of the annual celebrations during the week of Pentecost (Whitsuntide) reveals the importance of the Pinkster festival for slaves living in the parts of New York and New Jersey that had once formed the Dutch colony New Netherland (1614–1664). Brought to North America by seventeenth-century Dutch settlers, Pinkster came to be known as a predominantly African American celebration by the nineteenth century. It was, as Edwin Olson has argued, "their greatest festival until the Civil War period."[2] Sources indicate that, during Pinkster, slaves were given exceptional liberties by their Dutch American masters. They did not have to do any work for a period of at least three days and in some cases were given an entire week off; they were allowed to leave the premises at any time during the festivities; they could make money by selling products in the week anticipating the festival; and they could enjoy unrestrained dancing, flirting, and drinking side by side with black and white participants at the festivities. In places such as Albany they used to organize a procession in honor of their "king" that was allowed to start in the most noble part of town.[3] These remarkable liberties slaves enjoyed during Pinkster were at odds with the usual restrictions they had to endure, summarized by Herbert Aptheker as follows: "it may be stated that slaves were forbidden to assemble without the permission and presence of responsible whites . . . [they] were not to trade, buy, sell, or engage in any other economic activity without the permission of their masters, were not to be . . . on the city streets after nine or ten in the evening without written permission."[4]

The background of the Pinkster festival therefore raises many questions. According to Shane White, Pinkster is "one of the most important and revealing cultural phenomena in the history of the black experience in America" but also "one of the least well understood aspects of black life in New York."[5] Dena

Epstein confirms that "research in colonial archives and manuscript records is badly needed to satisfactorily document this rich cultural tradition."[6] Due to the Dutch name of the tradition, the earliest studies on Pinkster leave little doubt that it began as a Dutch holiday that for unknown reasons was later taken over by the slave community. In *Antiquities of Long Island* (1874), Gabriel Furman argues that "from a very early period, probably from the first settlement of the country, until about the commencement of the present century, Pinkster was a holiday among our Dutch inhabitants" and, while "this day was a species of negro jubilee upon Long Island at the same time that it was observed as a festival by the white population," it "eventually became entirely left to the former."[7] In *A History of the City of Brooklyn* (1867–70), Henry Stiles suggests that the Dutch never cared much about Pinkster. Whereas their main holiday was Easter and "it was evidently impolitic to allow the negroes the opportunity of being 'elevated' on the same day with their masters, who were apt to need their sober services and attention, the following Monday (Whitsuntide) was allowed to the slaves as their especial festival."[8] And in *Dutch and English on the Hudson* (1921), Maud Wilder Goodwin argues that "at first all was innocent merriment . . . but for some unexplained reason this festival was gradually relegated to the negroes . . . barbaric dances began, and fun so far degenerated into license that the white people and their children shunned the festivity."[9]

This theory of transition also returned in later scholarship. White, for instance, assumes that Pinkster "stretched back to seventeenth-century Holland" and that the Dutch community abandoned this tradition after the American Revolution when a process of Americanization had set in, whereupon it was gradually taken over by the black community. While Pinkster used to be small-scale and entirely Dutch, he claims, they transformed it into a big, predominantly African American celebration that reached its apogee in the late eighteenth century but faded away when city rulers imposed sanctions in the early nineteenth century. So, according to White, big African American Pinkster celebrations lasted only for about a quarter of a century.[10] Claire Sponsler similarly claims that "Dutch assimilation and a growing black presence in Albany perhaps set the stage for the transfer of Pinkster." By highlighting similarities between the African American Pinkster parades in the historically Dutch city of Albany—formerly called Beverwijck—and Dutch medieval Pentecost processions, Sponsler also argues that when the black community took over the tradition, "the potential meanings of black usurpation were disguised under customary behavior . . . African American Pinkster wasn't something new, it was instead a version of something familiar."[11] Graham Russell Hodges explains the importance of Pinkster by interpreting it as a festival used by the Dutch to engage in a "religious interaction" with their slaves, whereby "ecstatic moments of the Holy Wind" during Pentecost allowed for a "spiritual conversion." Hodges also links Pinkster to "rudimentary self-help organizations" among slaves and sees the festival as a sign that, by the late eighteenth century, "enslaved Africans in the mid-Atlantic were moving from tribal affiliation to a new concept of nationhood based on slave culture."[12] Considering the alleged transition from a Dutch into an African American celebration, several scholars have claimed that Pinkster should be considered a syncretic Dutch-African tradition. According to White, "Pinkster was not simply an African survival transplanted to the New World, but a complex syncretization of African and Dutch cultures forged on the Hudson River within the context of American slavery."[13]

Several words of caution are required at this point. Not a single explicit reference has been found about a Pinkster festival for the entire period of English colonial rule in America, either as a Dutch or as an African American celebration. Following the English takeover of New Netherland in 1664, an Anglo-Saxon cultural model became dominant in New York and New Jersey, which marginalized the Dutch community. As the Pinkster tradition indicates, however, it would be wrong to assume that specifically Dutch traditions ceased to exist or that the Dutch-owned slave community became simply part of an English slave system. Although it is estimated that as late as the mid-eighteenth century some 16 to 20 percent of the slaves in New York and New Jersey still spoke (some) Dutch, little specific data exist on America's Dutch-owned slave community.[14] The same applies to Pinkster, where the few existing sources transmit almost exclusively the point of view of outsiders.

Many of the misconceptions about Pinkster can be traced to the dominant Anglo-Saxon perspective in the late-eighteenth- and early-nineteenth-century American press. Unfamiliar with both Dutch and African American traditions, Anglo-Americans perceived Pinkster either as an exotic tradition or a despicable custom. Due to a lack of familiarity, their accounts of Pinkster are fraught with cultural misunderstandings. A revealing example is how Sojourner Truth's *Narrative* ended up being distorted by her amanuensis Olive Gilbert when the latter structured and complemented Truth's words according to her own Anglo-Saxon cultural conceptions. As is confirmed by Erlene Stetson and Linda David, the *Narrative* retains traces "of Truth's dialogic strivings with her interpreter."[15] For Truth, whose native language was Dutch and who spent the first thirty years of her life in a predominantly Dutch-speaking environment in the Hudson Valley, Pinkster was part of normal life. For Gilbert, on the other hand, it was an exotic custom. Thus, when Truth narrates how on Pinkster's eve (of the year 1827) she believed her master would come by to see if he could take her with him (to the festival), Gilbert misinterprets this as a mysterious prophecy. Because of Gilbert's unfamiliarity with Dutch American traditions and her subsequent misinterpretation of Truth's words, this trivial observation came to be seen by later generations as a revelation of supernatural powers to the point that Arthur Huff Fauset even suggests that Truth's "vision" was a likely example of African black magic.[16]

It should, however, be acknowledged that it was precisely their unfamiliarity with Pinkster that prompted Anglo-American authors to write about the festival in the first place. Members of the Dutch community hardly felt an urge to report on a tradition that was normal to them. In the existing data on Pinkster, the Dutch American voice has remained conspicuously silent. This Dutch silence makes it difficult to know precisely how this community celebrated Pinkster and how its slaves participated in the festivities.

In the absence of substantial documentary evidence on this festive tradition, any interpretation of Pinkster is speculative to a certain degree. One way of approaching the existing scholarship on Pinkster with a new theory despite the paucity of historical sources is by using a comparative method. In 1984 David Cohen showed that Pinkster celebrations by slaves in New York were remarkably similar to black performance traditions in other parts of the Americas.[17] Naturally, the observation that a similar tradition existed in more than one place does not automatically imply that the origin and historical development of one corresponds to that of the other. Yet as Samuel Kinser explains about his decision to use a comparative perspective in his groundbreaking study on Mardi Gras, "my suggestions about the parallels between African and Afro-American festive behavior are hypothetical. The hypotheses, as presented, may turn out upon further testing to be untenable. But the problem provoking the hypothesis is as real as the maskers whose behavior I am trying to explain."[18] Despite the speculative character of his comparative approach, Kinser's *Carnival, American Style* (1990) is today considered one of the most influential works on African American performance culture.

My decision to carefully reread the available data on slave culture in New York and New Jersey in search of traces of Pinkster and to compare these traces with those of festivals by slaves elsewhere in the Americas made me conclude that the traditional interpretation of Pinkster needs revision. Rather than claiming a transition from a purely Dutch to a syncretic Dutch-African festival, I have come to the conclusion that the roots of the African American celebrations during the Pinkster festival are to be found in Africa. Scholars who have presented a predominantly Afrocentric perspective on Pinkster have argued similarly. Sterling Stuckey, for instance, has claimed that Pinkster allowed the transmission of African traditions, values, and religious practices among slaves in the American diaspora.[19] However, the absence of a comparable indigenous tradition in anthropological studies on African modes of festive and religious expression has made it difficult to interpret the meaning of the African American Pinkster festivities from an Afrocentric perspective. In fact, such studies have either remained inconclusive about which indigenous African traditions, values, and religious practices were transmitted in the context of these celebrations or have presented conclusions that are purely speculative. For instance, several scholars have claimed that African Americans used Pinkster celebrations to honor an indigenous African god called Toto or Totau, whereas no anthropological study on indigenous African practices ever identified the existence of this mysterious god.[20]

While I do not wish to deny that indigenous African traditions were an important factor in the development of African American Pinkster celebrations, I believe that the complexity of the phenomenon cannot be captured with a one-dimensional connection between Africa and America as presented in the tradition of Melville Herskovits. In *The Myth of the Negro Past* (1941), Herskovits convincingly challenges the traditional assumption that African cultures had had no impact on the cultural forms adopted by descendants of African slaves in the American diaspora and fiercely rejects the claim that "the American Negro" was "a man without a past."[21] His study made a contribution of crucial importance to the field by exposing indigenous African influences in African American culture. It suffered, however, from an important weakness. Herskovits neglected the fact that by the time the first African slaves were brought to North America, many of them came from parts of Africa that had already acquired a syncretic Atlantic character. As Ira Berlin has demonstrated, due to intercultural contacts in the Atlantic world a large percentage of the earliest African slaves in North America and their European enslavers shared—to varying degrees—knowledge of and familiarity with certain cultural concepts.[22] Since the early sixteenth century, African rulers had become key players in the Atlantic trade. These transatlantic connections had brought new ideas, cultural concepts, and products as diverse as Chinese silk, Brazilian cassava, Indian textiles, Maldivian cowries, Mexican maize, Dutch gin, and Portuguese church bells to Africa, where they had strong impact on local cultures.[23] As a result of these intercultural connections, not all African cultural elements—or what Herskovits called "Africanisms"—that slaves brought with them to the New World were of purely indigenous African origin. Several of these elements had a syncretic character. As Kristin Mann and Edna Bay have observed, cultural influences between Africa and the Americas "moved not only back and forth between specific regions of Africa and the Americas. Indeed, they circulated in flows of differing reach and proportion all around the Atlantic basin."[24] From the sixteenth century on, the Atlantic basin was one gigantic intercultural zone, marked by inter- and extra-African cultural mixtures to which not only Arab-Islamic but also European-Christian—predominantly Iberian-Catholic—cultural elements contributed substantially.

My research has convinced me that Pinkster should be understood as a prime example of such a syncretic cultural continuity from Africa in the

Americas. While scholars have repeatedly highlighted the syncretic character of the Pinkster festival and other African American festive traditions, they generally assume that syncretism is a phenomenon that only set in upon the slaves' arrival in America. In this book, I intend to demonstrate that before arriving on the American East Coast, the essence of what came to be known as the African American Pinkster festival already existed as a syncretic phenomenon that mixed indigenous African and European cultural elements. In this respect, historical documents about sixteenth- and seventeenth-century Africa were more useful to understand the meaning of African American Pinkster celebrations than nineteenth- and twentieth-century anthropological studies that have analyzed African performance traditions as culturally isolated phenomena.

Like the vast majority of Africans who were brought to the Americas as slaves in the early seventeenth century, the charter generation in New Netherland predominantly consisted of West-Central Africans.[25] Their Lusitanian baptismal names such as Manuel, António, Sebastião, Isabel, Madalena, and Maria indicate that virtually all of them had gone—with varying degrees of exposure—through a process of Iberian acculturation before they had been shipped to America.[26] The fact that they proudly used their Portuguese, Catholic names to identify themselves in the New World shows that this acculturation had not occurred under pressure but rather that these men and women had voluntarily embraced certain Iberian cultural and religious elements as part of their own identity.

This was not a unique phenomenon. Our understanding of the black community in New Netherland becomes much clearer when considered against the background of what was happening elsewhere in the Dutch overseas empire.[27] A comparative analysis with the slave population in Dutch Brazil (1630–54) reveals that the charter generation in New Netherland formed a largely homogeneous group with well-established and mutually shared Afro-Iberian traditions.[28] As scholars such as Sidney Mintz, Richard Price, and Gwendolyn Midlo Hall have convincingly demonstrated, charter generations often managed to set a cultural pattern that was emulated by slaves who arrived in later decades.[29] My research on Pinkster has made me conclude that such a pattern must also have existed in the case of New York and New Jersey.

In order to truly understand syncretic phenomena such as Pinkster, one needs to use a framework that goes beyond the borders created by European colonizers in the Americas. Paul Gilroy, in his seminal work *The Black Atlantic* (1993), urges scholars to analyze the Atlantic World "as one single, complex unit of analysis" and to study the cultural behavior of slaves by adopting "an explicitly transnational and intercultural perspective."[30] The adoption of such an intercultural perspective naturally requires the use of research materials in languages other than English, a decision which not only distinguishes this book from the existing scholarship on Pinkster but also from many other studies on African American performance culture. Unless otherwise indicated, all translations from sources in languages other than English are my own. With its multilingual focus on syncretism in the analysis of a large palette of historical documents from the early decades of the slave trade, linked to a comparative perspective that connects North America to the entire Atlantic realm (the Iberian Peninsula, West and West-Central Africa, the Caribbean, and Latin America), this book presents a new methodological approach to the study of African American festive traditions.

This emphasis on the transatlantic character of African American Pinkster celebrations also corresponds to a growing concern in historical studies for a culturally centered approach to the analysis of slavery in the Americas. An increasing number of scholars have in recent years emphasized the need to focus on transatlantic slavery not only quantitatively and in terms of the labor needs of the plantation system but also from the perspective of cultural identity. Linda Heywood and John Thornton, in particular, have opened new paths in the analysis of slavery in the Atlantic world by using such a transnational and intercultural perspective. This book owes much to their pioneering work on West-Central Africa and the kingdom of Kongo in particular. As Heywood and Thornton have argued, little attention has traditionally been given in American scholarship to the fact that following the arrival of the Portuguese in Sub-Saharan Africa in the late fifteenth century, a syncretic culture emerged that was adopted by a significant percentage of Africans who later left the continent as slaves. As Thornton writes in his groundbreaking study *Africa and Africans in the Making of the Atlantic World* (1992), "European influences on African life ... were often encountered first in Africa and only later transferred to the Americas. Thus, where Africans have borrowed from Europeans they often did so willingly and on their own terms in their home territories, and not always under the stultifying influence of slavery."[31]

The assumption that our understanding of African American cultural performances gains strength if we take into consideration that the charter generations had often already been influenced by European rituals before they were brought to America as slaves has prompted me to question the traditional interpretation of Pinkster as a carnivalesque festival of reversal in the tradition of Victor Turner's theory on status reversal as a ritual process.[32] White, for instance, argues that Pinkster temporarily relieved pressure from the slave system, similar to festivals of misrule. The point of reference for this brief bacchanalian interlude, he claims, was always the order and certainty of the "normal" social structure. Hence the playful role reversals, a tradition that was also common practice during carnival in early modern Europe. White therefore believes that the Pinkster tradition primarily served the interests of the masters.[33] Terrence Epperson takes this interpretation to the extreme by reducing African American Pinkster celebrations to spectacles staged for the amusement of slaveholders.[34]

My research on Pinkster has convinced me that while the festival may have been perceived by slaveholders as a safety valve for their slaves, it meant something different to the slave community itself. I therefore subscribe to Bratford Verter's opinion that "of the various historiographical interpretations of Pinkster, least satisfactory is this characterization of the holiday as a carnival of inversion."[35] Following Joyce Goodfriend's argument that "portraying colonial slaves as dupes of unscrupulous whites hardly herald[s] recognition of the role of black actors in [New York]'s history," I add a focus on what Pierre Bourdieu calls "social capital" to the traditionally dominant perspective on political and financial capital in the study of slave societies.[36] I do so because I am convinced that African American Pinkster celebrations were not impromptu social gatherings. Rather, the complexity of this festival that in Albany attracted up to a thousand spectators must have required a team that coordinated activities, made decisions, and assumed responsibilities for the execution of a carefully planned program. By highlighting the cooperative spirit that characterized the Pinkster festival, my approach underlines the importance of the slave population's social capital.

Building on a theory first presented by Hodges in *Root & Branch* (1999), I relate the slaves' social capital to the establishment of mutual-aid organizations, which I trace back to Afro-Iberian brotherhood traditions introduced by the charter generation. This focus on brotherhoods not only allows me to provide a plausible answer to the Afro-Iberian characteristics of Pinkster celebrations but also an explanation for one of the greatest enigmas in African American history: the sudden rise of hundreds of fraternal and benevolent societies in the early nineteenth century. In his study on the history of New York's African American community, Craig Steven Wilder argues that this explosive growth of mutual-aid associations could not have come out of nowhere and suggests that these organizations "drew on traditions that enslaved Africans brought to New Amsterdam."[37] Berlin also claims that many of these institutions rested upon "clandestine associations black people had created in slavery."[38] My research confirms this theory and specifies the nature of these traditions with reference to mutual-aid associations in the tradition of Afro-Iberian brotherhoods established by the charter generation. Mitch Kachun's suggestion that Pinkster laid the foundations for commemorative traditions that would become important components of a maturing free black culture in antebellum New York therefore needs clarification.[39] Not the festival itself, but rather the brotherhoods that organized it are the crucial factor in understanding the assertive participation of the African American community in the public sphere.

It would, in fact, be wrong to narrowly reduce Pinkster to its festive nature. Rather, the spectacular African American celebrations were just one manifestation of a well-organized cooperative structure that implied black group solidarity as well as tactical negotiations with slaveholders. As Geneviève Fabre has argued, the black Pinkster king was essentially a "mediator between two racial worlds."[40] The finding that cooperation was part of a broader strategy in dealing with the harshness of slavery has required me to distance myself from Aptheker's conclusions on the African American response to life in bondage. By drawing a clear distinction between "passivity and docility" on the one hand and "rebelliousness" on the other, Aptheker naturally groups festivals such as Pinkster and other "safety-valves letting off some of the steam accumulated by abuses, grievances and oppressions" under the category "The Machinery of Control."[41] His view corresponds to the opinion expressed by Frederick Douglass, who considered traditions such as Pinkster "among the most effective means in the hands of slaveholders of keeping down the spirit of insurrection."[42] My research on Pinkster has led to a different conclusion and suggests that "docility" and "rebelliousness" complemented rather than contradicted each other in the sense that organized slave communities realized that there were times when more was to be gained with the former approach and times when more could be gained with the latter.

I have decided to use the term "cooperative resistance" to define the strategy of slave brotherhoods in New York and New Jersey that celebrated their leaders or "kings" during Pinkster. Their policy of cooperative resistance aimed to secure and gradually expand a set of minimal rights and human dignity in exchange for loyalty and commitment, by taking advantage of what Mintz and Price have phrased as "the [constraint of the] masters' monopoly of power . . . by their need to achieve certain results in terms of production and profit, but also by the slaves' clear recognition of the masters' dependence upon them."[43] As these scholars have persuasively argued, one should not be blinded by the necessity of slaveholders to maintain loyalty and guarantee minimal levels of labor performance by their slaves. While the whip may have been the principal technique for this purpose, it could not be, and never was, the only such technique. As Berlin confirms, "though imposed and maintained by violence, [slavery] was a negotiated relationship."[44] Unlike Berlin, however, I do not believe that the slaves' capability and talent to take advantage of this relationship should be limited to what he has called the "Atlantic Creole" charter generations of the seventeenth century. While it is true that later generations of slaves faced increasing difficulties in gaining their freedom, the case of Pinkster shows that slaves continued to use strategies similar to those of the charter generations to mitigate their life in bondage. As Melvin Wade has observed about eighteenth-century New England, "black captive and white captor existed in a relationship of give-and-take that permitted enough autonomy for blacks to assert themselves in a culturally continuous and complex fashion."[45] This also applies to

New York and New Jersey, where the Pinkster festival shows that negotiations and concessions between slaveholders and slaves were not a prerogative of the seventeenth-century charter generation but rather continued as long as slavery itself existed. Whereas the standard expression "paternalistic compromise," coined by Eugene Genovese, conveys the assumption of slave passivity, the term "cooperative resistance" highlights the active role of organized slave communities in obtaining concessions from slaveholders.[46] Not without reason, Thornton credits such slave associations with a revolutionary potential because "they were one segment of slave society that was more or less under slave control," and he underlines that even if slaveholders took a supportive approach to the leaders of these associations, they "still feared them."[47] In fact, the concessions made by slaveholders should not be reduced to mere paternalism. Although humanitarian concerns may occasionally have played a role in concessions, they were primarily a form of self-interest, if not self-preservation.

This book further explores the origin, development, and demise of Pinkster in the broader context of the transatlantic slavery and of master-slave relations in those parts of New York and New Jersey that had once formed New Netherland. It begins with an analysis of Pinkster as a Dutch tradition, both in the Netherlands and in New Netherland on the North American East Coast. This chapter, "Celebrating Pinkster as a Dutch Tradition," shows that Pinkster has two different, even opposing meanings in Dutch culture. While the term can refer to the Christian holiday known as Pentecost or Whitsuntide in English, Pinkster is also used in reference to popular celebrations rooted in pre-Christian fertility rituals that the Reformed Church had been unable to eradicate in the Dutch Republic. This chapter will show how the latter occurred in the context of *kermises* (outdoor fairs) that in the seventeenth century were introduced by Dutch settlers in North America, where they continued to exist until the early nineteenth century.

The next chapter focuses on the way the African American community celebrated the Pinkster holiday. The chapter "Celebrating Pinkster as an African American Tradition" shows how the most spectacular African American Pinkster performances were the king processions in Albany and highlights how different these slave celebrations were from those of the Dutch. It also corrects the assumption that Pinkster was a predominantly rural phenomenon by providing new evidence that the festival was still celebrated by African Americans in the heart of Manhattan in the early nineteenth century.

The following chapter, "In Search of the Pinkster King," explores different theories on the origins of the African American Pinkster celebrations by analyzing parallels to black performances elsewhere in North America, the Caribbean, and Latin America. This comparative analysis reveals that celebrations with characteristics highly similar to that of Pinkster existed all over the Americas, from New England all the way to Argentina, which makes me conclude that the African American Pinkster celebrations should be understood as a specific variant of a much broader cultural phenomenon.

The fourth chapter demonstrates how African American Pinkster celebrations in North America can be traced back to performance traditions that had developed in the context of Afro-Catholic brotherhoods in parts of Africa with a strong Portuguese influence. "Slave Kings and Black Brotherhoods in the Atlantic World" presents the history and importance of "black brotherhoods," Afro-Catholic mutual-aid associations that existed in Africa beginning in the late fifteenth century and flourished in the kingdom of the Kongo and Angola in the sixteenth and seventeenth centuries. It also shows how slaves with roots in West-Central Africa and other parts of Africa with a strong Portuguese influence introduced in the Americas mutual-aid associations modeled upon Afro-Iberian brotherhoods. In the context of these brotherhoods, they elected and celebrated their leaders or "kings" with Afro-Iberian performances.

The transfer of this Afro-Iberian tradition from West-Central Africa to Manhattan is apparent when seen in the context of the Dutch involvement in the transatlantic slave trade in the seventeenth century. In chapter 5, "The Pinkster King as Leader of a Brotherhood," demonstrates how the charter generation in New Netherland established a cultural and social pattern modeled upon Afro-Iberian customs that for many decades would continue to influence both African American celebration culture and the master-slave relationship in Dutch-speaking areas in New York and New Jersey. The chapter shows that the Pinkster celebrations were not only important from a cultural point of view but also served as inter-social negotiations both within the African American community and between masters and slaves.

A final chapter, "The Demise and Legacy of the Pinkster Festival," analyzes the circumstances leading to the prohibition of Pinkster celebrations in Albany in 1811. It explains how the Pinkster festival in New York and New Jersey came to an end and explores its continuous legacy in North American religion, parade culture, music, and literature. It pays particular attention to black fraternities, African American evangelicalism, minstrelsy, and the long-lasting impact of James Fenimore Cooper's interpretation of Pinkster in the novel *Satanstoe* (1845). It shows how Cooper's questionable decision to interpret slavery in a Dutch American tradition as a benevolent system changed the perception of Pinkster in the printed media. The same festival that until the mid-nineteenth century had almost exclusively been portrayed as a symbol of immorality now came to be perceived as an occasion of racial harmony. The chapter ends by showing how it was this change in perspective that led to a revival of Pinkster celebrations in the late twentieth century and ultimately to a repeal of the 1811 Pinkster ban in the year 2011.

• 1 •

CELEBRATING PINKSTER
AS A DUTCH TRADITION

The Netherlands

As the Dutch word *Pinkster* or, more commonly, *Pinksteren*—Pentecost—indicates, this festival has its roots in the Netherlands, where it is celebrated on the seventh Sunday after Easter to commemorate the descent of the Holy Spirit upon Christ's disciples. Formerly, *Pinksteren* was also known in the Netherlands under the name *Sinksen*, as derived from the Medieval Latin *cinquagesima*, the fiftieth day after Easter.

As elsewhere in Western Europe, the month of May traditionally was accompanied in the Low Countries by celebrations rooted in pre-Christian fertility rituals relating to the arrival of summer. Such celebrations usually began with a lot of noise to awaken everyone and to urge people to join the festive crowd. May festivities typically included the erection of the *meiboom* (maypole), a tree that was placed in the center of the village around which different types of popular entertainment were organized, from innocent games such as *zaklopen* (sack racing), *eiertikken* (egg tapping), *eierlopen* (running while holding an egg on a spoon), and *ringsteken* or *ringrijden* (attempts to lance a ring while riding a horse at a gallop) to rougher forms of entertainment such as *hanengevechten* (cockfights), *katknuppelen* (cat clubbing, or taking turns clubbing a suspended barrel containing a cat until it shatters and releases the animal), *ganstrekken* or *gansrijden* (goose riding, or pulling the neck off a goose smeared with oil and hung upside down while riding a horse at a gallop) and charivari or mock serenading of the *luilak* (late sleeper). May festivities were occasions during which established borders in society could temporarily be crossed with impunity.[1]

By the early Middle Ages, these traditional May festivities had become incorporated into a Christian worldview and had been given a new interpretation that related them to Pentecost. Typical Dutch Pentecost customs were the brewing of *pinksterbier* and the distribution of milk by farmers to young people, the so-called *pinkstermelken*. Youths used to collect money when they accompanied the *pinksterbruid* (Pinkster bride) or *pinksterbloem* (Pinkster flower), the latter being a young girl wearing a wreath, called *pinksterkroon* (Pinkster crown), who danced and sang around the village. This pre-Christian fertility ritual had come to be seen as a celebration in honor of the Virgin Mary. Other fertility traditions such as *ringsteken* came to be associated with St. George's fight against the dragon. The encounter with parrots during the Crusades resulted in a new Pentecost tradition, also dedicated to St. George: *papegaaischieten* (parrot shooting) or *koningschieten* (king shooting). Members of the *schuttersgilden* (shooting guilds) shot at a figure in the form of a parrot that had been placed on top of a pole. The winner of the shooting tournament received the title of "king" or, if he won three years in a row, "emperor."[2]

As the earliest dedications of churches in the Netherlands had traditionally occurred on Pentecost, these celebrations often coincided with the *ker(k)mis* or *foor*, an outdoor fair to commemorate the dedication of the local church. At those fairs, music was played, people danced, and booths sold drinks and food. Waffles and *oliekoeken* or *oliebollen* (a Dutch variety of dumplings) were typically associated with kermises, as were ring-dances to the rhythm of the bagpipe and the *giga*, a three-stringed violin. Pentecost fairs typically included boxing tournaments, horse races, and wrestling matches; they attracted conjurers, acrobats, quack doctors, and fortune-tellers; and they were stages for the exhibition of deformed or exotic people and animals.[3] Thus, the assumption by White that Pinkster in America began as a serious religious celebration that gradually "developed into a more commercialized entertainment" needs revision. Commercialized entertainment had been part of Pinkster festivals ever since the Middle Ages.[4]

Pentecost festivities in the medieval Low Countries were traditionally inaugurated with a procession. One of the most famous Pentecost processions occurred near Brussels, in honor of the Black Madonna of Halle. Jan Mostaert's early-sixteenth-century *Portrait of an African Man* depicts a black man wearing a hat badge that indicates a visit to the Madonna of Halle. The fact that he has a golden badge indicates that this unidentified man was not a casual visitor. He may have been a personal guard to Charles V, who visited the Black Madonna in 1520 on his way to Aachen, where he would be crowned Emperor of the Holy Roman Empire.

From the late fourteenth century on, a slow secularization of this Christian tradition set in when lay corporations came to play an increasingly important role in city festivities. As a result, processions evolved into spectacular parades with music, theatre, and dance that became known as *ommegangen* (circumambulations). *Ommegangen* were also organized for political and economical purposes to strengthen community ties and feelings of civic pride. It became a tradition to hold an *ommegang* at the occasion of *blijde inkomsten* (joyous entries), welcoming ceremonies for members of foreign aristocratic families

Jan Mostaert, *Portrait of an African Man*, ca. 1520. This unidentified sixteenth-century black man wears a hat badge that indicates a visit to the Black Madonna of Halle, who is honored every Pentecost with a procession. Courtesy the Rijksmuseum, Amsterdam.

who ruled over (parts of) the Low Countries. These rulers had to pledge adherence to the customary liberties of the city or the region. The *ommegang*, then, served both as a festival to welcome a new ruler and a reminder that local liberties were to be respected.[5] The political dimension of *ommegangen* was of particular importance during Pentecost. Since Charlemagne, Pentecost had been remembered as the day upon which the king or emperor used to hold court. Due to this political connotation, it was traditionally seen as a time when disputes were to be settled and harmony was to be re-established. *Van den vos Reynaerde*, the famous thirteenth-century Dutch beast epic, begins with the king gathering his court on Pentecost to debate political matters. Similarly, the thirteenth-century Dutch Carolingian novel *Reinout van Montalbaen* begins with the announcement that Charlemagne planned to hold court in Paris on the Tuesday after Pentecost.[6]

Cities tried to one-up each other by adding exotic and spectacular elements to their *ommegangen* such as wild animals, monsters, devils, giants, stilt walkers, sword dancers, and Morris dancers. The connection between the Low Countries and Spain, achieved by the House of Habsburg in the late fifteenth century, introduced the participation of Africans, such as a "Moorish princess" in the 1496 *ommegang* that welcomed Joanna of Castile to Brussels and a "black Caspar" on one of the camels carrying the Biblical Magi in the Antwerp *ommegang* in 1520. In cities engaged in international trade, it was common practice that the *vreemde naties* (foreign nations), representatives of foreign trading partners, participated. In the 1549 *ommegang* that welcomed the Spanish crown prince Philip in Antwerp, for instance, the English, Portuguese, Spanish, Eastern European, German, and Italian "nations" all joined the *ommegang* with their delegations.[7]

With the arrival of Protestantism in the Low Countries at a time when it was ruled by the Catholic House of Habsburg, the traditional balance of power between sovereign and local authorities came under pressure.[8] Based on the argument that the Spanish King Philip II disrespected the traditional liberties of the Low Countries, the States General of the Netherlands issued in 1581 the *Plakkaat van Verlatinghe* (Act of Abjuration) that rejected the Habsburg monarch as its legitimate ruler. As a result of the violent uprising against Spanish rule, the Low Countries became divided. While the southern provinces—known as the Spanish Netherlands and later as Belgium and Luxembourg—remained under Spanish rule, the northern provinces became an independent nation—de facto in 1609, officially in 1648—known as the Republic of the Seven United Netherlands or, simply, the Dutch Republic.

In the Catholic Spanish Netherlands, many of the popular Pinkster traditions continued to exist until the nineteenth century. Some have even survived until the present day. The biggest annual celebration in Antwerp, for instance, is the *Sinksenfoor* or Pentecost kermis. Despite increasing secularization since the mid-twentieth century, smaller towns in Belgium such as Londerzeel, Werchter, and Hoeselt still initiate their Pentecost kermis with a Catholic procession.

In the Dutch Republic, where Calvinist-reformed Christianity became the public religion, these popular traditions came under pressure. Protestant church leaders perceived Pinkster kermises as typical of the Catholic tendency to incorporate pagan rituals and customs into Christian practices, which corrupted Christianity. Their eagerness to purify Christianity in the Dutch Republic put pressure on the remaining Catholics. Although Catholics were not persecuted in accordance with the freedom of conscience expressed in Article 13 of the 1579 Union of Utrecht charter, their churches were confiscated, stripped of Catholic elements, and then reused as Reformed churches. While Protestants living in the Spanish Netherlands migrated massively to the Dutch Republic in the early seventeenth century, Catholics in the Dutch Republic—roughly thirty percent of the population—opted for a strategy of accommodation rather than migration to the Spanish Netherlands or other Catholic areas in Europe. Much to the dismay of orthodox Calvinists, civil authorities in the Dutch Republic facilitated this with a policy of pragmatic tolerance of which the *schuilkerken*, buildings that were not recognizable from the outside as Catholic churches, are a famous symbol.

Under Calvinist pressure, processions were prohibited and almost all Catholic holidays were eliminated in the Dutch Republic. Hardliners considered even the observation of major holidays such as Christmas, Easter, and Pentecost a "popish" vestige and ruled that ministers had to discourage any type of popular celebrations.[9] This negative attitude in Calvinist circles toward the traditional celebration culture also reflected an increased concern with morality and sinning. While in a Catholic tradition, sins could be confessed and pardoned, this was no longer possible in the Reformed Church. As Peter Burke has shown, Calvinists denounced kermises and other popular revelries as encouraging servitude to the world, the flesh, and the devil.[10] Dancing, in particular, was considered dangerous. According to Arie van Deursen, "the wickedness of dancing was so absolutely evident to the preachers that they seldom gave their reasoning for the prohibition." For devout Calvinists, he claims, "the dance hall was an anti-church, a synagogue of Satan."[11] By the late sixteenth century, not only the Reformed Church but also civil forces began to distance themselves from kermis entertainment, which they increasingly considered incompatible with modern, "civilized" norms and values. Seventeenth-century paintings in the Dutch Republic indiscriminately portray people participating in kermises as gross and primitive.[12]

Despite all discouragements and prohibitions, many people remained attached to pre-Christian festive traditions and continued to organize them.[13] Although strict Calvinists often decried such celebrations as surreptitious attempts by Catholics to preserve "popish" rituals in the Dutch Republic, it can be doubted that these boisterous events had a religious significance for the participants. Rather, the survival of Shrovetide revelries and Pinkster kermises illustrates the failure of the Reformed Church to impose its strict moral values on the Dutch population. The obligations to which one had to submit oneself to be accepted as a *lidmaat* (communicant member) of the Reformed Church were such that many churchgoers opted to be "adherents" only, what the Dutch called *liefhebbers* (sympathizers). The status of *liefhebber* allowed a certain leeway. Despite being part of the Reformed community, an "adherent" could occasionally set aside the strict church regulations. The number of communicant members of the Reformed Church in the seventeenth-century Dutch Republic did not exceed 20 percent of the total population.[14]

Pinxter Blom tot Schermerhorn.

Anonymous, *Pinksterbloem Parade in Schermerhorn*, ca. 1750. Four girls carry a Pinkster Flower Girl in the Dutch village of Schermerhorn. Courtesy the Rijksmuseum, Amsterdam.

Since they were well aware of the fact that many of their own church members struggled with the strict moral regulations of the Reformed Church, moderate Calvinist ministers tended to take a pragmatic attitude. In Amsterdam, for instance, the Reformed Church typically avoided any communion services as long as the city kermis lasted. Eventually, even the most militant members in the Reformed Church realized that it was impossible to ban all popular festivities from Dutch soil and began to give priority to the prevention of attempts by Catholics to reintroduce *paapse stoutigheden* (popish pranks) such as processions. A similar attitude reigned among secular authorities. Despite the growing disgust in elitist circles for popular festivals, civil authorities rarely cared to enforce prohibitions and turned a blind eye to popular celebrations as long as no recognizably Catholic traditions were observed. As a result of this ambiguous policy, many pre-Christian traditions that had been given a Christian character in the Middle Ages survived the Reformation in a de-Catholicized form. This was, for instance, the case with *Sinterklaas*, which lost its connection to the Catholic St. Nicholas but continued to be celebrated nationwide as a children's feast.[15] The same thing happened with Pinkster kermises. These celebrations continued but the traditional processions and other recognizably Catholic elements disappeared. In Dutch villages such as Cromvoirt and Luyksgestel, the Pinksterbloem tradition is still observed on Pentecost Monday. In Cromvoirt, girls aged six to twelve walk around the village singing and dancing. They form a circle around the girl who has been elected as Pinksterbloem and parade throught the village, while last year's Pinksterbloem collects money from door to door. This girl is known as *het Judasje* (the little Judas) and uses an eggshell to collect the coins. With the revenue, food and drinks are bought for the feasting children.[16]

Orthodox Dutch Christians celebrated Pentecost in church only. Despite the fact that it was recognized as a major Christian holiday in the Reformed Church, Pinkster never acquired the importance of *Pasen* (Easter) or *Kerstmis* (Christmas). Churches tended to collect much less money on Pentecost than on the latter holidays.[17] For devout members of the Reformed Church, Pentecost offered little more excitement than a special church service. For less devout people in the Dutch Republic, however, Pinkster was a time of unrestrained merriment. Pentecost celebrations in the Dutch Republic remained, in the words of folklorist Johannes ter Gouw, "a Bacchanalia" during the seventeenth century and only began to lose importance in the eighteenth century.[18]

Following the emancipation of the Catholic minority in the 1870s, Pentecost traditions experienced a revival in the Netherlands. In traditionally Catholic areas of the country, people provocatively ignored the controversial Article 167 of the 1848 constitution that prohibited the organization of religious processions and re-established the old Catholic procession culture during the Pinkster holidays. Due to increasing secularization in the 1960s, most of these processions have disappeared. Nevertheless, Pentecost continues to be a hallmark of Dutch popular culture to the present day thanks to Pinkpop, the world's longest-running pop music festival, which since 1970 has been organized uninterruptedly during the Pentecost holidays in the historically Catholic village of Landgraaf.

New Netherland

Dutch settlers who migrated to *Nieuw Nederland* (New Netherland) in the early seventeenth century brought their festive traditions with them to North America. First governed by a group of merchants who had formed the New Netherland Company in 1614, the territory between the fortieth and forty-fifth degrees of latitude in eastern North America was taken over by the newly created West India Company (WIC) in 1621. The WIC board of directors, known as the *Heren XIX* (Lords Nineteen), was hesitant about investments in a colony that promised little profit and was at risk of being claimed by England. There were also disagreements among members of the board whether the main focus of their policy in North America should be on fur trade with the indigenous populations or on colonization. In 1624, a modest beginning of a colonization policy was undertaken by sending a group of Walloons, Protestant immigrants in the Dutch Republic with roots in the French-speaking provinces of the Spanish Netherlands. This first immigration effort was not a success. Displeased with the harsh living conditions and the constraints imposed by the WIC, many Walloons returned after only two years. Those who stayed were joined the next year by a new group of settlers. Under company director Peter Minuit, who ruled New Netherland from 1626 until 1632, the colony grew to about three hundred inhabitants clustered in two centers: *Fort Oranje* (Fort Orange) in the Upper Hudson Valley and *Nieuw Amsterdam* (New Amsterdam) on the island of Manhattan.[19]

In 1629 the colonization faction among the WIC board of directors managed to push through a decision to stimulate population growth of the American colony via the *patroon* system. The Dutch *patroonship* allowed large tracts of land to investors promising to bring a substantial number of settlers to the colony. The patroon was not only entitled to the profits from his investment but also had the prerogative to establish his own court. Among the wealthy investors who tried to establish a patroonship in New Netherland was Michael Pauw, who obtained land on the west shore of the *Noordrivier* (North River, later Hudson River) in present-day New Jersey. Samuel Godijn planned an estate on the banks of the *Zuidrivier* (South River, later Delaware River), while Samuel Blommaert hoped to establish a patroonship in the valley area of the *Verse Rivier* (Fresh River, later Connecticut River). All these investments failed to bear fruit. The only successful patroonship was Rensselaerswijck, located near Fort Orange and owned by the Amsterdam diamond trader Kiliaen van Rensselaer.[20] Fort Orange itself, including the land within three thousand feet around its walls (the length of a cannon shot), was put under the exclusive jurisdiction of the WIC. Within this land, the town of Beverwijck (the later Albany) was founded and quickly developed into the center of the fur trade with the Native American population. Later, additional settlements such as *Wiltwijck* (the later Kingston) and Schenectady developed in the mid- and upper Hudson Valley. Under director Wouter van Twiller, in office from 1633 until 1638, settlers were encouraged to develop *Staten Eiland* (Staten Island, named after the Dutch States General) and *Lange Eiland* (Long Island) on patents that became known as *Nieuw Amersfoort*, the later Flatlands. When a ferry service between New Amsterdam and Long Island was established, another settlement called *Breuckelen* (Brooklyn) developed near its landing place. The Swedish attempt to build a colony on the South River in 1638 ended in 1655 when the territory was reconquered by the WIC. In recognition of the support provided by the city of Amsterdam to this military campaign, the main fort in the area was rechristened New Amstel (today's New Castle) and became a city-colony of Amsterdam.

Despite increasing tensions with Native Americans, which evolved into a major uprising in 1643–44, New Netherland experienced a steady, moderate growth in population. By 1650 the colony counted about two thousand inhabitants. The boom years of New Netherland began in 1654. Following the Portuguese reconquest of Dutch Brazil, the North American colony suddenly acquired strategic relevance for the WIC. Many of the resources intended for Brazil now found their way to what up to then had merely been a provincial outpost in the Dutch maritime empire. WIC employees who had lost their possessions in Brazil were granted land in New Netherland as compensation, which encouraged at least two hundred soldiers and colonists to move to the North-American colony.[21] Among them were twenty-three Jews. Long Island, in particular, attracted new settlers who founded *Midwout* (Midwood in today's Flatbush), *Boswijck* (Bushwick), and *Nieuw Utrecht* (New Utrecht) in the late 1650s and early 1660s. Upon taking an oath of allegiance, English settlers from New England were also given permission to settle on Long Island. Thus developed *Heemstede* (Hempstead), *'s-Gravesande* (Gravesend), *Rustdorp* (the later Jamaica), *Vlissingen* (Flushing), and *Middelburg* (the later New Town, now Astoria). From New Amsterdam, settlers also established *Nieuw Haarlem* (Harlem) at the north end of Manhattan and crossed the Harlem River and the East River to develop what came to be known as *Broncks Land* (the Bronx) and *Jonkheers Land* (Yonkers). By 1664 New Netherland had grown from a small trading post with only a few hundred inhabitants to a colony with about eight thousand colonists, some two thousand of whom lived in New Amsterdam and about a thousand in Beverwijck.[22]

Most colonists in New Netherland originated from the Dutch Republic, yet the percentage of Europeans with foreign roots was high. Besides people with roots in the Spanish Netherlands, New Netherland also counted several hundred inhabitants of German, Scandinavian, French, British, and even Bohemian and Italian origin. It was, by far, the most heterogeneous colony in North America. Dutch was the dominant language in the colony.[23] This should not come as a surprise, since many of the "foreign" settlers from the Spanish Netherlands were native speakers of Dutch dialects. Due to the similarity to German dialects, German immigrants also switched easily to Dutch. Most of the other European "foreigners" in New Netherland had previously lived in the Dutch Republic or had worked as sailors or soldiers on WIC ships and likely gained some knowledge of Dutch before they arrived in America. New Amsterdam's multicultural character hardly differed from that of Amsterdam and other major cities in the Dutch Republic, where a comparable percentage of the population consisted of foreign immigrants.[24] Acculturation to Dutch standards was, thus, the general rule in New Netherland. It was only on Long Island that English-speaking communities composed of immigrants from New England managed to resist assimilation successfully.

From the very beginning, blacks also contributed to the building of the colony. The first Dutch traders, who spent the winter of 1613–14 on the American East Coast, had been accompanied by the free black man Juan Rodriguez, a mulatto from Santo Domingo in Hispaniola.[25] In later decades, enslaved Africans arrived in New Amsterdam. While the slave population of the Dutch colony will extensively be discussed in the next chapter, it should be stressed that Africans played a crucial role in the development and expansion of New Netherland. In 1639 Jacob Stoffelsen van Ziericksee testified that company slaves were involved in "building Fort Amsterdam, which was completed in the year 1635, also in cutting building timber and firewood for the Large House as well as the guardhouse, splitting palisades, clearing land, burning lime and helping to bring in the grain in harvest time, together with many other labors."[26] In 1652, when new fortifications were needed, the company relied again on the African slave population to do the heavy work; and in 1658, slaves were used to build "a good wagon road" from New Amsterdam to Nieuw Haarlem "so that people can travel to and from it on horseback and with a wagon."[27] When European settlers such as Elias Emmens, Gijsbert Cornelisz Beijerlandt, William Pietersen, Peter Hendricksen, Nicholas Albertsen, and Claes Michielsen were convicted for crimes in New Netherland, they were sentenced to "work with the Negroes," the backbreaking work enslaved Africans had to do in the Dutch colony.[28]

Unlike in New England, hardly any immigrants came to New Netherland for religious reasons. As in the Dutch Republic, the Reformed Church was privileged in the colony and other religions were tolerated as long as their members refrained from public worship and proselytizing. As the charter of *Vrijheden ende Exemptien* (Freedoms and Exemptions) confirmed, "no other Religion shall be publically admitted in New Netherland except the Reformed, as it is at present preached and practiced by public authority in the United Netherlands . . . without however persecuting anyone on account of his religion, but leaving to everyone the freedom of conscience."[29] New Netherland counted several religious minorities among its settlers: a substantial number of Lutherans and Quakers and a small number of Mennonites, Jews, and Catholics. While the majority of people in the colony adhered to the Reformed Church, only a minority of them were communicant members. The number of communicant members in the Reformed Church consisted at most of 20 percent of New Netherland's population.[30]

Although there can be no doubt that the church played a crucial role in the lives of most settlers, it did so primarily as a place of social gathering and the maintenance of traditions such as baptism, marriage, and burial.[31] This does not mean that these people did not consider themselves Christians, yet they simply could not imagine a life without drinking, dancing, and erotic pleasures. English Puritans in Massachusetts considered themselves elevated above the Dutch in New Netherland and claimed that New Amsterdam was a cesspool of vice. As David Pietersz de Vries put it in his *Korte Historiael* (1655), "these people give out that they are Israelites and that we at our colony are Egyptians."[32]

Director Willem Kieft (1638–47) and, in particular, his successor Petrus Stuyvesant (1647–64) made serious efforts to change this reputation.[33] Stuyvesant, the son of a minister and former student at the Calvinist University of Franecker in Friesland, was an adherent of strict Calvinist doctrine. As did many militant Calvinists in the Netherlands, he had felt attracted by the WIC's ambition to continue the struggle against Spain, the country's Catholic archenemy.[34] Stuyvesant joined the WIC in the 1630s and eventually was appointed ruler of the Antillean island Curaçao in 1642. In April 1644, when attacking the Spanish-held island of Saint Martin, he had lost the lower part of his right leg to a cannonball. After his injured leg was amputated and replaced with a wooden peg, he returned to the Netherlands. From there, he was sent to New Amsterdam as director-general of New Netherland and the Dutch Caribbean islands. Upon arrival in New Amsterdam in 1647, Stuyvesant felt that the Reformed community in the colony was a "feeble, lukewarm and fainthearted congregation," and he made the exaggerated complaint that "nearly the just fourth of the city of New Amsterdam consists of brandy shops, tobacco or beer houses."[35] Stuyvesant took harsh measures to curb the city's nightlife by closing taverns and places of morally dubious entertainment. In 1656 he imposed the Sabbath as a day of rest by prohibiting "exercises and plays, excessive drinking bouts, the visiting of taverns and saloons, [or that] dancing, playing cards, backgammon or *ticktack*, ball, ninepins, pleasureboating, driving about in carts or wagons be carried on before or during divine service."[36]

Stuyvesant also tried to curb festive traditions. Not surprisingly, New Netherland's celebration culture had been following a Dutch pattern. As Janny Venema argues in her study on Beverwijck, "people basically followed a Dutch way of life. . . . Celebrations took place in a way similar to the ways of the fatherland."[37] Evidence shows that settlers in New Netherland discharged firearms in the air on New Year's Eve, held charivari on Shrove Tuesday, planted maypoles in late spring, and reveled on Pinkster.[38] They also organized kermises. Beginning in 1648, New Amsterdam had an annual Free Market on the first Monday after St. Bartholomew's Day (August 24) that lasted for ten consecutive days. This fair corresponded "to the legal Amsterdam Fair," which means that it was accompanied by a kermis.[39] The most unruly celebrations traditionally took place at the occasion of Shrovetide. In 1663 a group of men organized a charivari upon hearing the news that Pieter Jansz Slot was to be married. They placed a maypole in front of his door and decorated it with ragged stockings, insinuating that his bride was not a virgin. Three times, Slot cut the pole down, but every time the group reappeared, parading through the streets with kettle music and resurrected the pole. When the *schout* (sheriff) tried to intervene, he was threatened with axes and firearms.[40] Such actions deeply upset the devout community, all the more since Shrovetide was a tradition that had its origin in the Catholic era as a day of unrestrained joy in anticipation of Ash Wednesday, the first day of Lent. A reflection of these concerns can be found in the petition submitted by the consistory of Wiltwijck in 1664 with the urgent request to the magistrates to prohibit "the public, sinful and scandalous Bacchanalian days of Shrovetide (descended from the Heathen from their idol Bacchus, the God of wine and drunkenness: being also a leaven of Papacy, which the Apostle, I Cor. 5, has warned us to cast off)."[41]

Stuyvesant shared these concerns. In 1654 he had prohibited *gansrijden* and imprisoned a few farmers who had disobeyed his orders.[42] To no avail, then, in February 1655 Fiscal Cornelius van Tienhoven told the court that "he had been informed that the country people intended riding the goose again as they did last year."[43] Well aware of the difficulties of imposing such a ban, local administrators showed reluctance to support Stuyvesant's prohibitions.[44] Although they concurred with Stuyvesant that it "is considered entirely frivolous, needless and disreputable by subjects and neighbors, to celebrate such heathenish and popish festivals and to introduce such bad customs into this country," they pointed out that these customs "may be tolerated in some places of our Fatherland or winked at." They complained that Stuyvesant had "without their knowledge interdicted and forbidden certain farmers' servants to ride the goose on the feast of Bacchus at Shrove-tide" and claimed that one should not forbid the "rabble to celebrate the feast of Bacchus without the advice, knowledge and consent of the Burgomasters and Schepens [aldermen]."[45] In 1664 they even refused to communicate a new law on compulsory rest on Sundays to the population because they felt it was "too severe and too much opposed to Dutch liberties."[46]

These discussions also affected Pinkster. The word *Pinxteren* is mentioned for the first time in New Netherland in 1628, in a letter of Reverend Jonas Michaëlius.[47] Since Pentecost is a major Christian holiday in the Reformed Church, it is only natural that it was celebrated in New Netherland as soon as a church community was established. As with other major Christian holidays, the Dutch Reformed Church in New Netherland celebrated Pentecost with two religious services, both on Sunday and on Monday.

As in the Dutch Republic, however, the solemn celebration of Pentecost in church had to compete with boisterous popular festivities. We can assume that the "weekly Market-Day, to wit Monday [the Monday after Pentecost]" in New Amsterdam was accompanied by a kermis.[48] Also in Beverwijck, there were popular celebrations on Pentecost. On May 9, 1655, a week before Pentecost, the Court of Fort Orange and Beverwijck gave permission to Hendrick Joachemsz, a tavern owner and lieutenant in the town's burgher guard, to have the burgher guard *"den Papegay te laaten schieten* [shoot the parrot]" on "the third day after this coming *Pijnghsteren* [Pentecost]."[49] Although Joachemsz had promised to keep good order, the Pinkster festivities ended up being so boisterous that the authorities announced that damage done to property should be reported to them and that reparations would be paid. Stuyvesant himself also intervened in December 1655, arguing that "whereas experience has demonstrated and instructed that on New Year and May days with the shooting, May pole planting and excessive drinking, besides unnecessarily wasting powder, much drunkenness and other insolences are committed, in addition to other sad accidents leading many times to injuries." He therefore decided to "forbid henceforth shooting and planting of May poles on New Year and May days within this province of New Netherland; also, any noise making with drums or dispensing of any wine, brandy or beer upon those occasions, and this only to prevent further accidents and trouble."[50]

However, just as in the *patria*, such prohibitions had no lasting effect. Rowdy popular entertainment continued to be part of Dutch celebration culture long after Stuyvesant surrendered the colony to the English in 1664. In 1677, for instance, the authorities in the still heavily Dutch town of Albany issued a proclamation to punish "all misdemeanors which have occurred here on Shrove Tuesday, *viz.*, riding at a goose, cat, hare, etc., etc., on a penalty of £25 sewan."[51]

Stuyvesant's efforts to impose the Sabbath rest also had borne little fruit. When he visited New York City in 1697, Benjamin Bullivant commented that "the Dutch seeme not very strict in Keepeing the Sabath, you should see some shelling peas at they^r doors children playing at they^r usuall games in the streetes & ye taverns filled.["][52]

New York and New Jersey

On September 6, 1664, Stuyvesant surrendered the Dutch colony to the English commander and governor-designate Richard Nicolls. In order to avoid resistance, Nicolls had ensured that the articles of capitulation were relatively mild. All European inhabitants of New Netherland were given the status of "free denizens," which opened the possibility of recognizing the legality of Dutch contracts and property, including that of slaves. Local officials were temporarily allowed to stay on, and direct trade with the Dutch Republic and the Dutch Caribbean islands could continue. As a result, a large majority of the population remained in what was now an English colony.[53]

Scholars disagree as to how negatively the English takeover affected the Dutch community and other Europeans who had assimilated to Dutch cultural standards. While some have claimed that it resulted in a rapid decline of Dutch economic and social dominance, others have argued that the Dutch only gradually lost ground to the English. A revealing example of the reluctance to accept English rule can be found in Jeremias van Rensselaer's complaint about having to learn English in a letter to his mother in Amsterdam in 1668: "Now it seems that it has pleased the Lord that we must learn English. The worst of it all is that we have already for nearly four years been under this jurisdiction and that as yet I have learned so little. The reason is that one has no liking for it."[54] The enthusiasm among members of the Dutch community in July 1673 over the temporary Dutch reconquest of the colony is also indicative of widespread dissatisfaction with English rule. With the Treaty of Westminster in February 1674, however, Dutch rule over the territories once composing New Netherland definitively came to an end.[55]

While Dutch and Dutch-related elite families such as the Philipses, Steenwycks, Van Cortlandts, Bayards, Livingstons, and DeLanceys were compensated for their loyalty to the new rulers with extensive land patents and prestigious positions in the new administration, the middle class had more reason to worry about the preservation of rights and privileges they had enjoyed under Dutch rule. Among strict Calvinists, the ascension of the Catholic King James II to the throne of England in 1685 added a religious element to their concerns. It does not surprise that when the news about the victory of the Protestant Dutch stadtholder William III of Orange-Nassau over James II in the Glorious Revolution of 1688 reached the American colony, many not only reacted with relief but also with contempt for those in their own community who had been overeager to anglicize in the conviction that Dutch rule was a thing of the past.

Despite the fact that the Dutch community in New York welcomed the new king of England unanimously, William's ascension to the throne soon led to tensions.[56] In 1689, the New York City militia captain Jacob Leisler, a former WIC soldier of German origin, forcefully removed the English Lieutenant Governor Francis Nicholson from power and announced that he would rule New York until King William had sent his new officials. It is noteworthy that this rebellion took place during the week of Pentecost. Among Leisler's supporters were many members of the Dutch community who felt threatened by the English and resented the anglicized Dutch upper-class who had thought it wiser to remain loyal to Nicholson until further notice.[57]

Religion also played a role in the uprising, which Leisler portrayed as a struggle against "popery and slavery" in defense of the true Protestant faith.[58] Despite the anti-Catholic character of the rebellion, Leisler was not supported by the leading representatives of the Dutch Reformed Church, who cautiously followed the example of the Dutch elite. This decision caused anger among Leisler's supporters. As Randall Balmer has shown, many predominantly lower-class Dutchmen were so disillusioned with their religious authorities that the Reformed Church became the focus of popular disaffection.[59] In a dramatic letter to the *classis* (the Reformed Church's administrative body) in Amsterdam, the ministers Selijns, Van Varick, and Dellius presented a gloomy picture: "Bergen, Hackensack, Staten Island and Harlem have deserted us, yielding to the power of evil. They say they can live well enough without ministers or sacraments."[60]

In the summer of 1690, King William disavowed Leisler, who was taken to the gallows. With Leisler's execution, the division in the Dutch community between "whites" (anti-Leislerians) and "blacks" (pro-Leislerians) reached its height. Anti-Leislerians were granted substantial favors for their loyalty by William's representatives in New York, which included manorial patents such as the Philipsburgh Manor (1693) and the Van Cortlandt Manor (1697). In October 1698, when Leislerians regained control of the New York assembly, Leisler's body was exhumed and reburied in the Dutch Reformed Church on Garden Street.[61] Some twelve hundred Leislerians paraded on that day through the streets of Manhattan with the body of their executed leader.[62] In 1703, New York's Governor Cornbury still believed that Leislerians would "never be reconciled to an English Government, nor to an English Governour, unless they can find one who will betray the English Laws and interest to the Dutch."[63] In the following years, however, the division between pro- and anti-Leislerian factions subsided.[64]

The influence of the Dutch community in Manhattan had by that time already diminished considerably. This loss of influence had been accompanied by a growing anti-Dutch mood in New York City, where the increasingly dominant English elite did not hide its contempt for everything Dutch. Significantly, Robert Hunter's satirical play *Androboros* (1714) deliberately uses Dutch phrases such as "*Wat is dat Lating? Ick forestae't niet* [What is that? Latin? I don't understand that]" to transmit an image of boorishness.[65] This negative image of the Dutch undoubtedly accelerated the process of anglicization in Manhattan. In 1754 William Livingston wrote that "the Dutch tongue, which, though once the common dialect of the province, is now scarcely understood, except by its more ancient inhabitants."[66] In 1764 the Reformed Church, the last Batavian bulwark in this once proudly Dutch city, began to offer sermons in English.[67]

The Dutch influence in New York City also declined due to migration. Leisler's execution had accelerated a process of Dutch migration from Manhattan to the Hudson, Mohawk, Hackensack, Passaic, and Raritan valleys, even as far as Pennsylvania, in search of cheap farming land.[68] Rather than becoming tenants on one of the big manors, they preferred to have their own farms. In 1700 New York Governor Bellomont commented: "What man will be such a fool to become a base tenant to Mr. Dellius, Colonel Schuyler, Mr. Livingston when, for crossing Hudson's River, that man can for a song purchase a good freehold in the Jersies?"[69]

In Albany, on the western part of Long Island, on Staten Island, and in several small, self-sufficient communities in rural New York and New Jersey, traditionally Dutch social patterns and cultural practices survived much longer than on Manhattan.[70] Visitors usually characterized those insular Dutch communities as traditionalist, frugal, and primitive. In 1732, for example, the newly arrived Dutch Reformed minister Cornelius van Schie wrote about his parishioners in Poughkeepsie and Fishkill: "Many people here were born, and grew up, in the woods, and know little of anything else except what belongs to farming. . . . Most of these people can neither read nor write."[71] Pehr (Peter) Kalm, a Swedish traveler who visited the Hudson Valley in 1749, observed that "[t]he inhabitants of Albany and its environs are almost all Dutchmen. They speak Dutch, have Dutch preachers, and divine service is performed in that language: their manners are likewise quite Dutch."[72] The American variant of Dutch spoken by descendants of seventeenth-century settlers in New Netherland was known as Low Dutch, probably derived from the term *Nederduits* that was commonly used to refer to the Dutch language at that time, unlike *Nederlands*, the modern term. Sometimes Dutch was simply called the *taal* or, in anglicized form, *tawl*, meaning "the language."[73]

Many of those who had become disappointed with their church leaders in the context of Leisler's rebellion felt attracted by a Pietist countercurrent in

Dutch Calvinism known as the *Nadere Reformatie* (Further Reformation). The desire for "religious improvement" within this movement related to disappointment over the fact that the daily lifestyle of most Dutch Christians did not correspond to the moral and spiritual teachings of the Bible. Although in name they had become Reformed Christians, these people contented themselves with outward confession just like they had done during the Catholic era. Unlike the traditional Calvinist sermon that laid heavy emphasis on biblical exegesis and reasoned argumentation, Pietist preaching stressed spontaneity in order to touch the soul of the churchgoers. The conviction that a true reformation of piety, behavior, and morality required rebirth as a Christian explains the central focus in the Further Reformation on the Holy Spirit. Pietist circles firmly believed that it was the Holy Spirit that revealed to the sinner his lost condition before God and drove him or her to Christ for mercy and salvation.[74]

Although earlier Dutch Reformed ministers such as Everardus Bogardus, Johannes Cornelisz Backer, and possibly also Jonas Michaëlius had Pietist inclinations, the arrival of Dutch Pietism in America is traditionally linked to Guiliam Bertholf, a zealot of the radical Pietist Jacobus Koelman. Attempts by traditionalists in the Dutch Reformed Church in America to stop Bertholf failed, and he managed to establish several new churches in New Jersey in the early eighteenth century.[75] Bertholf also paved the way for the legendary Theodorus Jacobus Frelinghuysen, whom some scholars credit to have been a herald of the First Great Awakening in the Middle Colonies. By organizing bilingual (Dutch-English) preaching sessions in cooperation with the Presbyterian William Tennent, Frelinghuysen crossed denominational borders. Through Tennent, Frelinghuysen befriended the Anglican revivalist George Whitefield and influenced his method of preaching.[76] Soon after his arrival in the Raritan Valley in January 1720, Frelinghuysen's confrontational attitude brought him into conflict with some of his parishioners. In fact, the new minister had not minced his words when addressing his parishioners: "Come here . . . you proud, haughty men and women; you seekers after pleasure; . . . you hypocrites and dissemblers. How do you think the Lord will deal with you? . . . Be filled with terror, you impure swine, adulterers, and whoremongers."[77]

Frelinghuysen and his followers excelled in their opposition against any type of "immoral" behavior. For these hardliners, even dancing was a sin. Eilardus Westerlo, the Pietist Calvinist who succeeded Frelinghuysen's son Theodor as head of the Reformed Church in Albany in 1760, explicitly warned Stephen van Rensselaer III that his land "should not be profaned by revelry and dancing."[78] Despite the emphasis they placed on the role of the Holy Spirit, Pietist circles were also strongly opposed to Pinkster kermises, which they saw as a pagan— or even worse, Catholic—vestige that needed to be fully eradicated. Jacobus Koelman, whose influence on Bertholf and Frelinghuysen is well known, even refused to observe Pentecost in church and vigorously opposed any type of popular Pinkster celebrations.[79] The records of a meeting in 1767 of the consistories of the Bedminster, Raritan, and North Branch Dutch Reformed churches show that a church member who had been observed dancing at a "shooting match"—probably parrot shooting—was suspended with the argument that "shooting matches . . . afford inducement for the assembling of many idle and fickle persons, where nothing is ever transacted except that which is utterly useless, and usually ungodly."[80]

One can assume that the Dutch community in America was divided during the week of Pentecost. For Pietists and devout Christians in general, the excitement of Pentecost was probably limited to church services and prayer sessions. Dina van Bergh's diary shows in the entry on Pentecost 1747 that for Pietist women like her, the Pinkster holiday was essentially a week of prayers. "On that Lord's Day, I was enabled to pray with great earnestness for the sending of the Spirit, with a more abundantly manifest outpouring," she writes and "so we also did on Wednesday in the public prayer meeting . . . I was greatly helped in prayer."[81] Other members of the Dutch community, however, looked for less devout entertainment during the Pentecost holidays. William Coventry's *Memoirs of an Emigrant* indicates that dancing on Pinkster and other holidays was still very popular among rural Dutch families in the 1780s, which shows that the Pietist crusade against the traditional celebration culture had had only moderate success.[82] This is confirmed by John Watson, who in his *Annals and Occurrences of New York City and State in the Olden Days* (1846) argues that "Dutch dances were very common . . . Rev. Dr. Laidlie, who arrived in 1764, did much to preach them in disuse."[83] In a description of a Pinkster festival in Albany in the year 1803, an anonymous author calling him- or herself A.B. argues that "a certain class of whites" attended the boisterous Pinkster kermises, whereas "the serious part of the Dutch congregation" opted to celebrate Pentecost in church only.[84] Robert Lowell's *A Story of Two from an Old Dutch Town* (1878) also reveals that devout members of the Dutch community strongly opposed Pinkster kermises. Born in Boston, Reverend Robert T. S. Lowell had moved to Schenectady around 1860. There he studied the town's Dutch history and wrote a collection of short stories about it. In one of these stories, "Master Vorhagen's Wife," Lowell describes how Dominie Van Schaats led a moral campaign against "the shame and sin of Pinkster."[85] These examples show that while devout Dutchmen tended to keep a distance vis-à-vis the popular revelries, others ignored the objections by the religious authorities and took an active part in the "Bacchanalian" Pinkster kermises. The rowdy character of the celebrations is notable in the anonymous Pinkster account published by the *Troy Daily Times* in 1872, according to which "Pingster sometimes brought excessive indulgence and genuine Dutch rows" and "led to many family quarrels and disagreements," one of which "set the whole Dutch community against the Van Buren family, and produced an ill-will towards them which continued so long as there was any one to remember it left."[86]

Several sources confirm that kermis attractions continued to accompany Dutch American Pentecost celebrations until the early nineteenth century. One of the most interesting sources on Pinkster is the lengthy article provided in the mid-nineteenth century by the physician James Eights, who was born and raised in Albany. In his childhood recollections, Eights offers a lively description of such a kermis scene. "The Pinkster grounds," he writes, "were quaintly laid out in the form of an oblong square, and closely hemmed in with the rude buildings on every side save one, and this was left free, so as to give entrance and freely to admit the crowd." Beyond this square were "various exhibitions, such as of wild animals, rope dancing, circus-riding and the playing ground of all simple gaming sports."[87]

Another (anonymous) description of a Pinkster celebration in the Mohawk Valley, dating to 1846, indicates how the Dutch American community continued to celebrate Pinkster in the early nineteenth century with ancient traditions such as ringrijden: "a small cord was extended across the road with a finger ring suspended to it by a small twig or thread" and "the competitors all being prepared and mounted on their prancing steeds, armed with sharp-pointed skewers held between the thumb and forefinger, with which to pierce the ring." Then, "each in his turn and on a full gallop would make the essay, and the one who was first to succeed in piercing and receiving the ring on the end of his skewer successfully three times and in his regular turn, was considered the winner." As soon as it was discovered who the winner was, "he was pursued pell-mell by all the rest, and if he escaped and reached the goal without being captured, his bill at the dance, for himself and girl, had to be footed by the rest of the company; but if he was so unfortunate as to be caught, he had to foot the bill of his captor."[88]

Dutch Americans also preserved certain elements of the Pinksterbloem parades. Eights's account reveals that children who assisted at the Albany Pinkster kermis in the early nineteenth century still used to be "gaily decorated with ribbons and flowers of every description."[89] The Dutch word *Pinksterbloemetje* (little Pinkster flower) survived in America in the English corruption *Pinkster-blummachee, Pinkster bloomitze,* or *Pinxter blumachy* in reference to the Pink Azalea (*azalea nudiflora*).[90]

Although there can thus be no doubt that several elements of nineteenth-century Pinkster celebrations in New York—the name of the festival, the flowers, the kermis attractions—were related to traditions that had been introduced in America by Dutch settlers in seventeenth-century New Netherland, the American version of Pinkster cannot be reduced to simply an offspring of a

Dutch tradition. Due to the presence of slaves, Pinkster festivals in America developed differently. As the next chapter will show, American sources on Pinkster all confirm the massive participation of slaves, to such a degree that in the nineteenth century this originally Dutch festival was primarily perceived as a celebration of the black community.

•• 2 ••

CELEBRATING PINKSTER AS AN AFRICAN AMERICAN TRADITION

New Netherland

When the Dutch West India Company was created in 1621, its board of directors focused not only on trade. The Lords XIX also hoped to weaken the Spanish enemy by targeting its American possessions. To this purpose, they devised a strategy known as the *Groot Desseyn* (Great Design), an ambitious plan to gradually expand Dutch power in the Americas. Since the Iberian crowns were at that time merged, the WIC also considered Portuguese possessions and Portuguese ships legitimate targets in its war against Spain. In 1630 company forces conquered the province of Pernambuco in Brazil and hoped to dominate the lucrative sugar trade that the Portuguese had developed there since the early sixteenth century. The production of cane sugar relied heavily on slaves. Governor-General Johan Maurits, Count of Nassau, who ruled Dutch Brazil between 1637 and 1644, was clear that "[i]t is impossible to achieve anything in Brazil without slaves. Without them, the mills cannot crush the cane nor can the fields be tilled.... [I]f any man feels offended by this, his is a useless scruple."[1] While the Dutch impact on the Portuguese transatlantic slave trade had up to then been limited to the occasional capture of vessels carrying slaves, the WIC now began to target Portuguese slave-trading strongholds along the West African coast as well. In 1637 it obtained a major victory by seizing control of Fort Elmina, the main Portuguese stronghold on the Gold Coast. Later the WIC also launched a series of military operations in the Gulf of Guinea and in West-Central Africa, where in 1641 its forces conquered Luanda, Benguela, and São Tomé.[2]

Following these successive victories, several African leaders involved in the slave trade turned to the Dutch as potential allies. In 1642 a group of ambassadors representing Count Daniel da Silva of the rebellious Kongolese province of Soyo came to Dutch Brazil to discuss a possible alliance. Da Silva's rival, Garcia II, King of Kongo, also sent ambassadors to Pernambuco. These Kongolese rulers were well aware of the Dutch interest in slaves. Significantly, the count of Soyo offered Johan Maurits two hundred slaves to strengthen the new

Anonymous, *Dutch Diplomats at the Court of Dom Álvaro, King of Kongo*. This meeting relates to Dutch attempts to obtain Kongolese support for the planned attack on Portuguese Luanda in 1641. In Olfert Dapper, *Naukeurige beschrijvinge der Afrikaensche gewesten* (Amsterdam: Jacob van Meurs, 1668).

relationship, which offer was topped by the king of Kongo, who promised the WIC a gift of no fewer than seven hundred slaves. One of the presents from the Dutch the ambassadors took back to Kongo was an exquisite hat made out of beaver fur, New Netherland's main export product.[3]

Dutch Brazil was far more important to the WIC than New Netherland, as the profit to be made with Brazilian sugar exceeded that of North American beaver pelts by far. To the 4 to 7.5 million guilders of the total Dutch Atlantic trade in the early seventeenth century, New Netherland only contributed about 350,000 guilders at its highest point.[4] Despite the fact that the WIC had promised in Article XXX of the "Charter of Freedoms and Exemptions" (1629) that it would "endeavor to supply the colonists [in New Netherland] with as many blacks as it possibly can" and in Article XXXI of its (undated) "New Project of Freedoms and Exemptions" that each patroon [in New Netherland] would be allotted with "twelve black men and women out of the prizes in which Negroes shall be found," Dutch Brazil was systematically privileged in the distribution of slaves. In the 1620s and 1630s, only small numbers of slaves who had been captured by privateers on Iberian slave ships were brought to New Amsterdam.[5]

The earliest reference to slaves in New Netherland dates to 1628, when Dutch Reformed minister Jonas Michaëlius mentioned in one of his letters "Angolan slave women," whom he considered "thievish, lazy, and useless trash."[6]

As opposed to Dutch Brazil, where slave labor predominated from the very beginning, most of the hard and dirty work in New Netherland was initially done by European servants.[7] Only in 1644 did the WIC consider the option to "introduce a goodly portion of . . . negroes" to New Netherland in order to boost the colony's agricultural production so that "a great quantity of provisions could be exported thence to Brazil."[8] Since employers in New Netherland were dissatisfied with the demands and high costs of the few available European workers, Director Willem Kieft also suggested in 1644 that "it would not be unwise to allow . . . the introduction, from Brazil there, of as many Negroes as they would be disposed to pay for at a fair price." He predicted that these slaves "would accomplish more work for their masters, and at less expense than farm servants, who must be bribed to go thither by a great deal of money and promises."[9] As a result of this change in policy, the first major cargo of slaves arrived in New Amsterdam in June 1646,[10] brought from Dutch Brazil on the ship *Tamandaré*.[11] In January 1648 the States General made a lengthy report on the affairs of the WIC, suggesting that colonists and patroons in New Netherland should be allowed "to export their produce even to Brazil, in their own vessels . . . and to trade it off there, and to carry slaves back in return."[12] Due to increasing instability in Dutch Brazil, however, this plan was not realized. Until the mid-1650s, the only new slaves to arrive in New Amsterdam were brought there by privateers. In 1652, for instance, a group of forty-four slaves on their way from Jamaica to Cuba on a Spanish ship were captured by a privateer and subsequently sold to the Dutch in New Netherland. The ship's owner, Juan Gallardo Ferrera, later traveled to New Amsterdam and tried to get his former slaves back, in vain.[13]

Also in 1652, the WIC board of directors received a request from inhabitants of New Netherland to participate in the transatlantic slave trade, and it authorized them to "fetch from the coast of Africa as many Negroes as they shall require for agriculture."[14] There are no indications that such an endeavor ever took place. However, in 1654 two private traders from Amsterdam, Jan de Sweerts and Dirck Pietersz Wittepaart, petitioned the WIC for permission to buy slaves in Africa and sell them in New Netherland, which after a "lengthy discussion" was approved by the board of directors, since "it was understood that the same would tend to promotion of population growth and the improvement of the aforesaid place."[15] In the early summer of 1655, their ship *Wittepaart* arrived in New Amsterdam with some three hundred slaves from the Bight of Guinea. However, Stuyvesant complained that they were "exported from here without the honorable Company or the inhabitants of this province having derived any revenue or benefit thereby," which indicates that most of these enslaved Africans ended up elsewhere in North America. Stuyvesant thereupon decided that traders who brought slaves to New Amsterdam and wished to sell them outside of the Dutch colony had to pay "10 percent of their value or resale price."[16] In May 1660 a group of traders from New Amsterdam again petitioned Stuyvesant and the Council of New Netherland to allow them to engage in the transatlantic slave trade. Despite the fact that the WIC had already approved such activities in 1652, the Governor General and Council of New Netherland claimed that they considered themselves unqualified to take any decision on the matter without explicit approbation of the WIC directors in Amsterdam.[17] No further attempts by the traders to pursue this matter have been registered.

Meanwhile, the Portuguese reconquest of Luanda, Benguela, and São Tomé in 1648 as well as Dutch Brazil in 1654 forced the WIC to change its slave policy. While in past times the WIC slave trade infrastructure in Africa had almost exclusively served to supply plantation owners in Dutch Brazil, the company now decided to venture into new markets to make its remaining possessions in West Africa profitable. Ironically, the same WIC that had originally been created to fight the Catholic Spanish enemy now became the main slave supplier to Spanish possessions in the Americas. In the context of this new policy, the Antillean island of Curaçao acquired strategic importance for the WIC as a distribution center for tens of thousands of African slaves who were to be sold in Spanish America as well as to Dutch, Danish, French, and British plantation owners in the Caribbean. Approximately one third of these slaves were of West-Central African origin, while others were brought from the West African Gold Coast (Elmina, Bercu) and the Slave Coast (Ardra, Fida).[18] The small, arid island of Curaçao was soon overwhelmed with the arrival of so many slaves and could not supply sufficient foodstuffs, which eventually forced the WIC to ship provisions from Amsterdam to Curaçao.[19] Curaçao's difficulties in sustaining itself prompted Stuyvesant in 1659 to envision a strategic role of New Netherland in this new slave trading network. He suggested that the WIC board of directors "place a fair and fixed price upon negroes, whom your subjects might desire to import here for provisions, lumber, or otherwise," which would "undoubtedly increase the trade to Curaçao and provide the island from here with plenty of commodities."[20] At least four ships, the *Spera Mundi* with seven slaves, the *Eyckenboom* with nineteen, *Den Nieuw Nederlantschen Indiaen* in two journeys with ten and forty slaves, and the *Musch* with forty, sailed from Curaçao to New Amsterdam.[21] Encouraged by the profitable sale of these slave cargoes, the WIC board of directors planned to ship slaves from Curaçao to New Amsterdam not only for the local market but also for the neighboring English colonies.[22]

A first attempt, in 1663, with the *Wapen van Amsterdam* failed. The ship, carrying 101 men and women from Loango, was captured by English privateers near Curaçao and none of the slaves made it to New Amsterdam.[23] A second attempt

was successful. In July 1664 Simon Cornelissen Gilde's ship the *Gideon* arrived
with over three hundred slaves from Guinea and Angola in Curaçao with the
intention to continue his journey to New Amsterdam. However, since many of
them were infected with scurvy, Vice-Director Matthias Beck decided to keep
the majority of these slaves on the island and sent others to New Netherland
instead. The safe arrival of the vessel in August 1664 must have particularly
pleased the regents of Amsterdam, who had invested in the *Gideon* in exchange
for a fourth of the slaves they intended to use for the development of their city-
colony New Amstel. With the cargo of the *Gideon*, consisting of 153 men and 137
women, the total African slave population in New Netherland more than dou-
bled.[24] The plans to make New Amsterdam into the center of the North American slave trade failed, however, when only weeks after the arrival of the *Gideon*,
four English frigates sailed into the city's harbor and demanded the surrender of
the Dutch colony. In order to justify his decision to capitulate without any resistance, Stuyvesant later claimed in his "Report on the Surrender" (1666) that the
arrival of hundreds of "half-starved Negroes and Negresses who alone, exclusive
of the garrison, required one hundred *skepels* [twenty-two and a half bushels] of
wheat per week" had not left enough food supply to withstand a siege.[25]

The abundance of names ending in "Congo" and "Angola" indicates that the
overwhelming majority of slaves composing the charter generation in New
Netherland were of West-Central African origin. This is not surprising, since
Luanda was at that time the dominant source of American-bound slaves.[26] The
slaves' typically Lusitanian baptismal names such as Francisco, João, Manuel,
Luís, António, Sebastião, Bárbara, Catarina, and Maria as well as surnames such
as Britto [Brito], Premero [Primeiro], Albiecke [Albuquerque], and Portogys
[Português] also indicate that the large majority of them had gone—with various degrees of exposure—through a process of Iberian Catholic acculturation
before arriving in New Netherland. The fact that these slaves proudly identified
themselves with their Catholic baptismal names indicates that this acculturation must have occurred on a voluntary basis.[27] Other slaves with names such
as "Van Capo Verde," "Van St. Thomas" and "Santome(e)" must have come from
the Portuguese-controlled Cape Verde Islands and São Tomé. The slave called
Manuel the Spaniard probably lived on the Iberian Peninsula, as was the case
of a slave known as Anthony Ferdinand, who was identified as a "bachelor from
Cascalis [Cascais], in Portugal." Bastiaen from Santo Domingo and Jan Augus-
tinus from Cartagena must previously have lived in Hispanic territory in the
Americas. Others had lived in Brazil before they were taken to New Netherland.
One of them was Bastiaen, who was referred to as "from Pariba [Paraíba], Portuguese." Blacks with names such as Crioelje, Crioell, Criolyo, d'Crioole, Crioole, and Malaet were probably born in Spanish or Portuguese colonies and
may have been of mixed race.[28]

It can, in any case, be assumed that most of the slaves in New Netherland shared familiarity with Iberian culture. According to Heywood and Thornton, "this background with its engagement with European culture, and particularly its Christian and Catholic component, as well as the contact that the Dutch had with them in Angola and in Brazil, shaped the way in which they integrated into Dutch society in New Netherland."[29] Significantly, slaves in New Amsterdam opted for monogamous marriages for which they sought a blessing in church and were eager to have their children baptized.

Since Afro-Iberian culture served as their model of reference, it would be wrong to assume that New Netherland's charter generation had to construct a completely new identity in the Americas. As Joyce Goodfriend has rightly argued, the Africans in New Netherland brought to America a "cultural compass, which they used to orient themselves to their new environment."[30] Slaves who were brought to New Amsterdam from places as far away from each other as Portugal, the Cape Verde Islands, Angola, and Brazil shared an Afro-Iberian cultural compass. So, when Francisco van Capo Verde married Anna van Angola in New Amsterdam, the couple shared a substantial amount of Afro-Iberian cultural commonalities despite the fact that their ethnic and geographical origin was very different.[31]

Sources indicate that slaves in New Netherland shared for several decades a language of intercommunication that was not Dutch. In 1665, for instance, Domingo the Negro was called to court to translate for Jan Angola.[32] It is not known what this language of intercommunication was. Considering Jan's Angolan origin, they probably spoke Kikongo or Kimbundu. However, due to their exposure to Portuguese culture and due to the fact that many had previously lived in Brazil, Portugal, São Tomé, or the Cape Verde Islands, the lingua franca of the black community in New Netherland may also have been an Afro-Portuguese Creole language, similar perhaps to Curaçaoan Papiamentu or Surinamese Saramaccan that are still spoken in formerly Dutch colonies in the Caribbean.[33] Documents from the seventeenth-century Dutch Cape Colony referring to the use of Portuguese words by slaves of Kongolese and Angolan origin confirm some degree of familiarity with the Portuguese language among West-Central Africans.[34] One other element that speaks in favor of Portuguese is that slaves in New Netherland were known by their Portuguese names or the Dutch translation of those names, but not by the indigenous Kikongo version of the names, such as (M)fûnsu for Afonso, (M)pêtelo for Pedro, Dyôko for Diogo, (N)dîki for Henrique, or Zabiele for Isabel.

Since not only some of the slaves but also members of the Dutch community had lived in Brazil before coming to New Netherland, we can assume that Portuguese occasionally served as a language of interracial communication in the colony. For instance, a court case from 1662 reveals that Resolveert Waldron, who had previously lived in Brazil, communicated in Portuguese with a black man called Mattheu in New Amsterdam. Mattheu, a slave of Cornelis Steenwyck, was also involved in another court case, together with a certain Swan and Frans. Frans's real name was Francisco. In 1652 he was transported from Jamaica to Cuba on a Spanish ship that was captured by a privateer, who subsequently sold him in New Amsterdam. The identities of Mattheu and Swan are unknown. Blacks with similar names in New Netherland are Mattheus de Angola (Mateus de Angola), Swan van Loange (João de Luango) and Swan van Angola (João de Angola). In 1662 Frans, Mattheu, and Swan requested Resolveert Waldron to be their interpreter in court, which indicates that they too were able to communicate in Portuguese. The fact that Waldron spoke Portuguese may also explain why he was put in charge of a group of slaves who had to strengthen the ramparts of Fort Amsterdam.[35]

In the early decades of the colony, slaves remained mostly in New Amsterdam, where they worked at the service of the WIC. The company provided them with housing and medical care, granted them a small garden, and occasionally paid them for extra work.[36] Slaves were forced to do not only hard but also dirty and shameful work, such as clearing the streets of animal carcasses, the flogging of criminals, and the execution of convicts.[37] It is, therefore, no coincidence that the first slave mentioned in the Hudson Valley in 1646 is Rensselaerswijck's hangman Jan de Neger.[38]

In 1656 the WIC directors expressed concern about the fact that "too many of these Negroes are employed in private service."[39] This evolution proved to be unstoppable. The more slaves that arrived in the colony, the more private ownership increased. In 1657 slaves were sold in New Amsterdam at public auctions, where anyone could buy them with cash, beaver pelts, or other provisions.[40] In the final years of New Netherland, individuals in all economic strata except the lowest were represented among the slaveholders. The practice became so popular that some settlers bought slaves as an investment and leased them to others.[41]

In total, at least 467 slaves were brought to New Netherland. In the final years of the colony, blacks, both enslaved and free, made up to about 6 to 8 percent of the population. This percentage was higher in New Amsterdam, where it is estimated to have been between 10 and 17 percent.[42] Although they originated from a country where slavery was prohibited, the Dutch seem to have had few concerns about the morality of this practice. Significantly, Jan Baptist van Rensselaer was so unconcerned about slavery that he felt tempted to have a slave sent over to the Dutch Republic after he had moved there in 1659. When he requested his brother Jeremias to send him his slave Andries, Jeremias refused with the argument that "it would [be] but foolishness to have him serve you in a free country."[43]

The WIC did not adopt a strict slave code in New Netherland. Slaves enjoyed a limited number of privileges such as the right to marry, the right to hire oneself out for wages, the right to farm one's own garden and to sell products on the open market, the right to own cattle and graze animals on company land, and even the right to sue Europeans in court. The courts in New Netherland showed little distinction between blacks and whites.[44] On several occasions they showed a surprising leniency for crimes committed by slaves. In 1664, for instance, the female slave Lysbeth Antonissen was pardoned even though she had been convicted of arson.[45] The only slave known to have been executed in the Dutch colony was Jan Creoly after he had been condemned for acts of sodomy with the ten-year-old slave boy Manuel Congo in June 1646. Remarkably, the legal proceedings in this case were the result of a denouncement by members of the black community who had accused Creoly "of having committed sodomy by force." Manuel himself was spared, probably at the request of the other slaves.[46]

Religion played a crucial role in the master-slave relationship in New Netherland. Militant Calvinists had been among the strongest supporters of the creation of the WIC since they believed that the Dutch people had the divine task to continue the struggle against the Spanish Catholic enemy and to make America into a "truly Christian" (meaning: Reformed) continent.[47] The illusion that Calvinism was bound to succeed Catholicism in the Americas initially fostered the adoption of a flexible attitude in guiding to "God's true Church" those who—from a Calvinist point of view—had been misguided by Catholics. The ambition to prove that Calvinists were the better Christians implied a strong dedication to community-building by opening the Reformed Church to all those who had knowledge of Christ but had not yet encountered His "true Church." Initially, the Reformed Church had the intention to build on the foundations established by the Catholic Church in the Americas. Dutch Calvinists compared Catholics in biblical terms to Samaritans, who despite having abandoned the right path still had to be considered legitimate children of Israel. The Catholic churches that the Calvinist Dutch encountered in their Brazilian colony were therefore not to be destroyed but rather to be transformed into "truly Christian" churches, and people who had acquired knowledge of Christ through a Catholic baptism were not to be re-baptized but rather to be guided to a church where they would acquire a "true understanding" of His message. This welcoming attitude was not limited to people of European origin but included the indigenous populations in the Americas as well as those who had been brought there from Africa.

In the early decades of New Netherland, the Dutch Reformed Church was eager to reach out to the slave population. This turned out to be more complicated than expected. While their Catholic rivals provided anyone access to baptism, Calvinist baptismal practice was rooted in the concept of the Thousand-Generation Covenant. This limited baptism to children who had at least one ancestor within the last thousand generations who was a believer in Christ. Since the Reformed Church did not question the legitimacy of Catholic baptism, the Thousand-Generation Covenant included children with a Catholic forefather but it excluded Jews, Muslims, and pagans. Children of the latter group had to provide proof of a thorough understanding of Calvinist doctrine as adults before baptism could be considered.[48]

In 1618 the Synod of Dordt—the council of Reformed theologians from the Dutch Republic, the German states, Scotland, and Geneva that established the tenets of Calvinist orthodoxy—introduced a specification regarding slave children. In *De Ethnicorum Pueris Baptizandis* (1618), the synod presented a reasoning based on Gen. 17:11–13: God's command to Abraham to circumcise all males in his household, including those who had been bought with money. As circumcision was considered to be the equivalent of baptism, it was assumed that members of the Reformed Church were morally obliged to grant all children in their household access to baptism, regardless of skin color, ethnicity, and social status. It also implied that the head of the household had to guarantee a Christian education for the baptized child. If this head of the household failed to provide the child with a decent Christian education, this task had to be fulfilled by its godparent.[49]

In the colonies this rule caused confusion. For instance, it was unclear what had to be done with mulatto children with a Dutch father. Such children also existed in New Netherland despite the fact that the Colonial Council had proclaimed in 1638 that everyone should refrain "from adulterous intercourse with heathens, blacks, or other persons."[50] Captain J(oh)an de Vries' son Jan, for instance, was born out of a relationship with *Swartinne*, meaning "black woman"; and in 1650 the German Harmen Janszen married a (mulatto?) woman of Angolan origin called Maria Malaet.[51] As long as the father was present, the baptism of mulatto children did not represent a challenge to Dutch Reformed doctrine. More difficult was the case of those whose Dutch father could not be identified. While there could be no doubt that such children had to be accepted for baptism, there was no reliable head of the household who could guarantee a Christian education. For those cases, a Christian school was considered an acceptable alternative to the head of the household's role to ensure that these children would grow up with knowledge of the principles of the Reformed Church after their baptism. Yet establishing schools and finding qualified teachers turned out to be an expensive and cumbersome endeavor. A reflection of this can be found in the African Gold Coast. In 1626 Reverend Jonas Michaëlius accepted several mulatto children with unidentified Dutch fathers for baptism after the WIC director in Mouree had reassured him that he would include the children in his household in order to guarantee a Christian education. Michaëlius also founded a school in Mouree and planned to send two baptized mulatto children to the Dutch Republic where they would be prepared to assist him in his work. However, a year later he returned to Europe and subsequently traveled to New Netherland to become minister in New Amsterdam.[52] He was succeeded on the Gold Coast by Laurentius Benderius, who complained that Michaëlius's school bore no fruit since the teacher did not speak the local language(s).[53]

The implementation of *De Ethnicorum Pueris Baptizandis* in the colonies also confronted the Reformed Church with the difficult question of how to approach slave children with two African parents. In accordance with the Thousand-Generation Covenant, the *classis* in Dutch Brazil had decided in 1637 that in those cases a distinction had to be made between baptized and unbaptized slave parents: children whose parents "had been baptized and profess Jesus Christ may and should be allowed for baptism," whereas *heidenkinderen* (children whose parents were pagans) had to wait until their parents had been baptized first or until they themselves were old enough to provide proof that they understood the principles of Calvinist Christianity. In Dutch Brazil, some six hundred black children were baptized in the Dutch Reformed Church.[54]

Since virtually all slaves in New Netherland had already been baptized by a Catholic priest, Reverend Everardus Bogardus accepted many slave children for baptism in the Reformed Church during his time in office in New Amsterdam between 1633 and 1647. Records of the Reformed Church in New Amsterdam show that at least fifty-five children of black parentage were baptized in fifteen years time. Their baptismal witnesses were in most cases members of the black community who had joined the Reformed Church, but Bogardus himself, his wife Anneke Jans, and other members of the white community sometimes assumed this role. In 1641 the Reformed Church in New Amsterdam reported that "the [Native] Americans come not yet to the right knowledge of God; but the Negroes, living among the colonists, come nearer thereto, and give better hope."[55]

By accepting these slave children for baptism, Bogardus displayed a flexible attitude regarding the Christian identity of their parents. This flexibility is surprising since Calvinists tended to be skeptical about the degree of knowledge of Christianity among Catholic Africans. Significantly, Pieter Moortamer reported from Luanda to the Council of Dutch Brazil that the religion of the local population consisted of "superstitions they had learned from the Portuguese."[56] Olfert Dapper claimed that the Kongolese "only pride themselves to be Christians . . . in the presence of Europeans . . . because they known that this is in their interest . . . but in reality they are heretics and idolaters."[57] Johan Maurits was also skeptical about their Christian identity and claimed that the knowledge of Christianity among blacks in Dutch Brazil hardly went beyond "the muttering of Ave Marias while telling rosary beads."[58] This widespread skepticism explains why Reformed ministers who excelled in the baptism of slave children also insisted time and again on the importance of a school. Vincent Soler, who baptized most of the slave children in Dutch Brazil, requested an annex to the church in Recife in 1636 in order to cater to the Christian education of these children.[59]

Bogardus—who as *ziekentrooster* (comforter of the sick) had assisted Benderius on the Gold Coast, where he familiarized himself with Michaëlius's school—was responsible for establishing the first school in New Netherland where baptized slave children would learn the Dutch language and the principles of Calvinist doctrine. In 1636 he asked the West India Company to send a schoolmaster to New Amsterdam in order "to teach and train the youth of both Dutch and blacks in the knowledge of Jesus Christ," and eventually made it possible that Adam Roelantsz van Dokkum was appointed for this task in 1638.[60] This concern indicates that Bogardus did not trust African parents who had been baptized as Catholics and feared that even though they had joined the Reformed Church, they would be unable or unwilling to give their children a "truly Christian" education. Bogardus's leniency in accepting slave children for baptism as well as his insistence on a schoolmaster for these children corresponds to Leendert Joosse's argument that the main objective of this Dutch minister was not proselytizing as such but rather the "extermination of 'Popish' influences" in the American colony.[61]

Following the loss of Dutch Brazil in 1654 and the adoption of a new policy that primarily focused on selling slaves on the Spanish-American market, the WIC no longer concerned itself with the Christianization of slaves. A revealing case of this change in policy is Curaçao. Considering that the bulk of slaves taken to Curaçao would be sold to Catholic plantation owners anyway, the Company considered further attempts to stimulate the baptism of slave children a waste of time and resources. It even allowed Catholic priests from the South American mainland to come to Curaçao in order to baptize slave children, probably because this would make it easier to sell them to Catholic plantation owners.[62] In 1660 Michiel Zyperius informed the Amsterdam classis from Curaçao that "Papists . . . who sometimes arrived there" were baptizing slave children on the island.[63] In the early decades following the conquest of Pernambuco, such news would have provoked a fierce reaction. However, now that Dutch Brazil was lost and the WIC had implemented a new slave policy that was primarily oriented toward Catholic plantation owners, the Reformed Church no longer seemed to care and refrained from intervening in Curaçao.

This decrease of interest in missionary work was accompanied by a tightening of Calvinist orthodoxy. In 1661 the classis reacted angrily to the news that Reverend Adrianus van Beaumont had baptized fifteen slave children in Curaçao. It reproved the minister and made clear that "as long as the parents are actually heathens, although they were baptized in the gross (by wholesale, by Papists), the children may not be baptized."[64] With this regulation, the classis indicated that even Catholic slaves—those who had been baptized "by Papists" in Africa or the Americas—were now officially to be treated as pagans. By excluding African Catholics from the Thousand-Generation Covenant, the children of Catholic slaves could no longer be baptized until their parents had been baptized in a Reformed Church or they themselves had provided proof of understanding Calvinist doctrine in a confession of faith. This made it much more difficult, if not virtually impossible, for slaves to have their children baptized. Van Beaumont, who had previously served in Pernambuco, repented his actions with reference to Dutch Brazil, where "baptismal practices had been very liberal," and promised that he would henceforth adopt "a stricter policy."[65]

In New Netherland, only wealthy Dutch slaveholders, who had the means to provide education, occasionally still cared for the baptism of slave children. A notorious example is that of Stuyvesant, who continued to take his role as head of the household very seriously. Domine Henricus Selyns wrote in October 1660 that forty blacks lived in Stuyvesant's *bouwerij* (farm).[66] When he learned in 1664 that a group of slaves from New Netherland, including children his wife Judith Bayard had presented for baptism, had accidentally been sent to Curaçao and sold to Spaniards from Cartagena, where they were to be raised as Catholics, Stuyvesant ordered Vice Director Beck to do everything possible to repurchase these slaves, an effort that was in vain.[67] Stuyvesant's case was exceptional. Dutch Reformed proselytizing efforts among the slave population owned by the WIC almost came to a standstill in the final years of New Netherland. By that time, individual slaveholders had also become reluctant to welcome slaves in their church community. This related to the uncertainties about the long-term consequences of slave baptism. It was, for instance, unclear who had to assume the role of the head of the household in rural areas where there was no Christian school and, more importantly, whether slave children could still be considered slaves after receiving baptism. Concerning the first question, the Christian slaveholder was supposed to assume the role of the head of the household in places where there was no school. On the second question the Synod of Dordt had not provided a clear answer. There were different opinions, one of which was put forward by the Genevan theologian Giovanni Deodatus. Basing himself on Leviticus 25:39–40, which stipulated that no Israelite could hold another Israelite in perpetual bondage, Deodatus argued that "those baptized should enjoy equal right of liberty with all other Christians and that, concerning the danger of apostasy, they be safeguarded, as far as it can be done, by the prohibiting for the future of all selling and transferring of them to another . . ."[68] The ellipsis at the end was crucial. If "another" meant "another pagan," it implied that these children could still be sold as long as their new owner was also Christian. If "another" meant "another person," it implied that the baptized child could no longer be considered a slave in the sense of saleable property. In his influential book *'t geestelijk roer van 't coop-mansschip* (The Spiritual Rudder of the Merchant's Ship, 1638), Godefridus Ude-mans follows the latter interpretation and argues that "if [slaves] want to submit themselves to the lovely yoke of our Lord Jesus Christ, Christian love requires that they be discharged from the yoke of human slavery."[69] The consequence of these uncertainties was that Dutch slaveholders began to obstruct the baptism of slave children.[70] Not only did baptism imply that they had to make sure these children were provided with a Christian education but there was also a risk that they would not be able to sell them once they were old enough to work.

These changes did not affect those members of the black community who had already been baptized. They continued for several generations to marry and bap-tize their children in the Dutch Reformed Church. Baptism had also facilitated their requests to obtain freedom. In 1644 a group of eleven men—Paulo Angola, Big Manuel, Little Manuel, Manuel de Gerrit de Reus, Simon Congo, Anthony Por-tugis, Gracia, Peter Santomee, Jan Francisco, Little Anthony, and Jan Fort Orange—had been the first to petition the WIC for liberty for themselves and their families using the argument that they had faithfully served the company for eighteen to nineteen years. Eventually a deal was reached in the form of "half-freedom," which meant that they were set "free and at liberty, on the same footing as other free people here in New Netherland, where they shall be able to earn their livelihood by Agriculture, on the land shown and granted to them" on the condition that their children continued to belong as slaves to the WIC and that they had to pay an annual tax of "thirty *skepels* . . . of Maize, or Wheat, Pease or Beans, and one Fat Hog, valued at twenty guilders" to guarantee their liberty. "If anyone of them shall fail to pay the yearly tribute," the Company warned, "he shall forfeit his freedom and return back into the said Company's slavery."[71] In 1649 some members in the Dutch community believed this policy to be unethical and blamed the WIC for the fact that "children of manumitted slaves were retained in slavery, contrary to all public law."[72] Stuyvesant defended himself by answering that by that time only three children of these half-free slaves were still owned as slaves.[73]

In later years, many more slaves requested, and obtained, conditional free-dom from the WIC. In some cases, slaves were assisted by members of the Dutch community. In 1646, for instance, Minister Johannes Megapolensis requested and obtained the freedom of Jan Francisco, on the condition that the latter would annually pay the company ten *skepels* of wheat, or its value.[74] Occasion-ally, slaves owned by individual slaveholders also managed to obtain freedom through negotiation. In 1649 Philip Jansz Ringo granted his slave Manuel the Spaniard freedom on the condition that the latter would pay him one hundred guilders per year for a period of three years. Other slaves were granted manu-mission in wills, which was, for instance, the case of a female Native American slave called Cicilje in Jan Jansz Damen's will in 1649.[75]

By 1664 New Netherland counted some seventy-five free blacks. Since many of them were still relatively young when they obtained freedom, several members of the colony's free black community managed to acquire modest wealth. By 1643 there were black land owners on Manhattan.[76] The free black man Augustyn de Caper even had the means to hire Maritie Hendricks as a contract worker in 1663.[77] In general, however, free blacks remained at the bottom of society. No former slaves were listed among the burghers in New Netherland, nor were they included in the burgher guard.[78]

Several free blacks had been granted land by the WIC near a pond known as the *Kolck* (Fresh Water Pond, near today's Chatham Square) and along the *Wagenweg* (Wagon Road, near today's Fourth Avenue) on the outskirts of the town, close to Stuyvesant's *bouwerij*.[79] Those who lived there had to provide part of their harvest to the WIC and had the obligation to render support in case of a Native American or English attack. Free black landowners and poor whites who lived there side by side occasionally cooperated to defend common interests.[80] The multiracial neighborhood also had its weekly market.[81] This cooperation fostered biracial relationships.[82] In their *Journal of a Voyage to New York* (1679–80), Jasper Danckaerts and Peter Sluyter observe: "We went from the city, following the Broadway, over the *valey*, or the fresh water. Upon both sides of this way were many habitations of negroes, mulattos and whites."[83]

Blacks and whites also shared the same space for entertainment and celebrations. In 1661, for instance, the white settler Cors Jansen authorized Domingo Angola to use his home for a celebration by New Amsterdam's black community.[84] Certain taverns in New Amsterdam were known to have a multiracial clientele.[85] Whether blacks joined Dutch popular revelries during the Pinkster holidays is unknown. In one of the first studies on slave culture in New York, William Stuart argues that "without doubt the . . . Dutch . . . permitted [their slaves] to participate in the . . . annual fairs of their masters," but does not provide evidence to sustain this claim.[86] Willie Page also fails to provide evidence for his assertion that "very early in New Netherland, the African slaves began to celebrate *Pinkster*."[87] Although it is likely that slaves and free blacks participated in Pinkster kermises under Dutch rule, there is no proof that they did. However, the massive participation of African Americans in this originally Dutch tradition is evident in accounts on Pinkster festivals that appeared one century after the demise of New Netherland.

New York and New Jersey

The number of slaves in New York increased quickly in the decades following the Dutch surrender. While the charter generation in New Netherland had been predominantly of West-Central African origin, the slave population became more diverse under English rule. Until the mid-eighteenth century, the majority of new slaves were brought from Caribbean islands such as Jamaica, Barbados, and Antigua. Slaveholders tended to prefer such "seasoned" slaves since they were considered less vulnerable to diseases. Some slaveholders were convinced, however, that slaves imported from the Caribbean were of poor quality and claimed that all the good ones were kept on the islands or sold to plantation owners in Spanish America. They were among the earliest advocates of direct African slave trade—mostly from West Africa but even from as far as Madagascar—which became increasingly popular after the slave "plots" of 1712 and 1741 when many believed that plotting was less likely to occur among slaves who came directly from Africa. Slave imports directly from Africa boomed in the 1740s and reached their high point in the 1770s and 1780s.[88]

A large number of these slaves were acquired by Dutch families, who had decided to remain in America after Stuyvesant's surrender. It is estimated that by the mid-eighteenth century, slaves comprised up to 20 percent of the population in areas in New York and New Jersey with a strong Dutch element. According to data provided by the 1790 New York State Bureau of Census, 27.9 percent of the Dutch living in the state of New York owned slaves, compared to only 16 percent of the Scotch, 15 percent of the Irish, and 11.3 percent of the English and Welsh. The highest density was found in Harlem, the Bowery, and on the western part of Long Island, where up to 60 percent of Dutch households owned at least one slave.[89]

Under English rule, slavery became formally codified and slaves could no longer hold property or conduct business and were no longer considered equal to free persons in court. While in 1664 nearly 20 percent of the black population in New York had been free, this had dropped to about 7 percent by 1724. In a society that became increasingly divided between enslaved blacks and free whites, the position of free blacks came under pressure. Not surprisingly, thus, many of them accompanied the Dutch exodus from Manhattan to rural parts of New York and New Jersey. By the end of the seventeenth century, most black landowners had sold their land on the Fresh Water Pond and along the Wagon Road. Many of them bought shares in the Tappan Patent in the upper Hackensack Valley, from where some later moved to the isolated Ramapo Mountain areas.[90]

Slaves owned by Dutch families in rural areas were mainly employed in agriculture, a task often combined with that of household servant. In 1794 William Strickland wrote that people living on the western part of Long Island were mainly "of Dutch descent whose chief occupation is that of raising vegetables for the supply of the market of New-York." He also argued that Dutch farmers in America were completely dependent on their slaves: "Many of the old Dutch farmers in the county has 20 or 30 slaves about their house. To their care and management everything is left; the oldest slave manages the lands, directs the cultivation of it and without consulting him the master can do nothing."[91] In his description of Kings County (Brooklyn) in 1776, where many Dutch families lived, the Hessian officer Carl Baurmeister confirmed that in "[n]ear every dwelling house negroes (their slaves) are settled, who cultivate the most fertile land, pasture the cattle and do all the menial work."[92] Similar observations were made about Dutch families in the Hudson and Mohawk Valleys. During a visit to Coxsackie in 1787, Alexander Coventry observed that "each individual family had more or less black slaves who did all the work on the farm, and in the house"; and traveling in Ulster County in 1796, the French exile François Alexandre Frédéric, duc de la Rochefoucauld-Liancourt, characterized the local inhabitants as "dull torpid Hollanders" and observed that "each of the families, in some instances even the poorest has one or two negroes or negresses."[93]

While some slaves also worked in mills and on vessels, others were trained in crafts or trades. Among wealthy families, domestic slaves functioned as a status symbol.[94] The oldest image of an African American resident in Albany is a painting known as the "Boy of the Van Rensselaer Family." The painting dates to ca. 1730 and is attributed to John Heaton. The boy's expensive clothes—knee socks out of wool or silk, shoes with buckles, a jacket and a shirt out of linen or cotton—reveal a tendency among Dutch elite families to use slaves as a way to display wealth.[95] The painting may also relate to a custom in Dutch American elite families to "present" children with a slave of roughly the same age in their early childhood years.[96] According to the Scotswoman Anne Grant, who spent her childhood years from 1758 until 1768 with the Dutch Schuyler family in Albany, "when a negro-women's child attained the age of three years, the first new year's day after, it was solemnly presented to a son or daughter, or other young relative of the family, who was of the same sex with the child so presented."[97] A similar custom existed among Dutch families in Suriname, where the *lijfslaaf* (body slave) was usually a child taken from one of the domestic slaves. These children grew up together and knew everything about each other. When the *masra* (master) or *misi* (miss) married, the *lijfslaaf* accompanied him or her to the new house.[98]

Such practices, however, should not obscure that Dutch slaveholding families were careful to preserve enough distance from slaves so as not to tarnish their reputations. Unlike in Iberian colonies, where it was common practice that male members of slaveholding families had slave mistresses, sexual involvement with a slave could ruin one's reputation in the Dutch community. Grant mentions the case of a member of the Schuyler family who had fathered a child to a "favorite negro-woman . . . whose color gave testimony to the relation." The family educated the biracial boy named Chalk, but made sure that he remained

Attributed to John Heaton, *Boy of the Van Rensselaer Family*, ca. 1730. This painting is the oldest image of an African American resident in Albany. It depicts a young daughter of the Van Rensselaer family with a flower, a small bird, a dog, and a jingle as well as a black male child. The bird and flower are common *vanitas*—symbols of mortality. The obedient dog symbolizes the girl's good education. Her jingle with a whistle and teether out of red coral indicates that the girl's permanent teeth were erupting, which usually occurs at the age of six. The boy is about twice as old as the girl. Since he is wearing breeches, he must be at least ten. Current repository: Ms. and Mr. Rodman C. Rockefeller.

out of sight: a farm "in depth of woods embraced" was arranged for him, as well as a marriage to a "destitute white woman, who had somehow wandered from the older colonies."[99] It is also revealing that baptismal records of the Dutch Reformed Church in Albany omitted the parents' names of the four children (Jeptha, Pieter, Dina, and Maria) baptized in 1704 as "children of a Christian father and a Negro mother."[100]

One reason for the prevalence of slavery among Dutch families is that it was not a new phenomenon but only the intensification of a custom that had been initiated under Dutch rule. One can also suspect a causal relationship between the eagerness of these families to preserve a Dutch identity and the prevalence of slavery. Francis Harrison, a customs official in New York City, argued in the 1720s that "especially the Dutch ... are unwilling [to] take any white servants."[101] In fact, the Dutch resistance to anglicization naturally implied reluctance to hire Anglophone workers. Due to the lack of new Dutch immigrants willing to come to America, the use of slaves was a logical alternative for a community that stubbornly resisted assimilation to the dominant Anglo-American culture.

Slaves who grew up in insular Dutch communities adopted the Dutch language.[102] Runaway slave advertisements show how prevalent the use of Dutch was in New York and New Jersey. Hodges and Brown's anthology with advertisements dating from 1716 until 1783 includes 186 references to slaves who spoke English, while fifty-eight spoke (Low) Dutch, compared to only thirteen who spoke French, seven who spoke Spanish, and four who spoke German or High Dutch (*Hochdeutsch*). Among those who spoke Dutch, most were bilingual (English-Dutch) and some spoke as many as three languages. For instance, William Smith, who ran away from his master Arent Bradt in Schenectady, spoke "English, High and Low Dutch"; John Watson, who left his master Cornelius Wynkoop in Bergen spoke "English, French and Dutch"; and Cato, who abandoned his master Cornelius Low in Raritan Landing, spoke "very good English and Dutch, also pretty good High Dutch."[103]

Not all slaves were multilingual. Those who had lived all their lives in a Dutch-speaking environment often had difficulties speaking other languages. For instance, a slave called Hank, who ran away from his master John Mersereau on Staten Island, spoke "better Dutch than English"; Cyrus, who abandoned his master Jeremiah Stanton on Staten Island, spoke "Dutch and very bad English"; and Adonia, who left her master Johannes Blauveldt in Orange County, spoke "pretty good Low Dutch" but "little English."[104] When Alexander Hamilton (not to be confused with the founding father of the same name) was on his way to New York City in 1744, his slave, Domo, asked directions from a black woman on Coney Island who could only speak Dutch: "'Dis de way to York?' says Domo, 'Yaw, dat is Yarikee,' said the wench, pointing to the steeples. 'What devil you say?' replys Domo. 'Yaw, mynheer,' said the wench. 'Damme you, what you say?' said Domo again. 'Yaw, yaw,' said the girl. 'You a dam black bitch,' said Domo, and so rid on."[105] When writing down his memoirs in 1839, the Dutch immigrant Harm Jan Huidekoper recalled that in the late eighteenth century, "low Dutch was [on Long Island, in New York, along the North River, at Albany, Schenectady, etc.] the common language of most of the old people, and particularly of the Negroes."[106]

Another revealing case is that of Sojourner Truth, who grew up in rural Ulster County. When she was sold to the English-speaking Neely family around 1807, she had tremendous difficulties understanding her new masters. "If they sent me for a frying pan," she says in her *Narrative*, "not knowing what they meant, perhaps I carried them the pot-hooks and trammels."[107] Apparently, she did not learn much English during the short period she stayed with the Neelies because Gertrude Dumont, the daughter of John Dumont who bought her around 1810, recalls that upon arrival "she could neither talk nor understand anything but Low or Holland Dutch."[108] Gertrude Vanderbilt confirms that some older black women in Flatbush who had been slaves of Dutch families still spoke Dutch amongst each other in the late nineteenth century.[109] An article about Bergen County, New Jersey, in the *Troy Daily Times* of August 1885 pointed out that many older people there still spoke "Jersey Dutch" amongst each other and that "the curious lingo is also preserved by the old colored folks. . . . Nearly all the negroes in this section are descended from slaves who belonged to farmers whose families still own the land."[110]

Some slaves developed a strong emotional attachment to the Dutch language. Significantly, John Jea claimed in his *Life History* (1815) that he experienced a divine revelation in which God had promised him he would be taught how to read the Bible "both in English and in Dutch."[111] Such emotional attachment to the Dutch language is also revealed in the recollections by blacks with roots in the Hudson Valley. One of them mentioned during an interview that "for as long as anyone in my mother's family can remember, the men of the family have wandered the West Shore Valley of the Hudson from Kingston to Albany. They were Ten Broecks, Cantines, and Van Ettens. They were Dutch and proud of it." He also recalled "my Aunt Sebania telling me about her great-grandmother, a stern old lady who both spoke and understood English, but who refused to speak it except in the privacy of her home. In public she spoke Dutch, as any proper person should do, a dignified language."[112]

Several outsiders who became acquainted with the Dutch community in New York and New Jersey have argued that there was less distance between masters and slaves among the Dutch than among the British. The English captain Alexander Graydon, who in 1776 and 1777 had been a prisoner on Long Island during the War of Independence, familiarized himself with the island's Dutch community and described how at the house of a certain Jacob Suydam "a black boy too was generally in the room; not as a waiter, but as a kind of *enfant de maison*, who walked about, or took post in the chimney corner with his hat on, and occasionally joined in the conversation." Graydon assumed that "it is probable, that but for us, he would have been placed at the table; and that it had been the custom before we came." It made him conclude that "the idea of equality, was more fully and fairly acted upon in this house of a British subject than ever I have seen it practiced by the most vehement declaimers for the rights of man among ourselves."[113] In her bucolic childhood recollections *Memoirs of an American Lady* (1808), Grant went even further, arguing: "Let me not be detested as an advocate for slavery when I say that I think I have never seen people so happy in servitude as the domestics of the Albanians."[114] Her surprisingly mild judgment of slavery among the Dutch corresponds to that of Alexander Coventry, who observed in his diary that "although the blacks were slaves, yet I feel warranted in asserting that the laboring class in no country lived more easily, were better clothed and fed, or had more of life, than these slaves."[115] This statement corresponds to the judgment by the Scotsman James Flint, who visited Dutch families on Long Island during his American journey between 1818–20 and observed that "there are still a considerable number of slaves in Long Island; they are treated with a degree of humanity that slaves in some other parts of the world never experience; they are well fed, and the whip is very seldom resorted to."[116]

Such statements can easily transmit the false impression that slavery among the Dutch was a benign system. They run the risk of concealing the bitter truth that the very institution of slavery denied not only the equality but also the humanity of people. The answer of a slave to the suggestion by James Flint that he was probably happier than some poor free people since his Dutch American master fed him well makes precisely this point: "That may be true, Sir, but put bird in cage, give him plenty to eat, still he fly away."[117] There is also no reason to assume that punishments among the Dutch were less severe or less frequent than among other slaveholders. The earlier quoted article on Bergen County in the *Troy Daily Times* shows that cruel punishments of slaves also occurred on a regular basis among the Dutch. The author refers to an eighteenth-century report on the case of "two slaves [who] were subjected to 500 lashes each, 100 inflicted on each succeeding Saturday, for an assault upon a man whereby his life was endangered. One of the slaves died on the fourth Saturday." The author also quotes from a report, dated October 28, 1767, stating that "last week the Negro that murdered Tuers was burned at Hackensack, agreeable to his sentence," the evidence against him being that "when he touched Tuers's corpse blood flowed from its nostrils." The author also refers to a bill of one Daniel Hansome "for wood carted for burning two Negroes" and mentions that by the late nineteenth century, older people in Bergen Country still recalled "the burning of two Negroes at the other side of the Hackensack, near the house of Dewerk Van Horn."[118] The quotes by Graydon, Grant, Coventry, and Flint should thus not be misinterpreted as reflections of a racially harmonious society.

This also applies to religion. The presence of slaves in the Dutch Reformed Church was neither a common nor an undisputed phenomenon. While the transition from Dutch to English rule undoubtedly brought the Dutch American community closer to slaves for whom Dutch had become the native language, this process of Dutch acculturation rarely extended to religion. Most blacks who continued to marry and baptize their children in the Reformed

Church were descendants of those who had once been baptized in New Netherland. An interesting case is that of the free Dutch-speaking black man Aree van
Guinee, who entered history by hosting the first Lutheran service by Reverend
Justus Falckner in his house near what is now Franklin Township, New Jersey,
on August 1, 1714.[119]

While most Dutch churches had a section reserved for slaves, documents
from the Reformed Church dating back to the colonial period rarely mention
slaves and reveal that Dutch congregants tended to be hostile to their admis-
sion.[120] The case of Rachel, who in 1703 was baptized aged seventeen in the
Reformed Church of Kingston, is revealing of the concerns among the Dutch
that baptism would lead to pleas for freedom: the records explicitly mention
that "besides the points required of her in the formula of baptism, she also
promised the congregation to serve her mistress, Catharin Cottyn, faithfully
and diligently until the death of her mistress, and after that to serve her master,
Jan Cottyn, and afterwards she shall be at liberty and free."[121] In 1708 the Anglican missionary Elias Neau complained that he had not been able to catechize
in New Jersey because "they are almost all Dutch there and for they that live in
town are afraid that their slaves may demand their freedom after Baptism."[122]
According to Chaplain John Sharpe, one of the slaves involved in the 1712 plot
in New York City had attended Neau's catechism classes secretly and "had made
some proficience but was not admitted to baptism through the reluctance of
his [Dutch] master [Hendrick Hooghlandt], whom he had often solicited for
it."[123] Ira Berlin has indicated that less than a tenth of the black population in
New York attended church by the middle of the eighteenth century. Strangely,
he interprets this low number as a sign of "rejection of Christianity" by blacks
despite "decades of proselytization."[124] This dubious interpretation certainly
does not apply to Dutch-speaking areas. Among the Dutch, there was hardly
any proselytization among the slaves after the mid-seventeenth century, and
whenever outsiders attempted to reach out to Dutch-owned slaves, their masters thwarted these efforts.

The way the Dutch Reformed Church struggled with the question of slave
baptism is notable in the case of Theodorus Frelinghuysen's slave James Albert
Ukawsaw Gronniosaw.[125] Gronniosaw's *Narrative*, published around 1770, shows
how the famous Pietist minister dutifully assumed the role of head of the household in preparing his slave for baptism. Frelinghuysen taught him how to pray,
explained the basics of Christianity to him, and sent him to school to learn
Dutch. Despite all those efforts, Frelinghuysen remained hesitant to baptize
Gronniosaw. He planned to take Gronniosaw with him to Amsterdam in order to
have the classis take a decision on his baptism, but passed away before he could
do so.[126] Gronniosaw's case indicates that the fact that slaves owned by Dutch
families were not baptized does not necessarily imply that they had no notion

of Christianity. This is also visible in Truth's *Narrative*. Although Truth's mother was not baptized, she nevertheless taught her daughter the Lord's Prayer.[127]

It can, in any case, be concluded that only exceptional ones in the Dutch American slave community were admitted to the Reformed Church, and that those who became members maintained a secondary position. This spiritual neglect was later recognized by the Dutch Reformed Minister David Demarest, who in 1896 admitted that "the constitution of the Dutch Church provided that Masters ought to have slave children baptized and religiously educated. But all this was sadly neglected. . . . The religious welfare of the negroes was not cared for."[128]

Religious segregation, not only in Dutch but also in British families, caused a deep gap in social life between slaves and masters. It also fueled distrust and irritation about slave gatherings, especially when such meetings disturbed the Sunday rest. Documents reveal countless complaints and attempts to prohibit such gatherings. There were also fears that free blacks would use those gatherings to reach out to newly arrived slaves. In 1671, for instance, the New York City authorities accused the free black tavern owners Manuel Angola and Domingo of "entertaining sundry of the burgher's Negroes to the great damage of the owners" and charged them henceforth "not to entertain any Servants or Helps, whether Christian or Negro on pain of forfeiting their freedom . . . or harboring any Servants or Helps longer than twenty-four hours."[129] In 1682 the New York Grand Jury complained about blacks "gathering themselves togather in Greate numbers of the Lords Day and att other unseasonable times useing and exerciseing Severall Rude and Unlawfull sports and Pasetimes to the Dishonour of God." And despite the 1683 ordinance that prohibited the unsupervised assembly in New York City of more than four slaves at a single time and place, the Grand Jury again complained in 1692 about "the frequent randivouzing of Negro Slaves att the houses of the free Negroes" and about slaves "found playing or making any hooting or disorderly noise in the Street on the Lords days."[130]

Although New York City's Common Council had prohibited the sale of liquor to slaves without their masters' consent in 1691, many tavern owners flouted this law.[131] In 1710, for instance, Elizabeth Green was taken to court for allowing "Negro Slaves to assemble and meet together to feast and Revel in the Night Time."[132] It was clear that as long slaves had money, it was virtually impossible to impose such restrictions. In vain, the authorities of New York City in 1681, New Jersey in 1682, and New York Colony in 1684 prohibited slaves to sell products. The parallel economy by slaves proved to be unstoppable.[133]

In 1696 Mayor William Merritt of New York City personally experienced how difficult it was to enforce slave ordinances. When he tried to disperse a group of slaves and threatened to take them into custody, one of them slapped him in the face.[134] In November 1697 the Grand Jury in Kings County again complained of "great concourse and Mobbing of Negroe Slaves from Yorke and other places to this Place on the Sabbath Day."[135] In April 1700 the Supreme Court criticized the New York City mayor for failing to address "the Generall breach & profanation of the Sabbath by the frequent meeting of negroes in tumultuous crowds."[136] While the number of slaves allowed to assemble in New York City was theoretically limited to three in 1702, Elias Neau complained in 1703 that "on Sundays ... the Streets are full of Negroes who dance & divert themselves."[137] Following the insurrection of 1712, the "Act for Preventing, Suppressing and Punishing the Conspiracy and Insurrection of negroes and other Slaves" restricted even more the slaves' freedom of movement.[138] However, contemporaries were well aware of the fact that such prohibitions only created the illusion of control. As Thelma Foote confirms, "the colonial authorities never instituted fully effective mechanisms for policing the city's enslaved population."[139] Although occasional punishments did occur, the regulations were generally poorly enforced and masters often found it convenient to close their eyes to violations so long as their slaves rendered satisfactory service.[140]

New York slaveholders were also inclined to make other concessions to their slaves in order to stimulate them to work hard and to remain loyal. For instance, it was common practice that slaves would negotiate conjugal or family visits and a number of free days during holidays before moving to a new master.[141] One example is that of a slave called Yat, who negotiated with his new owners that he would be permitted three days off for Christmas, two for New Year, two for Easter, and three for Pinkster to "go Fiddling."[142] Like Yat, slaves owned by Dutch families were usually given three or more days off to celebrate Pinkster. One source about Pinkster even mentions how "the negro slaves had done practically no work for a week in anticipation of the holiday."[143] Pittstown Farmer Simeon Button's account book also reveals that cash advances used to be paid to black workers on the occasion of Pinkster.[144] During Pinkster, slaves were free to leave the premises. This leeway was granted despite the fact that some tried to take advantage of the situation to flee. In July 1803, for instance, the sixteen-year-old slave Tone of a Dutch farmer in Albany had planned not to return to his master after the Pinkster festival was over.[145]

The earliest source on slaves participating in popular Pinkster celebrations is an indirect reference in Grant's *Memoirs of an American Lady* (1808). In her childhood memories from the 1750s and 1760s, Grant does not explicitly mention Pinkster celebrations in Albany but refers to certain "licentious and idle habits" that were particularly strong during "three stated periods in the year, when, for a few days, young and old, masters and slaves, were abandoned to unruly enjoyment, and neglected every serious occupation for pursuits of this nature."[146] One can assume that Pinkster was one of these three periods. The fact that Grant does not tell her readers anything specific about these celebrations indicates that elite families such as the Schuylers considered the festival inappropriate for a young girl.

The first explicit reference to African American participation in Pinkster celebrations dates to 1786, when Alexander Coventry, a Scottish medical doctor residing in the Hudson Valley, comments: "It is all frolicking to-day with the Dutch and the Negro. This is a holy day, Whitsunday, called among the Dutch 'Pinkster.'" Two days later, he notes: "Still frolicking and dancing for Pinkster." In April 1789 Coventry also explained that before an African American man called Cuff agreed to be his slave, he negotiated with his new master a certain number of free days for the upcoming holidays: "Van Curen's negro Cuff came to me in the morning. I asked him if he would live with me. He said he would. . . . Cuff . . . wanted two days next week to keep Paas [Easter]" and then continued his diary in June with the news that Cuff was "keeping Pinkster, a festival or feast among the Dutch."[147] Grant Thorburn, an immigrant from Scotland who came to New York City in 1794, recalled that in those years "Paus [Easter] and Pinkster were of universal observance." On those holidays, he claims, "all made it an idle day—boys and negroes might be seen all day standing in the market place, laughing, joking, and cracking eggs. In the afternoon, the grown up apprentices and servant girls, used to dance on the green in Bayard's farm in the Bowery."[148] Similarly, in 1797 the playwright William Dunlap observed on a journey from Manhattan to New Jersey that "[t]he settlements along the river are Dutch, it is the holiday they call pinkster & every public house is crowded with merry makers & wagon's full of rustic beaux & belles met us at every mile. The blacks as well as their masters were frolicking and the women & children look'd peculiarly neat and well dressed."[149] Unlike Grant's observations, these three other references to Pinkster—the only ones dating back to the eighteenth century—do not refer to elite families but to how ordinary Dutch families and their slaves celebrated the holiday. These authors do not portray the festival as morally dubious entertainment. On the contrary, people dress up nicely, the children participate and the type of frolicking on Pinkster seems to be as innocent as egg coloring. Although neither source explicitly mentions that masters and slaves celebrated the Pinkster holiday together, the authors make no reference to any specifically African American performances.

This is different in nineteenth-century sources, two of which provide a lengthy description of the African American performances that occurred during Pinkster celebrations. The oldest describes the Pinkster festival in Albany in the year 1803 and is provided by an anonymous eyewitness calling him- or herself A.B. In the account that was published in the newspaper the *Albany Centinel*, A.B. highlights that the African American community usually began its preparations for the festivities in the week anticipating the holiday, when "the negroes patrol the streets in the evening more than usual and begin to practice a little upon the Guinea drum."[150] The expression "more than usual" shows that it was not uncommon in early-nineteenth-century Albany to see blacks walking on the street after working hours. The account also highlights the importance of playing on the "Guinea drum." Since Guinea was then an unspecified geographical reference, the expression "Guinea drum" does not necessarily mean that the percussion instrument observed by A.B. was effectively from Guinea or the Gulf of Guinea. The term "Guinea" could in those years refer to any place along the West African coast from Senegal down through Angola.[151]

According to A.B., the center of Pinkster celebrations in Albany was a hill appropriately called "Pinkster Hill." There the slave community prepared a type of amphitheater, with all kinds of booths, similar to those typically used at a Dutch kermis. "The place of encampment is along the great western road," A.B. specifies, and "on each side of which arbors of different sizes and figures are erected." The camp is built in the following manner: "A number of long stakes are stuck in the ground enclosing the space intended to be occupied as a bower. Between these stakes the pine bush is woven . . . [and] the covering is of the same material, sometimes woven and sometimes thrown loosely over the cross-sticks or rafters," so that "the whole scenery at a distance, especially when the wind puts the shrubby texture of these airy cottages in motion, assumes the appearance not of art but nature, and forms a beautiful contrast with the forbidding nakedness of the surrounding hills." "These arbors," A.B. explains, "are divided into different apartments, filled up with seats, and stored with fruit, cakes, cheese, beer and liquors of various kinds. In the center of this villa, and in front of the royal arbor, a sort of Amphitheatre is laid out, where the Guinea dance is to be performed." Pinkster Hill was an isolated area in Albany, near the slave cemetery and the gallows. It is unlikely that the Dutch community would have chosen such a remote area for its Pinkster kermis. Probably, Pinkster Hill was the place where the slaves traditionally gathered to stage their own celebrations during the Pinkster holidays, separate from those of the Dutch. This view corresponds to Grant's observation that slaves in Albany had been granted cottages by their masters on the hills above the town, which served "as a place of joyful liberty."[152]

By the year 1803, however, this once isolated area located at the end of State Street—where the New York State Capitol would be built in 1867—had become more easily accessible and attracted a large crowd of spectators. "On Monday morning," A.B. explains, "the blacks and a certain class of whites, together with children of all countries and colours, begin to assemble on *Pinkster Hill* collected from every part of the city and from the adjacent country for many miles around, forming in the whole a motley group of thousands," presenting "a kind of chaos of sin and folly of misery and fun." A.B.'s expression "a certain class of whites" suggests that members of the white elite were not to be seen on Pinkster Hill, which corresponds to Grant's experience while living with the Schuylers.

Less affluent whites did, however, gather in great numbers on Pinkster Hill to watch the arrival of a procession, which, according to later sources, started in the city center and then went up State Street.[153] According to A.B., this procession featured a black king and other black dignitaries: "An old Guinea Negro, who is called *King Charles*, is master of ceremonies, whose authority is absolute, and whose will is law during the Pinkster holiday. On Monday morning between the hours of ten and twelve o'clock, his majesty after having passed through the principal streets in the city, is conducted in great style to *The Hill* already swarming with a multifarious crowd of gasping spectators." "Before *him* is borne a standard," A.B. explains, "on which significant colours are displayed, and a painting containing his *Portrait*, and specifying what has been the duration of his reign." Then, "two pedestrians, in appropriate badges, lead a superb steed, of a beautiful cream colour, on which their fictitious sovereign rides in all the pomp of an eastern *nabob*—whilst a large procession of the most distinguished and illustrious characters follow after." Later sources have identified Charles as one of the slaves owned by Volkert Petrus Douw, a descendant of Volkert Jan Douw, who immigrated to New Netherland in 1638. Volkert P. Douw was related to the Van Rensselaer family and to Anneke Jans, the wife of the New Amsterdam minister Everardus Bogardus.[154] Douw was one of the most influential and wealthiest men in Albany. He had served as mayor between 1761 and 1770 and as a New York senator between 1786 and 1793. He owned about fourteen slaves who worked on his estate called Wolvenhoeck (Wolves' Corner) or, in anglicized form, Wolvenhook, about a mile south of the Albany city center.[155] One of these slaves was the African-born Charles, who passed away in the year 1824 at very old age.[156]

According to A.B., the Pinkster festivities served as a source of income for Charles and the organization he directed: "[A]fter the ceremonys in honor of his arrival are ended, he proceeds to collect his revenue. This consists in a levy of one shilling upon every black man's tent, and two upon every tent occupied by a white man." "Compliance with this requisition is indispensable to the occupying of a tent within the limits of the encampment," A.B. explains, because "if any individual refuses to comply, his tent, by the direction of the King, is instantly demolished." Once the tax collection is completed, dances are performed: "The most singular of these sports and the only one which I shall particularly notice, is what the Negroes call Toto, or the Guinea dance." "In the centre of the *villa*," A.B. explains, "there was a kind of Amphitheatre allotted for that purpose. On the one side of which is the royal tent fronting the dancing ground, where the parties perform and around which the spectators are assembled." At the entrance of this tent "sits their chief musician dressed in a horrid manner—rolling his eyes and tossing his head with an air of savage wildness; grunting and mumbling out certain inarticulate but hideous sounds and at the same time malling with both hands upon the hollow sounding Guinea drum." A.B. continues the description with a focus on "two imps, one on each side decorated with feathers and cow's tails," who "copy his uncouth and terrifying grimaces, and thumping on two similar but smaller instruments imitate his sounds of frightful dissonance." According to A.B., the dance consists "in placing the body in the most disgusting attitudes and performing, without reserve, the most lewd and indecent gesticulation, at the crisis of which the parties meet and embrace in a kind of amorous Indian hug, terminating in a sort of masquerade capture."

The second lengthy description of a Pinkster celebration was provided in the mid-nineteenth century by the physician James Eights (1798–1882), who grew up in Albany. Eights first published his childhood recollections of the festival in the Albany newspaper the *Cultivator,* and in 1867 this lengthy account was reprinted under the title "Pinkster Festivities in Albany Sixty Years Ago" by Joel Munsell in the *Collections on the History of Albany.* Although Eights's recollections date back to a time when he was a young teenager and were written down when he was in his fifties, his account is very detailed. According to Eights, the festivities were coordinated by the slaves themselves and "the master of ceremonies, on this occasion—the Beau Brummel of the day—was Adam Blake, then body servant to the old patroon," to whom "was unanimously entrusted the arduous duty of reducing to some kind of order this vast mass of incongruent material, which his superior ability soon enabled him to accomplish with complete success."[157] Adam Blake, here referred to in connection to the English fashion icon George Bryan "Beau" Brummell, had arrived in New York in the late eighteenth century as a slave of the Dutch American Jacob Lansing and was later sold to the influential patroon Stephen van Rensselaer III.[158] The fact that both Charles and Adam Blake served among the most influential families in the region indicates that the wealth of the master corresponded to the position of the slave in the organizational committee of the Pinkster performances, which provides credibility to the assumption that these performances occurred with the support of elite families.

The celebrations on Pinkster Hill had a specific order: while celebrations on Pentecost Sunday were largely dedicated to the children, the following day was reserved for the king procession: "The hour of ten having now arrived . . . a deputation was then selected to wait upon their venerable sovereign king, 'Charley of the Pinkster hill,' with the intelligence that his respectful subjects were congregated, and were anxiously desirous to pay all proper homage to his majesty their king." Whereas A.B. refers to the Pinkster king as an "old Guinea Negro," Eights claims that "Charles originally came from Africa, having, in his infant days, been brought from Angola." He describes Charles as "tall, thin and athletic; and although the frost of nearly seventy winters had settled on his brow, its chilling influence had not yet extended to his bosom, and he still retained all the vigor and agility of his younger years." Eights describes his uniform as that "worn by a British brigadier of the olden time. Ample broad cloth scarlet coat, with wide flaps almost reaching to his heels, and gayly ornamented everywhere with broad tracings of bright golden lace." His clothes were "of yellow buckskin, fresh and new, with stockings blue, and burnished silver buckles to his well-blacked shoe." Charles also wore a "tri-cornered cocked hat trimmed also with lace of gold."

Eights then continues with a description of the dances that used to take place on Pinkster Hill: "It consisted chiefly of couples joining in the performances at varying times, and continuing it with their utmost energy until extreme fatigue . . . compelled them to retire and give space to a less exhausted set; and in this successive manner was the excitement kept up . . . until the shades of night began to fall." The principal musical instrument was "a symmetrically formed wooden article usually denominated an eel-pot, with a cleanly dressed sheep skin drawn tightly over its wide and open extremity—no doubt obtained expressly for the occasion from the celebrated Fish slip, at the foot of the Maiden's lane." The chief drummer was "Jackey Quackenboss, then in his prime of life and well known energy, beating lustily with his naked hands upon its loudly sounding head, successively repeating the ever wild, though euphonic cry of *Hi-a-bomba, bomba, bomba*, in full harmony with the thumping sounds." His vocal sounds, Eights explains, "were readily taken up and as oft repeated by the female portion of the spectators not otherwise engaged in the exercises of the scene, accompanied by the beating of time with their ungloved hands, in strict accordance with the eel-pot melody." Jackey Quackenboss is likely to have been one of the nine slaves owned by Hendrick Quackenbush, whose impressive manor house still stands.[159]

On the third day of the Pinkster festival, "the upper class of revelers had left the ground to seek entertainment elsewhere, or spend the evening in tea-party gossip. . . . On the succeeding fourth and fifth days," Eights continues, "the grounds were left to the free enjoyment of the humbler classes," which, "instigated by the more potent draughts they swallowed, speedily brought on wrangling discord" and "quickly succeeded by rounds of fighting, bruised eyes, and bloody noses unnumerated, big Jack Van Patten, the city bully, being unanimously declared the champion of the lists, having successfully overthrown all his numerous opponents." Eights thus indicates that the celebrations on Pinkster Hill observed a hierarchy and that people were well aware of who was supposed to be seen or not seen on which days.

These two lengthy descriptions are the most important and detailed sources of information on African American Pinkster celebrations. An additional source is Absalom Aimwell's *Pinkster Ode*, a literary text on Pinkster published in 1803. The ode is dedicated to "*Carolus Africanus Rex*" or, in the English form, "King

Charles, Captain-General and Commander in Chief of the Pinkster Boys." The author behind the pseudonym is unknown.[160] According to Aimwell, Charles was the son of an African king and "tho' for a sceptre he was born, / tho' from his father's kingdom torn, / and doom'd to be a slave; / still he retains his native majesty."[161] Although some scholars have quoted this passage as evidence that Charles was an African of royal descent, it should be stressed that the *Pinkster Ode* is a literary text that should be viewed with cautious skepticism.

Other accounts of Pinkster or references to the festival can be found in diaries, memoirs, newspapers, magazines, novels, and historical studies. The authenticity of these sources cannot always be guaranteed. Only in exceptional cases did nineteenth- and early-twentieth-century authors identify their sources of information. Many accounts on Pinkster in newspapers and magazines were published anonymously and, although the authors claim to have personally witnessed the festival, their descriptions may in some cases have been inspired by what A.B., Eights, or others had previously written about Pinkster. Due to the limited number of sources on Pinkster, however, the new information they provide should be taken into consideration in the analysis of the festival.

In one of those accounts, published anonymously in the May 1875 edition of the *Manhattan and de la Salle Monthly*, it is argued that Albany had a long history of black king elections; the dignity of these kings "was elective, and for life" and the "last monarch of that dynasty was Charley."[162] Other accounts of Charles's life give an ironic twist to their descriptions of "the black king" by adding humorous or demeaning anecdotes. An example can be found in *Harper's New Monthly Magazine* in 1857, where an Albany citizen calling himself "Knickerbocker—a Dutchman of purest Belgic blood" argues that he was a light child and that "on one occasion Charley took me on his shoulders and leaped a bar more than five feet in height. He was so generously 'treated' because of his feat, that he became gloriously drunk an hour afterward, and I led him home just at sunset."[163] In 1881 *Harper's* published another anecdote on King Charles by an unidentified author, who claimed that "although King Charley often boasted of his bravery, his master and fellow-servants would twit him with cowardice, and call out to him, 'Saratoga'—a most sensitive point with him." According to the author, Charles's master was "en route to join the army at Saratoga and Charles was following him on horseback as body-servant." It was moonlight, and "he saw moving with the wind a quantity of Indian salt, commonly known as *sumac*, which, when ripe, presents a red appearance." Charles mistook this for the enemy and cried out, "*Heer, ik zag een vyand*, [Master, I saw the enemy] and putting spurs to his horse, he rode in hot haste for home, proclaiming that his master had been captured, and he, after hard fighting, had escaped."[164] The same story includes, however, another anecdote that recognizes Charles's prestige by pointing out that he was the man chosen by Douw to ride his best horse in a bet

Anonymous, *King Charles Racing on Ice*. Artist's conception of Charles, the Pinkster king, winning a nightly horse racing competition for his master Volkert Petrus Douw against General Philip Schuyler. In *Harper's New Monthly Magazine* 62 (March 1881).

against General Schuyler. According to the author, Schuyler had offered to bet a large amount that his horse could beat a famous racehorse named Sturgeon, owned by Douw. Although it was in midwinter, the story goes that "Indians and negroes, under Peter Van Loan, the overseer, entered into the sport, cleared the ice, and stationed themselves with lanterns across and down the river. The race was run, old Sturgeon coming in first, amid the shouts and yells of white men, Indians, and negroes, his rider being King Charles, of Pinkster fame."[165] Since these stories were written several decades after Charles's demise, their content may be based more on legends than on actual eyewitness accounts.

Nevertheless, the anecdotes consistently show that there was a close connection between Charles and his master, which adds credibility to the assumption that the African American Pinkster celebrations in Albany occurred with the support of elite slaveholders.

Other sources provide more information on the mysterious "Toto dance." The author of an anonymous account in the 1836 edition of the *Family Magazine* claims that the "totaw" dance "was performed by the Blacks of both sexes, and somewhat resembled the Spanish Fandango."[166] In 1846 an anonymous account of a toto dance in the *Schenectady Cabinet* points out that dancers "would collect together in a hurly-burly manner" and then move "in a promiscuous manner, observing a gyratory movement around the musician, hopping and jumping, giving to their bodies every species of fanciful, fascinating and even lascivious motion bordering on the obscene, somewhat in the manner of the Egyptian dancing girls." The author also argues that the dancers ended up reaching a state of trance, characterized by "a profuse perspiration and a foaming at the mouth, and with a deep, concentrated effluvia emitted from their bodies."[167] Another anonymous account, published in the *Schenectady Daily Evening Star and Times* in 1866, claims that the name of the dance related to a song with a melody that sounded like "to-to-to-to-to-to-kicka knock a paw." It was allegedly sung "at first slowly and 'crescendo' gradually, until singing by the whole crowd of negroes and tom-tom beatings became one confused jargon." Allegedly, some "twenty or thirty wenches, aged anywhere from fourteen to eighty, and of all shades and dresses" would then step "into the ring" and express their loyalty to the Pinkster king by "sh[aking] him by the hand and kiss[ing] him." The king addressed them as "my old wo Flora" and "Liddle Bet" after which "they formed two lines and he would walk two or three times up and down between the lines, saying, 'I'se your master, I'se your King, and I take you all to Guinea wid me when I go dar on a white hoss, when I'se dead.'" After those words were spoken, "they danced around him to the music of the tom-tom and tambourine, until the old King fell down from exhaustion, when there was a struggle in the harem to see who should carry him to the nearest bough house, there to be regaled with spruce beer and hard cider."[168] In his *Collections on the History of Albany* (1867), the Albany publisher Joel Munsell not only reprinted James Eights's account but also added his own recollections of the Albany Pinkster festival. According to Munsell, the dances performed by slaves on Pinkster Hill were "the original Congo dances as danced in their native Africa" and King Charles "generally led off the dance" that consisted of a "double-shuffle" and "heel-and-toe breakdown."[169]

An account, published anonymously in the *Schenectady Daily Evening Star and Times* in 1866, shows that the Albany Pinkster kermises attracted black visitors from as far away as Boston. It deals with the pitching of coppers, a popular game of chance whereby a hole was dug in the ground and a pitching place chosen about ten feet from it. People then took turns pitching and flicking copper coins with their thumbs and tried to "shoot" the coin into the hole. The winner would collect the coins that had failed to reach the set target. According to the author, a group of free blacks from Boston had come to participate at the Albany Pinkster kermis and stole some cents during a pitching game. This was observed by a black man from Albany called Pero, who then cried: "Stop, stop! You, you nigga's! here's dese Boston free nigga's wid tar on dere heels, picking up our cents!" The author concludes the anecdote with the reference that "the way the wenches pitched into the Bostonians and drove them from the ground was never matched yet even by the driving of a refractory militia man from a general training."[170]

Albany was not the only place where King Charles had a performance during Pinkster. In 1836, the *Chittenango Herald* reported that Charles celebrated the Pinkster festival in "Schenectady and Albany alternately."[171] In his *History of the City of Troy* (1876), historian Arthur James Weise points out that King Charles also used to lead the Pinkster festivities in nearby Troy on "the old parade-ground, east of Fourth Street, between Broadway and Congress Street." There, "booths, for the sale of beer, cakes, &c., were erected, and at night lights were suspended from the trees to illuminate the scene." As in Albany, the African American community in Troy seems to have been in charge of the festivities that attracted a large white audience, since "crowds of white people thronged the common to observe the merrymaking."[172] In 1872 the author of an anonymous account in the *Troy Daily Times* argues that the Dutch had deliberately made Pinkster a "holiday time for the blacks" and had designated the "meadow in front of Col. Schuyler's house, between it and the river" for the celebrations by the city's African American population. According to the author, local slaves usually celebrated Pinkster in Troy but "occasionally they would go to Albany and aid their neighbors in drinking to Prince Charlie."[173]

Nearby Kingston also used to have its own Pinkster celebration. In an interview in the *Kingston Daily Freeman* in 1881, the former slave Henry Rosecranse Columbus Jr., who was born in 1804, recalled that "[t]here was the Pinkster holiday, the Great Holiday for the colored men. They used to meet at Black Horse Tavern (the building still stands on the lower end of Wall Street, across the street not far from Jacob Plongh's blacksmith shop)."[174] The anonymous author of a satirical article, published in 1804 in the *Balance and Columbian Repository*, points out that in and around Hudson in Columbia County, there were "many processions" by the black community during Pinkster and specifies that in Hudson "Wind-mill-hill was stormed."[175] This indicates that Albany was not the only place where blacks organized a procession during Pinkster and that, as on Pinkster Hill, slaves used to celebrate Pinkster in Hudson on top of Windmill Hill, today's Academy Hill.[176]

This reference to a Pinkster procession in Hudson shows that Charles was probably not the only Pinkster king. Other sources confirm this. The anonymous fictional story "Poor Harry—the Old Slave," published in 1859, describes the election of a Pinkster king called Harry:

> Early the next morning drams and trumpets echoed over the hills, and large parties from different directions were marching for Township lot on the old road. It was not to battle; it was the Slaves' yearly jubilee, which lasted three days. Bolivar had been fed and curried five years by Harry, and had seen the smoke of more than one battle; but never did he carry himself so proudly as at this time harnessed before the *calash* in which was Harry and his bride. When they arrived at the lot, Harry was declared by acclamation, martial for the celebration, and a wreath of Pinkster blossoms was carelessly thrown over Katy's head. Harry was beloved by all the colored population. If "King Charley" himself had been present, his hat would not have been filled with loose change sooner than was Harry's; he was the master spirit in that and all subsequent celebrations. In those times the Slaves had many holidays; on which occasions he always looked neat and had money to spend.[177]

David Murdoch, a preacher at the Dutch Reformed Church in Catskill, New York, also mentions the existence of a "slave king" in his novel *The Dutch Dominie of the Catskills* (1861), which is set in 1777 in the Catskill-Kingston area and includes ample information on Hudson Valley Dutch folklore. Murdoch describes how this "king," dressed with a "cocked hat . . . and a large towel tied around the neck," acted as a judge over other slaves, and organized secret dance gatherings during which one could hear slaves crying out loud the word *sangaree*, a term that will return in an entirely different context in chapter 4 of this book.[178] In her biographical novel on the life of Sojourner Truth, first published in 1967, Jacqueline Bernard claims that Kingston had its own Pinkster King called "Prince Gerald" but fails to provide evidence to sustain this claim.[179] The historical study *The Hoosac Valley* (1912) by Grace Niles provides more credible information on the existence of other Pinkster kings. According to Niles, there was a black king called Tom Mandolin in Schaghticoke, near Albany. He was a slave on Colonel Johannes Knickerbacker's mansion and died in 1850. Allegedly, he told Washington Irving the adventures of Ethan Allen, Ignace Kip, Mallery, Spook Hollow, and Schaghticoke Plains. During Pinkster, Niles argues, not only King Charles in Albany but also King Tom in Schaghticoke was "clad in gold-laced scarlet coat and yellow breeches, and amused the crowd with antics and songs."[180] These references corroborate Sterling Stuckey's assumption that besides Albany, slaves in other parts of New York and New Jersey also used to elect a Pinkster king.[181]

Pinkster Celebration in Early America, c. 1800

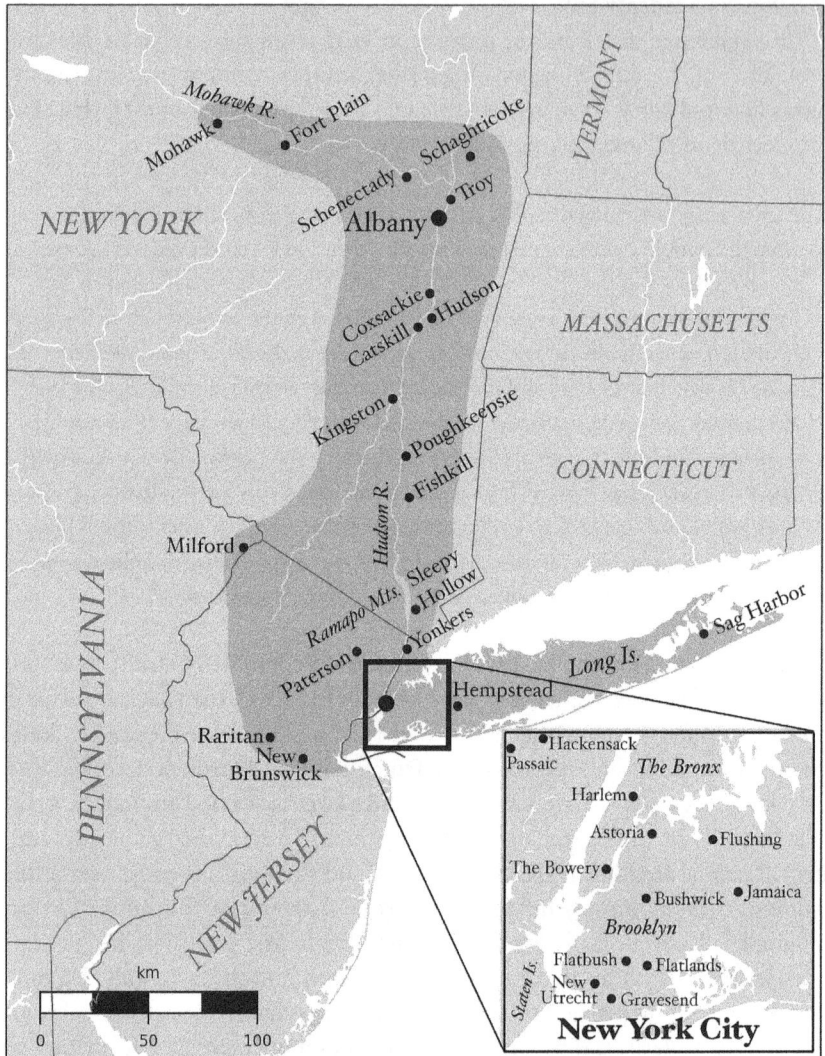

Shading denotes areas with recorded Pinkster celebrations.

Pinkster Celebration in Early America, c. 1800. Map made by Flynn Walsh.

Evidence indicates that the area in which African Americans celebrated Pinkster was vast. In New Jersey, Pinkster celebrations covered the entire northern part of the state, where in places such as Paterson it continued to be a holiday until the late nineteenth century.[182] The rowdy nature of Pinkster celebrations in Paterson is noted in an anonymous article published in 1850 in the *Evening Post*, in which the author argues that the boisterous atmosphere at the occasion of an execution "seemed . . . more like a gala-day, a general training, or a pinxter-festival, than like a solemn ceremony in vindication of the law."[183] In 1810, Rachel Van Dyke mentions in her diary how on Pentecost Monday (June 11), the black population of New Brunswick gathered to celebrate what is likely to have been a Pinkster festival. The gathering took place at Halfpenny Town, an area where mostly fishermen and boatmen lived, and where "the negroes were all assembled in their Sunday clothes, as happy and as merry as Lords and Ladies. Some were gambling for Cents, some dancing to the violin other talking and laughing—and all appeared to be without care—only regardful how they might enjoy the passing moment."[184] In upstate New York, Pinkster celebrations took place at least as far to the west as Fort Plain, along the Mohawk River, where, according to historian Nelson Greene, African Americans used to celebrate Pinkster at Wagner's tavern with "a peculiar dance they called To-to dance" and "as (this part of) Fort Plain had no name, it was commonly known as 'To-to-ville.'"[185]

Alice Morse Earle mentions the existence of Pinkster celebrations in Maryland, but does not provide evidence to sustain this claim.[186] We do know for sure that Pinkster celebrations spread to the Pennsylvania border. In his memoirs *Recollections of Men, Customs and Events in Milford Pennsylvania and Vicinity* (1889), Charles Rockwell mentions how Old Adam, a black man nicknamed "the Governor" and "the King," still celebrated Pinkster in the mid-nineteenth century. Having visited Old Adam's house as a teenager, Rockwell remembers that the "red letter day of the year was 'Pinkster' a prominent holiday that was always celebrated by a dance." On Pinkster day, "the stove was taken out and all furniture removed except a wooden bottom chair in each of two corners of the room on which stood the two old negroes Harry and Frank, one to call off and the other to play the violin." According to Rockwell, "the floor creaked and the window sash rattled in the frames as young and old men and women seemed to unlimber as they shook off the steps . . . and circulated around the music of the violin."[187]

Another black community leader known as "the Governor" shows up in documents relating to the Cooper family. In Cooperstown, James Fenimore Cooper's parents had a slave called Joseph Stewart, who everyone respectfully called "the Governor." Unlike other slaves who were buried in what was known as the "Nigger Heaven," Governor Stewart received an honorable place in the Cooper family's burying ground.[188] In Cooper's fictional work, we find indications that Pinkster celebrations were not only a rural phenomenon. In his novel *Satanstoe; Or, the Littlepage Manuscripts. A Tale of the Colony* (1845), Cooper offers a detailed description of a Pinkster festival in New York City. In a passage of the novel set in the year 1757, he describes how slaves used to celebrate Pinkster in the old Common on Manhattan:

> The next day was the first of the three that are devoted to Pinkster, the great Saturnalia of the New York blacks. Although this festival is always kept with more vivacity at Albany, than in York, it is far from being neglected, even now, in the latter place.... After showing Jason the City Hall, Trinity Church, and the City Tavern, we went out of town, taking the direction of a large common that the King's officers had long used for a parade ground, and which has since been called the Park, though it would be difficult to say why, since it is barely a paddock in size, and certainly has never been used to keep any animals wilder than the boys of the town.... Jason was at first confounded with the noises, dances, music, and games that were going on. By this time, nine-tenths of the blacks of the city, and of the whole country within thirty, or forty miles, indeed, were collected in thousands in those fields, beating banjoes, singing African songs, drinking, and most of all laughing, in a way that seemed to set their very hearts rattling within their ribs.... The features that distinguish a Pinkster frolic from the usual scenes at fairs, and other merry makings, however, were of African origin. It is true, there are not now, nor were there then, many blacks among us of African birth; but the traditions and usages of their original country were so far preserved as to produce a marked difference between this festival, and one of European origin. Among other things, some were making music, by beating on skins drawn over the ends of hollow logs, while others were dancing to it, in a manner to show that they felt infinite delight. This, in particular, was said to be a usage of their African progenitors. Hundreds of whites were walking through the fields, amused spectators.[189]

The area known as the Common had originally served as a place that could be used by anyone to let cattle graze or to collect firewood. Part of the Common was later also used as a cemetery for deceased slaves. This graveyard was discovered during construction work in Manhattan in 1991, which led to the erection of the African Burial Ground National Monument.[190] In a source dating to 1713, Chaplain John Sharpe explains that blacks in New York City used to be "buried in the Common by those of their own country and complexion without the office, on the contrary the Heathenish rites are performed at the grave by their countrymen."[191] In 1847 David Valentine remembered the place as a "desolate, inappropriate spot," used by the black community to bury its members retaining "native superstitions and burial customs, among which was that of burying by night, with various mummeries and outcries."[192] One can therefore assume that the Common served as a semi-autonomous social space for New York City's black population, where there was only minimal interference by local authorities.

Several scholars have, however, expressed doubts about the authenticity of Cooper's description. Shane White argues that Cooper's account of Pinkster is not credible because it is part of a work of fiction set at a time when Cooper was not yet born.[193] In the historical edition of *Satanstoe*, editor Kay Seymour House claims that Cooper probably did not invent the scene but transferred— for unknown reasons—a Pinkster celebration he had witnessed in Albany to Manhattan. According to House, "the Pinkster celebration which Corny Littlepage describes as being 'kept with more vivacity at Albany than in York' is nonetheless transferred to York," whereby Cooper "was undoubtedly drawing on his memories of the Albany Pinkster . . . which made an impression on him when he was in school there."[194] James Pickering also challenges the location of the Common, arguing that Pinkster celebrations only occurred in the periphery of Manhattan, such as Brooklyn, and that the authorities would not have tolerated such a massive gathering of slaves in the heart of city.[195]

Stuckey has argued differently. He considers Cooper's text "a brilliant re-creation of Pinkster," which can serve as a historical source. Stuckey even suggests that the skeleton of a black man "buried in a British Marine officer's coat," discovered in 1992 in the Burial Ground, must have been that of a former Pinkster king.[196] Following Stuckey, historians such as Terrence Epperson and Leslie Alexander have indeed treated the passage in Cooper's novel as an authentic account of Pinkster.[197]

Concerning the authenticity of Cooper's account, it is important to point out that several sources confirm Pinkster celebrations by the African American population on nearby Long Island. Historian John Watson observes in his *Annals and Occurrences of New York City and State in the Olden Time* (1846) that at the occasion of Pinkster, "the negroes on Long Island . . . came in great crowds to Brooklyn and held their field frolics." And in *A History of the City of Brooklyn* (1867–70), Henry Reed Stiles explains that the old Ferry Market in Brooklyn used to be a center of the island's African American Pinkster celebrations. According to Stiles, "the village was fairly black with them; they came trooping into Brooklyn from the island, men, women and children, sometimes as many as two hundred. They danced for eels around the market; they sang; 'tooted' on fish horns; [and] played practical jokes on one another." Pinkster, he claims "was a scene of the broadest good humor—where every sort of common game and of uncommon drollery was in requisition, and drinking was by no means neglected." Since so much alcohol was consumed, "on the following morning as many as twenty-five or thirty would usually be brought up before old Squire Nicolls on a charge of disorderly conduct." The squire, however, "knowing that 'Pinkster' came but once a year . . . always treated the culprits with leniency; and, summarily confiscating whatever funds remained in their pockets after their 'spree,' dismissed them."[198] Although Brooklyn undoubtedly hosted the largest Pinkster festival on Long Island, the assumption by historian Gabriel Furman in *Antiquities of Long Island* (1874) that it was celebrated "especially on the west end of this island" can be complemented by an anonymous article from the *Corrector* indicating that in 1882, "old fellows from Orient and . . . from Shelter Island" still used to "keep Pinkster" in Sag Harbor, in the extreme east of Long Island.[199]

There is also evidence that Pinkster activities occurred in Manhattan. In his *Market Book* (1862), Thomas De Voe highlights how African Americans from Long Island used to cross the East River to Manhattan to sell "roots, berries, herbs, yellow or other birds, fish, clams, oysters, &c." on Catharine Market in order to make some pocket money in anticipation of the Pinkster festival.[200] Others sources indicate that African Americans not only came from Long Island to Manhattan to make some money but also to celebrate the holiday itself. An anonymous article in the *Public Advertiser* from 1809 confirms that Pinkster festivals were still taking place in "the Park" in the early nineteenth century. The article informs that "Whitsun Monday called by the negroes of Long and Staten Island 'PINGSTER HOLIDAY' is also known as sweep-chimney's holiday."[201] On this day, "all the negroes of Long and Staten Island obtain permission from their masters to visit New York to participate in the amusement of the day." On their arrival in the city, they "repair to the Park, which is the general rendezvous, where they meet their friends the sweeps—after reciprocating the usual congratulations, they divide into different groups, some of these engage in pitching and tossing coppers, others in leaping, jumping and a great variety of extraordinary feats of agility." According to the author, May 22, 1809, "brought a return of this joyous anniversary, which affords so much gladness and mirth to our fellow citizens of colour." The author informs that the "Tories of this city having for some time contemplated an extraordinary exhibition of the art of catching gulls," meaning the organization of a circus. The New York City authorities eventually decided to have the circus coincide with "Pingster Monday, when from the number of strangers of distinction who visit N. York on that day, they would not only command a full house, but receive some additional performers." The article ends with a reference to dissatisfaction among African Americans over the fact that they had to organize their Pinkster performances in a circus tent: "Public notice was accordingly given that the circus would be opened at 12 o'clock on that day. Fortunately some heavy showers of rain fell about noon, which removed all the objections of the coloured citizens against their usual place of performance."

The park that is mentioned here as the original venue of the festival is in all likelihood City Hall Park, the area formerly known as the Common where Cooper set the stage of Pinkster. Other references confirm that African American Pinkster celebrations used to take place in City Hall Park as well as on Chatham Square. In 1876, for instance, the *Sun* writes that "in the old Dutch times, the limits of the Park were known as the Vlacte or Flat, and was the scene of many a Paas and Pinxter festival." In 1878 the *New-York Times* writes that "'Pinkster' is the Dutch word for Whitsunday, or Pentecost. Among our forefathers the Pinkster feast lasted a whole week. . . . On Whit-Monday all manner of shows were exhibited in the Park and Chatham Square." And in 1880 the *New York Evening Express* writes that "the Dutch are particularly famous for their wholesouled enjoyment of Whitsuntide. . . . In this city, too, in the days of the Knickerbockers, Pinkster was a time for universal merriment. Park Row and Chatham Square were alive with all manner of shows, and young and old flocked to see them."[202] These references corroborate Stuckey's assumption that Cooper's description of the Pinkster festival, despite being presented in a work of fiction, is reliable. They also show that Pinkster was not just a rural festival. Rather, the area in which it was celebrated in the nineteenth century roughly coincided with that of the seventeenth-century Dutch colony of New Netherland, including its former capital New Amsterdam.

However, it remains unclear why African Americans became so attached to Pinkster and continued to celebrate the festival long after Americans with Dutch roots had lost interest in their forefather's kermis traditions. The fact that this holiday traditionally had been a time of liberty, during which behavior that otherwise would not be tolerated was winked at, undoubtedly contributed to the continuous popularity of Pinkster. One can assume that slaves considered the exceptional leeway granted during Pinkster a license to stage performances that otherwise would not have been tolerated and felt increasingly attached to a holiday that meant something different to them from what it meant to the Dutch community. Several scholars have interpreted the remarkable African American attachment to this originally Dutch tradition as a reflection of Pinkster's syncretic, Dutch-African nature. This possibility will be further explored in the next chapter.

— • 3 • —

IN SEARCH OF THE PINKSTER KING

Dutch-African Roots

Several scholars have interpreted Pinkster as a syncretic Dutch-African tradition and assume that by celebrating the Pinkster holiday with their Dutch masters, African American Pinkster celebrations were a mixture of Dutch and indigenous African elements. Shane White, for instance, has claimed that "Pinkster was not simply an African survival transplanted to the New World, but a complex syncretization of African and Dutch cultures forged on the Hudson River within the context of American slavery."[1] Andrea Mosterman also refers to Pinkster as a "truly African-Dutch festival ... the main example of African-Dutch traditions in North America."[2] This brings up the question of what exactly can be considered Dutch about the way African Americans celebrated Pinkster. It should in this respect be underscored that Pinkster in itself cannot be considered a type of celebration. Rather, Pinkster was the Dutch name of the Pentecost holiday that gave occasion to different kinds of popular entertainment, some of which also occurred on other holidays.

The arguments used by Mosterman to sustain her claim that Pinkster should be understood as a syncretic, Dutch-African tradition are the presence of 1) a large white audience that attended the black performances, 2) booths owned by white people on Pinkster Hill, and 3) a white man called Old Platt, who used to play the violin during the celebrations on Pinkster Hill. "Even though whites were not the focus of attention," Mosterman argues, "their presence was nevertheless an important part of the festival." She also assumes that the black king processions during Pinkster relate to the Dutch Pinksterbloem parades, whereby Dutch girls had over time been replaced by other "people who had the least social and political power," namely slaves.[3]

The few existing eyewitness accounts and recollections about the Pinkster festivities describe the tradition in different ways. While some authors paint bucolic scenes of whites and blacks celebrating the holiday together, others describe Pinkster celebrations as anything but harmonious biracial entertainment. In 1846, for instance, an anonymous account about Pinkster in the *Schenectady Cabinet* reports that "[a]s the morning advanced, groups of old and young would arrive on the ground until they became a multitude of old and young, white and black, all congregated together in one heterogeneous mass," which seems to confirm the assumption that Pinkster celebrations were a mixture of Dutch and indigenous African elements.[4] However, the type of celebrations mentioned in the same article do not point in the direction of syncretism but rather suggest that both communities celebrated the holiday in their own way: while the white "Dorponeans"—a reference to the Dutch word *dorp* (village)—engaged in the typically Dutch ringrijden (riding the ring), slaves used the liberty granted to them on the Pinkster holiday to dance with their "king" to drum music. In his *Antiquities of Long Island* (1874), Gabriel Furman also argues that both communities celebrated the holiday differently. According to Furman, Pinkster was "a species of negro jubilee ... at the same time that it was observed as a festival by the white population."[5] In his *History of the First Reformed Dutch Church of Jamaica* (1884), Henry Onderdonk paints a much less harmonious scene and even claims that Dutch slaveholders felt intimidated by their slaves during Pinkster because "they roamed about the neighborhood, calling at every house for a drink, and late at night returned home reeling, noisy, and quarrelsome, disobedient to the mistress and sulky to the master" and that "it required another day or two to get the negroes in working order."[6]

Although Mosterman rightly claims that African American Pinkster celebrations often attracted a large white crowd, the presence as such of white spectators is no reason to assume syncretism. It should also be said that the presence of white spectators at black performance spectacles was not unique to Albany's Pinkster Hill. In many other places in nineteenth-century North America examples can be found of white fascination, albeit often mixed with disgust, for black dancing. A famous example is New Orleans' Congo Square, where black dancing even became a sort of tourist attraction. As Henry Castellanos observed in 1895, "white people, from motives of curiosity or fun, invariably attended these innocent pastimes."[7] Moreover, many of the white spectators mentioned in nineteenth-century sources on Pinkster were of non-Dutch origin. In his *Pinkster Ode*, Aimwell describes the people at Pinkster Hill as the world in miniature:

> There, among the sons of Herman,
> You'll meet with many an honest German,
> Who will smoke and see it out,
> *Mit* cool strong *peer* and sour crout.
>
> The *Burgomaster* in his place,
> Will move along with sober pace;

Smoking, foremost of the train,
Mynheer will answer *yaw* and *nayn*.

And next the Yankee, deep in trade,
Riding on his pacing jade,
Full of learning, courage too,
He whistles yankee doodle do.

Brisk French Monsieurs, who come from far
Talk all at once, *we, we, be gar*;
Sing *Carmanole* and *libertie*,
With *footre jang* and *sac cra je*.

The solemn Scot, whose ancient blood,
Swell'd royal veins form Noah's flood.
Can prove the kirk of Scotland stands
Higher on hills than level lands.
Explains predestination's law,
Kens the who' plan of Adams's fa';
Claims right divine to heap abuse
On Papists, Turks, and stubborn Jews:
And will from 'lection creed not swerve;
He'd sooner hang, or burn, or starve.

Saint Patrick's sons will here and there
Give you a bold and manly stare,
For *Shela's* children when they roam,
Oft lave their modesty at home;
Or wear it out by travelling far,
And fighting either side, in war.

From high Welch mountains there will be
Saint Davy's sons, the brave and free.
Peace to these good industrious men,
May every one increase to ten.
May every ship find pleasant gales,
That brings the honest sons of Wales.

A few, who came from Albion's isle,
With envious, or contemptuous smile,
Will look around, surcharg'd with spleen,

And tell what they've in London seen.
And how their beef is better far,
Than ours, which smells so strong of tar.
How pitch-pine-knots ar'n't half so good
As English coal, for dressing food;
Declare we mostly cook our meat,
Not fit for gentlemen to eat—
Yet eat, and stuff themselves so full,
We shall find them proud and dull.[8]

Aimwell mentions German, Dutch, New England "Yankee," French and Québecois, Scottish, Irish, Welsh, and English spectators. It can thus be assumed that many of the white owners of booths on Pinkster Hill were not Dutch. This is probably also the case of the violin player Old Platt, whose name indicates English, French, or German origin rather than Dutch.

A stronger argument in favor of the syncretic nature of African American Pinkster celebrations can be made with reference to the king parades in Albany. Since King Charles and his companions used European-style military uniforms, hats, and banners that clearly point at a European influence, the syncretic nature of these parades can hardly be denied. Although Mosterman does not provide evidence to sustain her claim that they derived from the Dutch Pinksterbloem parades, there are some indications that this Dutch tradition might, in fact, have influenced the slave community. In his *History of Schoharie County* (1845), Jeptha Simms claims that on Pinkster "the blacks are seen with smiling faces on that day, clad in their best apparel, going to visit their friends—often bearing flowers called by them *Pinkster-bloomies*"; the 1875 May edition of the *Manhattan and de la Salle Monthly* mentions that the women who danced with King Charles on Pinkster Hill were as "rosy as the *bloomies* which they bore in their hands"; and in her study on *The Hoosac Valley* (1912), Grace Niles argues that "on Pinxster Day, Whitsun Monday in May, began a week's holiday for the Negroes on Pinxster Hill in Albany or in Troy, where they gathered Pinxster-flowers . . . and paraded the village streets."[9] Whether these vague and late references are enough evidence to claim that the African American Pinkster parades are derived from Dutch Pinksterbloem traditions can be doubted, all the more since Mosterman does not provide a convincing explanation for the reason why a fertility tradition that celebrated a young girl covered with flowers transformed into a parade honoring an older man dressed as a European monarch.

Claire Sponsler and Donna Merwick, who also believe Pinkster to be a syncretic Dutch-African tradition, have argued differently. Possibly misguided by Mariana Schuyler van Rensselaer's inaccurate claim, in her *History of the City of New York in the Seventeenth Century* (1909), that Whitsuntide in New

Netherland used to be "celebrated by the Dutch Calvinist as heartily as by any Catholic," Sponsler and Merwick claim that African American Pinkster parades are rooted in medieval Dutch procession culture.[10] As has been demonstrated, however, the Reformed Church in New Netherland did not approve of any type of public celebrations during Christian holidays and, although it begrudgingly tolerated the "pagan" Pinkster kermises, would never have allowed Dutch or other European settlers to introduce the Catholic practice of organizing processions on that holiday.[11] Although one can assume that Catholic Europeans might have liked to organize a procession during Pentecost, they only formed a small part of the population in New Netherland. There are no indications that the Catholic minority in New Netherland ever defied the mighty Reformed Church by manifesting itself publicly during religious holidays. Such attempts would have led to an immediate reaction by the authorities and the ensuing discussions would have been mentioned in the official documents that painstakingly recorded daily life in New Netherland. As Fred van Lieburg has argued, "Catholics and Mennonites were the Calvinists' most prominent competitors, but these minority confessions were of little consequence in New Netherland."[12] Jaap Jacobs also confirms that "incidents did not take place with the Roman Catholics. Only a few of them lived in New Netherland, and they seem to have obeyed the edicts against conventicles and probably limited their worship to the family circle."[13]

Graham Hodges has explained the importance of the Dutch Pinkster festival for the African American community from a Christian perspective. According to Hodges, the Pinkster festival served as the primary occasion for a religious interaction between the Dutch and their slaves, whereby "ecstatic moments of the Holy Wind" during Pentecost allowed for a "spiritual conversion."[14] But in fact, the religious celebration of Pentecost in the Dutch Reformed Church and the popular Pinkster kermises were two very different things. Although both celebrations were called Pinkster, they had nothing in common. Popular Pinkster kermises had their roots in pre-Christian fertility rituals that had no relation whatsoever with the Christian feast of Pentecost as celebrated in the Reformed Church. Devout Calvinists abhorred Pinkster kermises and the Reformed Church did everything it could to keep its members away from these popular celebrations. It is hard to imagine that people who ignored these objections by church authorities would consider the boisterous, bacchanalian Pinkster kermises an opportunity to have a "religious interaction" with their slaves.

Other scholars have claimed that the African American Pinkster parades have their roots in Dutch carnival traditions. According to White, the parade in honor of a black king during Pinkster should be understood as "the world turned upside down," whereby "for a short period those at the bottom of the social hierarchy . . . reversed their lowly status and lack of power."[15] This theory corresponds to the assumption by Roger Abrahams that many black folkloric traditions in the American diaspora can be traced back to European carnival traditions due to the fact that slaves often worked side by side with indentured workers of rural European origin.[16] In the Netherlands, medieval rituals of inversion from the pre-Lenten period such as charivari and mock king celebrations on the feast of Shrovetide did, in fact, include parades with characteristics similar to those of the African American Pinkster parades that have been observed in Albany.[17] While no traces of Catholic processions have been found in New Netherland, this is different with Shrovetide parades. In 1654, for instance, a group of people in Beverwijck "clothed themselves in strange customs, and put on women's clothes, therein publicly paraded as harlequins through the city and streets, in the sight of the inhabitants, and besides did other scandalous and unseemly things."[18]

In the medieval Low Countries, Shrovetide used to be a heyday for corporations of marginalized people who were known as *rabauwen* or, in the French-speaking provinces, *ribauds*. These ribalds, as they were called in English, had a reputation of dissoluteness and suffered from a series of discriminations. Like prostitutes, ribalds were not allowed access to certain hospitals; they were charged with risky operations during wars, the execution of convicts, and other forms of dangerous, dirty, and shameful labor. Despite their low social standing, the ribalds functioned as a type of guild and elected their own leader who was known as "king." This *Rex Ribaldorum* (King of the Ribalds) had real power, because city authorities required him to control other marginalized groups that were potentially troublesome: prostitutes, vagabonds, lepers, and mentally ill people. There was an intimate connection between this corporation and local performance culture. In the Flemish city of Ghent, for instance, the annual *Auweet* (torch parade) on the Thursday, Friday, and Saturday before Laetare Sunday in mid-Lent was traditionally initiated by the ribalds. Similar corporations were known as *moorkinderen*, *moerkinderen*, *meuraers*, or *muederaers*. The Dutch words *moor, moer, meur,* or *mueder* refer to mud or blackness, which relates to the dirty work these people had to do such as cleaning cesspits, sweeping streets, removing animal carcasses, and other tasks that correspond to the type of work slaves performed in New Netherland. They also elected their own leader, who was known as their "king" or—in the case of Flanders—"count" or "dean." Moorkinderen traditionally played a prominent role in the revelries at the occasion of Shrove Tuesday.[19] By the sixteenth century, their tasks were gradually taken over by the city authorities and the corporations disappeared. In the seventeenth-century Dutch Republic, however, rowdy young males still used to form fraternities called "kingdoms" that were possibly inspired by the medieval corporations of ribalds and moorkinderen. These "kingdoms," which were ruled by a mock king who provocatively ignored city bans on gambling, drinking, and dancing on Sundays and Christian holidays, were responsible for many of the charivari in the pre-Lenten period.[20]

The interpretation of African American Pinkster parades as a carnivalesque tradition implies that they functioned as mockeries of serious customs by their masters. Kevin Dawson, for instance, has argued that King Charles's extravagant clothing used at Pinkster parades served to caricature the type of clothing worn by elite whites, who unknowingly "laughed at representations of themselves."[21] It should, in this respect, be acknowledged that the aggressive policy in the Netherlands toward the medieval Catholic procession culture did not imply a ban on secular parades. In the city of Leiden, for instance, a spectacular annual thanksgiving parade known as *Leidens Ontzet* (Leiden's Relief) used to be held on October 3 to remember William of Orange's liberation of the city from a Spanish siege in 1574.[22] It was also common practice that the *burgerwacht* (burgher guard) or *schutterij* (militia) organized a military parade on the occasion of a kermis or fair.[23] Both Beverwijck and New Amsterdam had a burgher guard. We can assume that, as in the fatherland, these groups used to hold parades in which they marched in traditional clothing through town while beating drums and upholding pennants. This Dutch parade culture had a remarkably long existence in America. In 1814, when news of the liberation of the Netherlands from Napoleonic rule reached the United States, several groups of Dutch American citizens expressed their joy by staging parades. This was the case in the town of Utica, New York, where "descendants of Dutchmen evinced their affectionate remembrance of the land of their forefathers" in a procession that "moved from Mr. Welles' Tavern through Whitesboro' and Church Streets to the Presbyterian Church, where the U[nited] States and Orange standards were fancifully displayed on each side of the pulpit."[24]

The only reference to a Pinkster kermis in New Netherland—in the town of Beverwijck in 1655—explicitly mentions the involvement of the town's burgher guard.[25] It also informs that members of the Beverwijck militia organized parrot shooting, a tradition whereby the winner of the tournament received the title of *Pinksterkoning* (Pinkster King) and was subsequently paraded through town wearing a fake crown. While no evidence has been found of slaves participating in and/or mocking Dutch parrot-shooting tournaments, a source from Louisiana indicates that such practices did occur. In his *Journal of a Tour in America* (1824–25), Edward Derby described a "negro fête" on the Michel Labranche plantation, situated in the Parish of St. Charles about twenty-seven miles north of New Orleans. According to Derby, a gaily beribboned oxcart appeared on the last day of harvest, surrounded by "singing, dancing and laughing" slaves, who were accompanied by a band. They then performed "a Congo dance . . . chiefly a sort of shuffle, and a violent agitation of all the muscles of the body." Throughout these performances, some slaves approached the white bystanders and asked "for small supplies of silver." Afterwards, the slaves went to the front lawn of the big house, where they erected a pole "with a popinjay figure of a bird on the top" and "an old merry looking negro, a native Guinea man, came out with a crooked stick which he carried in imitation of a gun, to perform a series of pantomime." This older slave "shouldered his gun, presented it at the bird . . . fired, and was knocked backwards by the recoil—a dénouement which seemed to afford infinite amusement. He then returned, and made a speech, in what language I know not, in a sort of recitative, several others occasionally joining in a chorus."[26] Derby's description of the Congo dance as well as the subsequent collection is reminiscent of what occurred during Pinkster celebrations in Albany, while the concluding scene is most likely a mockery of parrot shooting, a tradition known in Louisiana as *atirer au papegay*.[27] However, a striking difference between this scene and the descriptions of African American Pinkster celebrations is that the latter do not include signs of mockery. While many scholars assume Charles to have been a mock king, all accounts by those who effectively witnessed the Pinkster celebrations in Albany show that his dignity was real and that African Americans who participated in the celebrations treated their "king" with unfeigned respect.

As the parallels to the event in Louisiana indicate, African American celebrations with characteristics similar to the ones observed during the Pinkster festival in Albany have been recorded in areas far beyond the borders of what used to be New Netherland. The fact that slaves organized dancing performances on the occasion of fairs was not exclusive to New York. In his *Annals of Philadelphia and Pennsylvania* (1830), historian John Watson recalled how "many can still remember when the slaves were allowed the last days of the fairs for their jubilee, which they employed . . . in dancing the whole afternoon in the present Washington square, then a general burying ground." As in Albany, slaves traveled from far and wide to participate at these annual gatherings in Philadelphia. According to Watson, "in that field could be seen at once more than one thousand of both sexes, divided into numerous little squads, dancing, and singing, 'each in their own tongue,' after the customs of their several nations in Africa."[28] Parades similar to the ones in Albany have also been observed elsewhere. A notorious example is the African American Christmas parade witnessed by the missionary worker Henry Benjamin Whipple, who during a trip through Georgia in 1843 observed "a corps of staff officers with red sashes, mock epaulettes & goose quill feathers, and a band of music composed of 3 fiddles, 1 tenor & 1 bass drum, 2 triangles & 2 tambourines and they are marching up & down the streets in great style." They were followed by "others, some dancing, some walking & some hopping, other singing, all as lively as lively can be. . . . Here they come again with flags flying and music enough to deafen one & they have now two fifes to increase their noise." As in Albany, they "levy contributions on all the whites they see & thus find themselves in pocket money."[29] These similarities indicate that while the syncretic nature of African American Pinkster parades cannot be denied, the European elements of the tradition are not necessarily of Dutch origin.

Anglo-African Roots

Since African American Pinkster parades have only been recorded on paper for about a century and half after the demise the New Netherland, the possibility cannot be excluded that they were inspired by a European tradition with roots outside of the Netherlands. One possible model in this respect is that of the English "muster day" or "training day." First established in 1675 as a consequence of the frequent fighting with Native Americans in New England, this annual military training day was later also introduced in New York, where it roughly coincided with Pentecost. When the Dutchmen Jasper Danckaerts and Peter Sluyter visited New York in 1679–80, they observed military training that took place on the day before Pentecost.[30] Training Day existed for a long time. The New York Militia Law of 1792 still required a training session and parade on the first Monday of June, which roughly corresponds with Pentecost. The annual Training Day is known to have been a major social event with a parade that was followed by public entertainment.[31] In his memoirs from 1889, Andrew Mellick recalled a Training Day in New Jersey with "acres of people all dressed in their Sunday best, before whom the troops deployed, marched, and countermarched to the inspiring music of drum, fife, and bugle." After the parade, "booths were set up for the sale of cakes, pies, beer, and rum; ... When the drills and ceremonies of the militia were concluded, all kinds of shows and games were instituted for the amusement of the people." He also remembered how "the Bedminster colored people always celebrated" and that "general training, usually occurring in the middle of June."[32] When she was interviewed in 1883, the former slave Silvia Dubois did not even mention Pinkster and claimed that "training day" was the most important festive event for her and other African Americans in New Jersey.[33]

The military parades on Training Days also served as inspiration for the Victory Parades following the Revolution. Significantly, when the city of Albany celebrated in August 1788 America's independence and the new constitution, a parade was organized that was similar to the available descriptions of the African American Pinkster parades in that city. It began in the center of town, where Albany troops of light horse, full uniform, and with Captain Leonard Gansevoort at their head marched through the street to the top of the hill. They were followed by a band of musicians, people holding standards of the United

States and the eleven states of the Federal Union, as well as representatives of the trades of the city and its hinterland, who carried the tools of their trade.[34] The connection between Training Day parades and African American Pinkster parades is also notable in the anonymous article "Corporation of Albany vs. The State of New-York," published by the *Balance* in 1811. After the State of New York imposed a new law that required everyone to participate in the annual militia training, the newspaper questioned whether this law potentially violated the ban on Pinkster that had been issued earlier that year and that prohibited "any person or persons, on the days commonly called Pinkster (one of which is the first Monday of June) to march or parade, with or without any kind of music, in any of the public streets of this city, on pain of forfeiting ten dollars, or suffering imprisonment not more than five nor less than two days."[35] Despite similarities, this article clearly shows that Training Day and Pinkster were not synonyms for the same event. The reference in the *Evening Post* in 1850 that the boisterous atmosphere at the occasion of an execution in Paterson "seemed . . . more like a gala-day, a general training, or a pinxter-festival" also indicates that Pinkster and Training Day were similar in nature, though different types of events.[36]

The African American parades during Pinkster are also reminiscent of the popular white marches, known as "Fantasticals," mocking the annual United States' Victory Parades. In his *History of Kingston* (1888), historian Marius Schoonmaker provides a witness account of a Fantastical composed of people using "grotesque arms of various descriptions, from the old musket to the cane and broomstick," who were wearing "fantastic dresses to match" and drew "large crowds of admirers to their parades."[37] One of the nation's most famous Fantasticals was formed in Philadelphia in the 1820s. It was led by a certain "Colonel Pluck," whose cocked hat and ceremonial military dress resembled that of King Charles.[38] Similar parades known as "Callithumpians" were charivari of working-class whites with blackened faces who paraded with brooms in outlandish clothing while beating drums, pots, pans, and kettles. They intimidated random people in the streets whose only chance of liberating themselves was to give some cash or to donate alcohol.[39] Similar in nature were the parades on "Pope's Day," an anti-Catholic festival on the November 5 when grotesque representations of the Pope and a Catholic pretender to the English throne were carried around towns in a mock procession.[40] Despite remarkable parallels to the Pinkster processions in Albany, it should again be stressed that accounts of Pinkster do not include signs of mockery that are so obvious in Fantasticals, Calithumpians, and Pope's Day marches.

The fact that by the beginning of the nineteenth century blacks dominated the chimney-sweeping business and that the Pinkster festival in New York City was also known under the name "Sweep-Chimney's Holiday" indicates a possible link to another English tradition that has its roots in mumming plays:

Anonymous, *Colonel Pluck*. Colonel Pluck was the leader of one of the nation's most famous Fantasticals, formed in Philadelphia in the 1820s. During parades, he would wear a cocked hat and ceremonial military dress that resembled that of Charles, the Pinkster king. Courtesy the American Antiquarian Society.

the "May-Day Sweeps."[41] In the second half of the eighteenth century, chimney sweeps in England had appropriated traditional May festivities known as "Whit Fairs" or "Whitsun Ales." During these festivities, a king and queen of the day were chosen, there were archery competitions, games, Morris dancing and "Whit Walks," parades with brass bands. In their Whitsun festivities, chimney-sweeps with unwashed or blackened faces featured a Lord, who was dressed in the garb of Morris dancers.[42] The anonymous description of a May-Day Sweeps festival in London in 1825 shows that the Lord's outfit was conspicuously similar to that of Albany's King Charley: "The chimney-sweepers' jackets and hats are bedizened with gilt embossed paper; sometimes they wear coronals of flowers in their heads; their black faces and legs are grotesquely coloured with Dutch-pink." Similar to the African American Pinkster king in Albany, the king's size in May-Day Sweeps is notorious because "the Lord is always the tallest of the party, and selected from some other profession to play this distinguished character." Headwear and uniform are also similar, since the May-Day king "wears a huge cocked hat, fringed with yellow or red feathers, or laced with gold paper; his coat is between that of the full court dress, and the laced coat of the footman of quality." We also learn about the May-Day king's clothing that "in the breast he carries an immense bunch of flowers; his waistcoat is embroidered; his frill is enormous; his 'shorts' are satin, with past knee-buckles; his stockings silk with figured clocks; his shoes are dancing pumps, with large tawdry buckles; his hair is powdered, with a bag and rosette"; and "he carries in his right hand a high cane with a shining knob and in his left a handkerchief held by one corner, and of a colour once white."[43] While the parallels are striking, it is unlikely that Pinkster celebrations are an African American variant of May-Day Sweeps. Besides the omission of mockery in Pinkster festivals, there is no convincing argument to explain why only Dutch-owned slaves in New York and New Jersey would have copied this English tradition for their celebrations at the occasion of the Dutch Pinkster holiday.

No other festive tradition has more characteristics in common with African American Pinkster celebrations than New England's "Negro Election Days." As Sterling Stuckey confirms, the "Election Day ceremony [served] much of the same function for blacks [in New England] that Pinkster served for New York blacks."[44] Like Pinkster, "Election Days" usually occurred in May or June and just as Albany had its King Charles, Lynn had its King Pompey, South Kingstown its King Prince Robinson, and Portsmouth its King Nero Brewster.[45]

Election Days have been recorded from the mid-eighteenth until the mid-nineteenth centuries in Rhode Island, New Hampshire, Massachusetts, and Connecticut. On those days, the slave community elected a "governor" and/or "king" and sometimes also a lieutenant governor, treasurer, judge, sheriff, deputy, and other officers. The first reference to this tradition dates to 27 May

1741—the Saturday after that year's Pentecost—when Benjamin Lynde of Salem noted in his diary that he had given his slaves "Scip 5s and Wm 2s 6d" for a "Negro's Hallowday."[46] The earliest extensive description dates back to 1756 and was recorded in Newport, Rhode Island, where "the election declared, a general shout announced that the struggle was over—and here, contrary to the masters' practice, the vanquished and victors united in innocent and amusing fun and frolic." The festivities that followed the king/governor election were "accompanied with the music of the fiddle, tambourine, the banjo, drum, etc." and a parade when "the whole body moved in the train of the Governor-elect, to his master's house, where, on their arrival a treat was given by the gentlemen newly elected, which ended the ceremonials of the day."[47]

Participation in the election was of great importance to slaves. William Bentley observed in his diary that slaves "were too restless at home to be of any use till [the Election Day] was over."[48] In 1817 a black seaman angry at having been prevented from attending the election ceremony blew up the quarter deck of a packet boat in the Boston harbor.[49]

Just as Albany's King Charles was "tall, thin and athletic," physical appearance seems to have played a key role in the election of kings and governors in New England. Governor Eben Tobias, whose son was to become the US minister to Haiti during Reconstruction, was "tall, well proportioned"; Governor Quosh was "a native African of immense size and Herculean strength"; and King Mumford was recalled as "a big, burly, powerful fellow."[50] A remarkable case is that of Salem-born Richard Crafus, also called Seaver, a "black Hercules," who was "six feet five inches in height and proportionately large."[51] After he had been arrested by the British Navy and sent to jail in Dartmoor, Crafus became known among the black prisoners as "King Dick," which historian Jeffrey Bolster related to the "Negro Election" tradition in his native Salem, where blacks "select[ed] their own dignitaries," whose task it was to "maintain order in a disorderly world" and who formed "a nation-within-a-nation."[52] Wearing a bearskin grenadier's cap and carrying a huge club, King Dick maintained order among the inmates. While in prison, he formed an alliance with a black priest known as Simon, who led Christian services that were apparently inspired by Methodism. The king honored and protected the priest and the latter ensured respect and obedience to the former. According to one of the inmates at Dartmoor, "the musical performances at these meetings were in a wild, but not unpleasant style." Although the services "were carried out entirely by the blacks," whites were occasionally also "taken into the Black Society."[53] After his repatriation to United States, Crafus maintained his royal air while acting as a special aid to the Boston Police in the period 1826–35. According to George Crichton, he was "a well-known character ... [who] lived in one of the crowded tenements on Botolph Street and was the focus of all the colored population of that district." Wearing a red vest and white shirt, crowned with "an old style police cap" and "swinging an immense cane" he used to serve as master of ceremonies on Election Days in Boston. Crafus also led an annual parade or procession on the Boston Common.[54]

Like Pinkster celebrations, Election Day festivals were commonly held in an open field in the outskirts (gallows places, the top of a hill, slave burial grounds) or at a place that traditionally had been claimed by marginalized people (the Common), where there was little interference from the authorities.[55] In his memoirs published in 1868, Sol Smith recalls that in Boston, he and his white friends had the habit of chasing "all the niggers off the Common ... except on what was termed 'nigger 'lection'" because then "the colored people were permitted to remain unmolested on Boston Common."[56] Witness accounts show that the election procedure was accompanied with a lavish meal and dance performances that included a parade during which salutes were fired and occasionally mock stick fights were performed.[57] In Connecticut, the newly elected governors were honored with a sash, and kings were given a crown, a sword, and other emblems of royalty.[58] One of them paraded through town "on one of his master's horses, adorned with plaited gear, his aides beside him à la militaire ... moving with a slow majestic pace."[59]

As during Pinkster celebrations, there was a hierarchy among the slaves on Election Days, whereby those who had "a master of distinction" occupied leading positions.[60] According to historian William Piersen, who focused on Election Day in his study *Black Yankees* (1988), slaves who became elected king or governor occupied leading positions in the slave community, such as the general supervisor of a farm.[61] Besides the election of a leader or leaders, Joseph Barlow Felt pointed out in his *Annals of Salem* (1845–49) that slaves also "adopted regulations as the circumstances of their association required," which indicates that these elections provided the structure for some type of self-government.[62]

Slaveholders did not attempt to prevent such forms of self-government. On the contrary, as Wilkins Updike's account of Election Day in his *History of the Episcopal Church in Narragansett* (1847) shows, they supported it and took pride in clothing slaves on Election Day with some of their finest luxuries because "the slaves assumed the power and pride and took the relative rank of their masters, and it was degrading to the reputation of the owner if his slave appeared in inferior apparel, or with less money than the slave of another master of equal wealth." Also the horses of the wealthy landowners were on this day "surrendered to the use of slaves, and with cues, real or false, heads pomatumed and powdered, cocked hat, mounted on the best Narragansett pacers, sometimes with their master's sword, with their ladies on pillions, they pranced to election," and the election treat "corresponded in extravagance in proportion to the wealth of his master."[63] Other accounts make reference to slaveholders paying for the funeral ceremonies of slaves who had served as governor or king and show that these men, despite being slaves, commanded some respect among white people.[64]

The fact that slaveholders tolerated and even supported this tradition indicates that they perceived it as useful. As in the case of the king of the ribalds in the medieval Netherlands, the slave king or governor in New England was expected to take charge of misdemeanors and other minor grievances against slaves that arose during his term of office.[65] This is confirmed by historian Orville Platt, who mentions the existence of "a sort of police managed wholly by the slaves," and a black "court," whose punishments had more of an effect since "people of their own rank and color had condemned them, and not their masters."[66] Piersen cites the case of a slave called Prince Jackson who was found guilty of stealing an axe, whereupon he was given twenty lashes by King Nero's deputy sheriff.[67]

As in the case of Albany's King Charles, white people reporting on Election Day were inclined to give this tradition an ironic twist by adding a humorous or demeaning anecdote on the elected king or governor. Pierson quotes the examples of Governor Peleg Nott whose horse allegedly ran away during the parade and "bespattered his Excellency from head to foot with mud and water," and of King Nero who allegedly was so thin that he "required padding in the back of his borrowed silk stockings," but then lost the padding during the parade.[68]

Like Pinkster, New England's Election Day ceremonies have traditionally been understood as the imitation or mockery of white procedures. Eyewitnesses doubted that African Americans had the necessary skills to create such an organizational system on their own. Writing about an election ceremony in Windsor, Connecticut, in 1859 the physician Henry Reed Stiles went so far as to justify his skepticism with the argument that the "spirit of emulation and imitation . . . is peculiar to their race and the monkey tribe."[69] Even authors who sympathized with African Americans assumed that the practice could only have been a form of imitation. Significantly, when recalling an election ceremony in Lynn, Massachusetts, in 1897 James Newhall commented that "so long as slavery existed in Massachusetts, our colored brethren . . . were accustomed then, in imitation of their masters, to assemble on Boston Common or in some other convenient place, and proceed to elect rulers from their own ranks; or rather imitation rulers, rulers without authority and without subjects."[70]

Folklorists and historians, including Piersen, have generally been inclined to understand Election Day as a carnivalesque festival of reversal. However, the available sources on African American celebrations on Election Day do not contain signs of mockery. Original accounts indicate that members of the slave community had a strong respect for their elected "governors" and "kings." White's suggestion that these festivals functioned as a "safety valve allowing a cathartic release from the pent-up frustrations both of the long winter and of

Anonymous, *Parade of the Black Govenor of Hardford*. Artist's conception of a black governor parading in Hartford, Connecticut. In *Connecticut Magazine* 9, no. 3 (Summer 1905).

the institution of slavery" therefore requires some differentiation. Although this
tradition may have been perceived in that way by the slaveholders, all sources
indicate that Election Day festivals had a different meaning for the slave community itself. While White is undoubtedly correct in assuming that "the point of
reference . . . was always the order and certainty of the 'normal' social structure,"
Pinkster and Election Day indicate that this "order" was not simply imposed but
rather involved some type of negotiation between the master and the leader(s)
of the slave community.[71]

It can also be doubted that the parades celebrating the newly elected black kings and governors were a mere imitation of European traditions. Quite remarkable in this respect is the observation by Joseph Felt in 1849 that the way Election Day had traditionally been celebrated by the slave community "was followed by a small proportion of whites until a recent period."[72] Similarly, Platt claimed in 1898 that popular parades by white Americans in New England had been inspired by black parade culture.[73] These suggestions indicate that the conspicuous parallels between African American Pinkster parades and phenomena such as Fantasticals and Callithumpians may relate to black influence on white popular culture rather than the other way around. While this possibility will be explored later in this book, further analysis based on parallels to African American traditions outside of Anglophone America shows that king election ceremonies involving parades were not unique to North America.

Luso-African Roots

The presence of elected "slave kings" has been observed far beyond the borders of New England and New York. Several accounts of New Orleans' Congo Square, for instance, refer to "black kings." In her study on popular culture *American Humor* (1931), Constance Rourke writes that "many who heard the minstrels in the Gulf States or along the lower Mississippi must have remembered those great holidays in New Orleans early in the nineteenth century when hundreds of Negroes followed through the streets a king chosen for his youth, strength, and blackness."[74] In fact, writing about New Orleans in 1823, Timothy Flint mentions how "some hundred of negroes, male and female, follow the king of the wake, who is conspicuous for his youth, size, the whiteness of his eyes, and the blackness of his visage." The king "produces an irresistible effect upon the multitude. All the characters that follow him, of leading estimation, have their own peculiar dress, and their own contortions. They dance, and their streamers fly, and the bells that they have hung about them tinkle."[75] As Samuel Kinser rightly observes in *Carnival, American Style* (1990), "the richly ornamented king of the wake whom Flint saw at New Orleans [was] not carnivalesque."[76]

Many more references to king celebrations by slave communities can be found in the Caribbean. In Martinique in 1758, for instance, the French governor reported that at a Corpus Christi celebration "several [slaves] were richly dressed to represent the King, Queen, all the royal family," and that in one of the parishes of the island, "the priest had the year previously introduced the two darkies who imitated the King and Queen into the sanctuary where they were both placed into the chairs."[77] In 1843 James Phillippo wrote about Jamaica that "each of the African tribes upon the different estates formed itself into a distinct party, composed of men, women, and children. Each party had its King or Queen, who was distinguished by a mask of the most harlequin-like apparel." These slave communities "paraded or gamboled in their respective neighborhoods, dancing to the rude music."[78] In 1844 Henry Breen reported about the slave community in St. Lucia that "each society has three kings and three queens, who are chosen by the suffrages of the members. The first, or senior, king and queen only make their appearance on solemn occasions, such as the anniversary of their coronation or the *fête* of the patron saint of the society."[79] On the Danish Virgin Islands, Thurlow Weed wrote in 1866 that "the slaves on each estate elect their Queen and Princess, with their King and Prince, whose authority is supreme. These have their Maids of Honor, Pages, &c., &c. . . . In the Town the Free Colored People and House Slaves form their parties, elect their Kings, Queens, &c., and Dance in like manner."[80] In his *History of British Guiana* (1893), James Rodway argues that "it had been customary for years for the negroes of every nation in a district to choose head-men or 'Kings,' under whom were several subaltern officers of the same nation." The duties of the Kings were "to take care of the sick and purchase rice, sugar, &c., for them, to conduct the burials, and see that the corpse was properly enclosed in a cloth, and that the customary rites and dances were duly observed." Rodway specifies that the burial and mutual-aid society he had discovered had been established by blacks of West-Central African origin and that members had the power to force their leaders to step down: "An end was put to these 'Companies'—as they were called—among the Congoes, by a quarrel between them and their 'King,' who at a certain burial declared that he had no money, although the people believed he had enough for the purpose, as it was impossible that their contributions could all have been exhausted." In consequence, "the 'Company' was abolished, and on each estate they had since taken care of their own dead." Rodway continues by saying that "from the confessions of the Congoes, it appeared they had a 'King,' Governor, General Drummer and a Doctor or Lawyer."[81] Father Marie Bertrand de Cothonay reports in his *Journal d'un missionnaire dominicain des Antilles anglaises* (1893) from Carénage on the island Trinidad, where former slaves used to organize a celebration that started with a High Mass and a procession that took them to "a bamboo hut, covered it with *carate*-leaves, to which they had given the pompous name 'palace.'" They had also "named a black man as their king." During the following three days and nights, "bacchanalian celebrations took place" and "the king, who was elected by acclamation, had arranged the necessary funding, invited the guests, presented the blessed bread, etc. and opened the dance."[82] In 1843 the French abolitionist Victor Schoelcher witnessed in Haiti a carnival celebration, where he saw "companies" of blacks, each with "its own name, its own flag and a king." The latter was wearing a "feathered turban as his crown" and a "cloak of satin embellished with sequins in gold and silver." "Most of these companies," he claimed, "are composed of blacks who descent exclusively from a certain African nation."[83] Parades featuring a king, princes, marquises, and counts are still a common phenomenon in Trinidad folklore and in Haitian traditions such as *Les Rois Diables* and *Rara*.[84]

The earliest reports on black king elections and parades in the New World can be found in a Latin-American context. In the early sixteenth century, Bernal Díaz del Castillo described how, during a celebration in Mexico City, a group of fifty sumptuously dressed black men and women escorted "their king and queen" in a parade.[85] In 1715, the French traveler Guy Le Gentil de la Barbinais observed how African slaves in Lima were divided into "tribes" that were commanded by their respective "kings," who were responsible for order and justice in their communities. According to Le Gentil de la Barbinais, the city authorities of Lima used to give a financial compensation to the owner of the slave who "had been chosen as king."[86] In the 1830s, John Wurdemann witnessed a slave celebration in Cuba where "each tribe, having elected its king and queen, paraded the streets with a flag, having its name and the words *viva Isabella*, with the arms of Spain on it.... [T]hese parties stopped at the doors of houses, which they frequently did to collect money." The king and queen "wore dresses in the extreme of the fashion, and were very ceremoniously waited on by the ladies and gentlemen of the court, one of the ladies holding an umbrella over the head of the queen."[87] Describing the *Día de los Reyes* (Epiphany) celebrations in Santiago de Cuba in 1873, Walter Goodman commented on a *comparsa* (festive parade) of "Congo Negroes," who were "headed by a brace of blacks, who carry banners" and are followed by "a battalion of colonels, generals, and field-marshals, in gold-braided coats and gilded cocked-hats.... These are not ordinary masqueraders," he claimed, "but grave subjects of his somber majesty King Congo, the oldest and blackest of all the blacks: lawfully appointed sovereign of the coloured community."[88] According to one of Lydia Cabrera's informants on slave culture in Cuba, the Congo slaves of the *cabildo* (brotherhood) of Congos Reales in Trinidad formed a "real Congo kingdom with a King, a Queen, court and vassals . . . the King of the *cabildo*, also called a *capataz*, is wearing a frock coat trimmed with braid, shoes with buckles and a sash across his shoulder. Instead of a sword he carries a stick with a tassel. On his head is a three-cornered hat with feathers."[89]

In places with a high concentration of slaves, like Cuba and Brazil, one finds an abundance of such references to black king elections and subsequent parades. As Daniel Walker confirms in his study on slave culture in Cuba: "One account after another mentions the fact that Havana's mutual-aid agencies, called *cabildos*, conducted a highly reverential ritual that paid homage to the 'king' and 'queen' of each association."[90] Until abolition in 1888, Brazilian documents include hundreds of references to the election of slave kings without the slightest trace of irony. This indicates that in places with a large slave population, the election and celebration of a black king was not perceived as an odd habit but as a well-established tradition.[91]

Black king elections and subsequent parades or processions with flags and music bands have, in fact, been observed all over the Americas, from New England all the way to Argentina.[92] This corresponds to Walker's theory that African American Pinkster parades in New York may have been part of a much larger performance tradition carried out by people of African descent in the Americas.[93] In the 1980s, folklorist David Cohen had been the first to highlight parallels between African American Pinkster celebrations and black coronation festivals in the Caribbean and Brazil.[94] Around the same time, Piersen's research on "Negro Election Days" in New England also made him conclude that slave king elections in Brazil bore "striking similarity to the eighteenth-century Yankee pattern."[95]

Contemporary scholars have argued that such pan-American parallels in black performance traditions should be traced back to the establishment of secret slave associations in the American diaspora, which were modeled upon Efik, Igbo, Ogboni, Ekpe, Poro, Sande, Lemba, Nkimba, Ndembo, or Kimpasi religious and/or mutual-aid societies.[96] However, the use of flags, banners, and European-style crowns in king parades along with the use of European aristocratic titles cannot be convincingly explained with reference solely to indigenous African traditions.

One of the few African American witness accounts on Pinkster celebrations allows a different interpretation. John Williams, a former slave from Albany, argued in the late nineteenth century that "Pinkster Day was in Africa a religious day, partly pagan and partly Christian, like our Christmas day. Many of the old colored people, then in Albany, were born in Africa, and would dance their wild dances and sing in their native language."[97] Williams's statement points in the direction of the Afro-Catholic culture(s) that flourished in Kingdom of Kongo and in Angola, from where the charter generation in New Netherland originated. It corresponds to the assumption by Giovanna Fiume that slave king celebrations in Colombia, Haiti, Martinique, Jamaica, Cuba, Venezuela, Uruguay, Argentina, Peru, and Brazil all relate to Afro-Catholic brotherhoods.[98]

By 1921 the Cuban ethnographer Fernando Ortiz Fernández had already suggested that the election and celebration of African kings in the New World related to an Afro-Catholic, Hispano-Portuguese custom.[99] In the 1960s, Roger Bastide argued that black king election ceremonies with flags, banners, and parades must originally have been introduced in the Americas by Bantu peoples from West-Central Africa.[100] In a recent study, Brazilian historian Marina de Mello e Souza claims that king election ceremonies in Brazil and possibly also elsewhere in the Americas reflected an "African heritage linked to the Catholic

Kingdom of Kongo."[101] De Mello e Souza's findings correspond to Linda Hey-wood's argument for "an early and continuing Central African cultural pres-ence in the American diaspora" and that "a significant percentage of the Central Africans who left the region as slaves had participated in, or had at least been influenced by, the Afro-Portuguese culture (Creole) that had emerged in and around the Portuguese settlements."[102]

In their study of the *Cofradía de los Congos del Espíritu Santo* (Kongo Broth-erhood of the Holy Spirit, 1997) in the Dominican Republic, Carlos Hernández and Edis Sánchez highlight that on the feast of Pentecost, locally known as the *Fiesta del Espíritu Santo*, slaves used to elect and celebrate their kings. Even today, the black community of Villa Mella in the Dominican Republic still hon-ors its kings on Pentecost. According to Hernández and Sánchez, "on the eve before the feast, Saturday night, the kings representing the different communi-ties in Villa Mella gather at the church square, wearing their crowns." Initiated by a spectacular firework, "the kings, the gathered public and members of the brotherhood carrying musical instruments enter the church, where the rituals of the last night of the nine days of prayer [in anticipation of the arrival of the Holy Spirit on Pentecost] take place as well as several cultural performances." After the Mass has ended, "a procession takes place through the village" and after the procession, "all members of the brotherhood gather in the park of Villa Mella where they play their songs and drink rum. They play music, sing and dance until the night falls."[103] Hernández and Sánchez point out that a compara-tive study of similar black performance traditions in Brazil, Cuba, and Panama reveals that "these groups have in common that they organize feasts in honor of the patron saint of their respective Catholic brotherhood (*hermandad, cabildo, cofradía*) as well as on other special occasions in which they parade through the city playing instruments, singing, and dancing." All these groups share the char-acteristic of being organized in kingdoms, "in the context of which they recall the kings of Kongo and Angola."[104]

The assumption that the African American Pinkster parades in Albany could also relate to Afro-Catholic, Luso-Kongolese traditions corresponds to the observation by Willem Frijhoff, one of the Netherlands' leading experts in religious culture, that all available data on the African American Pinkster parades indicate that they followed a pattern rooted in Catholic procession cul-ture. Since "the religious practices of blacks in New Netherland were strongly influenced by Portuguese Catholicism," Frijhoff argues, "one can assume that this Catholic heritage survived for a long time, which explains the origin of the Pinkster processions."[105] Frijhoff's conclusion raises a range of new questions on the origin, nature, transmission, and survival of Afro-Catholic cultural elements with roots in West-Central Africa in the American diaspora. These questions will be further explored in the following chapter.

• 4 •

SLAVE KINGS AND BLACK
BROTHERHOODS IN THE
ATLANTIC WORLD

Portugal

Since the European Middle Ages, Catholic associations of lay people known as brotherhoods (*irmandades/hermandades*) or confraternities (*confrarias/cofradías*) played a crucial role in Iberian procession culture. Brotherhoods were dedicated either to a Catholic saint or to the Virgin Mary and annually celebrated the day dedicated to their patron, who was represented on the brotherhood's banner. Traditionally, the festivities of the brotherhood's patron coincided with the election of the new board. This was accompanied by a banquet offered by the brotherhood's leader to all members. Each brotherhood had its own regulations for membership, and the type of brotherhood to which one adhered corresponded to one's standing in society. Certain brotherhoods consisted exclusively of members of aristocratic families, while others were restricted to members of certain professional corporations or to inhabitants of certain neighborhoods. Even marginalized groups such as beggars and the blind could have their own brotherhoods. Following a European medieval procedure for dealing with potentially troublesome minority groups, the authorities expected the leaders of such brotherhoods to act as representatives of the entire group and held them accountable for acts of misconduct by their members. In urban centers with large African slave populations such as Lisbon, Cádiz, and Seville, so-called "black brotherhoods" developed, composed of free blacks and black slaves.

In Portugal the first reference to the presence of blacks in brotherhoods dates to 1484.[1] Most Portuguese confraternities associated with the black community were dedicated to Our Lady of the Rosary. The original Confraternity of the Holy Rosary was founded in 1468 in Douai, a French-speaking city in the southern Low Countries, by the Dominican Alan of Rupa. Other Dominicans followed his example. One of the most successful rosary confraternities was founded in 1475 by Jakob Sprenger, dean of the faculty of theology at the University of Cologne. In his role as inquisitor, Sprenger considered the concept of confraternity a useful instrument to combat pre-Christian traditions related to ancestor worship. Sprenger dedicated considerable attention to fraternal solidarity between the dead and the living and opened the brotherhood to the poorest of the poor without regard to ethnicity, gender, or social status: "In our brotherhood no one will be kept out, no matter how poor he may be; but rather the poorer he is, the more disdained and despised, the more acceptable, beloved and precious will he be in this brotherhood."[2]

In the late fifteenth century, a Confraternity of Our Lady of the Rosary was established in Lisbon. Like other brotherhoods, it was a complex and heterogeneous organization with a broad range of interests among its white and black members. It also underwent considerable changes in the course of its existence. In 1518 it received the privilege of requesting manumission for any slave who had proved to be a faithful member. Around 1540 the black community separated itself and applied for its own charter as *Irmandade de Nossa Senhora do Rosário dos Homens Pretos* (Brotherhood of Our Lady of the Rosary of the Black Men), which it received in 1565.

By the end of the sixteenth century there were at least nine black brotherhoods in Portugal, most of them dedicated to Our Lady of the Rosary. Allegedly, the popularity of Our Lady of the Rosary among blacks relates to a miraculous apparition of the Virgin Mary in the form of a statue. After several fruitless attempts by white Christians to take the statue into their chapel, black Christians approached the statue with beating drums and dance. Where the whites had failed the black men succeeded, and ever since, Our Lady of the Rosary was seen as the "friend of black Christians." Since Our Lady of the Rosary was often venerated as appearing above the waters of the sea, her popularity among slaves may also relate to the ocean that connected them to their native Africa.[3]

Black brotherhoods possessed a hierarchical structure in which European aristocratic titles were used. This strict hierarchy was accompanied by a democratic decision-making process. According to Chapter XXVI of the black brotherhood of Our Lady of the Rosary in Lisbon, members willing to be candidates for prince, count, judge, treasurer, superintendent, scribe, administrator, and king had to submit their requests to an electoral commission. During processions, the king and queen were usually protected from the sun by a sunshade held by one of the members and wore a crown or a hat covered with pieces of gold, silver, or anything shiny to make it look like a crown.[4] In places with a large number of slaves, several black brotherhoods could develop that were subdivided according to the slaves' origins or "nations," named after the place or region in Africa from where they had been shipped, such as Kongo, (São Jorge da) Mina, or Mozambique.[5]

Since the kings of brotherhoods had real power, it would be wrong to reduce their presence in processions to a carnivalesque inversion of the established order. While the use of aristocratic titles by slaves can easily be misconstrued as a form of parody, an interpretation of these organizations based on the importance of their social capital in the sense coined by Pierre Bourdieu shows that these titles functioned as a strategy to foster unity and stability. "If the internal competition for the monopoly of legitimate representation of the group is not to threaten the conservation and accumulation of the capital which is the basis of the group," Bourdieu explains, "the members of the group must regulate the conditions . . . to set oneself up as a representative (delegate, plenipotentiary, spokesman, etc.) of the whole group, thereby committing the social capital of the whole group." Accordingly, "the title of nobility is the form *par excellence* of the institutionalized social capital which guarantees a particular form of social relationship in a lasting way."[6]

Black brotherhoods usually had a white treasurer and had to submit their *compromissos* (statutes) for approval to the city authorities. This has prompted scholars to argue that brotherhoods essentially served the interests of slaveholders by having blacks accept the rules and standards of a society that repressed them.[7] However, it should be stressed that these organizations were not forced upon the black community. Documents indicate that the desire to create a brotherhood came from within the slave community itself. This is not surprising considering that brotherhoods strengthened black solidarity, enabled the maintenance or construction of a collective identity, provided a mutual-aid system in order to care for the needy, and secured a minimal social mobility that, in exceptional cases, could lead to manumission. In fact, the collection of money to liberate brothers and sisters from the bonds of slavery was one of the main goals of black brotherhoods. Moreover, brotherhoods functioned as a means of cultural affirmation as they provided blacks with a chance to have their own chapels, to participate in processions with their own performances, to have Masses for the souls of the living and dead members, and to make sure that members received an honorable funeral and burial place.[8] As Didier Lahon has shown, the latter was a major concern to slaves living in Lisbon, where until the creation of the first black brotherhoods deceased slaves used to be thrown "at the mercy of the raving dogs" on a heap of ordure by the banks of the Tagus.[9]

Therefore, Marina de Mello e Souza rejects the assumption that black brotherhoods were an instrument of oppression. She refers to brotherhoods as "channels of negotiation" and argues that they were transcultural organizations that functioned on the basis of interdependency between masters and slaves.[10] Elizabeth Kiddy also maintains that it would be wrong to consider brotherhoods a form of accommodation as opposed to the resistance of slaves who attempted to run away in order to form maroon settlements. According to Kiddy, the establishment of maroon settlements and the decision to form a brotherhood represent the same impulse: the recreation of black community life within a new, alienating environment.[11]

Despite the fact that negotiations played a key role in the modus operandi of black brotherhoods, it would be wrong to assume that they essentially functioned on the basis of cooperation. Rather, brotherhoods used a strategy of cooperative resistance, which means that the balance occasionally tilted more toward tactical cooperation and sometimes more toward protest. Their strategy corresponded to that of slaveholders and white authorities who in their interaction with black brotherhoods also adopted an attitude that wavered between repression and support. During negotiations and disputes, representatives of black brotherhoods insisted on their equality as Christians. Some black brotherhoods went as far as sending procurators to the Holy Office in Rome to defend their cause. One example is the journey to Rome in the 1680s by Lourenço da Silva de Mendouça, procurator of the black brotherhood of Our Lady Star of the Negroes in Madrid and of Our Lady of the Rosary in Lisbon.[12]

The participation at processions and subsequent festivities during which collections were held and booths sold food and drinks served as an important source of income for black brotherhoods. Other forms of revenue were dues, donations, the collection of alms, the organization of paid funeral marches, and testaments. Some brotherhoods also used games of chance such as lotteries to make money, and even placed collection boxes for donations in taverns. Members also donated jewelry to embellish the statues of the brotherhood's patron saint or the Virgin Mary. Not surprisingly, black brotherhoods were often accused by slaveholders of handling stolen goods.[13]

Processions and celebrations primarily occurred on holidays that were intimately related to the black community such as the feast day of Saint Moses the Black, an ascetic monk from Egypt (August 28); Saint Iphigenia, a legendary Nubian Princess (September 21); Saint Benedict—*il Moro*—of Palermo, whose parents had been African slaves (October 5); Saint Elesbaan, formerly known as King Kaleb of Axum in today's Ethiopia (October 27); and Our Lady of the Rosary (first Sunday in October), all of whom were venerated with specific *loas* (veneration songs). The black community in Portugal also venerated a black Saint Anthony, called Santo António de Notto, who originated from Libya and had been a slave in Sicily.[14]

Black brotherhoods were often accused of celebrating holidays in a disrespectful way because during processions their members would wear African clothing, play African instruments, and perform African dances.[15] On August 5, 1633, for instance, an unknown Spanish Capuchin observed a procession of thousands of slaves in Lisbon. He wrote that they were dressed "in accordance

Saint Elesbaan and Saint Iphigenia, 18th century. Statues of two black saints in the Santa Clara Church, Porto. Picture: Inez Lopes.

with their native customs and walk around half naked, with sashes tied around their heads, arms and chests and colorful cloths covering their bottoms," that they carried "bows and arrows according to their customs" and that while "many sing while playing viols, drums, flutes and other instruments according to their customs, they dance with castanets and perform savage dances."[16]

The kings of black brotherhoods usually served wealthy masters and expected the latter to support the annual celebration of the brotherhood.[17] This is notable in the description provided by António de Oliveira de Cadornega, shortly before he left for Angola in 1639, about the king of the black brotherhood in Vila Viçosa. Since this slave king worked in the local ducal palace, his master allowed him to annually invite all the members of his brotherhood for a banquet at the palace in honor of Our Lady of the Rosary.[18]

Other important holidays for black brotherhoods were Corpus Christi, Epiphany, Easter, Pentecost, All Saints' Day, All Souls' Day, St. John's Day (June 23), and St. James's Day (July 25). Corpus Christi is celebrated on the Thursday after Trinity Sunday, which is the first Sunday after Pentecost. The holiday has its roots in the mystic traditions of the Low Countries, where it was promoted by the thirteenth-century Augustinian nun Juliana of Liège. Juliana claimed to have seen the moon shining as brightly as the sun. This was followed by a vision of Christ who explained to her that the moon represented the militant Church, which had to be restored in its former glory by means of a feast that in its splendor was as brilliant as the sun.[19] Similar to the Dutch ommegangen, Iberian Corpus Christi processions typically included people carrying statues of saints, candle-bearers, girls decorated with flowers, musicians playing bagpipes, drums, tambourines, flutes, and trumpets, stilt walkers, sword or stick dancers who staged mock fights at the sound of the drum, mummers dressed as animals, devils, angels, or dragons, elaborately adorned oxen and wagons with *tableaux vivants* featuring biblical scenes such as the creation of the world, Adam and Eve, St. George's fight with the dragon, Noah and the ark, the fall of Lucifer, and David and Goliath. Another typical feature of Corpus Christi parades was the inclusion of "kings" and "emperors" in accordance with the words of Psalm 71:X–XI, "the kings of Tarsis and of the islands shall offer presents; the kings of the Arabians and of Saba shall bring gifts. And all kings of the earth shall adore him: all nations shall serve him."[20] For instance, a document on the Corpus Christi celebration in the Portuguese city of Coimbra in 1517 indicates that the guild of the potters performed a sword dance, the guild of the cobblers presented a *mourisca* (mock war dance), and the guild of the drapers formed a parade featuring an emperor and empress accompanied by eight maids of honor.[21] The expansionist character of Corpus Christi also implied the presence of

Christian monarchs representing foreign nations. Therefore, the kings of black brotherhoods who participated in the procession represented African kings whose conversion to Christianity symbolized the steady spread of the Catholic faith around the world.[22] A similar situation occurred during processions on the feast of Epiphany, during which the black brotherhood's king symbolically represented one of the three Magi.[23]

The Portuguese *Festa do Divino Espírito Santo* (Feast of the Divine Holy Spirit) on Pentecost originated in the fourteenth century and was allegedly based on one of the many miracles involving Queen Consort Elizabeth of Aragon, better known as *Rainha Santa Isabel* (Holy Queen Elizabeth). Elizabeth is said to have had a dream in which God asked her to build a church to honor the Holy Spirit in Alenquer, Portugal. When the workers arrived, the foundations of the church had already miraculously been prepared. The celebration of the Holy Spirit also served to strengthen the position of the monarchy as the godly guardian of the Portuguese empire, hence the use of the term *divino* and the importance of the imperial standard, the crown, and the scepter during the procession. These symbols linked the Portuguese monarch to the legendary Charlemagne, the *Rex Christianissimus* and father of the *Imperium Christianum* that the Portuguese monarchy wanted to extend to all corners of the globe.[24] Research by Carlos Francisco Moura also revealed that the election and parade of an "emperor" during the Feast of the Divine Holy Spirit was the most popular paratheatrical tradition performed on Portuguese ships during the Age of Discovery.[25] It should, as such, not surprise, that the tradition left traces in all parts of the world with a history of Portuguese rule.

The information gathered so far allows us to highlight some remarkable parallels to African American Pinkster and Election Day celebrations. Like black brotherhoods in Portugal, these celebrations involve the election of a community leader called "the king." This king dresses as a European monarch and marches in procession through town. At the beginning of the procession we find someone holding a banner. The procession ends at a "palace," where dances and a banquet take place. Members use the occasion to raise money for the brotherhood and to ask for donations in order to provide assistance to members in need. Slave masters provide tactical support, while holding the king accountable for problems within the slave community. All these characteristics correspond to the way black brotherhoods in Portuguese societies operated. Moreover, the event in Albany coincides with a major Portuguese holiday, the Feast of the Divine Holy Spirit on Pentecost. These surprising parallels raise the question how an originally Portuguese custom could possibly have ended up celebrated among slaves in North America, requiring a closer look at the role of brotherhoods in the context of the Portuguese expansionist policies.

Africa

It is well known that the Portuguese exported brotherhoods and their inherent rituals overseas, where they were responsible for making the religious cult
a part of daily life in settlements they established in Asia, Brazil, and Africa.[26]
The first black brotherhood in Africa, dedicated to Our Lady of the Rosary,
was established in the year 1495 on Santiago, one of the islands of the Cape
Verde archipelago.[27] It had considerable influence on local performance culture.
Documents indicate that in the mid-eighteenth century it was still common
to see "gatherings of the kings of the brotherhood of the Rosary" on Santiago
and that "in all neighborhoods of the island women and men were elected to
serve as kings and queens, who every Sunday and holiday stage parades with
their drums and flutes in order to collect money."[28] Other eighteenth-century
documents refer to parades of "black kings with their soldiers" on Santiago, and
to a "governor of the blacks," who had "judges" and "an army composed of free
blacks and black slaves . . . with lieutenant generals, colonels, sergeants and captains of infantry."[29] Similar groups exist today under the name *tabanca*, a Guinean term for "settlement." Like the ancient brotherhoods, tabancas function as
mutual-aid associations in the island's poorest neighborhoods and ensure that
their members receive a decent funeral. They are led by a "king" or a "governor,"
who has his own delegates and "army" and who represents the community in
negotiations with the authorities. On the feast day of the tabanca's patron saint,
dues are collected, a procession is organized, members gather for a communal
dinner, drums are played, and dances takes place.[30]

The Cape Verde Islands functioned as a complement to a range of Portuguese trading posts along the West African coastline in places such as Arguin,
Shame, Elmina, and Accra. To manage the administration, the crown appointed
an authority at each post, usually with the title of "Captain of the Portuguese" or
"Governor of the Portuguese."[31] A syncretic Luso-African culture developed on
the nearby West African shore when men born on the Cape Verde Islands or in
Portugal settled along the Guinea coastline and rivers to engage in trade. These
so-called *lançados* or *tangomaos* established relationships with local women and
gave origin to the development of a Luso-African community characterized by
a syncretic form of Christianity. Although they did not completely abandon
their traditional African beliefs and customs, these Luso-Africans considered
themselves to be Portuguese and Christians. In 1738 Francis Moore observed
in his *Travels into the Inland Parts of Africa* that "they reckon themselves still
as well as if they were actually White, and nothing angers them more than to
call them Negroes, that being a Term they use only for Slaves."[32] These Luso-
Africans promoted the use of Kriol—a creolized form of Portuguese—as the
lingua franca used for business in the Guinea region.[33] Closely related to them

were the Kristons or Grumetes, Africans who had converted to Christianity. According to Gerhard Seibert, "their communities were organized on the basis of Catholic brotherhoods (*irmandades, confrarias*). These brotherhoods celebrated Catholic feasts and provided support for members in need."[34] As George Brooks has shown, a distinctive feature of Kriston culture was *folgar*, the celebration of Catholic holidays with music and dance according to a Portuguese model.[35] By the seventeenth century, Christianity had spread along the Guinea coastline to Sierra Leone.[36] Although the total number of converts to Christianity in Upper Guinea remained fairly limited, the Portuguese cultural, linguistic, and religious influence in the region was considerable, even among those who rejected Christianity.[37]

In 1526 a black brotherhood dedicated to Our Lady of the Rosary was established on São Tomé, an originally uninhabited island in the Gulf of Guinea.[38] It strongly influenced the island's performance traditions. In 1836 Raimundo da Cunha Matos reported that "a lot of confraternities and poor brotherhoods" still existed on the island and that "the feasts of the Rosary" were among the most splendid ones, although "the degree of profanation and irreverence during the feast of the Rosary has declined in comparison to what it used to be in the past."[39] São Tomé was originally used for the production of sugar cane, as on the island of Madeira. According to Luiz Felipe de Alencastro, it functioned as a laboratory of what Brazilian slave society was to become.[40] The establishment of a brotherhood was the result of a petition by the local black population and should be seen as recognition by the colonizers that they could not rule the island in the same way as Madeira. On the latter island, white settlers dominated, whereas the idea of forming a white working class on São Tomé by sending for convicts and Jewish "orphans"—mostly children who had been taken away from their parents—failed, as many of them perished due to tropical diseases.[41] African slaves soon formed the overwhelming majority of the population on the island, which led to the decision to grant *cartas de alforria* (letters of manumission) to a select group of blacks.[42] Decisions regarding alforria were coordinated in the context of the brotherhood, whose charter granted the possibility of requesting freedom for any slave, male or female, who was a distinguished member. Although freedom remained an unreachable goal for the large majority of slaves, the system at least offered some hope since it allowed negotiation and opened the possibility to raise of one's own social status or at least that of one's children. This encouraged slaves to adopt Portuguese customs and to demonstrate their loyalty. It was, for instance, common practice to employ slaves as agents in slave trading operations and to form black militias that assisted regular soldiers in military campaigns. As Toby Green has shown in relation to the Cape Verde Islands, respect for alforria was of crucial importance to the local black population. Significantly, the news that the free black

man Rodrigo Lopez had been smuggled onto a ship and sold as a slave in Hispaniola in 1526 almost provoked an uprising.[43] The Dutch were familiar with
this sensibility. When John Maurice of Nassau ordered the assault on Luanda
in 1641, he made it clear that no blacks who had been granted alforria by the
Portuguese could be enslaved.[44]

In 1533 both São Tomé and Santiago became dioceses, which meant the
Christian mission in Africa was no longer coordinated from the archdiocese of
Funchal, on the island of Madeira. From São Tomé, Catholicism reached parts
of Lower Guinea, such as Allada and Ouidah in Benin and the Kingdom of
Warri in the Niger Delta area, but failed to take root.[45] As had happened along
the Upper Guinean coast, a Portuguese Creole language also spread from São
Tomé to the Lower Guinea region where it became a lingua franca in international trade. For a while, Portuguese was the only foreign language that the kings
of Dahomey authorized. According to the seventeenth-century Jesuit Alonso de
Sandoval, the best way to communicate with slaves from Lower Guinea was in
the "language of São Tomé," which he defined as "a corrupt and complicated
version of Portuguese."[46]

Portuguese missionary work in East Africa was initially coordinated from
the Jesuit stronghold in Goa, India. In 1511 a brotherhood of Our Lady of the
Rosary had been established in Goa and, according to Leopoldo da Rocha,
countless other brotherhoods of Our Lady of the Rosary followed in other parts
of Asia that the Portuguese brought under their control. Goa was known for
its vivid procession culture, in which African slaves also participated.[47] From
Goa, Portuguese missionaries were active in Ethiopia, but failed to reconcile
the Ethiopian church to Rome.[48] A separate diocese, detached from Goa, was
established in 1610 on the island of Mozambique. There the Dominican convent
had a black brotherhood dedicated to Our Lady of the Rosary. From a small
island off the African coast, which the Portuguese called Mozambique, several
attempts were made by Jesuits and Dominicans to convert inland rulers. From
there, missionaries were also sent to the island of Madagascar. Despite some
successes—most notably the 1652 conversion of the King of Mutapa, whose
kingdom stretched between the Zambezi and Limpopo rivers of southern
Africa—Catholicism failed to take root. The assumption by Hodges—that slaves
from Madagascar, who were brought to New York in the late seventeenth and
early eighteenth centuries, were Catholic converts—can be doubted. Portuguese
missionary efforts in the area had been largely unsuccessful.[49] In East Africa,
little more was achieved than the formation of small Catholic enclaves popu-
lated by Portuguese men, their African wives, and their mixed-race children. At
least one of these enclaves, Sena, had a Rosary brotherhood.[50]

The main focus of Portuguese missionary efforts on the African continent
was the Kingdom of Kongo and Angola. Catholicism had been introduced

Anonymous, *Mbanza Kongo, São Salvador*. Seventeenth-century drawing of São Salvador/ Mbanza Kongo, the capital of the Kingdom of Kongo. Buildings marked with a C are Catholic churches. In Olfert Dapper, *Naukeurige beschrijvinge der Afrikaensche gewesten* (Amsterdam: Jacob van Meurs, 1668).

in West-Central Africa in the late fifteenth century, when Portuguese missionaries baptized the ruler of the Kongolese province of Soyo (or Nsoyo) in April 1491. The following month they also baptized the Manikongo Nzinga a Nkuwu as King João I of Kongo, which was also the name of the king of Portugal at the time. Whereas Nzinga a Nkuwu/João I remained hesitant to fully embrace the new faith, Catholicism truly expanded in Kongo under the king's son Mvemba a Nzinga, better known under his Catholic baptismal name Afonso. With Portuguese military support, Afonso was able to defeat his pagan half-brother Mpanzu a Kitima in a power struggle over succession in 1506. In accordance with the new faith he had embraced, Afonso dedicated his victory in the Battle of Mbanza Kongo to a miraculous intervention by São Tiago (St. James the Greater).[51] This paralleled the alleged intervention of St. James, the "Moor-slayer" (Santiago Matamoros/São Tiago Matamouros), in the battle of Clavijo in Spain in 844. The king's name Afonso also linked him to the Battle of Ourique in 1139, in which the Portuguese King Afonso Henriques had defeated the Moors thanks to a miraculous intervention by St. James. In the capital city of Mbanza Kongo, later also named São Salvador, King Afonso I cut the trees on the royal cemetery and used the site to build a church. This church, dedicated to Our Lady of Victory, symbolized the central position of the new religion in the Kongo kingdom. By destroying the old cults, King Afonso set up a new structure to develop a new religion under his control. The spread of Catholicism went hand in hand with the struggle against "pagan" enemies who potentially represented a threat to the king's power.[52] King Afonso even requested a Bull of Crusade from the Vatican, so that his expansionist policies could be justified as an attempt to spread the "true faith." Accordingly, members of influential Kongolese families who supported him in this effort were not only granted titles of European nobility—such as duke, count, or marquis—but also borrowed key attributes of Portuguese noblemen and were knighted in the Order of Christ.[53]

While it was long assumed that the impact of Catholicism in the region had been fleeting, superficial, and had affected only a slim minority of Kongolese people in upper-class circles, there is a growing consensus in contemporary scholarship that by the end of the sixteenth century Catholicism had become an important source of Kongolese identity.[54] Even people living in isolated areas of Kongo eventually came to accept the principal rituals and symbols of Catholicism.[55] A list of questions, submitted to the ambassador of the Kingdom of Kongo in Lisbon in 1595, reveals that by the late sixteenth century the capital of Kongo already counted six confraternities: Our Lady of the Rosary, the Holy Sacrament, Saint Mary, the Immaculate Conception, the Holy Spirit, St. Ignatius, and St. Anthony. Early-seventeenth-century documents also indicate the existence of a brotherhood linked to a *Santa Casa da Misericórdia* (Holy House of Mercy), Portugal's main charitable institution. Membership in a confraternity was initially the exclusive privilege of the kingdom's elite and therefore conferred great prestige.[56] According to Raphaêl Batsîkama, the St. Anthony brotherhood, in particular, had a long-lasting impact on Kongolese religious culture.[57]

The fact that the authority of a newly elected king had to be confirmed by a coronation officiated over by a Catholic priest allowed the Portuguese to use religion as a means to interfere in local affairs. King Afonso and his successors constantly complained about Portuguese abuse of the *padroado*, the patronage of the Church granted by Pope Leo X in 1514 to increase Portugal's political influence in the region.[58] This discontent explains the Kongolese attempt to win papal support for the creation of a local diocese through which they could bypass the Portuguese bishop in São Tomé and negotiate religious affairs directly with the Vatican. However, Portugal consistently thwarted any decision that questioned its religious monopoly as established in the padroado and boycotted the establishment by Pope Clement VIII of a new diocese in Mbanza Kongo in 1596 by insisting on its right to appoint the bishop and eventually moving the seat of the diocese to Luanda in Portuguese-controlled Angola.[59]

Continuous conflicts with the kings of Kongo, in fact, prompted the Portuguese to expand their stronghold in Luanda, which they had established in the southern edge of the kingdom in 1576. From Luanda they developed new trade routes that bypassed the king of Kongo, making it into the West-Central African center of the transatlantic slave trade.[60] Although the penetration of Catholicism in Angola was not as strong as in Kongo, it was substantial in all areas under Portuguese control. Since Luanda became the de facto seat of the diocese that was supposed to be in the Kongolese capital, it was the center of Portugal's missionary ambitions in the region. In 1628 a black brotherhood of Our Lady of the Rosary was established in Luanda. Every first Sunday of the month, this brotherhood would organize a procession on the streets of Luanda.[61] Several other black brotherhoods existed in Portuguese-controlled areas in Angola, even in places as far in the interior as Massangano.[62] Members of Angolan brotherhoods expected to be treated as equals to white Catholics. Significantly, when Portuguese residents in Luanda tried to prevent members of a black brotherhood from using the city's Portuguese cemetery, the latter complained to the bishop and insisted that Christians were "all equal in the eyes of God." As in Kongo, the local procession culture in Angola continued to include many indigenous elements. The eighteenth-century Portuguese historian Elias Corrêa disparagingly referred to these processions as "celebrations without religion."[63] As had happened in Guinea, Afro-Catholic influences also spread along the Angolan coast as well as in the Benguela highlands thanks to ethnically mixed and autonomously operating Luso-African communities composed of merchants who claimed a Portuguese and Catholic identity.[64]

In 1640 the quarrel over control of Catholic policy in West-Central Africa led to the decision by Pope Urban VIII to send "neutral" friars, mostly Italians, of the Order of Friars Minor Capuchin to perform the sacraments in Kongo.[65] These Capuchin missionaries established dozens of new confraternities—dedicated to St. Francis of Assisi, the Immaculate Conception, Our Lady of the Rosary, the Cord of St. Francis, St. Bonaventure, Saint Claire, the Slaves of Mary, etc.— as a way to spread and solidify the new faith as well as to "purify" Kongolese Catholicism by eradicating indigenous traditions they perceived as "diabolic superstitions."[66] The importance of confraternities to the Capuchin's missionary strategy is apparent in the case of the Flemish missionary Joris van Geel—one of the few non-Italian Capuchins operating in the Kongo—who carried with him several prewritten documents with the text "Rules of the brotherhood of ____, founded at the Church of ____" when he started his mission in 1651.[67] Capuchins founded brotherhoods far into the interior of Africa. Even the Kingdom of Matamba had its confraternity of Our Lady of the Rosary in the early seventeenth century.[68]

The role of the Capuchins in spreading Catholicism in West-Central Africa should not be overstated, however. The expansion of Catholicism in the region was not primarily the result of successful European missionary work but rather of the decision by King Afonso and his successors to embrace and promote the new faith. Christianity in Kongo did not depend on European missionaries to thrive, because an active local laity took their place. European Capuchins worked alongside local interpreters, catechists, and churchwardens and in practice very much depended on them. These lay ministers, called *mestres de escola* (schoolmasters), generally belonged to the local nobility. They not only spread the new faith in the Kingdom of Kongo but were also employed in missionary activities in the kingdom of Ndongo, the Mbundu regions, and Loango.[69] "Even in remote regions far from the established parishes and missionary convents, and even outside the territories controlled by the kingdom," Cécile Fromont writes, "crowds of men and women could experience memorable, if few, Christian rituals and see or own modest Christian images. . . . Christianity, then, was part of the world of many Central Africans."[70]

Thornton argues that thanks to these lay ministers, "Christianity conquered Kongo peacefully—but at the cost of adapting itself to the 'conquered' people's conception of religion and cosmology," as happened with the Chinese rites in China and the Malabar rites in India, which respectively combined Catholicism with local Confucianist and Hinduist elements.[71] It is therefore likely that Kongolese brotherhoods had characteristics in common with indigenous societies such as *kimpasi*, which made them differ considerably from the Portuguese model they were derived from.[72] Catholicism did not, in fact, superimpose itself on indigenous beliefs in Kongo. Kongolese Catholicism was a profoundly syncretic variant of Catholicism that stood close to indigenous beliefs. The translation of Christian terms into local Kikongo occurred on the basis of words and expressions already rooted in animistic traditions. For instance, Catholic saints were converted into ancestors' souls (*moyo*), so that the Holy Spirit was called *Moyo Ukisi*. The Portuguese Feast of the Holy Spirit had, as such, a Kongolese counterpart.[73] Christian objects such as crosses, crucifixes, and rosaries were decorated with Kongolese motifs and interpreted as new and stronger *minkisi*, magic complexes that gave protection against evil forces. Many Kongolese considered Catholic baptism to be a rite that protected against disease and witchcraft, hence the Kongolese tradition to place a grain of salt in the mouth of the supplicant in accordance to the traditional belief that salt protected against witches. In fact, the Kikongo term for baptism was *curia mungua* (modern: *kudia mungwa*), meaning to eat salt.[74] Even those who rejected the official Kongolese Catholicism that was propagated by the local nobility and either remained loyal to indigenous cults or joined new ones such as Dona Beatrice's St. Anthony Movement frequently adopted Catholic elements.[75]

In view of the fact that Kongolese Catholicism adapted itself to the indigenous conception of religion and cosmology, there are doubts as to whether this religion should be considered a local variant of Catholicism or whether it was Catholic only in name and hardly affected existing indigenous beliefs. These

Crucifix from the Kingdom of Kongo. Crucifix with *minkisi*, illustrating the syncretic character of Kongolese Catholicism. HO.1955.9.3, collection Royal Museum for Central Africa, Tervuren (Belgium); picture: J. Van de Vyver. Courtesy the Royal Museum for Central Africa, Tervuren.

doubts not only divide contemporary scholars but were also a matter of dispute among Jesuit and Capuchin missionaries. Some of these missionaries adopted a more flexible attitude than others. The Italian Capuchin Girolamo Merolla, for instance, was well aware of the fact that the Kongolese gave their own interpretation to the Catholic elements they embraced, but he did not consider this a reason to question their Catholic identity. He openly admitted that people of his mission were not afraid to confront hostile members of animist cults because they wore medals "given to them by us as preservatives against sorcery."[76] Others, however, did not allow any compromise to Catholic orthodoxy. In accordance with the strict norms of the Counter-Reformation, they claimed that a considerable part of Kongolese Catholicism such as curing, healing, and divination was of diabolical nature and had to be destroyed. For instance, the Italian Capuchin Lorenzo da Lucca argued in the early eighteenth century that the Kingdom of Kongo had always remained a pagan society and that the population's Catholic identity did not go beyond baptism and occasional Mass attendance.[77]

A crucial, though often neglected, element in discussions on Kongo's Catholic identity is that the Portuguese had introduced their religion in Africa before the foundation of the Society of Jesus and the Counter-Reformation, at a time when it was still common practice in the Lusitanian motherland that girls would rub their genitals against the tomb of St. Gonçalo to increase their fertility, people would laugh and shout at actors performing devils in stage performances inside the churches, and lascivious dances would take place during processions. Even white Catholic brotherhoods in Portugal were full of "superstition." The Brotherhood of the Cross, for instance, did not allow its *mordomo* (chief administrator) to touch any object of iron on the day of his installation on the grounds that this would bring down a pestilence on the village.[78] At that time, the borders between traditional beliefs and Christianity were still very blurred in Portugal. As George Brooks has argued, sixteenth-century Portuguese and West Africans "shared similar beliefs concerning the causes and cures of disease, and in the efficacy of amulets."[79] Speaking about the Cape Verde Islands, the African scholars José Maria Semedo and Maria Turano confirm that "there is a tendency here to assume that popular beliefs and 'superstition' are all of African origin, but many of these traditions can easily be traced back to Portuguese popular culture."[80] Belief in divination, cures, amulets, and witchcraft, elements cited by some contemporary scholars to question Kongo's Catholic identity, were common in sixteenth-century Portugal.[81] Not surprisingly, thus, even deeply Catholic Portuguese adopted indigenous beliefs and traditions while living in Africa. A famous example are the amulets known in eighteenth-century Portugal as *bolsas de mandinga*, which people would carry on their body at all times except when entering a church.[82]

It is undeniable that interaction with the Portuguese beginning in the late fifteenth century affected local traditions in the Kongo region.[83] Portuguese culture had, in fact, strong impact on Kongolese society: the Kongolese aristocracy adopted Portuguese names, titles, coats or arms, and styles of dress, and imported material goods from Portugal. The king of Kongo sent youths from the elite families to Europe for education and had one of his sons consecrated in Rome as a bishop. Members of the Kongo elite became literate and were ordained as priests in the local church, while the king sent embassies to Rome and maintained correspondence with the popes. Christian festivals were observed, churches and chapels were erected, and local craftsmen made

Christian religious artifacts. Religious brotherhoods were founded and orders of knighthood instituted in imitation of Portuguese practices.[84]

This impact also applies to music and festive traditions. Garcia de Resende's early-sixteenth-century chronicle about the Portuguese King João II reveals how a group of Kongolese, who had been taken to Portugal and later returned to their homeland, had "learned our language and our customs" while living in Portugal.[85] In his *Relação do Reino do Congo* (Account of the Kingdom of Kongo, 1492), Rui de Pina mentions that King João II not only sent crucifixes, chalices, banners, and candlesticks to the King of Kongo, but also church bells and pipe organs.[86] According to the anonymous author of the early-seventeenth-century *História do Reino do Congo* (History of the Kingdom of Kongo), the Portuguese king Manuel I sent instructors to Kongo to make locals literate and to teach them "how to sing plainchant to organ music."[87] In 1512 Simão da Silva mentions a long list of Portuguese presents for the King of Kongo, including mirrors from Venice, lace from Bruges, and textiles from India but also a frame drum, small bells, and trumpets. The committee that was to deliver these presents in Kongo included a bagpipe player and an organ player.[88] Trumpets of European design were commonly used in the Kongolese court by the mid-seventeenth century.[89] In 1642 Pieter Mortamer reported from Luanda to the Council in Dutch Brazil that among the things they should prepare to please the King of Kongo was a committee that included a "young black boy who is reasonably well versed in playing the trumpet."[90] In the chapter on "Ethiopians in the Congo and Angolan kingdoms" in his *De instauranda Aethiopum salute* (On Restoring Spiritual Health to Africans, 1627), Sandoval also mentions that "among them are many black men who are great Christians. Much of the clergy is this color, and they pride themselves on knowing how to play the organ."[91] It would thus be wrong to assume that only upon arrival in the Americas did Central Africans become exposed to and influenced by European music. Naturally, this influence was mutual. Documents from the Age of Discovery also refer to Portuguese sailors entertaining themselves on board with "African dances."[92]

Brotherhoods played a crucial role in the development of a Kongolese variant of Iberian Catholic procession culture, including its most militant expressions involving self-flagellation.[93] One of the earliest references to Catholic procession culture in Kongo dates to 1582, when Carmelite missionaries staged a solemn procession with a statue of the Virgin Mary in the Kongolese capital.[94] The mixture of Portuguese and Kongolese elements is notable in the descriptions provided by the Italian Capuchin Andrea da Pavia of the processions he observed in Soyo in the late seventeenth century. On Corpus Christi, for instance, he witnessed how the people collected branches in order to "decorate the church interior with greenstuff and flowers." Then several cannons and muskets were brought to the church square, where there was "a large pathway that leads to a type of theater . . . in the middle of which a magnificent altar is made." When these preparations are concluded, "children initiate the procession, carrying the cross, then the congregationists follow in due order, then the members of the confraternity of the holy sacrament with their red capes, then the lay priests wearing their surplices, then comes the canopy carried by six of the most noble men of the county, all dressed ceremoniously." The prince "walks behind the holy sacrament and wears clothing decorated with gold, silver and jewels," while the procession is accompanied "by a great number of people playing musical instruments."[95]

On Easter, da Pavia observed how "the great prince makes his apparition in gala costume with his entire court." After receiving his blessing, the prince takes his sword and shield and "begins a war dance which in their language, they call *sangare*. The dignitaries do the same while shouting loudly. After a while, they exchange the swords for bows and arrows and repeat the same dance."[96] Da Pavia also observed a "great celebration with fires" in honor of St. John and was deeply impressed by the celebrations on St. James's Day, when nobles from all over the kingdom gathered in the capital to pay tribute to the King of Kongo. The solemnities in honor of St. James the Greater lasted for eight days and ended with "a general banquet for everyone." But before this happened, "all the chiefs must pay their contribution to the prince during these eight days." The day after the banquet, the prince inspected his troops and war dances were performed: "They call this in their language *sangamento*. All the chiefs must parade in front of the prince and execute a war dance and other military maneuvers. All this takes place on the church square [where] a large gallery, decorated with rugs and other tapestries, has been built at the order of the prince."[97]

According to the Capuchin missionaries Giuseppe-Maria da Bussetto and Giovanni Francesco Romano, similar processions and celebrations occurred on Pentecost.[98] Kongolese *ku-sanga* war dances, which the Portuguese called sangamentos, had traditionally been performed at a time of transition in power. Whenever a new King of Kongo or one of his regional governors was elected, sangamentos were performed as part of the delegation of power.[99] The fact that sangamentos later became so intimately related with St. James's Day corresponds to the link between the saint and King Afonso I, the founding father of the Christian kingdom of Kongo. Kongolese kings positioned themselves in the lineage of Afonso I, using his coat of arms and Portuguese-style symbols of royalty such as the crown, sword, and cape to legitimate their claim to the throne. Although white Portuguese brotherhoods also performed mock war performances with swords or sticks during the celebrations of Corpus Christi and other major religious holidays, Heywood and Thornton assume that mock war battles and stick fights during king election ceremonies by black brotherhoods with roots in West-Central African were inspired by sangamento rituals relating to king elections in the Kingdom of Kongo.[100]

An anonymous description of the celebrations in Luanda following the canonization of the Jesuit Francis Xavier in 1620 prominently highlights the importance of such mock war performances in West-Central Africa. According to the author, the first thing they did was make "a banner and a portrait of the saint." Then began a procession in honor of St. Francis Xavier and "in front one could see three giants . . . followed by Creoles from São Tomé, who performed their dances . . . and amongst them was their king, before whom they gave speeches, according to their custom." Then the confraternities of the city followed: "the confraternity of St. Lucia, of the Holy Mary Magdalene, of the Holy Body (Corposant), of St. Joseph, of the Souls of Purgatory, of St. Anthony, of Our Lady of the Rosary, of Our Lady of the Conception, of the Most Holy Sacrament, all with their respective pennants." Then one could see a ship "that represented how the saint traveled to India. . . . Behind the ship one could see a swordfight that was as well performed as the best one can see in Portugal." Then the sons of the city's dignitaries marched by, "who were all very talented dancers and who, after several variations, performed a dance with sticks. . . . So many people assisted at the procession that there was not enough space for them on the streets, which never before had happened in Angola." Then a theatre play was performed, "whereby the Kingdom of Kongo welcomed the saint." Finally, on the eighth day of the celebrations, "a scene from the life of St. Francisco Xavier was performed about the time when he was preaching in Malacca and prophesized that the Portuguese would obtain a victory against those from Ache, which involved a great spectacle of war."[101]

Catholic symbols and rituals, many of which were linked to the Order of Christ, continued to be used in the Kongo region long after the last Capuchins had left Central Africa in the early nineteenth century.[102] When visiting the coastal region of Soyo in 1816, British officer James Tuckey noted how local "Christians after the Portuguese fashion" were "loaded with crucifixes."[103] In a letter dating from June 1855, King Henrique III of Kongo approached the Portuguese authorities in Luanda with the request to send him priests. He expressed concern about the fact that "all Christians are required to go to confession at least once a year because otherwise they go to hell" and excused himself that he had "nothing to offer, because nowadays slaves are no longer in demand."[104]

Afro-Iberian performance traditions also continued. During his journey through northern Angola in 1873, Joachim John Monteiro witnessed a sangamento with Catholic characteristics. He observed how the King of Matuta "shook his sword at [the visitors] like a harlequin at a clown in a pantomime, [his men] all rose and followed him for a few paces, and then dropped on their knees whilst he went through the dance and sword exercise again." After the dance was finished, the guests presented their offering, including palm wine, which was handed to the marquis, who according to Catholic ritual "made the sign of the cross over it with his hand, repeating at the same time some words in Latin."[105] In the late 1870s, Alfredo de Sarmento witnessed in northern Angola a parade of the *dembo* (ruler) of Mbwila (or Ambuila), Dom Álvaro Afonso Gonçalves, that was initiated by musicians playing "*marimbas* [xylophones], *batuques* [drums] and a type of tooter made with pieces of ivory that produce a screeching and unpleasant noise. Then the *macotas* follow, who ... are his secretaries, counselors and aids.... Some of them carry two heavy sunshades to protect the king from the sun." All this was accompanied "by dances and mock war performances." The festive clothing of the dembo consisted of "a tricorn hat, a blue shirt embroidered with gold, a red vest on top of a longer waistcoat of blue satin with silver embroidery, around his waist a piece of blue satin braided with silver and white fringes, black silk socks and Chinese shoes embroidered with gold." The macotas were wearing "big crucifixes made of yellow metal around their necks."[106] According to José Redinha, king processions were still a common phenomenon in northern Angola and Cabinda in the mid-twentieth century. In 1943 Redinha witnessed a procession in Dundo, where "in front, one can see the King and Queen.... Their costumes are inspired by Portuguese gowns of nobles and captains of the discoveries ... and others carry banners, pennants, standards, flaming adornments that represent emblems, weapons and sticks." According to Redinha, these processions were "a mix of Christian faith and popular superstition ... and include elements of Catholic procession culture, of Portuguese traditions from the era of the discoveries and of the embassies sent by Zambi-Apombo (King of the World), as the Atlantic Angolans once used to call the Portuguese king."[107]

One can thus conclude that a vivid procession culture developed in the context of Afro-Catholic brotherhoods on the African Atlantic islands and in areas on the African continent with a strong Portuguese presence. These performances had a syncretic character that combined Iberian and indigenous African elements. In a West-Central African context, many of the rituals probably also related to traditional king election ceremonies in the kingdom of Kongo.

Considering the important role of this institution, we can assume that Africans who originated from areas with a strong Portuguese influence or who had spent considerable time in such areas must have been familiar with brotherhoods and the organizations' inherent rituals. The fact that the vast majority of members of the charter generation in New Netherland originated from the Kingdom of Kongo and Angola provides a credible explanation for the remarkable parallels between Afro-Portuguese brotherhood rituals and African American Pinkster celebrations. This theory is strengthened by the fact that Charles, the famous Albany Pinkster king, was of Angolan origin. In the case of Africans originating from the Kongo region, brotherhoods probably meant more than just institutions of mutual aid, since they allowed continuation of rituals relating to Afonso I, the founding father of the Catholic kingdom of Kongo. It is credible to assume that there was a strong attachment to Luso-Kongolese brotherhood rituals among the charter generation on Dutch Manhattan and a desire to pass these traditions on to future generations. This assumption requires, however, further investigation into the development of black brotherhoods in the Americas.

Latin America

The earliest reference to the existence of a black brotherhood in the Americas dates back to 1540 and was found in Lima, Peru. In 1549 the municipal council in Lima complained that the black brotherhood's meetings only served to revel and to plan robberies. However, since it relied on a black militia to keep a slave population of about fifteen hundred under control, it never considered prohibiting the organization. Forty years later, the same authorities who had previously criticized the brotherhood now requested that its members perform the dances "they have been accustomed to do in past years" on the feast of the Most Holy Sacrament.[108] Something similar has been observed in Cuba in 1573, where local authorities requested the black slave community on the island to enrich the upcoming Corpus Christi procession with "inventions and plays."[109] The first references to black brotherhoods in Brazil and Mexico date to the late sixteenth century.[110]

It is unknown whether these early brotherhoods were created by the church authorities or on the initiative of slaves themselves. Writing about the island Hispaniola in the early 1540s, Giralmo Benzoni noted that "the blacks make common cause among themselves" and "each nation recognizes its own king or governor," which seems to indicate the latter.[111] In his description of early-seventeenth-century Cartagena, Sandoval also noted that slaves "depended on their brotherhoods to bury them."[112] This was of vital importance, he noted, as nobody else cared for the piles of slave bodies left unburied, "thrown in the rubbish dump, where they will be eaten by dogs."[113] Nicolás González, another Jesuit, explained in 1658 that such funerals were social occasions, where "certain assemblies of Moors of the same nation meet when someone of their nation dies." These assemblies were not informal groups, he specified, as they had "chapters," like brotherhoods.[114]

Other sources confirm that certain groups of slaves imported Afro-Catholic traditions in the New World.[115] A well-known example comes from Pernambuco, Brazil, where the Italian Capuchin Dionigio de Carli stopped on his way to Kongo in 1666. According to de Carli, he saw a "black woman, who kneeled, beat her breast, and clapped her hands upon de ground." Upon inquiring what the woman meant by those motions, a Portuguese bystander answered: "Father, the meaning of it is, that she is of the Kingdom of Congo, and was baptized by a Capuchin; and being informed you are going thither to baptize, she rejoices, and expresses her joy by those outward tokens."[116] Another example comes from Cuba, where one of Lydia Cabrera's informants on slave culture recalled that a local brotherhood used to be known as "el cabildo de los congos portugueses" and that the "saint" of these "Portuguese Kongolese" was called "Gangasímba," a likely corruption of the Kikongo expression "Nganga a Nzambi," meaning priest of God. Another informant told her that "Jesus Christ, in ancient times, went to Kongo. . . . And there were churches over there and a lot of Christian Kongolese." Cabrera also refers to the sixteenth-century Spanish playwright Lope de Rueda, in whose comedy *Los Engañados* (The Fooled) one of the African characters speaks in a mixture of Portuguese and Spanish about a "very religious cousin" who is a "nun, prioress, abbess in my country, the land of the honorable Manicongo."[117]

It is also striking that certain maroon communities established by runaway slaves in Latin America consciously preserved Catholic elements. If Catholicism had been forced upon these former slaves, one would expect them to quickly liberate themselves from all Christian ballast in their maroon societies. However, this was not the case in the seventeenth-century maroon community of Palmares in Brazil, founded primarily by slaves from Angola and Kongo. Dutch and Portuguese sources point out that people in Palmares had erected a church in the center of the settlement; that there was as chapel with images of the Christ-child, Saint Blaise, and Our Lady of the Conception; and that Zumbi, the king of Palmares, did not allow the presence of "fetishists." Documents also show that Palmares had a priest who baptized children and married couples and that its inhabitants followed Catholic rite, although according to Francisco de Brito, they did so "in a stupid fashion."[118] Other maroon communities in Brazil had Catholic names: São Sebastião, São Luís, São Benedito do Céu, Cris-Santo, etc.[119] A similar case has been observed in Veracruz, Mexico, where a certain Yanga was elected a king of a *palenque* (maroon community). Yanga ended up giving away the location of his settlement to secure the assistance of a Catholic priest. When soldiers eventually conquered his maroon village, he was found in his chapel saying prayers.[120] The leaders of another palenque called Matudere, located near Cartagena, also came in search of a Catholic priest whom they took to their settlement in order to baptize the newborn and consecrate marriages. According to Father Zapata, people in Matudere "lived in Christianity, knew the prayers, sustained the church and prayed the rosary." Domingo, the founder of Matudere, had an Angolan father.[121]

In regard to West-Central African slaves in Brazil, Marina de Mello e Souza has therefore argued that "Catholicism represented a link to their native Africa."[122] Ronaldo Vainfas also claims that "African Catholicism, as it existed in Kongo and Angola, influenced the way Catholicism developed within the black community in Brazil, with its brotherhoods of Our Lady of the Rosary and its celebrations at the occasion of the coronation of black kings."[123] One can assume that many slaves of West-Central African origin and other parts of Africa with a strong Portuguese influence were indeed familiar with Catholicism and the concept of brotherhoods before their arrival in the New World. Others, who came from parts of Africa with little or no Portuguese influence, probably only learned about brotherhoods in the context of the "religious instruction" they received before and/or after their shipment to the American continent. It is known that the early-seventeenth-century missionaries Alonso de Sandoval and Pedro Claver separated slaves upon arrival in Cartagena according to their "nation," and assigned groups of ten slaves from a given "nation" to a catechist who spoke their language.[124] One of Claver's assistants was a Kongolese slave named José Monzolo, who had been baptized in eastern Kongo and had learned the catechism in both Kikongo and Kinzolo. Another assistant was Ignacio Angola, who testified that he accompanied the friar every Sunday on a procession through the streets of Cartagena, carrying a standard and a cross, and at the end of which he translated the Spanish sermon into Kimbundu.[125] These assistants were likely transmitters of Afro-Catholic brotherhood traditions to newly arrived slaves.[126]

There are also indications that some Afro-Catholic slaves provided "religious instruction" to others without supervision by the official church authorities. In Brazil a Kongolese slave called Pedro Congo was arrested in 1754 for proselytizing activities among slaves from the Mina "nation" with roots in West Africa. Congo defended himself by pointing out that he was doing Catholic missionary work. However, the authorities interpreted the Kongolese variant of Catholicism he was teaching as sorcery, and he was punished accordingly.[127]

One of the earliest extensive descriptions of a king election ceremony in the Americas, dating back to 1666, comes from Pernambuco, Brazil. It was penned by the French traveler Urbain Souchu de Rennefort, according to whom "after celebrating Mass, a group of about four hundred men and one hundred women elected a king and a queen, marched through the streets singing and reciting improvised verses, playing drums, trumpets and frame drums. They were wearing the clothes of their masters and mistresses, including golden chains and pearls; some wore masques."[128] Although Souchu de Rennefort does not mention that these slaves belonged to a brotherhood, a complaint in 1641 by the *classis* in Dutch Brazil that members of the brotherhood of Our Lady of the Rosary had dared to hold "a procession of the idol Rosário" in Sirinhaém, Pernambuco, and that "good [Protestant] Christians ... who witnessed it and refused to honor [the Virgin] were not only treated disrespectfully but even beaten up," indicates that black brotherhoods must already have existed at that time in Pernambuco.[129] Another source shows that Recife's black Rosary Brotherhood elected a *Rei dos Angolas* in 1674.[130]

Later sources provide more detailed descriptions of king election ceremonies. A famous example is that of Henry Koster, who during his stay in Brazil between 1809 and 1815 witnessed a brotherhood king election in Pernambuco. In his diary, the English coffee-grower mentions that "in March took place the yearly festival of our Lady of the Rosary, which was directed by negroes; and at this period is chosen the King of the Congo nation, if the person who holds this situation has died in the course of the year, has from any cause resigned or has been displaced by his subjects." According to Koster, "the Congo negroes are permitted to elect a king and queen from among the individuals of their own nation, the personages who are fixed upon may either actually be slaves or they may be manumitted negroes." These sovereigns "exercise a species of mock jurisdiction over their subjects which is much laughed at by the whites; but their chief power and superiority over their countrymen is shown on the day of the festival." Standing at the door of his house, Koster witnessed "a number of male and female negroes, habited in cotton dresses of colours and of white, with flags flying and drums beating; and . . . we discovered among them the king and queen, and the secretary of state. Each of the former wore upon their heads a crown, which was partly covered with gilt paper." Koster also explains that the expense of the church service was to be provided for by members of the black community and that "there stood in the body of the church a small table, at which sat the treasurer of this black fraternity and some other officers, and upon it stood a box to receive the money."[131]

Similar Afro-Catholic processions can be witnessed in Brazil today. This is especially the case during Pentecost, when the *Folias do Divino* are celebrated. As a combination of dance, music, theatrical performances, and processions, these feasts are called *autos*.[132] The processions traditionally begin with a group of standard-bearers, followed by a dancing crowd honoring the king or emperor and his court or *embaixada*, all of whom are wearing the clothes of noblemen. The procession organizers are called *mordomos*; they execute the demands of the king, which in past times even included the liberation of a number of prisoners. The *juízes de prenda* take care of the financial side of the festival and organize collections. The procession, accompanied by firecrackers symbolizing salutes, ends at the *império do divino*, a decorated space that symbolizes the royal palace. At its center, where the altar is found, Kongo dances take place as part of a ceremony to invest divine emperorship. Kongo dances are known in Brazil as *congadas, congados*, or *(autos dos) Congos*. The dancers, called *soldados*

Johann Moritz Rugendas, *Feast of Our Lady of the Rosary*. Procession of a black brotherhood in Brazil in honor of Our Lady of the Rosary. The brotherhood's king and queen are at the center. In Johann Moritz Rugendas, *Voyage pittoresque dans le Brésil* (Paris: Engelmann, 1835).

(soldiers), use swords, cudgels, or sticks and are grouped in *ternos* or *batalhões* (battalions). The commander of the *soldados*, the *capitão* (captain), serves as a guard to the court. Congadas represent both African and European themes, including battle scenes between Moors and Christians based on the Carolingian *Song of Roland* and others between the pagan African Queen Nzinga and the Christian King of Kongo.[133] According to Marlyse Meyer, this merger of African and Carolingian elements transforms the King of Kongo during Brazilian Pentecost celebrations into an African variant of Charlemagne, a *Carolus Magnus, Africanus Rex.*[134]

Comparing Brazilian black king festivals to the available sources on king election ceremonies in the Kingdom of Kongo, Cécile Fromont confirms that "the comparison . . . holds true across all descriptions" and that rituals relating to King Afonso I of Kongo must have served as a model to king elections in Kongolese brotherhoods in the American diaspora.[135] Marina de Mello e Souza has come to a similar conclusion and argues that even in analyzing a ritual court "whose members wear European clothing and that celebrated a Catholic saint, we can discern the direct link to . . . an African past that was already infused with European elements . . . which were widely used by Kongo elite ever since the beginning of the sixteenth century."[136] In fact, when the English geographer

Richard Burton, who had previously traveled in the Kongo region in Africa, observed a congada in Brazil in the mid-1860s, he immediately recognized parallels to the Kongolese tradition. According to Burton, the people in the procession were "dressed, as they fondly imagined, after the style of the Agua-Rosada House, descended from the great *Manikongo* and hereditary lords of Congo land.... All were armed with sword and shield, except the king, who, in sign of dignity, carried his scepter, a stout and useful stick."[137]

Sources indicate that Kongolese slaves were often pioneers in introducing Afro-Catholic brotherhood traditions in the Americas. According to one of Cabrera's informants on slave culture in Cuba, "it was always the Kongo brotherhood that initiated the procession [on Epiphany], followed by the other brotherhoods."[138] Elizabeth Kiddy demonstrated that in eighteenth-century Pernambuco, slaves belonging to different "nations" were only allowed to create their own brotherhoods with explicit approval of the king of the Kongo brotherhood. We can assume that brotherhoods established by slaves of other "nations" did not simply copy the Luso-Kongolese model but rather developed specific variants of it, with their own rituals. Significantly, when embassies of other "nations" had come to pay homage to the ambassador of the king of Kongo, who visited Dutch Brazil (Pernambuco) in the mid-seventeenth century, they did so "according to the ceremonies used among their nations."[139] It is likely that brotherhoods composed by slaves from parts of Africa with little Portuguese influence had rituals that differed even more from the original Iberian model than in those of Kongolese brotherhoods. Significantly, a 1780 report about the festival of Our Lady of the Rosary in Recife, Brazil, shows that a brotherhood composed by slaves from the Mina coast had statues of indigenous African deities in its temple and that its members would anoint themselves with oils and animal blood in preparation for religious services.[140]

Although there can be no doubt that slave communities in the Americas also established groups that had no connection to Afro-Catholic brotherhoods, slave organizations in the context of which kings were elected, processions were held, European-style crowns were used, and aristocratic titles were chosen must have been influenced directly or indirectly by Afro-Iberian cultural concepts. The remarkable proliferation of Afro-Iberian king election ceremonies all over the Americas can only be explained with reference to the crucial impact made by the charter generations. This impact of the first slave generation was related to the fact that newly arrived Africans were generally not put to work until they had completed some form of "training," which involved socialization and adjustment to new customs under the guidance of an older slave.[141] This practice stimulated the transmission of cultural patterns, even among slaves who originated from different parts of Africa than the charter generation.[142]

As Green has demonstrated, the overwhelming majority of slaves who arrived in the New World until the mid-sixteenth century had previously lived on the Iberian Peninsula, the Cape Verde Islands, or São Tomé.[143] From the late sixteenth until the mid-seventeenth centuries, Luanda was the dominant source of America-bound slaves, which Heywood and Thornton have labeled "the Angolan wave" in the history of the transatlantic slave trade.[144] As Joseph Miller has argued, upon arrival in the Americas these West-Central African slaves lived in intimate contact "with predecessors who had arrived in small numbers from backgrounds in slavery in late medieval Iberia" and "particularly those coming through Kongo channels, must have had a useful familiarity with Portuguese Christianity and used it to find places for themselves without relying on the more 'African' aspects of their origins."[145] This is confirmed by Heywood, who argues in relation to West-Central African slaves in Brazil that "many Kongos and not a few Angolans had been Christians before their enslavement in Brazil. Thus they would have been familiar with the brotherhoods in Luanda, Soyo, and Kongo, and the central role they played in the creole society of Kongo, Angola, and São Tomé."[146] Nicole von Germeten's research on black brotherhoods in Mexico also concludes with the claim that "some Central Africans probably took part in social and religious brotherhoods and sisterhoods before crossing the Atlantic."[147]

Due to their familiarity with Iberian culture, these charter generations, which some scholars refer to as "Atlantic Creoles," must have been the ones who introduced the first brotherhoods in the Americas that were further developed by their Creole (American-born) offspring. Heywood and Thornton are convinced that many of the Afro-Iberian traditions imported to the Americas by West-Central African charter generations provided "a crucial cultural model for the waves of captives, mostly from West Africa brought in by the slave trade after 1640," and that "the Atlantic Creole Charter Generation possessed the means to set down their own cultural pattern in the Americas, even where they were subsequently outnumbered by new arrivals with no Creole background."[148] This theory implies that in many cases, the concept of brotherhoods must also have been adopted—albeit in an adapted form—by slaves in the Americas who originated from parts of Africa with little or no Portuguese influence.

It should also be said that after the mid-seventeenth century, the "Angolan wave" diminished in strength but did not disappear completely. 39.6 percent of the slaves who arrived in the Americas between 1651 and 1675 were still of West-Central African origin, which declined to about 26 percent for the period between 1676 and 1700.[149] These numbers account for a steady influx of West-Central African slaves, many of whom were familiar with Afro-Catholic traditions, until the eighteenth century.

In conclusion to this section, it is worth pointing out that Brazilian conga-das reveal additional parallels between Afro-Iberian brotherhood rituals and African American Pinkster and Election Day celebrations, such as the refer-ence to "Congo dances," the use of the term "captain," and the presence of "sol-diers." These parallels give more credibility to the assumption that the African American Pinkster celebrations in New York and New Jersey were inspired by Afro-Iberian brotherhood rituals that had been introduced by the Kongolese and Angolan charter generation. Also important to comparisons with Pinkster are the indications that slaves in Latin America must have taken the initiative to organize themselves in organizations modeled upon Afro-Iberian brother-hoods. If this was the case in Latin America, the question arises whether slave communities in other parts of the Americas also formed brotherhoods. This possibility is explored in the next section.

The Caribbean and North America

As Ira Berlin rightly observes, brotherhoods played a crucial role in the inter-continental networks that developed in the context of transatlantic slavery. However, like most scholars, Berlin perceives brotherhoods as an essentially Iberian phenomenon that was crucial to the development of black identity in Latin America, and differing from that in North America, where "numer-ous informal connections between black people" developed, but not brother-hoods.[150] This raises the question of how merely "informal connections" can explain the organization of a Pinkster festival that in Albany attracted up to a thousand spectators. This question is all the more pertinent because no other black cultural tradition in the Americas has more characteristics in common with Albany's African American Pinkster celebrations than Afro-Iberian king election ceremonies organized in the context of black brotherhoods. Although Berlin confirms that Atlantic Creoles "created an intercontinental web of *cofra-dias* ... so that, by the seventeenth century, the network of black religious broth-erhoods stretched from Lisbon to São Tomé, Angola, and Brazil," he believes that those Atlantic Creoles who ended up in Dutch, French, or English colo-nies refrained from doing so since the "comparable institutional linkages" to brotherhoods failed in those parts of the Americas.[151] Berlin's assumption thus presupposes that brotherhoods could only be established with institutional sup-port and excludes the possibility that slaves themselves took the initiative to create such organizations.

This assumption has been questioned by Jorge Cañizares-Esguerra, Matt Childs, and James Sidbury, according to whom "approved institutional struc-tures authorized by the Catholic Church were not always necessary for Africans and their descendants to build fraternal structures."[152] Moreover, several documents show that certain slave communities living outside of the Iberian realm in the Americas remained attached to the Afro-Catholic traditions they had brought with them from Africa. When visiting the island of Barbados in 1654, the French priest Antoine Biet wrote that "if any of them have any tinge of the Catholic Religion which they received among the Portuguese, they keep it the best they can, doing their prayers and worshipping God in their hearts. . . . They were extremely sorrowed to see themselves sold as slaves in an island of heretics."[153] In the late 1680s, the French Jesuit Jean Mongin reported from St. Christopher that all the slaves of Kongolese origin on this Caribbean island were familiar with Catholicism.[154] In the 1720s the French clergyman Jean-Baptiste Labat made similar comments about Kongolese slaves on other islands in the Caribbean, which in the case of Haiti was later confirmed by Médéric Moreau de Saint-Méry.[155] In French Guyana, Jean Goupy des Marets noted in 1690 that all the slaves with West-Central Africa roots on the Remire plantation, who had been brought there by Dutch traders, identified themselves as Catholics and had been baptized in Africa.[156] Newspaper descriptions of fugitive slaves in Jamaica in the 1790s refer to a "Negro woman with a crucifix necklace," another bearing a "cross shaped Spanish mark," and a third one as "speaking Portuguese."[157] John Storm Roberts pointed out in 1998 that the roots of black culture in Jamaica were "always regarded as Ashanti" until "strong Congolese elements were discovered about fifteen years ago" that "are to be found in Afro-Christian . . . sects."[158] In a letter dated 1885, Father de Cothonay mentions that in Saint-Dominic'-village, in Trinidad, "almost all men are members of a brotherhood dedicated to Saint Dominic . . . they have pennants, flags, musical instruments and firecrackers." According to de Cothonay, their procession "deploys itself in an orderly fashion along the flanks of Papuré Hill" and after Mass, a celebration takes place, whereby "the king of the brotherhood appears with his diadem in gold paper and his clothes covered with fake gold. One could also see the Queen wearing the most magnificent clothes . . . she presides with the king over a feast . . . that takes place in a house called the *palace*."[159] Research by Maureen Warner-Lewis has also revealed how people of Kongolese descent in Trinidad passed on stories about Catholic legends, rituals, and practices from West-Central Africa. She found evidence that in one Trinidadian town, members of the black community used to be called *Koongo Za Nguunga*, an expression derived from *Kongo di Ngunga*, meaning "Kongo of the (church) bell" or Catholic Kongo.[160] The same reference to *ngunga* (church bell) was found in one of the folksongs Kenneth Bilby and Kia Bunseki Fu-Kiau collected from a group known as the "Bongo Nation" in eastern Jamaica, that is assumed to have Kongolese roots.[161]

A remarkable example of Afro-Catholic identity in the Caribbean comes from the Danish Virgin Islands, where the Moravian missionary worker Christian

Georg Andreas Oldendorp noted in the 1760s that it was common "primarily by the Negroes from the Congo" to perform "a kind of baptism . . . characterized by pouring water over the head of the baptized, placing some salt in his mouth, and praying over him in the Congo language." "Before the baptism," he argues, "an adult *Bussal* [a slave who arrived directly from Africa] must receive five to six lashes from the baptizer for the sins which he had committed in Guinea. Afterwards there is a Negro celebration, provided by the more prosperous of the slaves." According to Oldendorp, these slaves had "recognition of the true God and of Jesus Christ" and had learned these baptismal rituals from Portuguese priests in Africa. Oldendorp also explains that the practice involved baptismal fathers and mothers who "adopt those whom they have baptized . . . and look after them as best they can. They are obliged to provide them with a coffin and burial clothing when they die. Usually, the baptizer buries those whom he has baptized." The fact that these Kongolese catechists catered to the needs of these newly arrived slaves and ensured that they would receive a Christian burial suggests that they operated in the context of a brotherhood-related organization.[162] As Warner-Lewis suggests, the rituals observed by Oldendorp "may have derived from practices within the Catholic fraternity in Koongo [*sic*]."[163] In fact, in the 1840s Thurlow Weed identified several slave king elections on these islands, and the 1839 Von Scholten's Report identified the majority of slaves on the islands of St. Croix and St. Thomas as Catholics.[164]

Oldendorp's reference to baptism rituals on the Virgin Islands corresponds to the observation by Moreau de Saint Méry that Creole slaves in Saint-Domingue, later Haiti, looked down on newly arrived *Bossals* who had not yet been baptized.[165] In Haiti, king election ceremonies in the context of organizations with characteristics similar to Afro-Portuguese brotherhoods were a common phenomenon. According to David Geggus, an anonymous description of slave culture on the island's North Province, where many African slaves were of Kongolese origin, revealed that the slaves in Le Cap "have organized separate rankings among themselves. They have gathering places, kings and queens, sashes of different colors with different types of gold and silver braid that they wear on their jackets, and the women wear round their waist." Members of these associations paid "a subscription of several *portugaises* [a gold coin worth 66 livres] and burial fees which the others inflate as they feel like it. These funerals give rise to big processions, at which the sashes are worn."[166]

The importance of king elections to slave communities is particularly notable in the context of Haiti's 1791 revolt. In the North Province, where the rebellion started, the slave Makaya respectfully referred to the king of Kongo as "master of all the blacks" and descendant of "one of the three Magi."[167] Romaine Rivière, an insurgent leader who claimed to be the Virgin Mary's godson and adopted the name Romaine-la-Prophétesse, expressed his intention to become "king of

Santo Domingo."[168] The anonymous report from a French militiaman on the Haitian revolution shows that the election of a king in a ceremony involving a Capuchin friar was one of the first things that occurred in each liberated quarter. On September 5, 1791, he wrote that "the Negroes celebrated two marriages in the church at L'Acul. On the occasion they assumed titles, and the titled blacks were treated with great respect, and the ceremony was performed in great pomp." A Capuchin called Cajetan was retained among them, and "has been obliged to officiate. Their colors were consecrated and a king was elected. They have chosen one for each quarter."[169] After Jean-Jacques Dessalines's assassination in 1806, his brother-in-arms Henri Christophe assumed the title of Henry I, King of Haiti, and established a Haitian nobility that consisted of princes, dukes, counts, barons, and knights. As pointed out by Laurent Dubois, "the institutional heart of Christophe's regime . . . was the European-style hereditary landed aristocracy, complete with heraldic crests and mottoes that he created to administer his kingdom."[170] While this emergence of a Haitian aristocracy with European titles has long puzzled scholars, the parallels to brotherhoods are apparent. Henri Christophe's kingdom in North Haiti that lasted until 1820 inspired blacks elsewhere in the Caribbean. In the context of Cuba's Aponte Rebellion in 1812, Joaquín Belaguer, king of the Kongo brotherhood in Puerto Príncipe, admitted that his involvement in the uprising had been inspired by Henri Christophe's coronation in Haiti. According to Matt Childs, members of the Kongo brotherhood in Puerto Príncipe not only spread rumors about support by the king of Haiti to their revolt, but even by the king of Kongo himself.[171]

As noted in chapter 2, Pinkster celebrations in Albany were marked by a song with the words "hi-a-bomba, bomba, bomba."[172] The word *bomba* could refer to the slave overseer or driver in Caribbean slave societies, who in order to command respect from his fellow slaves traditionally wore a military uniform similar to that of King Charles in Albany.[173] The term is also used in reference to a type of drum that became popular in Puerto Rico, where a *baile de bomba* has been recorded with the words "Aya, bombe, quinombó! Ohé, ohé mano Migué! Ayayá, sagú, carú! Ohé, ohé, quinombó." Anthropologist John Alden Mason links these bomba dances to the town of Loiza Aldea in Puerto Rico, where many slaves of Kongolese and Angolan origin lived and where the famous *Fiestas de Santiago Apóstol* in honor of St. James the Greater developed.[174] It is remarkable that the words "hi-a-bomba" and "aya, bombe" correspond roughly to the expression "aya bomba ya bombai," recorded in South Carolina by William S. Simonise, a native of Charleston who had been for many years a resident of Haiti.[175] This Haitian connection is reinforced by the fact that a similar expression—"eh! eh! Bomba, hen! hen!"—was recorded by Moreau de Saint-Méry in 1797 in a Haitian Vodou initiation ceremony that was allegedly led by a "queen" and a "king" who brought the initiates into a circle and then tapped them on the head with a piece of wood.[176] In 1814 Louis Drouin de Bercy recorded the words "a ia bom-baia bombé" in rituals he assumed to be part of Vodou initiation. According to Drouin de Bercy, the group he observed had a "black king" as leader and referred to itself using the term *confrérie* or brotherhood.[177] While the mean-ing of the words in these Haitian songs still divides scholars, there is a growing consensus that they are Kikongo. If *bomba* is indeed a Kikongo term, it could possibly refer to the Kongolese rainbow and snake god Mbumba, who may be associated with the Vodou god Damballah and his many representations on Haitian Catholic lithographs of Moses and St. Patrick. However, *bomba* can also mean "secret" or "mystery" in Kikingo, whereas *bombe* can mean "buffoon."[178]

The likely Kikongo origin of the words corresponds to Thornton's theory that although the term Vodou derives from the West-African Fon *vodu(n)* (God), Kongolese Catholicism had a strong impact on the development of Haitian Vodou.[179] Following Thornton, Hein Vanhee and Terry Rey have argued that a set of lay Catholic roles was brought to the island by West-Central African slaves and that in the absence of a formal church organization, these roles were incorporated in a complex of practices that we now denote as Vodou. Whereas it was traditionally assumed that Vodou consisted of a set of West-African—pre-dominantly Yoruba, Ewe, and Fon—religious practices that were later overlaid with (European) Catholic elements, Vanhee and Rey claim that many of the Catholic elements in Vodou relate to Kongolese Catholicism. They argue that the roots of Vodou are to be found in the blending of Catholic and indigenous Kongolese traditions in the sixteenth- and seventeenth-century Kingdom of Kongo and that West-African elements were only added later, in Haiti.[180]

This theory could explain the continuous presence of Luso-Kongolese elements in contemporary Haitian Vodou such as the fact that St. James the Greater is worshipped as the deity of war and that the Portuguese brotherhood term *loa*—pronounced as *lwa*—is used in reference to saints. As a Haitian infor-mant once mentioned to the anthropologist Alfred Métraux: "One has to be Catholic in order to be able to serve the *loas*."[181] In light of this connection to the Kingdom of Kongo, the assumption by Harold Courlander that "the Haitians ... have come to confuse some of the *loa* with Catholic saints" needs revision. It is not the Haitians who are confusing things, but Western scholars who have failed to recognize the impact of Kongolese Catholicism on the development of Vodou.[182] In fact, as Elizabeth McAlister has shown, the Haitian king procession known as *lwalwadi* or *rara* "recalls and activates religious principles from the African kingdom of Kongo."[183] These processions take place on Catholic holi-days and feature flag bearers, musicians, and a king. At the end of the proces-sion, donations are collected. These parallels to Luso-Kongolese brotherhood traditions require a correction of Courlander's disparaging characterization of *rara* as "a mammoth parade of sensual exhibitionism . . . imbued with half-clear ideas of Christian crusades . . . it is simply *Rara*, loud noise."[184]

This connection to the Kingdom of Kongo is in accordance with Geggus's revelation about the Haitian Revolution (1791–1804) that "insofar as the black Revolution expressed an attitude to Christianity and the Catholic Church, it was surprisingly favorable."[185] Geggus found evidence that slaves in the northern Cap Français region used to hold their own meetings in Catholic churches during the afternoon siesta and at night, often without the presence of a priest. These predominantly West-Central African slaves had named their own choir leaders, beadles, and church wardens. Some were known to catechize and preach, not only in the church but in the town and on surrounding plantations.[186] According to Félix Carteau, a local merchant, these slaves regarded baptism as a status symbol, packed churches for Mass, and massively participated at Afro-Catholic processions.[187]

The presence of Kongolese elements in Vodou could account for the parallels between the words recorded at the Albany Pinkster festival and those at Haitian Vodou ceremonies. Considering the impact of the "Angolan wave" all over the Americas, the connections between Haiti, Brazil, Cuba, South Carolina, and New York may indeed relate to a shared West-Central African origin of slaves. For instance, several accounts from South Carolina confirm that West-Central African slaves brought Afro-Catholic traditions with them from Africa. Seventeenth-century records from the South Carolina Lowcountry list dozens of slaves with Iberian Catholic baptismal names such as António, Maria, Francisco, Emanuel, and Isabel.[188] When the English missionary Francis Le Jau approached the slave community in South Carolina in 1710 he was surprised to find that some "were born and baptized among the Portuguese," which prompted him to impose as a rule that they would only be admitted to communion upon renouncing the "errors of the Romish Church." He clarified that he "framed a short Model of Submission grounded upon some Popish Tenets which they told me of their own Accord, without troubling them with things they know not: I require of them their renouncing of those particular points, the Chief of which is praying to the Saints."[189] The anonymous English author of the "Account of the Negroe Insurrection in South Carolina" in early October 1739 observes that "amongst the Negroe Slaves there are a people brought from the Kingdom of Angola in Africa, many of these speak Portugueze . . . and . . . profess the Roman Catholic Religion." He continues: "On the 9th day of September . . . Some Angola Negroes assembled . . . and one who was called Jemmy was their Captain. . . . Several Negroes joined them, they calling out Liberty, marched on with Colours displayed, and two Drums beating."[190] Considering the strong Catholic identity of these rebellious slaves, historian Mark Smith has claimed that Kongolese slaves in South Carolina deliberately linked the Stono Revolt in 1739 to their veneration of the Virgin Mary.[191] African American attachment to the Virgin Mary has also been registered by the New England abolitionist Thomas W. Higginson, who recorded religious songs of the first freed slave regiment that fought against the Confederacy. One of their favorite songs was "Hail Mary."[192] Another example comes from the isolated Sea Islands in South Carolina, where many blacks had Central African roots. When Thomas Turpin arrived there in 1834 to do missionary work, he observed that the black population had "societies organized among themselves" that "appeared to be very much under the influence of Roman Catholic principles."[193] When interviewed in 1960, Sam Gadsden, a black man born on the island of Edisto in 1882, recalled that "we had some Black kings around here in the old days . . . and they really ruled the colored people."[194]

In spite of the virulent anti-Catholic mood in eighteenth-century New York and New Jersey, Afro-Catholic elements have also been identified among the slave community in these states. Besides the continuous influence by the West-Central African charter generation in New Netherland on their descendants and on slaves who arrived after the demise of the Dutch colony, later slaves also brought new Afro-Catholic elements to New York and New Jersey. Despite the fact that only a small number of the new slaves in New York and New Jersey were directly imported from West-Central Africa—the Trans-Atlantic Slave Trade Database indicates a total number of about five thousand—it should be pointed out that about thirteen percent of the slaves who arrived in New York via the British Caribbean were of West-Central African origin.[195] Among these Caribbean slaves with roots in West-Central Africa, some are likely to have had some exposure to Catholicism before being enslaved. Mary Jorga, who in a report from New York dated 1741 is referred to as a "free Portuguese baptized negress," was probably one of them.[196] A reference in the New-York Gazette of August 1733 to a runaway slave from Jacobus van Cortlandt called Andrew who "professeth himself to be a Roman Catholic" confirms the continuous existence of Afro-Catholic elements within the Dutch-owned slave community in New York. Andrew's case is all the more interesting since he had shirts with him that were "marked with a cross on the left Breast."[197] In the Kingdom of Kongo, the use of shirts with an embroidered cross was a prerogative of those who had been granted knighthood in the Order of Christ. According to the Capuchin Raimondo da Dicomano, knights of the Order of Christ in the Kingdom of Kongo enjoyed "the privilege to put lots of crosses made with pieces of cloth in several colors on their capes." When traveling through the north of Angola in the late nineteenth century, Alfredo de Sarmento observed that it was still common to meet people who claimed to be knights in the Order of Christ and who "wear the cross of the order made with pieces of cloth in several colors."[198]

In the case of New York, it should also be added that during the wars between England and Spain from the 1680s until 1750s, many black, mulatto, and mestizo soldiers were captured on Iberian vessels and subsequently sold as slaves.[199] In a petition to New York Governor Robert Hunter in the early eighteenth century, a group of captured Afro-Iberians complained that "they were free men, subjects to the King of Spain, but sold here as slaves."[200] Research by Eliga Gould confirms that in many cases, these so-called "Spanish Negroes" and "Spanish Indians" were indeed free men who were enslaved illegally by the British. Some of these soldiers were of high rank, such as Francisco Menéndez, who was the captain of a black militia.[201] As will be shown in the next chapter, "Spanish Negroes" were known in New York for their involvement in slave conspiracies and secret organizations that had many characteristics in common with brotherhoods. This may not be a coincidence, because there can be no doubt that Catholic "Spanish Negroes" must have been familiar with Afro-Iberian brotherhoods.[202] These "Spanish Negroes" were not only to be found in New York City. A runaway advertisement from 1765 indicates that the Albany skipper Abraham Douw, who was related to King Charles's master Volkert Petrus Douw, owned a "Spanish negro man named Tom" who "pretends to be a free man and speaks very good English and Spanish" and who ran away "in the company of a mulatto Spaniard belonging to Mr. Barent Ten Eyck, of Albany."[203]

While the role of "Spanish Negroes" will be explored further in the next chapter, the many parallels between the descriptions of African American Pinkster processions on one hand and king election rituals by Afro-Iberian brotherhoods on the other—the form of the procession, the organization of the amphitheater, the election and celebration of the king, the king's Angolan background, the king's clothing, the Congo dances, the word "captain-general" for the leader of the band, the mutual aid in the organization of the festival, the collections— are so overwhelming that White's claims that "the overall structure of Pinkster was clearly Dutch," that slaves in Albany "created something new," and that "the black version of the carnival was of much more recent origin" are in need of revision.[204] The abundance of parallels between both traditions show that the African American king celebrations at the occasion of Pinkster correspond to a pattern that has been observed all over the Americas. This makes it much more likely that the African American celebration on Pinkster holidays developed out of Afro-Iberian brotherhood traditions introduced by the charter generation than out of Dutch Pinkster traditions or English festive traditions.

This assumption corresponds to Bradford Verter's argument about Pinkster that "preparing for the holiday must have involved knowledge passed down through generations" and that "of the various historiographical interpretations of Pinkster, least satisfactory is this characterization of the holiday as a carnival of inversion."[205] In contrast to Graham Hodges's suggestion, it can, indeed, be doubted that Charles's election was "a mock election of a monarch."[206] By placing the king celebrations in Albany in a broader Atlantic context, it becomes clear that blacks in Albany and New England were not playing as if they had elected a king but that they really did so. Although certainly not as influential as his mid-nineteenth-century Brazilian counterpart Cândido Fonseca Galvão, known as King Obá II, who became an advisor to the Emperor Pedro II, King Charles must have been a prestigious leader of Albany's black community.[207] The next chapter will further analyze the question of whether the king celebration at the occasion of Pinkster could have been a ceremony relating to a self-governing institution by slaves that was rooted in Afro-Iberian brotherhood traditions.

·• 5 •·

THE PINKSTER KING AS
LEADER OF A BROTHERHOOD

New Netherland

In 1996 Ira Berlin made the claim that slaves in New Netherland aptly used their "Atlantic Creole" talents of negotiation to secure a minimal set of rights and privileges.[1] Three years later, Graham Hodges argued that individual slaves would not have been able to achieve these results without some form of coordination and suggested that the charter generation in New Amsterdam had formed a community that "best resembled the confraternities or brotherhoods found among Kongolese and Angolan blacks living in Brazil."[2] Considering the West-Central African origin of the charter generation, its familiarity with Afro-Portuguese traditions, and its Afro-Catholic identity, Hodges's assumption is plausible.

It has been documented that the slave community in New Amsterdam often defended its interests as a collective group. Berlin himself acknowledges that the slaves in New Netherland developed "a variety of institutions that reflected their unique experience and served their special needs," Cynthia Van Zandt argues that they "formed links with one another as a way to influence the degree of Dutch control over their community" and Susanah Shaw Romney concludes that "the intimate network among Africans functioned not simply as a haphazard collection of relationships; instead, it had a particular shape, with nodes of authority and overlapping lines of respect."[3]

An example is the petition submitted by a group of five blacks to the West India Company in November 1635 requiring a settlement on their promised wages.[4] Another example of black solidarity is the reaction to the killing of West India Company slave Jan Premero by fellow slaves in January 1641. Instead of accusing one another, those involved in the crime assumed joint responsibility and let fate decide which one would be executed. When Manuel of Gerrit de Reus[5] was to be punished by hanging, both nooses around his neck broke and "the inhabitants and bystanders called for mercy and very earnestly solicited the same." Eventually, the authorities "graciously granted him his life

Anonymous, *Battle of Guarapes*, 1758. This eighteenth-century painting of the Battle of Guarapes in 1649 that ended Dutch rule in Brazil features in the lower left corner Henrique Dias's black regiment composed of slaves who were promised manumission for their military service. Courtesy the Museu Histórico National, Rio de Janeiro.

and pardoned him and all the other Negroes, on promise of good behavior and willing service." It is also remarkable that less than one year after Premero's killing, his widow Marie Grande married one of her former husband's confessed killers and that the accused were later among the first slaves in the colony to obtain freedom.[6]

Documents also make reference to a slave called Bastrijn, Bastiaen, or Sebastiaen (Sebastião) as the "Capt. van de Swarten" and "Captijn van de Negers" (captain of the blacks). He is likely to have been the same Sebastião who had the Lusitanian surname de Britto and was also referred to as "van Santo Domingo," which indicates that he had lived on the island of Hispaniola. In 1647 he became a free man and later a landowner in New Amsterdam. He married Isabel Kisana van Angola in the Dutch Reformed Church. Their son Franciscus Bastiaense later married Manuel of Gerrit de Reus's daughter Barbara Emanuel.[7]

It is likely that a man called Bastiaen, who together with a group of white settlers served as a witness for Captain J(oh)an de Vries's mixed-race son Jan, was this "captain of the blacks." J(oh)an de Vries had served in Brazil before coming to New Netherland. There, he befriended many blacks, leased land for them, and stood up in church as godfather to their children.[8] Since de Vries had previously lived in Brazil and brought a black Brazilian woman (later the mother of his son Jan) with him to New Amsterdam, it is likely that he and Captain Sebastião shared familiarity with Iberian traditions and military practices. They may even have communicated in Portuguese. In fact, Sebastião's assumption of the title "captain" corresponds to an Iberian tradition related to black militias. One of the most famous of these militias had developed in response to the Dutch occupation of Pernambuco in Brazil. It was led by Henrique Dias, who was called the *capitão dos negros* (captain of the blacks) and later even *governador dos negros* (governor of the blacks). Dias commanded the *terço da gente preta* (black regiment) and was granted the title of Knight in the Order of Christ for his contribution in expelling the Dutch from Brazil. As a beneficiary of these royal favors, he traveled to Lisbon in 1656 to request "recompense for his services carried out in the Brazilian wars" as well as freedom "for those who had joined his militia following calls by generals and governors who in Your Majesty's name had promised manumission." Both requests were granted.[9]

As in Portuguese slave societies, it is likely that the manumission of slaves in New Netherland was related to their participation and proof of loyalty in military and semi-military operations. It is known that in their Brazilian colony, the Dutch had adopted the Iberian custom of forming black militias and that they granted manumission to those who had proven themselves loyal on the battlefield. The first reference to black militias fighting with the Dutch in Brazil dates to 1624. Following the brief occupation of Salvador de Bahia, the WIC established a "company of blacks," of which "some were armed with bows and arrows, old Hispanic swords, rondaches, spears and chopping-knives" and "who chose among themselves a black man called Francisco as their captain."[10] In 1630 Dutch authorities in Recife also "founded a company of blacks, armed with bows and arrows, shields and swords, big clubs of hard wood and Bohemian Earspoons [polearms]."[11] One black militia in Recife was led by a black man named António Mendes, who assumed the title of "captain." Another militia, founded in 1648, was directed by "Captain" João de Andrade. This practice implied that the Dutch had to negotiate with these slaves, who subsequently seized the opportunity to petition for manumission.[12] In 1637 manumission was granted to slaves who had rendered the Dutch military support: "These blacks came from their masters to us, served us for four, five, six, even seven years faithfully, many of them carried arms in support of our case. . . . If we would now return them to the hands of their embittered masters, we would be very ungrateful."[13]

A similar situation later occurred in New Netherland, where the WIC regularly used slaves for military and semi-military operations. As Van Zandt confirms, WIC officials in New Netherland "actively considered using enslaved Africans as militia to help defend the colony."[14] During the war against Native Americans in the 1640s, the Commonality of New Netherland suggested to Director Willem Kieft that he arm the "strongest and fleetest Negroes" with a "small ax and half-pike."[15] This decision required negotiations with a group of enslaved men, all of whom later requested manumission.[16] Similar to black militias in the Iberian world, a group of blacks in New Netherland assisted the *fiscaal* (chief prosecuting officer) in maintaining order.[17] In 1643 Kiliaen van Rensselaer also considered asking Director Kieft to send "some of the negroes" to Rensselaerwyck in order to use them "as brute forces" against rebellious tenants.[18] Johan de Deckere, commissary at Fort Orange, ordered "his Negro and two soldiers" to keep watch on a prisoner.[19]

Under Stuyvesant's rule, blacks were employed to hunt down runaway slaves and were part of Captain Martin Crigier's company that conducted military operations against pirates and bandits in the borderlands between New Netherland and the English provinces.[20] When requesting additional slaves in 1660, Stuyvesant wrote that he intended to use them "in the war against the wild barbarians."[21] And while on a military campaign in the Esopus area in 1660, Stuyvesant asked the secretary and council in New Amsterdam to "let the free and the Company's Negroes keep good watch on my Bouwery."[22] Black soldiers were also included in the military force Stuyvesant sent out against the Esopus Munsees in 1663, and gunpowder was delivered to "4 gangs of negroes and the overseer."[23] Although there is no evidence that an actual black militia existed in New Netherland, the presence of a man known as "captain of the blacks" clearly points in that direction. The many parallels to black militias in Dutch Brazil also indicate that what Berlin vaguely identified as an Atlantic Creole pattern of negotiation used by slaves in New Netherland was essentially an Afro-Iberian pattern. In fact, the slave society in New Netherland functioned in a similar way to slave societies in Iberian colonies.[24]

The slaves' strategy, to promise loyalty in military operations in return for freedom, also provides a credible explanation for the sudden request for full freedom by a group of slaves on September 4, 1664, when English gunboats had arrived in the New Amsterdam harbor. One can assume that Ascento Angola, Christoffel Santome, Pieter Pietersz Criolie, Antony Antonysz Criolie, Salomon Pietersz Criolie, Jan Guinea, Lowies Guinea, and Bastiaen Pietersz took advantage of the situation to make their support in defense of the colony conditional on Stuyvesant's pledge to grant them full freedom. Despite the fact that there was no fighting involved in the surrender of New Netherland, Stuyvesant honored his word and granted all these men full freedom as well as land patents in December 1664.[25]

There are indications that Dutch WIC officials themselves were also inclined to use an Iberian model in their interaction with slaves. This should not come as a surprise. As Wim Klooster has shown, the WIC copied several aspects of the Portuguese imperial system, from the building of fortified trading posts and the designing of *factorijen* to the adoption of accounting practices.[26] Other studies on Dutch overseas settlements in the early seventeenth century confirm that the initial policies of the Dutch trading companies were often based on a Portuguese model.[27] This also applies to the way the WIC interacted with its slaves. As Hodges has indicated, "the Dutch had entered the slave trade in Africa in the late sixteenth century, borrowing methods of the Portuguese in Lower West Africa."[28] Brazil was the place where the company's policy on the treatment of slaves was initiated, and until the demise of the colony in 1654 it remained the center of Dutch slave operations in the Americas; the policy adopted by the Dutch in Pernambuco initially set the standard of how slaves were to be treated in other WIC possessions, including New Netherland. As José Gonsalves de Mello has shown, the Dutch adopted "a Brazilian and Portuguese model" in their treatment of the slaves in Pernambuco. In a more recent study on Dutch Brazil, Pedro Puntoni comes to similar conclusions, arguing that the Dutch "treated their slaves like the Portuguese used to do."[29] Even after the fall of Recife, the company continued to refer to its former Brazilian colony as a model on how to deal with slaves in New Netherland. In 1657, for instance, company directors suggested that "trades such as carpentering, bricklaying, blacksmithing and others ought to be taught to the Negroes, as it was formerly done in Brazil."[30] All this suggests that the master-slave relationship in New Netherland was deeply influenced by an Iberian model.

As was shown in chapter 2, in its interaction with slaves the Dutch Reformed Church also initially followed a policy that corresponded to the Iberian focus on proselytizing. However, after the fall of Recife in 1654 shattered the dream of a Calvinist American continent and forced the WIC to change the focus of its slave-trading policy, which ended up reducing Africans to a commodity for the international market, the Reformed Church reconsidered its policy vis-à-vis the slave population. This change corresponds to a general transformation of the Dutch Reformed Church in America from an all-embracing church to a church of the elected that placed great emphasis on orthodoxy.

By the time the Reformed Church revised its overseas policy, however, it had already formed a small Protestant black community in New Netherland. There has been much speculation about why slaves who had been baptized as Catholics in Africa were so eager to have their children baptized in the Reformed Church, whereas the Catholic nobility in Africa had always fiercely resisted Dutch attempts to introduce Protestantism.[31] For instance, Samuel Brun, a Protestant Swiss surgeon who visited Kongo on a Dutch ship in 1611–12, argued that "all people in this kingdom are Christians in the Iberian way" and that "the Iberians vilify us among the natives because we are not Catholic."[32] The Catholic Kongolese king Garcia II even went as far as to publicly burn a stack of Calvinist books in 1642.[33] It is unclear whether the eagerness of Kongolese and Angolans in Dutch Manhattan to have their children baptized in the Reformed Church implies, as Heywood and Thornton suggest, that "what mattered was the assertion of a Christian identity rather than a sectarian Catholic one," or that a Protestant baptism was considered a lesser evil than no Christian baptism at all by a community that intended to preserve some of its Afro-Portuguese, Catholic heritage.[34] The former seems more likely considering that the "black captain" Sebastião acted in at least four cases as the baptismal witness of children in the Dutch Reformed Church, which indicates that he, and probably also the group he was leading, did not oppose the switch from Catholicism to Protestantism. Moreover, his son Franciscus Bastiaense was part of the small group of black communicant members of the Dutch Reformed Church.[35] Frijhoff, however, assumes that the decline of slave baptisms in New Netherland was also connected to a tendency among the baptized black population to preserve a religious identity that was not in accordance with the Calvinist orthodoxy expected by Dutch ministers, especially after the mid-1650s.[36] This view is in line with the argument used by New Netherland minister Henricus Selijns. Writing to the Amsterdam *classis* in 1664, he claims that slave parents requesting baptism for their children "sought nothing else by it than the freeing of their children from material slavery, without pursuing piety and Christian virtues."[37] It should be pointed out that it was common practice among members of black militias in Iberian colonies to adopt certain cultural elements of those whom they served as a sign of loyalty. It may thus well be that the decision by slaves to join the Dutch Reformed Church was primarily intended as a symbolic act to build trust and to later capitalize on that trust to demand concessions and ultimately manumission for themselves and their families. If so, the slaves' eagerness to have their children baptized and to get married in the Dutch Reformed Church had more to do with tactics than with faith. This may also explain why so many slaves made a point of identifying themselves as Christians in their petitions for freedom and why some slave families reached out to members of the white community as witnesses for their children's baptisms. One of them, Anthony Ferdinandus, even chose Paulus Heymans, the Dutch overseer of the company slaves, as witness at his son's baptism.[38] This tactic corresponded to an Iberian pattern. As Gerald Cardoso has shown, it was common practice in Brazil that when the slave master or mistress accepted to be godparent of a slave child, this would "free the Negro baby at the baptismal font."[39]

Since their decision to join the Reformed Church had occurred at a time when the church leaders were less worried about Calvinist orthodoxy, it is possible that the black Protestant community in New Netherland preserved some of its Afro-Catholic rituals. This would mean that black conversion to the Reformed Church followed a similar pattern to that of Native American conversion. Research by Mark Meuwese on the Mohawk community has revealed that their conversion occurred primarily for tactical reasons and that those who had been baptized in the Reformed Church never abandoned completely their traditional beliefs nor some of the Catholic customs they had adopted earlier from French Jesuit missionaries. Some Mohawks were even witnessed attending Calvinist services while praying the rosary![40]

It should also be noted that only a minority of the slave community in New Netherland effectively joined the Reformed Church. Hodges, therefore, assumes that most members of the charter generation did not abandon their Afro-Catholic identity and that the black community secretly continued Afro-Catholic practices in New Amsterdam.[41] A similar attitude has been reported elsewhere in the Dutch colonial realm. In Ceylon, for instance, the Catholic indigenous population, converted under Portuguese rule, secretly continued to practice Catholic rituals during the time the island was occupied by the Calvinist Dutch.[42] In the absence of documentary evidence, the attachment to Afro-Catholic practices for New Netherland's charter generation and its descendants remains obscure. It is certain, however, that the change in policy by the Dutch Reformed Church in the late 1650s forced slaves to adapt their strategy in determining how mutual aid was to be secured. Had the Dutch baptism policy continued, mutual aid within the black community would most likely have come to be organized in the context of the Reformed Church. Cotton Mather's diary on life in Massachusetts reflects the desire of some slaves in late-seventeenth-century America to build a structure for mutual aid within the context of a Christian church. His entry from December 1693 reveals that "a company of poor Negroes, of their own Accord, addressed me, for my Countenance, to a Design which they had, of erecting such a Meeting for the Welfare of their miserable Nation that were Servants among us."[43] One can assume that blacks who joined the Dutch Reformed Church in New Netherland had similar hopes and expectations. The case of Bassie de Neger is exemplary. The Deacons' Accounts show that in 1671, this black member of the Dutch Reformed Church in Rensselaerswyck received food and money when he was in need. The church community later also paid for his coffin and funeral, including the brandy and beer for the reception that followed, all items which in Iberian slave societies were traditionally taken care of by brotherhoods.[44]

The revision of the Dutch Reformed policy in the 1650s, however, gave slaves no other choice but to develop their own mutual-aid system, for which the Afro-Iberian concept of brotherhoods formed—as Hodges suggested—the most likely model. Since the organization of a brotherhood with Afro-Catholic roots in a colony under Dutch Calvinist rule required secrecy, it must have occurred out of sight of the authorities and of those who chronicled life in New Netherland: on the Common, gallows-fields, slave burial grounds, the top of hills, and other isolated places. During the long winter months, taverns such as that of Andries Johemsen, where in 1662 the slaves Mattheu, Swan, and Frans were arrested, may also have played a role as secret meeting places.[45]

One can also assume that Dutch objections against the continuation of slave baptisms stimulated the black community to preserve its own heritage. Naming patterns reveal, in fact, a continuous attachment to Lusitanian, Catholic baptismal names. The assumption by Christopher Moore that, by dutchifying their names, all blacks in New Netherland quickly abandoned their Afro-Portuguese roots needs revision.[46] Although such cases existed, they were not the general rule. Moore's example of the rejection of a toponymic name by Emmanuel van Angola in favor of a patronymic name for his son Nicholas Manuel does not necessarily correspond to a Dutch model. In contrast to Moore's suggestion, it should be said that patronymic names were not the only standard in the seventeenth-century Netherlands.[47] Toponymic names beginning with "van" (meaning: from) were also common. Not by accident, a popular refrain in a late-nineteenth-century Dutch American song was "I'm a Van of a Van of Van of a Van of a Van of an old Dutch line."[48] Rather than a rejection of Afro-Portuguese roots, this change in name seems to correspond to an Iberian pattern exemplified by Heywood and Thornton with the name António Manuel, where the father's Catholic baptismal name was added as the second element to the child's name.[49] Remarkably often, the first names of members of the black community in New Netherland continued to correspond to Iberian names referring to Catholic saints.[50] All the popular intergenerational names that Joyce Goodfriend identifies for slaves in New Netherland—Anthony (António), Emanuel, Francisco, Jan (João), Domingo, Peter (Pedro), Anna (Ana), Catharina (Catarina), Cecília, Christina (Cristina), Elizabeth (Isabel), Lucretia (Lucrécia), Magdaleen (Madalena), Marie (Maria), and Susanna (Susana)—correspond to the list provided by Jean Cuvelier of *(n)santus*, Portuguese Catholic names adopted by West-Central Africans.[51]

According to Frijhoff, such Afro-Catholic traditions brought to New Netherland by the charter generation continued to exist precisely because the Dutch Reformed Church changed its policy in regard to slaves in the 1650s.[52] This argument may apply not only to names but also to Afro-Catholic performance traditions. Had black mutual aid come to be organized within the increasingly orthodox Reformed Church, Calvinist opposition against dances and processions undoubtedly would have led to the complete abandonment of the charter generation's Afro-Catholic performance culture. The Dutch Reformed change in policy, however, makes it likely that many descendants of the West-Central African charter generation kept on organizing mutual aid in their own way, even after the English took over the Dutch colony in 1664.

This assumption corresponds to Hodges's theory that the "association" built by the charter generation "provided a supportive model for newly arrived, enslaved Africans." The second part of this chapter will explore traces of a continuation of the charter generation's Afro-Iberian support model.

New York and New Jersey

As scholars such as Mintz, Price, Midlo Hall, Heywood, and Thornton have argued, the charter generations in the Americas often managed to set a strong cultural pattern that shaped black identity for many generations.[53] Considering that the charter generation in New Amsterdam was one of the most homogeneous groups of Africans to enter the Americas in the history of the slave trade, it is credible to assume that the predominantly West-Central African cultural identity of this group and its shared attachment to Afro-Iberian traditions had a substantial impact on the formation of an African American identity by the Dutch-owned slave community in New York and New Jersey.[54]

Evidence of the continuous existence in colonial New York of brotherhoods modeled upon the charter generation's Afro-Iberian traditions can be found in the 1738 report in the *New-York Weekly Journal* on a black association in Kingston, Ulster County, that organized a memorial service for its deceased king: "Several people have been amus'd here with Relation of a Discovery of a Plot concerted by the negroes at Kingston, but by good Information, we find it to be no more than an intended Meeting, to drink to the Memory of an old Negro Fellow, dead some Time ago, whom they used to call their King."[55]

Another intriguing source is a report by an anonymous author calling himself "the Spy" that was delivered to the *New-York Weekly Journal* in 1736 by a certain F.C. The Spy reports how his landlord's slave was tuning "his Banger" and upon asking "the Meaning . . . of his being so merry," the man answered "*Massa, to day Holiday; Backerah no work; Ningar no work; me so savvy play Banger; go yonder, you see Ningar play Banger for true, dance too; you see Sport to day for true. . . . Massa, you savy the Field, little Way out a Town, no Houses there, grandy Room for dance there.*" Together, they went to that place, where the Spy saw "the Plain partly covered with Booths, and well crowded with Whites, the Negroes divided into Companies, I suppose according to their different Nations." Some of them were "dancing to the hollow Sound of a Drum, made of the Trunk of a hollow Tree, othersome to the grating rattling Noise of Pebles or Shells in a Small Basket, others plied the Banger, and some knew how to joyn the Voice to it." The Spy also observed "several Companies of the Blacks, some exercising the Cudgel, and some of them small Sticks in imitation of the short Pike." Tired of the noise, the Spy left the scene and considered that "the Day, (being one of those set apart to commemorate the Resurrection of our Blessed Saviour) and the Diversions I had seen, I could not chuse but think that Holidays thus spent could be of very little Service."[56] In a later report, the Spy informed his readers that he "was pick'd up by one with whom I had been in Company before," who informed him that these pastimes were "practiced among the Fraternity called Gamesters." So, not only does the Spy use the terms "nations" and "fraternity" that are so intimately related to the concept of brotherhoods, he also reveals that the dances on the Christian holiday—probably Easter—involved a mock fight with sticks, similar to what typically occurs in Kongolese brotherhoods in Brazil and elsewhere in the Americas.

The event witnessed by the Spy has characteristics in common with what came to be known in Jamaica, Barbados, and other Caribbean islands as a "tea meeting," a fundraising event organized by a black mutual-aid association where alcohol was served, music was played, dances were performed, speeches were held, people performed mock stick fights, and in some cases a king and queen were elected.[57] As Thornton has suggested, the popularity of stick dances in slave communities of Kongolese descent in the American diaspora may relate to *sangamentos*.[58] It is, in this respect, surprising to find a scene in David Murdoch's novel *The Dutch Dominie of the Catskills* (1861) about a slave performance in rural New York where the word *sangaree* is shouted. The same novel, set in 1777 in the Catskill-Kingston area, also mentions the existence of a "slave king," who acted as a judge over other slaves.[59] Although Murdoch's references to Dutch folklore in the Hudson Valley are well researched, an actual connection to Kongolese sangamentos cannot be confirmed. In other parts of the novel, Murdoch uses terms such as *Unga Golah* and *greegee*, which he probably took from Theophilus Conneau's *A Slaver's Log Book* (1853) about the Pongo River region in Guinea. Although Conneau's book does not mention the term *sangaree*, Murdoch may have taken it from another source on Africa.[60]

It should also be pointed out that the British anthropologist John Weeks identified two types of war dances during his stay in the Kongo region in the 1880s, when what remained of the once mighty kingdom was ruled by King Pedro VI. One of the dances was called *nsanga*, a likely corruption of sangamento, which Weeks defined as "a crowd of folk who shout, wave knives, and fire off guns to the sounding beat of a big drum"; the other, called *etutu*, he defined as "dancers carry[ing] long sticks in their hands, with bells, or anything that jingles, fixed to the top ends. It is danced by a line of men and a line of women, who work their shoulders as well as their legs."[61] The latter dance corresponds better to the performance witnessed by the Spy in New York and provides a possible explanation for the reason why people would later also call the "Congo dances" on Albany's Pinkster Hill "Toto dances." If the Toto dance were indeed of Kongolese origin, its name might refer to *(n)toto*, meaning earth or soil, or *tóoto*, meaning arrow or stick in Kikongo.

There are also indications that the "hellish confederacy" Judge Daniel Horsmanden claimed to have detected in the context of the famous 1741 "slave plot" in New York City might have functioned as a brotherhood.[62] It all started when three slaves—Prince, Caesar, and Cuffee (two of whom had a Dutch master)—were arrested and investigations revealed that they were linked to an association

known as the "Geneva Club," named after the Dutch *jenever* (gin) they had stolen in 1738. Members of the Geneva Club would meet and probably also store
stolen goods at the tavern of the English cobbler John Hughson. Hughson's tavern was frequented by slaves, free blacks, and poor whites. One of the rooms was
paid for by Caesar to house a white, allegedly Irish, prostitute called Margaret
Sorubiero, known as Peggy Kerry, with whom he had a child. While the jury
investigated the case of the Geneva Club, the first of thirteen suspicious fires in
Lower Manhattan erupted in April 1741. Many New Yorkers still remembered
the slave uprising of the year 1712 and feared that these fires were part of a
plot. This theory was given credibility by Mary Burton, the young indentured
servant at Hughson's tavern, who informed Judge Horsmanden that slaves had
been using the tavern to conspire. Following General James Oglethorpe's warnings against Spanish secret agents operating in North American territory in the
context of the British-Spanish War of 1739–48, Horsmanden later also arrested a
man named John Ury, a teacher and scholar of Latin, whom Burton accused of
having been involved in the plot. Horsmanden believed this man to be a secret
Catholic priest and agent of the Spanish enemy. In total, one hundred and sixty
blacks and twenty-one whites were arrested in the case. A surprisingly large
number of these slaves were owned by Dutch American slaveholders such as
Varick, Vanderspiegle, Groesbeck, Ten Eyck, Roosevelt, DePeyster, Van Horn,
Van Zant, Tiebout, Van Courtlandt, Marschalk, Goelet, and Vandursen. Of those
who were arrested, thirty blacks and four whites were executed and seventy
blacks and seven whites were deported from New York.

Although the terms "black brotherhood" and "fraternal organization" have
often been used in relation to the Geneva Club and similar black associations
involved in the New York "plot" such as the Fly Boys and the Long Bridge Boys, it
is generally understood that these were little more than criminal gangs. Thomas
De Voe, for instance, argued that "many of these slaves had become otherwise
troublesome, as they held daily and nightly cabals, forming themselves into parties or clubs."[63] However, the titles attributed to the leaders of the Geneva Club
correspond surprisingly well to those commonly used in black brotherhoods
and militias. An anonymous account, published in the *New-York Gazette* in February 1738, spoke about the discovery of a "Company of Blacks," led by someone
using an Iberian honorific title—a certain "Mr. Don Dago" (Don Diego/Dom
Tiago?)—who had organized "an elegant Entertainment" for which "some of the
Fraternity . . . broke open a Cellar and stole a large Quantity of strong Liquor."
As punishment, their leaders were put on carriages and "were continually com-
plimented with Snow Balls and Dirt, and at every Corner had five Lashes with a
Cowskin well laid on each of their naked black Backs," whereby "sundry others
of the Brotherhood were lashed at the Publick Whipping-Post."[64] This article
was originally understood as a mere satire that alluded to an earlier article about

the city's white Freemasons in the *New-York Weekly Journal*.[65] When the *Weekly Journal* protested against this comparison, however, the author of the article in the *Gazette* reacted by pointing out that what he had reported was essentially true because the members of the Geneva Club had effectively formed an organization that resembled a Masonic brotherhood.[66]

The references in Judge Hormanden's *Journal* (1744) that the culprits had had "the impudence to assume the style and title of Free Masons," that "the negroes were flattered they were to be formed into companies, several officers of them were named for the purpose, captains, etc." and that "it was agreed among them, that Hughson was to be king, his wife queen, Vaarck's Caesar governor, and Peggy, his mistress, governess" also reflect the distribution of titles commonly used in Afro-Iberian brotherhoods.[67] The fact that they had decided to choose a white man to become their king is surprising. Although it was not uncommon for poor whites to join black brotherhoods, there are no references to them being elected as kings. A more credible version is that of the slave called Bastian, who clarified in his testimony that "Hughson was to have the goods that were stolen from the fire," whereas not Hughson but rather the black man Caesar "was to be king."[68] William Kane, a white soldier implicated in the conspiracy, also claimed that Caesar was to become "the Chief among the Negroes."[69] Furthermore, it was discovered that blacks had not only gathered at Hughson's tavern but also at the house of Gerardus Comfort. There an all-black organization, which included at least six "Spaniards," was led by a certain Jack, who, according to the witnesses Sarah and Sawney, "was to be a Captain."[70] Two other slaves involved in the "plot," the Spanish-speaking slave Curaçao Dick and one called York, were also "to be a Captain," while a slave called London was to be "an officer" under Captain York.[71]

The activities of those involved in the "plot" are remarkably similar to those of the fraternity of the "Gamesters" described by the Spy in his 1736 article. According to the Spy, the "fraternity" he visited raised money through gambling and cockfights, which corresponds to the type of illicit activities Sentry William Kane declared he had witnessed at the taverns where the black culprits had gathered.[72] Moreover, while the "Gamesters" celebrated the "Resurrection of our Blessed Saviour," Horsmanden's investigations make reference to a gathering of blacks at Hughson's tavern to celebrate Whitsuntide (Pentecost) with a lavish banquet. In their confessions, several slaves (Sterling, Scipio, London, Tom, and Henry) linked their first knowledge of the conspiracy to a gathering on Whitsuntide in 1740. The constables Joseph North and Peter Lynch argued in court "that there was a cabal of negroes at Hughson's last Whitsuntide" and that when they entered the room, "the negroes were round a table, eating and drinking, for there was meat on the table, and knives and forks; and the negroes were calling for what they wanted."[73] The assumption that this gathering occurred in the context of a brotherhood corresponds to Jill Lepore's analysis of the New York "plot." According to Lepore, slaves in New York traditionally "chose important, prominent men" on the occasion of Pinkster, who served "as respected leaders within the black community"; and long before Pinkster festivals were observed and recorded by whites, "black elections . . . must have taken place privately, at places like John Hughson's tavern."[74]

The presence of Catholic elements in the "conspiracy" also points in the direction of Afro-Iberian brotherhoods. Traditionally, scholars have been inclined to discard Horsmanden's suggestion that the slave conspiracy was part of a "Spanish and Popish plot," relating this suspicion to the anti-Catholic hysteria that had erupted in the aftermath of Britain's declaration of war against Spain in 1739.[75] It should, however, be pointed out that many of those involved in the "plot" were Catholic. Most of the white culprits were Irish Catholics and at least thirteen black culprits were so-called "Spanish Negroes," Spanish-speaking black or mestizo soldiers who had been captured and enslaved in New York despite their claims that they were free men.[76] According to Horsmanden, these "Spanish Negroes" had made a deal with the "York negroes" and then joined the "plot." All of them were claimed to have fighting experience while serving in the Spanish army.[77] In court, the Sephardic Jew Mordecai Gomez served as their interpreter. They insisted that they were free men who had been enslaved illegally and demanded to be identified by their proper names; not as "Powlis" but as Pablo Ventura Angel, not as "Tony" but as Antonio de St. Bendito, and so on. The Catholic identity of these "Spanish Negroes" is notable in the decision by Wan de Sylva (Juan da Silva) to pray and kiss a crucifix before his execution.[78] As the *New-York Weekly Journal* confirms, da Silva "died steadfastly in the Roman Catholick Profession."[79] Since they were deeply Catholic and had grown up in Iberian territory, there can be no doubt that these "Spanish Negroes" were familiar with brotherhoods.

General Oglethorpe's warnings against Spanish agents in disguise sent from Spanish Florida to provoke the slaves in North America may also have been closer to the truth than traditionally assumed. The black culprit Bastian confessed that slaves in New York City expected "that War would be proclaimed in a little time against the French; and that the French and Spaniards would come here," and Cato, another black culprit, claimed that "the Spaniards will come and take us all."[80] As Linebaugh and Rediker have argued, this was "not an idle fantasy," since "Spain had already done just that for many people of African descent in the New World."[81] According to Thornton, the Spanish authorities were well aware of the fact that many slaves in British-controlled territories in America identified themselves as Catholics.[82] Following the English and Dutch decision to establish colonies in Spanish-claimed territory in the New World, the king of Spain had decreed "to place in liberty all black slaves that flee the English and

Dutch colonies to my dominions with the pretext to embrace our Holy Catholic Faith."[83] The desertion of Afro-Catholic slaves from English colonies to Spanish territory was not a chimera. In 1716 the Spanish Governor Estivan Bravao de Rivero argued that numerous slaves had fled to Puerto Rico "in search of the Catholick Religion."[84] Sizeable groups of Afro-Catholic Angolan slaves also fled from South Carolina to Florida throughout the 1730s.[85]

Although there are good reasons to question the trustworthiness of Mary Burton's allegations, there might have been some truth in her testimony on a Catholic priest in disguise named John Ury, who allegedly baptized the conspirators while holding a crucifix over their heads.[86] Ury's secret missionary work among the slaves was, in fact, confirmed by other witnesses, and his journal contains evidence that—although unordained—he pretended to be a Catholic priest.[87] One witness, Elias DeBrosse, argued that Ury had approached him to buy sacramental wafers for a Mass and another one, William Kane, claimed to have witnessed Ury performed baptism by putting "salt into the child's mouth, sprinkled it thrice, and crossed it," which corresponds to the typically Kongolese Catholic habit of baptizing children with salt.[88]

All this seems to indicate that what the New York City authorities had actually discovered was not a "plot" but a network of secret slave associations that had characteristics in common with Afro-Iberian brotherhoods. The panic among local authorities over the amount of organizational skill displayed by the slave community parallels what happened in similar circumstances in other parts of the Americas. Reporting about Santiago, Chile, in 1609 Juan de Torquemada wrote about a "tumult and rumor of an uprising of Negroes" because "many of them had gathered and elected a king." However, "in all truth, it turned out to be an affair of the Negroes . . . and there was nothing to it."[89] In 1693 the authorities in Cartagena claimed to have uncovered a "slave conspiracy" and interrogated a certain Francisco de Vera about the city's black community. One of their questions was if he knew whether slaves had "their kings, governors, and captains, and if they meet in their councils to deal with the problems of their nation . . . and have their parties and festivities in which they join together." De Vera was surprised by the question and answered that he thought that the authorities were well aware of the fact that slave nations in Cartagena had their annual coronation festivals at which officials were appointed.[90]

A similar case took place on the Caribbean island of St. Christopher in 1770, where the authorities believed to have uncovered a "slave plot," which eventually proved to be "nothing more than a Meeting every Saturday night of the Principle Negroes belonging to Several Estates in One quarter of the Island called Palmetto Point, at which they affected to imitate their Masters and had appointed a General, Lieutenant General, a Council and Assembly."[91] In Trinidad in 1805, the authorities also claimed to have uncovered a "conspiracy" when slaves had been observed forming "convoys" or "regiments" that were led by a "king," who was wearing a "uniform comprising a hat with black cockade, a black jacket with scarlet collar, and a green ribbon over the shoulder." In their feasts, they drank toasts "to the King's health." Furthermore, they collected money, cared for the sick, and buried the dead. According to Michael Mullin, they also made a rebellious song, which played on elements of the Catholic communion service: "the flesh of white people is our bread, their blood is our wine."[92] In an alleged "conspiracy" on the island of Jamaica in 1806, slaves had formed "a Society," which according to the arrested was for purposes of mutual aid. Members of this "black society" were observed mustering with wooden swords and guns. They also appointed officers "from Generals to Sergeants and Corporals."[93]

Another case occurred in British Guyana, where an enquiry following rumors of a "slave plot" in 1808 led to the deportation of six and the execution of nine slaves when the authorities discovered the existence of several "Companies" among the slave population that were led by a "king."[94] In 1823 another court case was opened in Trinidad upon suspicion of a "slave plot." The investigation ended up revealing that among the slave population on the island there were "many Societies . . . under the Military designation of *Regiment* . . . to be used on the occasion of Dances on Holy days to denote different parties, tribes or nations such as *Regiment Congo*."[95] Eugene Genovese has famously interpreted the role of kings in these and other slave "plots" as a restorationist reflex among slaves in the American diaspora who tried to restore an African royal past.[96] More convincing, however, is Mullin's conclusion that "a better approach to the conspiracies" is to highlight the parallels to "the black religious brotherhoods of Brazil."[97]

These parallels to brotherhoods in Brazil do not imply that all the slaves linked to such associations had West-Central African roots and were all Afro-Catholic. This was certainly not the case in New York, where slaves with West-Central African roots had by the mid-eighteenth century become a small minority. The 1712 slave uprising in New York City is indicative of the fact that among Dutch families, there was a growing number of slaves with West African roots. About half the slaves involved in the 1712 uprising, whom contemporaries claimed to have been almost exclusively "of ye Nations of Cormantee & Pappa," had Dutch owners such as Vaninburgh, Philipse, Gouverneur, Coertens, Schuyler, Van Clyff, Vantilborough, Burger, Stouthenburgh, Lynsen, Provoost, Van Dam, Hooghlandt, Pels, Dekey, Roosevelt, and Vaarck.[98] Since no profound Portuguese influence on West African Coromantee (or Akan) and Pawpaw cultures has been reported, it is unlikely that the slaves involved in the 1712 uprising had ever come in touch with Afro-Catholic traditions. Whether this played a role in the apparent lack of support they received by descendants of the charter generation is unknown. It is certain, however, that the steady arrival of slaves with

West African roots must have had considerable impact on the Afro-Catholic traditions that had been introduced in Manhattan by the charter generation.

In this respect, a parallel can be drawn to the 1736 "slave plot" on the island of Antigua. Interestingly, one of the slaves sentenced in the New York "plot," a certain Will, was claimed to also have been involved in that Caribbean "plot."[99] The Antigua "plot" is well documented. The election of a certain Court as "king" of the Antigua slave community in October 1736 was (mis)interpreted by local authorities as the formation of a replacement government and hence a declaration of war. Court and some of his supporters were subsequently arrested and executed, despite protests of Court's master Thomas Kerby that the coronation was just "an innocent play." Like most slaves in Antigua in the 1730s, Court was identified as "Coromantee." However, Court's organization included several island-born Creoles of unknown African origin that were led by a certain Tomboy. Unlike the Coromantees, these Creoles could read and write and some of them were reportedly "initiated into Christianity according to the Romish Church," which points at a West-Central African origin or at least familiarity with Iberian culture.[100] To strengthen his alliance with the Creoles, Court had granted them honorific titles in his organization.[101] Despite the fact that they, as a minority group, had received several influential positions in the organization, some Creoles were anything but enthusiastic about the deal Tomboy had made with the Coromantees. Significantly, a description of Court's election ceremony reveals how a certain Maria and Tilgarth or Targut, both Creoles, did not hide their contempt for the West Africans. According to Targut, "Maria sat at the Table and She looked very Black on Seeing So many Coromantees there, and she and I made Signs of Contempt to Each Other."[102] It is unknown whether, as David Gaspar has argued, this Antigua "plot" was essentially an all-Coromantee affair organized according to Akan rituals or whether the rituals at Court's coronation were a mixture of newly imported West African Akan traditions with existing rituals that had been introduced by the forefathers of the island's Creoles. The latter theory corresponds better to the deal between Court and Tomboy. One could thus speculate that in Antigua an evolution had taken place whereby West African slaves had become so dominant that they eventually managed to assume control over the Afro-Iberian mutual-aid organization that had once been established by the island's charter generation. This theory would clarify why some of the Creoles in Antigua were anything but enthusiastic about the power-sharing agreement with the increasingly numerous West Africans.

Rivalries between descendants of the charter generation and later slaves from other parts of Africa or between slaves with West African and West-Central African roots were not unique to Antigua. For instance, the Our Lady of the Rosary brotherhood in Salvador, Brazil, continued to allow only Angolans

and their descendants to sit on its board at a time when the vast majority of
the brotherhood's members consisted of more recently arrived West-African
Jejes. In Minas Gerais, Brazil, a planned slave uprising in 1724 failed because the
West-Central African Angolan "nation" and West African Mina "nation" could
not agree on a single leader. In Barbados, descendants of the charter generation
planned an uprising against the white community in 1692, whereby they hoped
to overtake power on the island and subsequently use the recently arrived West
Africans as their own slaves.[103]

Something similar to what happened in Antigua may also have occurred
in New York. Although Lapore has claimed that the authorities uncovered "an
Akan-influenced brotherhood" in the 1741 New York "plot," it seems more likely
that the black mutual-aid organizations that were discovered in New York City
mixed elements relating to the Afro-Catholic traditions of the charter generation and of the "Spanish Negroes" with elements relating to indigenous rituals
from the increasingly numerous West African slaves.[104] The use of titles typically associated with Afro-Iberian brotherhoods and militias, the observation
of Pentecost, and the numerous Catholic elements make it highly unlikely that
the secret societies established by the New York City slave community were an
all-Akan affair.

Perhaps the most remarkable feature of the 1741 "plot" is that the harsh punishments inflicted on the city's slave population did not deter brotherhoods in
the New York area from continuing their traditional rituals. In January 1742,
only months after thirty blacks had been executed, Horsmanden reported that
"many cabals of negroes had been discovered in diverse parts of the country."
"Particularly in Queens County, on Nassau alias Long Island," he wrote, blacks
had "formed themselves into a Company about Christmas last; by way of play
or diversion (as they would have had it thought), had mustered and trained with
the borrowed arms and accoutrements of their masters (or we would rather
suppose, surreptitiously obtained)."[105] Similar practices continued to take place
in nearby states. On May 16, 1758 (the Tuesday after Pentecost), barely seventeen
years after the New York "plot," people in Salem, Massachusetts, wrote a petition
to the authorities complaining about the "great disorder . . . on Election days
by negroes assembling together, beating drums, using powder and having guns
and swords."[106] The fact that slaves involved in these performances publicly displayed arms they had borrowed from their masters indicates that the latter were
at the very least acquainted with these ceremonies and most likely lent some
support to it. The degree to which landlords in rural areas were willing to make
concessions to their slaves, even after the harrowing events in New York City, is
indicative of their dependence on the latter.

Not by accident, Sojourner Truth explained in her *Narrative* how slaves in
the Kingston area "us[ed] their influence" to obtain concessions from their

Attributed to John Heaton, *Van Bergen Overmantel*, ca. 1728–38. Martin van Bergen, a New York colonist of Dutch origin, commissioned this work to depict his farm near the Catskill Mountains. Intended to be displayed over the fireplace (thus the term *overmantel*), the work indicates the Dutch-style architecture of the farm. Most notably, the *overmantel* displays the ethnic diversity of New York in the 1700s, depicting Dutch American settlers, African American slaves, and two Native Americans. Courtesy the New York State Historical Association.

masters.[107] Born in 1797 to a Dutch-owned slave woman, Truth serves as an intriguing example of how Afro-Portuguese traditions survived among slaves for several decades after the demise of New Netherland. Research by Margaret Washington revealed that Truth's mother Elizabeth must have been of West-Central African descent.[108] Despite the fact that her mother had acculturated to Dutch customs and only spoke Dutch to her child, she nevertheless decided to give her daughter a typically Iberian Afro-Catholic name rather than a Dutch one: Isabel.[109] Not only does her given name link Truth to the Portuguese Rainha Santa Isabel, the mythical initiator of the *Festa do Divino* during Pentecost, but also the many references to the Virgin Mary in Truth's speeches and songs, as well as her decision to literally bargain with God over His assistance, point to an Afro-Catholic rather than a Calvinistic approach to the Divine.[110]

The tendency in the master-slave relationship in traditionally Dutch areas in colonial New York and New Jersey to negotiate the choice of slave master, the number of holiday vacations, conjugal and family visits, and in exceptional cases even manumission followed a pattern remarkably similar to that of the charter generation in New Netherland.[111] As such arrangements involved complex exchanges of information, slaves must have provided guidance to one another. According to David Gellman, "African American New Yorkers sought to maintain and deepen the bonds of family and community attachment as a counterweight to the burdens imposed upon them through slavery."[112] Truth's diary confirms this theory and shows that there was a lot of networking in the

slave community where she grew up. Considering the ease with which she was able to change to a new master when she disliked the previous one, Suzanne Fitch and Roseanne Mandziuk have argued that there "must have been a network that allowed blacks and whites to communicate other than on the master-slave level."[113] In Truth's *Narrative* one reads: "In this way the slaves often assist each other, by ascertaining who are kind to their slaves, comparatively; and then using their influence to get such a one to hire or buy their friends." Masters did not oppose this, because they "allow those they are about to sell or let, to choose their own places, if the persons they happen to select for masters are considered safe pay."[114]

Despite their wealth and influence, landlords in rural areas depended in practice a great deal on the loyalty of their tenants, contract workers, and slaves. From the very beginning of the colony, landowners had been forced to grant concessions to their workers in order to secure cooperation. Whenever these concessions were questioned, violence erupted.[115] During the 1750s the Livingstons faced fierce protests by their tenants; in the early years of the following decade, the Van Rensselaers and the Van Cortlandts were also confronted with acts of violence by theirs.[116] Although slaves were in a much weaker position than tenants, the landlords nevertheless practiced a cautious strategy to secure their support. Considering that the earliest landowners in the region such as Kiliaen van Rensselaer employed slaves to intimidate rebellious tenants, one could even speculate that leaders of black organizations in rural areas were involved in actions to enforce order at the request of the landlord. This would explain why slave "kings" and "governors" tended to be physically strong men who had an influential landowner as master. The story about King Charles accompanying his master as a bodyguard on the way to Saratoga during the Revolutionary War corroborates this assumption.[117]

There can, in any case, be no doubt that physical support by slaves in case of danger was crucial for those landlords who lived in isolated areas that were under threat of hostile attack. In the eighteenth century, people in places such as the Mohawk and upper Hudson Valleys lived in constant fear of a Native American assault.[118] Significantly, after French troops and their Native American allies killed sixty people in Schenectady in February 1690, the panic over this "Indian attack" was such that hundreds of settlers fled downriver toward New York City. Even in a big city like Albany, the population that had been 2,016 in 1689 dropped to 1,476 in the aftermath of this attack.[119] Especially in areas bordering Native American territories, slaveholders had every interest in securing the loyalty of their slaves through negotiations and concessions. It is, as such, only natural that Albany became a center of African American king election ceremonies.

It would, thus, be wrong to reduce concessions by slaveholders to paternalistic acts. Such an interpretation transmits the false impression that slaves were passive beings who completely depended on their masters' whims. The many references to the eagerness of slaves to form associations indicate that slaves aptly used the strength derived from their social capital to obtain concessions. However, slaves had no legal standing and could therefore not force binding contracts upon their masters. Since slaveholders could unilaterally revoke all previously made concessions, it was crucial for slaves to have the achieved concessions reconfirmed on a regular basis. One can assume that Pinkster fulfilled this role as an annual ritual.

An example of this social negotiation between a master and a representative of the slave community can be found in C. M. Woolsey's *History of the Town of Marlborough, Ulster County* (1908): "An old man with a large tract of land had among his slaves one called Harry. He was very large and a fine-looking fellow. He was the leader of a company or drilled as such. His old master was very proud of him, and he always rode his owner's big black stallion on such occasions."[120] The expression "leader of a company" corroborates the assumption that slave organizations must have existed in rural parts of New York. Woolsey's study on Marlborough also provides a fascinating example of mutual aid within the slave community. In 1812 a slave called Figarow (probably Figaroa or Figueroa) was set free by his master John Roberts. Two years later, Figarow appeared as a witness acknowledging the payment of one hundred dollars to John Roberts to set another of his slaves, Lewis Ciprienmango, free.[121] In 1849 a man now called

Fegarrow intervened to assist Margaret Ann Mango to vest a title of real estate in her name after her husband Lewis Ceprien Mango had died.[122]

All this indicates that the Pinkster festival should be understood in the context of a *modus vivendi,* both within the slave population and between masters and slave representatives. It cannot be a coincidence that slaves who occupied leading positions during the Albany Pinkster festival all belonged to influential families. King Charles's Pinkster procession could never have started from "young massa's house" on State Street, one of Albany's most noble districts, without consent of the city's white elite.[123] Elite families who had lived for several generations in the Albany area, such as the Van Rensselaers, Schuylers, Ten Broecks, Gansevoorts, Van Vechtens, Van Schaicks, and Douws, must have been aware of the existence of slave brotherhoods and must have realized that it was in their own interest to render some form of support to the annual king celebrations on Pinkster Hill.

However, the arrival of ever more new immigrants in the second half of the eighteenth century completely changed the social structure in upstate New York. As the following chapter will show, these dramatic changes not only gave the deathblow to Dutch identity in America but also to the traditional *modus vivendi* between masters and slaves.

6

THE DEMISE AND LEGACY
OF THE PINKSTER FESTIVAL

The 1811 Prohibition

While Dutch identity remained strong until the Revolution in Albany and parts of rural New York and New Jersey that had once formed New Netherland, this changed in the late eighteenth century with the arrival of thousands of New Englanders and European immigrants in search of manufacturing jobs and cheap farming land. In the once predominantly Dutch American city of Albany, for instance, the population quadrupled between 1790 and 1820.[1] Due to the steady arrival of new population groups, the Dutch American community in Albany and other parts of New York and New Jersey quickly became a small minority.[2]

This numeric decline of the Dutch population's percentage was accompanied by a process of anglicization. In Albany and its surroundings, the arrival of a large contingent of British soldiers in the context of the French and Indian War (1754–63) had already had a significant impact on local culture. The soldiers had introduced new customs in the area and had become role models for the younger generation.[3] A telling example of the tensions caused by these social changes is the controversy over the decision by British officers to perform George Farquhar's play *The Beaux Stratagem* in 1759, which involved the participation of male actors dressed as women and contained some cynical remarks about matrimony. Conservative people in the Dutch community were deeply upset about it and the Pietist Reverend Theodorus Frelinghuysen made it the topic of a sermon. The next morning, Frelinghuysen found a staff, a pair of old shoes, a loaf of black bread, and a coin on his doorstep—all items transmitting the unmistakable message that some people wanted him to leave, which he did.[4] The negative image of the Dutch among Anglo-Americans undoubtedly accelerated this process of anglicization. Immigrants from New England tended to highlight the qualities of the cultivated and enterprising Anglo-American by portraying people of Dutch descent as boorish and backward. Significantly, when the influential banker Gorham Worth was asked to explain why he had called Albany a "third or fourth rate town" upon his arrival in New York in 1825, he replied that he had done so because Albany was "Dutch, in all its moods and tenses; thoroughly and inveterately Dutch. The buildings were Dutch—Dutch in style, in position, attitude and aspect. The people were Dutch, the horses were Dutch, and even the dogs were Dutch."[5]

During his journey through rural New York and New Jersey in 1783–84, the native Dutchman Carel de Vos van Steenwijk had no difficulties finding older people with whom he could still speak his native language and observed with surprise "how incredibly content they were to see a Dutchman." Near Kingston, he even met with Dutch families who spoke hardly any English. Nevertheless, he acknowledged that in most families, children increasingly used English as their main language of communication and behaved in an "American" fashion.[6] During a trip to the Hudson Valley in 1794, William Strickland confirmed that "the Dutch, as Dutch in opposition to English, were fast wearing out in this country which a generation or two back might be said to have been entirely inhabited by such, and that they were assimilating themselves to the English or Americans."[7]

Once their Dutch heritage was no longer a matter of pride to these Americans, they naturally lost the desire to organize the traditional ring-riding and Pinksterbloem events on Pentecost. It would therefore be wrong to claim that Americans of Dutch descent consciously abandoned their Pinkster traditions. Rather, these traditions disappeared because an increasing number of people no longer considered "Dutchness" to be an important part of their identity. Pinkster celebrations only survived in small circles of people who consciously held on to their Dutch ancestry. This was, for instance, the case of the St. Nicholas Society and the Holland Society. In 1880, for instance, members of New York City's St. Nicholas Society still celebrated Pinkster with a lavish dinner in their clubhouse, which for the occasion had been "handsomely decorated with flowers" in the old Pinksterbloem tradition.[8]

The arrival of ever more white immigrants from New England and Europe not only affected the Dutch community. The percentage decline of Dutch Americans coincided with a sharp decrease in the percentage of African Americans. In Albany, for instance, blacks sank from 17 percent of the total population in 1790 to only 6 percent in 1820.[9] By the time the first extensive descriptions of Pinkster celebrations in Albany and elsewhere in New York and New Jersey began to appear, both the Dutch American and African American communities had become relatively small minorities.

During those decades of dramatic social change in once predominantly Dutch-speaking areas in America, slaves gave increasing signs of discontent. In 1775 there were rumors about a slave plot in Ulster and Queens Counties. Later that year, the town of Newburgh in Orange County passed new ordinances to curb some of the privileges of slaves. The same occurred in Albany in 1776 following an arson that was thought to be the result of a slave plot. During the war that erupted in consequence of the American Declaration of Independence, British Commander-in-Chief Sir Henry Clinton opportunistically offered freedom to those slaves who would abandon their patriot masters and support the British army. Lured by this promise of freedom, hundreds of slaves fled to the British.[10] In 1779 one slave in Albany was arrested for "seducing a number of Negroes to join the enemy" and another for trying "to stir up the minds of the Negroes against their masters and raise insurrection among them."[11] Despite attempts by George Washington at war's end to convince the British to restitute all runaway slaves to their American masters, some three thousand former slaves were declared free and entitled to safe passage to Nova Scotia and Great Britain under the peace agreement of November 30, 1782.[12] Some of these black Loyalists later migrated to Sierra Leone, where they established mutual-aid associations with festivals and customs that, according to David Northrup, "had no counterpart in their homelands" and were "strikingly similar to ... Catholic sodalities."[13]

Following the American independence, the ideal of liberty grew stronger. Although most whites excluded the slave population from their noble ideals, exceptional ones such as the Quaker community insisted that true liberty could not be achieved without the abolition of slavery. Critical voices on slavery could also be heard in the press. In February 1785, slavery was criticized in the *New-York Gazetteer* as "the deprivation of all the rights which nature has given to man" and an anonymous author provocatively argued in the *New-York Journal* that slaveholders deserved to be "plundered, tormented, and even massacred by the avenging hands of their purchased slaves."[14] In 1797 William Dunlap was overly optimistic in reporting that "within 20 years the opinion of the injustice of slave holding has become almost universal."[15]

The two main political parties of the time—the Democratic-Republican Party, formed by Thomas Jefferson in 1791, and the Federalist Party, formed by Alexander Hamilton in 1792—held different opinions on slavery. Although Federalists were divided on the issue of abolition, they tended to follow Adam Smith's economic theories that saw slavery as part of the old economic order.[16] Many Federalists had also interpreted the 1791 slave revolt in Haiti as a sign that the time had come to get rid of the increasingly demanding slaves and to replace them in the workforce by cheap immigrants from Europe.[17] Influential Federalists such as Alexander Hamilton and John Jay were founding members of the Manumission Society, who supported the opening of a chapter for free black voters in the Federalist fraternity known as the Washington Benevolent Society. As had traditionally happened in the Albany slave king procession, this Washington Benevolent Society commonly staged parades with participants carrying George Washington's portrait.[18]

Democratic-Republicans generally opposed abolition in order to secure the support of yeoman farmers who still relied on their slaves and of white laborers who feared black competition on the job market. The Tammany Society also denounced free blacks as the cause of low wages and long working hours. When free black Americans in New York who had enough capital to qualify as voters decided that they would unanimously support the Federalists in the 1808 elections, the Democratic-Republican party launched a racist campaign song beginning with "Federalists with blacks unite," whereupon Federalists reacted by insinuating that Jeffersonian Republicans purchased votes of noncitizen immigrants.[19] Well-to-do blacks tended, in fact, to side with Federalists.[20] In a public address to black New Yorkers in 1809, Joseph Sidney argued that his fellow African Americans should support their "Federalist friends" rather than Democratic-Republicans, whom he labeled as "enemies of our rights."[21] When black voters turned out to have been of crucial importance for the election of a series of Federalist candidates in 1813, Jeffersonian Republicans reacted by adopting measures to restrict voting rights for free people of color.[22]

Federalist support for black voting rights did not imply support for equal rights. Rather, Federalists favored a paternalistic policy whereby, after achieving emancipation, the black community would continue to rely on the political goodwill of the same white elite families that had previously enslaved them.[23] In this respect, Federalist attempts to make deals with the black elite in the context of the Washington Benevolent Society gave continuation to the traditional policy of slaveholders to ensure slave loyalty by granting tactical support to representatives of the slave community. This attitude should not be a surprise since several of the leading Federalist politicians in the young republic—such as Stephen van Rensselaer, Abraham ten Broeck, Leonard Gansevoort, Gulian Crommelin Verplanck, and Philip John Schuyler—belonged to prominent landowning families who had for decades been in charge of the slave system.[24] Although these families had supported the revolutionary cause, they remained deeply suspicious of democratic principles and attempted to use their wealth and influence to solidify their political power. If abolition turned out to be inevitable, they wanted at least to ensure their control over the black community. These Federalists abhorred nothing more than the notion of equality, which they associated with a lack of respect for authority, rebellion, and ultimately chaos. Significantly, Federalists consistently referred to slave revolts as evidence of what respectable citizens would have to endure once democratic ideas associated with the French Revolution became dominant in America.[25]

The debate on slavery also divided the Dutch American community. Following the adoption in 1780 of a law that gradually emancipated slaves in Pennsylvania, wealthy Dutch American slaveholders with Federalist sympathies realized that New York would follow sooner or later. Although the complete abolishment of slavery in the state of New York did not take place until 1827, most elite families had already begun to replace their slaves by cheap European immigrants in the early nineteenth century. However, the vast majority of Dutch Americans were yeoman farmers, who still relied heavily on slavery.[26] In Long Island, for instance, more than 60 percent of the families in areas with a traditionally strong Dutch character were still holding slaves.[27] They were among the fiercest opponents of Governor John Jay's Gradual Emancipation Law that would free all slave children born after the Fourth of July 1799. Dutch yeoman farmers accused the New York governor of wanting "to rob every Dutchman of the property . . . most dear to his heart, his slaves," and of forcing them to educate children of slaves "even if unable to educate their own children."[28] Delaware County politician Erastus Root recalled with reference to this debate that "the slaveholders at that time were chiefly Dutch. They raved and swore *dunder* and *blitzen* that we were robbing them of their property."[29]

In November 1793, in the midst of this tense discussion over slavery in the Dutch American community, a fire that had erupted in the stables behind Leonard Gansevoort's home in Albany burned out of control: twenty-six homes and almost an entire block in the city's business district burned down. Three slaves—two females (Dinah and Bet) and one male (Pomp)—were accused of arson and subsequently sentenced to death. Dinah belonged to Volkert Douw, King Charles's master. Bet was owned by Philip van Rensselaer and Pomp had been a slave of Mathew Visscher, who had died shortly before the arson took place. All three were influential landowning families of Dutch origin. Following the fire, the Albany Common Council established a night watch and enforced a curfew for slaves after 9 p.m. Despite these measures, another major fire destroyed some ninety-six houses in Albany in 1797. Although there were again rumors of a plot, this time no one was convicted.[30] Speaking about slavery in Albany in the late eighteenth century, Joel Munsell argued that "the slaves were much dreaded by their masters, and supposed to be capable of any villainy."[31]

These tensions also affected the annual Pinkster celebrations. The dark clouds forming over Pinkster Hill are clearly visible in Absalom Aimwell's *Pinkster Ode for the Year 1803*. The initially bucolic description of Albany in late May is suddenly interrupted when the poet addresses the black community:

Rise then, each son of Pinkster, rise,
Snatch fleeting pleasure as it flies.
See Nature spreads her carpet gay,
For you to dance your care away.
"Care! what have we with care to do?
Masters! Care was made for you.
Behold rich free-men—see dull care
Oft make their bodies lean and spare.

How many weave the web of life,
With wool of care, and warp of strife.
With care of state and statesman groans,
As if its weight would break his bones.
But what have we with care to do,
My Pinkster boys? 't is not for you."
Thus spake the genius of the day,
As up the hill she led the way.[32]

The *Ode* proceeds to a condemnation of slavery, which is paralleled by a speech in which King Charles calls for slave loyalty to their masters much along the lines of the *modus vivendi* of the past:

"Harken, ye sons of Ham, to me;
This day our Bosses make us free;
Now all the common on the hill,
Is ours, to do what e'er we will.
And let us by our conduct show,
We thank them as we ought to do. . . .
Let us with grateful hearts agree
Not to abuse our liberty.
Tho' lordlings proud may domineer,
And at our humble revels jeer,
Tho' torn from friends beyond the waves,
Tho' fate has doom'd us to be slaves,
Yet on this day, let's taste and see
How sweet a thing is Liberty,
What tho' for freedom we may sigh
Many long years until we die,
Yet nobly let us still endure
The ills and wrongs we cannot cure.
Tho' hard and humble be our lot,
The rich man's spleen we envy not.
While we have health, whence pleasure springs,
And peace to purchase fiddle-strings,
Let's with united voice agree
To hail this happy jubilee."[33]

With a racist undertone, the poet also comments on the responsibilities of the Pinkster King to keep the slave community under control:

Charles! didst thou ever see
A hundred monkeys on a tree,
A hundred more upon the ground,
With *orang outangs* playing round?
Such numbers there might be, and noise;
From such a multitude of boys.
But should the rubble, wrong and rude,
Dare on your dancing lines intrude,
Then beat the banjo, rub a dub,
And send the rogues to Beelzebub.[34]

Thereupon the *Ode* introduces a Jeffersonian Republican politician called "Jo Growler." In this passage, the poet ridicules the failed attempt by Democratic-Republicans to establish an alternative to the Federalist-controlled Bank of Albany.[35] Aimwell also makes a reference to salt, which relates to the demand of the petitioners of this new "State Bank" that it should grant them, exclusively, the rights over the Salina salt-springs:

Jo is a politician; he
Thro' thick and thin bawl'd Liberty!
Curst all the speculation laws,
Made but to pamper mister's maws.
Tells how the great Leviathan,
Last winter, "laid a monstrous plan;
And join'd the great ones of the deep—
First hush'd the centinels to sleep:
And then fell too with main and might,
Work'd double tides both day and night
And form'd a Bank, so strong and stout,
It damm'd the little fishes out.
Yes, friends, it was this monster's wish,
To eat up all the little fish.
And then to season such a fry,
He cast about with eager eye.
At length he spy'd (his nose's fault)
He spy'd the Onondaga Salt!
And with an appetite so keen,
He would have lick'd it all up clean;
And drank the lake, with every spring,
As if it were a little thing.

O had he swallow'd them by LAW!
They'd make a fire within his maw,
That soon would try his inward fat!
What! think to quiz a democrat!
Zounds! federals never us'd us so,
Nor gave us such a deadly blow.
By—whoever tempts the Western Whale
Must be more cautious of his tail.
O one of us! O Jefferson!
Where will thy head-strong children run!"[36]

The *Ode* ends with a reference to the African burial ground and the prospect of emancipation:

Now if you take a farther round
You'll reach the Africs' burying ground.
There as I rambled years ago,
To pass an hour of love-lorn woe;
I found a stone at Dinah's grave,
On which was carv'd the following stave:
Here lies Dinah, Sambo wife,
Sambo lub him like he life,
Dinah die 'bout sik week go,
Sambo massa tell he so. . . .
"Enough, says I, to Dinah's shade,
Thou too, wilt drudge no more, with spade,
Nor hoe, nor pot, nor washing tub,
Nor clean away-nor sweep, nor scrub.
Sleep on good wench, or only doze,
I'll not disturb thy blest repose.
Thy honest soul has wing'd its flight,
Beyond the reach of tyrant's sway;
In realms of everlasting light—
To meet good *Benezet* and *Lay.*"[37]

The mention of "Dinah's grave" is a likely allusion to the slave girl involved in the alleged 1793 plot, who after her execution was buried in the African cemetery near the place where the African American Pinkster celebrations occurred. Her death is connected to the names of Benjamin Lay and Anthony Benezet, two prominent Quaker abolitionists whom Aimwell highlights as models of patient reform.[38] The *Ode* should thus be understood as a call for patience to the slave community and an appeal to community leaders such as King Charles to ensure that slavery would come to an end without the eruption of more violence. This message of patient reform corresponds to early-nineteenth-century Federalist rhetoric in the political discussions over abolition.[39]

Journalists with Federalist sympathies also liked to make reference to the Pinkster festival when attacking or ridiculing their Jeffersonian Republican rivals. An article entitled "Duane's Jubilee (old style)" in the *Balance and Columbian Repository*, published in Hudson, Columbia County, in May 1804 mentioned that the black community "celebrated the glorious acquisition of Louisiana (old style) vulgarly called *Pinkster*.... We heard nothing about the festival, nor who was placed at the head of the table; and we wait for Capt. Stargazer to give us the toasts and to tell us whether they were drank intermingled with songs and great guns." It concludes with reference to "many processions," the storming of "Wind-mill-hill" and "salutes at noon (of night)—and that not only one Venus, but hundreds of them appeared to smile on the progress of democracy."[40] The content of this article reflects the virulent debate between the Federalist *Balance* and Charles Holt's newly founded Democratic-Republican *Bee*. The latter had moved from Connecticut to Columbia County in order to become the leading Democratic-Republican spokesperson in the region. The reference to Pinkster relates to the Louisiana Purchase in 1803, a decision by President Jefferson that had been bitterly opposed by Federalists. It also makes allusion to a dispute that had erupted in Pennsylvania in the aftermath of the purchase. The Pennsylvanian Democratic-Republican Party was divided between those who backed Governor Thomas McKean and a dissent faction, led by the influential *Aurora* newspaper publisher William Duane and the Philadelphia populist Michael Leib, that was dissatisfied with the governor's support for strong executive and judicial powers. To provoke Governor McKean, Duane and Leib had pointedly avoided toasting him at the celebration of the Louisiana Purchase in May 1804.[41] The bickering that followed was exploited to the maximum by the Federalist *Balance*, especially when it heard that its rival Holt had argued that an uncommon appearance of the planet Venus had occurred during the celebration, which he believed to be a sign of confidence in the progress of America's democracy. The *Balance* reacted to Holt's "vision" with a sarcastic reference to Pinkster as a festival "full of Venuses."

One of the very few articles on Pinkster reflecting a Dutch American perspective is a satirical piece about local politics in Federalist newspaper the *Albany Centinel*. In June 1805 an author with the Dutch name Snyder (Snijder) published an essay under the title "Alarm." In a parody allusion to Charles's royal status as "king" of the black community, Snyder playfully exploits the Jeffersonian Republican hatred of aristocratic rule, claiming that "from the manner in which Pinxter is observed in this city, by a part of the sovereign people, great danger is to be apprehended of the destruction of republicanism, and of the introduction of monarchy." He warns of "a man who styles himself a King, appears, dressed in robes of majesty, surrounded by a number of subjects, and lays the inhabitants under contribution. Some allege that there can be no danger, because the man is black. I beg such to consider that all men are equal, and to reflect on the conduct of him who is now the emperor of Hayti, and who is as back as jet."[42] Snyder then highlights a series of recent political failures and scandals involving members of the Democratic-Republican Party. Like Aimwell in his *Ode*, he makes allusion to the failed attempt to establish an alternative to the Bank of Albany and refers to Ebenezer Purdy, a Democratic-Republican politician who resigned from the Senate in 1805—pleading ill health—in order to avoid expulsion for bribery in connection with the Merchant's Bank Charter: "The king is old, and if he be not soon taken up, he may die, and thus elude the justice of a republican tribunal. . . . I would humbly suggest farther that if the Corporation will not interfere; whether the said king could not be brought before Judge Purdy (if alive) and have a fair trial, without bribery and corruption."[43]

These parody articles were written at a time when Federalist power in Albany had begun to crumble. By the 1780s yeoman farmers were about to constitute the majority of the population in counties that traditionally had been controlled by a handful of landowning families, which foreshadowed the inevitable shift in political power. In those years, the Albany Federalist Party was involved in an increasingly nervous power struggle. The landowning elite that had hoped that its wealth, prestige, and control over thousands of tenants would be sufficient to consolidate its power in the republic had, with the election of George Clinton as governor of New York in 1777, come to realize that the new political system represented a serious threat to its influence.

The worst nightmare of the landowning elite soon came true. In 1790 the antifederalist Abraham Yates was appointed mayor of the once-Federalist bulwark Albany. In 1800 the election of Jefferson as President of the United States represented a dramatic defeat for the Federalist party at the national level. Only one year later, the party suffered another major defeat in New York when its candidate Stephen van Rensselaer lost to Clinton his bid for the seat vacated by John Jay. With the introduction of universal manhood suffrage following the adoption of the constitutional convention of 1821, the political decline of the once almighty landowning families in rural parts of New York became unavoidable.

While many newspaper articles in those years brought up the topic of Pinkster with a satirical undertone, others highlighted the moral corruption—and thus the need for enlightened, Federalist guidance—of those who usually took part in the festival. As Simon Middleton has argued, the rural Federalist elite "agreed that all men were driven by natural appetites and passions, which only those of wealth and standing possessed the necessary virtue and refinement to overcome."[44]

Their conviction that the country would go to ruin without the moral guidance of an enlightened elite is reflected in an article from June 1803, allegedly consisting of a letter found on the street and submitted to the *Albany Centinel* by a certain A.B.: "The narration appears to have an allusion to this city but whether it was penned by some speculating Yankee or some ill-natured European . . . is uncertain. I hope . . . you will give it a place in your paper and that the corporation, and the inhabitants of our city, will, for the honor of human nature, make a wise improvement of it."[45] According to Bradfort Verter, A.B. possibly refers to Aaron Burr, who habitually signed his correspondence with this abbreviation. Although Burr loosely associated himself with the Democratic-Republican Party, his increasing distance from President Jefferson had attracted the attention of some Federalists, who hoped to use his political influence to build a common platform, hence his regular appearance in Federalist newspapers such as the *Albany Centinel*.[46] Whether A.B. actually refers to Aaron Burr is speculative. What can be affirmed with certainty, however, is that the article reflects the Anglo-American perspective of someone with Federalist sympathies, who is foreign to the Pinkster tradition.

A.B. clearly distinguishes himself from Albany's Dutch community. His unfamiliarity with the origins of the tradition is notable in the incorrect assumption that the Dutch American Pinkster festival had once been a purely religious feast that had only recently "degenerated into periodical seasons of dissipation." A.B. thus insinuates that what had been a decent celebration as long as it remained under the control of the Federalist elite got out of hand as soon as blacks and white, Democratic-Republican "rabble" took over the tradition. A.B. even raises the specter of miscegenation and the risk of America degenerating into a "mongrelized" nation if political leadership were taken out of the experienced hands of elite families. His typically Federalist conviction that only the guidance of a select group of wise men can prevent society from lapsing into chaos is evident in the article's final chapter: "These sports continue three days, and sometimes for four days and nights successively; during which and throughout the whole extent of the encampment, every vice is practiced without reproof and without reserve." According to A.B., "married negroes consider themselves as absolved, on these occasions, from their matrimonial obligations . . . all restraints are flung off, and nature, depraved nature, undisguised and without a veil, on every side is exhibited. Here lies a beastly black and there lies a beastly white, sleeping or wallowing in the mud or dirt." Nevertheless, "multitudes go up and reconnoiter the eminence on which the rare farrago are assembled, and where these shameful indecencies are tolerated, with as much apparent complacency as an eastern deacon going to a general training." And even worse, "parents, and Christian parents too, permit their children to go and even accompany them to this place of shameful dissipation—*Tell it not in Gath! Publish it not in the streets of Askalon*."[47] A.B.'s hope, expressed in the foreword, that the authorities would make a "wise improvement" of the letter indicates a desire to have the Pinkster festival prohibited. When the article was reprinted later that month in New York City, the *Daily Advertiser* included a note arguing that though "ancient inhabitants" might still remember Pinkster as a festival that formerly was "universally celebrated," "a change in manners" had "entirely abolished" the festival.[48] The decision by this New York City newspaper to emphasize the cultural distance between their readers and those of the "backward" Hudson Valley is remarkable, because other sources reveal that Pinkster was celebrated in Manhattan until at least 1809 and would continue to be celebrated on Long Island until the late nineteenth century. Rather than factual truth, this announcement about the end of Pinkster reflects an attempt to use the printing press as a means to attach opprobrium to Pinkster as an example of cultural backwardness and moral nuisance.

A negative bias also characterizes the reference to Pinkster in an anonymous article published in the *Albany Centinel* one year after A.B.'s detailed description of the festival. It reported on the "Death of Capt. Shawk," a black ferryman from Greenbush, near Albany, and reduced Pinkster to an ordinary drinking bout: "Upon that great Dutch holiday which they call Pinxster, he would dress himself in his best clothes, and indulge too much in idleness with his fellow blacks. This was the season in which he was most likely to be overcome with liquor." The author also argues that this was a general problem, since on Pinkster, "the servants wander abroad, drink, and frolic, all in honour of Pinxster; and have a license and opportunity of committing excess and lewdness which they have not upon any other day."[49] This bad reputation of Pinkster is also apparent in John Russell Bartlett's entry for "Pinxter" in his *Dictionary of Americanisms* (1848): "(Dutch, *pingster*) Whitsunday: 'On Pinxter Monday, the Dutch negroes of New York and New Jersey consider themselves especially privileged to get as drunk as they can.'"[50]

The negative publicity about Pinkster took effect. On July 17, 1804, the Albany Common Council passed a law "to regulate the amusements of the Negroes in the City of Albany during the Whitsuntide holidays," which stipulated that "no white persons shall during the Whitsuntide holiday erect or put up any Boothe Hut or Tent within the said City near to or where the Negroes shall erect or put up theirs, nor shall any white persons expose for sale any beer, Cyder, mead, spirituous liquors, or cake, crackers or any other kind of Refreshment at the place or places where the Negroes shall meet to carry on their said Amusements."[51] On April 28, 1811, the Common Council went a step further and prohibited the festival altogether because of "too much boisterous rioting and drunkenness," and determined that "no person shall erect any tent, booth or stall within the limits of this city, for the purpose of vending any spirituous liquors, beer, mead or cider, or any kind of meat, fish, cakes or fruit, on the days commonly called Pinxter," nor "to collect in numbers for the purpose of gambling or dancing, or any other amusements, in any part of the city, or to march or parade, with or without any kind of music, under a penalty of ten dollars or confinement in jail."[52]

It would be wrong to assume that these measures corresponded to the shift in power from the traditional elite composed by Dutch American, Federalist families, who had always tolerated and even supported the Pinkster festivities, to the new, Democratic-Republican, Anglo-American rulers. In fact, these prohibitions were all decided during the period 1799–1816, when Albany was ruled by the Dutch American, Federalist mayor Philip Schuyler van Rensselaer. Verter therefore claims that the Pinkster processions in Albany are to be understood as an expression of "democratic populism" that "challenged the settled power of the Federalist merchants who lorded over the local economy and the state government."[53] This theory is questionable because it fails to explain why a tradition that for decades had been tolerated and even supported by the landowning families would suddenly become directed against them. It can also be doubted that such a frontal attack on Albany's elite would have been allowed to begin in the noblest part of town, with a procession organized by slaves who were all owned by families whose power was allegedly being challenged.

Shane White has provided a different theory about the prohibition of Pinkster by the Albany city council. According to White, the prohibition related primarily to a growing concern with public morals in the context of the Second Great Awakening.[54] The prohibition of Pinkster coincided, in fact, with members of Albany's elite families supporting the "State Act for Suppressing Immorality" as well as the foundation of the "Albany Society for the Suppression of Vice and Immorality."[55] However, it should also be pointed out that by the time the Pinkster celebrations were prohibited, most elite landowning families in Albany were no longer in need of slave loyalty. While Dutch American yeoman farmers were still desperately trying to stop abolition, elite families such as the Gansevoorts had already divested themselves of their slaves and had hired cheap Irish contract workers instead.[56]

Pinkster's Demise

In his introduction to the 1867 reprint of James Eights's childhood recollections about Albany's Pinkster festival, Joel Munsell argues that "the excesses which attended these occasions were so great that in 1811 the common council was forced to prohibit the erection of booths and stalls, the parades, dances, gaming and drunkenness, with which they were attended, under penalty of fine or imprisonment" and, "being thereby deprived of their principal incitements and attractions, the anniversary soon fell into disuse, and is therefore unknown to the present generation."[57] While the decision by the Albany elite to withdraw their support and eventually to prohibit the annual celebrations at the occasion of Pentecost undoubtedly had an impact upon the tradition, it seems questionable that the ban alone put an end to the traditional Pinkster celebrations. As Verter has argued, "passing a law is easy, enforcing it considerably less so. Given the large number of regular attendants, enforcing a ban on Pinkster would have been very difficult indeed."[58]

Munsell uses another argument to explain the demise of Albany's African American Pinkster celebrations, suggesting that "on the death of King Charles, it was observed with less enthusiasm, and finally sank into such a low nuisance as to fall under the ban of the authorities."[59] This argument is even less convincing considering that king elections and celebrations must have had a long tradition and were unlikely to end because of the death of one specific king. Moreover, King Charles did not pass away before the 1811 ban but died in 1824, thirteen years later.[60] Munsell's affirmations on Pinkster should thus be taken with caution. In fact, in 1867 Munsell published his own recollections of a Pinkster celebration in Albany despite the fact that he only moved from Massachusetts to the Hudson Valley in 1826, fifteen years after the festival had been banned.[61]

One can thus assume that the festival continued to be celebrated in Albany long after the city ban, although on a more modest scale. This can be confirmed by the witness testimony in an 1844 court case in Troy, who affirmed: "I lived near the Steam Mill in Sandlake in the Spring of 1842; I recollect of Warger's going off to Albany to keep Pinkster."[62] In other areas, Pinkster celebrations continued until the late nineteenth century. In 1874 Gabriel Furman claimed in *Antiquities of Long Island* that "especially on the west end of this island, [Pinkster] is still much of a holiday," despite the fact that those celebrations could not be compared in size and importance to "the perfect saturnalia that was for a long period exhibited in its observance at Albany."[63]

Although small size Pinkster celebrations continued to be organized in isolated areas until the late nineteenth century, it cannot be denied that interest in the tradition among African Americans declined sharply in the first quarter of the nineteenth century. As White has observed, there was remarkably little concern among African Americans about the Pinkster tradition coming to an end.[64] This is confirmed by Claire Sponsler, who has showed that by the 1820s "respectable" blacks had begun to shun the festival.[65]

This increased concern for public morality and respectability among African Americans coincides with the foundation of the first black evangelical churches.[66] By 1815 10 percent of the members of Albany's Methodist Church consisted of African Americans, and soon the black Methodist community was big enough to form its own church. In 1820 the African Baptist Church also established its first congregation in Albany.[67] When evangelical churches began to reach out to the black community, their proselytizing activities undoubtedly had a negative effect on a popular festival like Pinkster that was at odds with Protestant morality. This was not a new phenomenon. The 1709 Communications of the Society for the Propagation of the Gospel had already explicitly mentioned that one of the conditions of slave baptism was the requirement not to "spend the Lord's Day in feasts, dances and merry meetings."[68] The anonymous account by a member of Albany's African American community confirms that in the early years of black Methodist and Baptist churches, "it was against church rules to indulge in dancing."[69] As Dena Epstein has argued in regard to the Second Great Awakening, the "repudiation of dancing was neither eccentric nor an isolated phenomenon, but widespread and quite general among both white and black converts to various evangelical sects."[70]

Charles Rockwell's childhood recollections of a Pinkster celebration in Milford, Pennsylvania, in the 1840s show that blacks who had become members of a Protestant church community refrained from dancing. Rockwell recalled the following conversation: "I said to the old woman, 'Peggy, why don't you dance?' To which she replied, 'I tell you, Charlie, I is just spilin' for a dance but my old man is de sexton ob de Presbyterian Church and dey don't like dancin.'"[71] Moral concerns about traditional Pinkster celebrations by those who joined an evangelical church community are also notable in the case of Diana Mingo, a former slave from Schodack, Rensselaer County, who moved to Albany after she had become free. In Albany she used to "take part in the unique celebrations of her race on 'Pinxter' . . . hill, just west of Eagle Street, beyond the hospital, in the company of 'King Charley' (a sort of leviathan Ethiopian dressed in scarlet coat with gold lace trimmings and other showy uniform)." But ever since she joined "the organization of the colored Methodist church . . . she has been an exemplary member" and "this half-heathen observance was strongly contrasted by the religious character of her long life in church."[72]

John Jea's *Life History* (1811) is indicative of the religious transition that took place within New York's black community in the first quarter of the nineteenth century. Jea was born in Nigeria in 1773 and grew up as a field slave of a Dutch or German family in rural New York.[73] While one can assume that he participated in Pinkster celebrations in his youth, he radically rejected any type of Dionysian pleasure after joining an evangelical church community. Significantly, Jea felt disgusted when he visited New Orleans and witnessed people dancing on Sundays and doing "every evil thing that could be mentioned."[74] Nevertheless, Pentecost remained important to him from a religious and communal point of view. In his *Life History*, Jea highlights how "at our watch nights and camp meetings, I have known one hundred and fifty, or two hundred, awakened at one time; by which it was evident that the time was like the day of Pentecost."[75]

It would, in fact, be wrong to interpret the conscious decision by African Americans to reject the boisterous Pinkster celebrations after they had joined an evangelical church community as a complete rejection of their social and cultural heritage. While the "immoral" aspects of these celebrations that proved to be incompatible with evangelicalism (the consumption of alcohol, sensual flirting, erotic dances) were rejected, the spiritual, emancipatory, and communal elements of the festival translated to the black evangelical churches. As Thornton has convincingly demonstrated, the evangelical wave of the Great Awakening was perceived as a revelation of the Holy Spirit.[76] For a community that prepared itself for life in a post-slavery society, it was an acceptable, even logical alternative for the traditional Pinkster celebration that was deeply marked by slavery. Those who had once emphatically celebrated Pinkster could easily make the transition from Afro-Catholic spirituality to black evangelical spirituality in the context of a new form of brother- and sisterhood that corresponded better to their new status of emancipated citizens.

As Michael Gomez has suggested, Afro-Catholic traditions with roots in West-Central Africa must have played a crucial role in the development of African American evangelical Christianity.[77] The latter was, in fact, not simply an imitation of white Christian churches. There is ample evidence that long before the first officially recognized black churches were established, Afro-Christian communities already existed in New York and New Jersey.[78] In 1775 an advertisement in *Rivington's New-York Gazetteer* mentioned the case of a runaway slave called Mark from Bergen County who was "a preacher."[79] In 1783 the *New-York Gazette and the Weekly Mercury* posted an advertisement on a runaway slave called Anthony who "pretends to be a preacher, and sometimes officiates in that capacity among the Blacks."[80] In 1786 the *New Jersey Gazette* mentioned the case of a slave called Gilbert who "can read very well, pretends to be religious, and sometimes undertakes to preach."[81] Other runaway slaves were described as "very religious, preaches to his colour, walks before burials, and marries" and "a great professor of religion, and has much to say on the subject."[82] In remote areas in New York such as Owego, the Bethel African Methodist Church even continued to organize colorful brotherhood processions to the accompaniment of the beating of a drum until the beginning of the twentieth century. According to the *Owego Gazette* of July 1911, these paraders "were grotesquely costumed, representing historical personages, who were gorgeously arrayed in discarded regalia of fraternal societies."[83]

As with the former brotherhoods, black evangelical churches gave great importance to burial procedures. Significantly, the African Society, the first known black evangelical society in New York City, founded in 1795, gave priority

to the purchase of land for its own cemetery.[84] Members were also greatly concerned about their coffins and, in times of need, the church community gathered together to purchase a decent coffin for deceased members.[85] Following an
old brotherhood tradition, these churches focused not only on the spiritual but
also the material needs of poorer members by collecting money, food, and other
necessities.[86]

This focus on the betterment of the African American population corresponded to that of the black mutual-aid societies that developed in the early
nineteenth century, many of which were linked to newly founded black evangelical churches.[87] As Craig Wilder and Ned Sublette have argued, the explosive
growth of black mutual-aid associations in North America in the early nineteenth century must have drawn on existing traditions of mutual aid within
the slave community.[88] Without the earlier presence of brotherhoods, this sudden proliferation of black mutual-aid associations can hardly be explained. This
evolution may, in fact, parallel the transition from brotherhoods to mutual-aid
societies in post-slavery Cuban society and other Caribbean societies.[89] In
their report on *Friendly Societies in the West Indies*, A. F. and D. Wells point out
that there are "interesting suggestions of mutual-aid movements . . . founded
upon traditions brought overseas by the slaves themselves."[90] And in his study
on early-nineteenth-century mutual-aid and burial societies in the Bahamas,
Howard Johnson observes that slaves used to form groups according to their
"nations" and suggests that "an organization of that type, on a more informal
basis, might have existed during the slavery era."[91] Remarkably, one of these
Bahamian mutual-aid societies was called the "Congo Nr. 1 Society." In August
1888 representatives of this society sent a letter in the name of the "Natives of the
Congo" to Leopold II, "King of the Belgians and King of the Congo Free State,"
with the request to allow them to return.[92] In Philadelphia one black mutual-aid
association called itself the Angolan Society, and thus probably kept the name
of the slave "nation" that once created the brotherhood.[93]

As William Kennedy has shown, early-nineteenth-century black mutual-aid
associations in Albany functioned as "fraternal organizations" that "cared for the
sick and buried the dead."[94] For instance, the United Society of Chimney Sweeps
in Albany gave priority to care for the burial of deceased members and the
maintenance of "mutual control over the members."[95] Another black mutual-aid
association in Albany, the Burdett-Coutts Benevolent Association, was presided
by Adam Blake, the son of a former slave with the same name whom James
Eights recalled as master of ceremonies in King Charles's Pinkster parades.[96]
As did brotherhoods, these mutual-aid associations excelled in organizing
parades.[97] For instance, the New York African Society for Mutual Relief marked
its anniversary in 1809 with a parade carrying silk banners; and on Emancipation Day 1827, a parade took place in Albany led by what the *Albany Argus*

and City Gazette described as "African bands and Marshals."[98] When abolition was announced, the Wilberforce Society even publicly displayed its mutual-aid fund, or treasury chest, that was "raised by weekly subscription, which is employed in assisting sick and unfortunate blacks." What for decades had to be kept hidden in shady taverns and other secret places could now proudly be shown to the public. The fund, contained in a blue box, "was carried in the procession; the treasurer holding in his hand a large gilt key; the rest of the officers wore ribands [*sic*] of several colors, and badges like the officers of free masons; marshals with long staves walked outside the procession. During a quarter of an hour, scarcely any but black faces were to be seen in Broadway."[99]

As Mitch Kachun has suggested, the parades organized by nineteenth-century black mutual-aid organizations must have been a continuation of the old king processions observed during Pinkster.[100] Significantly, on July 5, 1827 (Emancipation Day), "Grand Marshal" Samuel Hardenburgh paraded through the streets of New York City in the same way that "King" Charles had once done in Albany. Hardenburgh was wearing a "cocked hat and drawn sword, mounted on a milk-white steed." He was followed by "his aids on horseback, dashing up and down the line; then the orator of the day, also mounted, with a handsome scroll, appearing like a baton in his right hand." Then in due order, "splendidly dressed in scarfs of silk with gold-edgings, and with colored bands of music, and their banners appropriately lettered and painted, followed, The New York African Society for Mutual Relief, The Wilberforce Benevolent Society and The Clarkson Benevolent Society."[101] Unlike Charles, however, Samuel Hardenburgh was no longer a slave but a free man, and the organization he led was no longer a semi-secret brotherhood but an officially recognized mutual-aid association.[102]

While the former Pinkster parades in New York and Election Day parades in New England do not seem to have evoked negative reactions by white bystanders, parades in the post-slavery era were often met with violence and insults.[103] As is reflected in the infamous Boston broadsheets that ridiculed "de African Shocietee," its "sheef Marsal," and its "Bobalition parades," black mutual-aid associations were often the victim of white derision.[104] Alexis de Tocqueville's observation in *Democracy in America* (1835) that "the prejudice which repels Negroes seems to increase in proportion as they are emancipated" also applies to black parade culture.[105] African Americans were systematically excluded from ceremonial events in the new republic. Parades to mark Evacuation Day (celebrating the British retreat from New York), Washington's Birthday, the Fourth of July, and the ratification of the Constitution could be viewed by blacks, but only whites could march.[106]

This change in mood was a direct consequence of abolition. Festivals such as Pinkster and Election Day used to have the consent and even support of influential slaveholders who considered it useful to maintain a good relationship with the "kings" and "governors" of the slave population. Following abolition, however, such festivals and parades not only lost their importance for the white ruling class but now also represented a potential threat to its authority. Even Federalists who had favored abolition never wished to see the black community acting as self-confident citizens, prone to demand their place as equals in the public sphere. On top of that, the aggravation of job competition following the wave of white immigration intensified anti-black sentiments among the white working class, who feared blacks as competitors on the job market. These fears fueled popular white resistance against the right of blacks to make equal use of public spaces.[107]

However, within the black community itself there also was a growing opposition to the traditional African American procession culture.[108] As Kachun has shown, post-abolition black community leaders were concerned with inculcating a Protestant morality based on self-restraint, education, and sobriety among their members, and thereby distanced themselves from the "clouds of paganism and error" they identified in traditional cultural practices deemed inappropriate for respectable free citizens in the modern republic.[109] Since this attitude implied a growing concern with morally dubious behavior on the part of their members during festive parades, black community leaders launched a campaign against the traditional procession culture. *Freedom's Journal*, in particular, was engaged in this endeavor. Using many of the same moralistic arguments the Dutch Reformed Church had once used to oppose the popular Pinkster celebrations, this newspaper complained about "the insolence of certain Coloured females" and "debasing excesses." It claimed that blacks should spend their money on food and decent clothing rather than on silly costumes because "nothing is more disgraceful to the eyes of a reflecting man of colour than one of these grand processions, followed by the lower orders of society."[110] Community leaders such as Samuel Cornish and Peter William Jr. no longer wished to place themselves in the tradition of Pinkster, a festival with a dubious moral reputation that was incompatible with the Protestant morality of Cornish's Presbyterian Church and William's Episcopal Church. Frederick Douglass also lashed out to the participants in parades as "a vastly undue proportion of the most unfortunate, unimproved, and unprogressive class of the colored people."[111]

Such arguments corresponded to an international pattern. In post-abolition Cuba, for instance, a new generation of black community leaders also urged their members to rid themselves of traditional customs. One of them, Martín Morúa Delgado, argued that "an immoral people, a perverted people can never be free. . . . We ought to limit the number of dances because they only produce vicious acts and customs."[112] In similar terms, the Afro-Haitian writer Louis Joseph Janvier launched a campaign to eradicate all Afro-Catholic traditions on the island. Advocating the civilizing influence of Protestant Christianity, he went as far as to claim that "the Protestant is thrifty and self-reliant, he does not waste his money on carnivals and other frivolities. . . . The Protestant is almost always a more practical worker and a better citizen than the Catholic."[113]

The new generation of American black community leaders in North America disliked the traditional Pinkster and Election Day festivities not only because of moral concerns but also because these festivals were rooted in the old brotherhood tradition of "cooperative resistance" from the era of slavery, which clashed with their eagerness to debunk the stereotype of the black man as a subservient Uncle Tom. As Joseph Reidy has argued about Election Day, "generally unmindful of its earlier positive contributions, [new black community leaders] saw it only as an anachronism devoid of any tactical or strategic relevance."[114] In fact, the new generation no longer demanded small concessions, as the kings and governors of brotherhoods had done in the old days. They expected to be treated as equal citizens at all levels.

In 1827 a bitter debate took place among the representatives of New York's black population about the way emancipation had to be commemorated. The new generation that insisted on a low-key celebration "without any public procession" was countered by those who still placed themselves in the old brotherhood tradition and proposed a "Grand Procession, Oration and Public Dinner." Unable to reach a compromise, each group ended up holding its own ceremony: one group on the fourth of July, the other on the fifth.[115] In 1834 the new generation obtained a victory when the National Convention of Free People of Colour passed a resolution with the words: "[W]e disapprove, will discountenance and suppress, so far as we have the power or influence, the exhibition and procession usually held on the fifth of July annually, in the city of New-York; and all other processions of coloured people, not necessary for the interment of the dead." This resolution had passed with only two dissenting votes, one of which had come from Marshall Samuel Hardenburgh, who desperately held on to the old brotherhood traditions.[116]

However, the victory of the new black political elite over the old procession culture was deceptive. Despite the resolution being passed, many African Americans reacted in the same way as ordinary seventeenth-century Dutch people had done to pressure from the Calvinist elite: they ignored the concerns expressed by those who considered themselves their spiritual and moral leaders. In August 1840 Charles Bennett Ray's the *Colored American* angrily reported that some people had shamefully ignored concerns from the National Convention of Free People of Colour at the August First celebration in Newark and complained that "a number came in from the country, with a drum and fife, formed a procession, which was fallen in with by a few of the more thoughtless of the place, all of whom conducted themselves in a manner deeply mortifying to the mass of our people in Newark."[117]

African Americans also held on to traditional parade culture in other parts of the country. In January 1863, for instance, the *New York Herald* reported how blacks in Key West had celebrated emancipation with "about two hundred and fifty niggers, of all sizes, ages and complexions, marching in columns of twos, with proper officers . . . commanded by 'Sandy,' a venerable nigger of huge proportions." In the old brotherhood tradition, Sandy "was attired in a full suit of black, with a sash and rosette on his breast of enormous size and of the most gaudy colors; he has suspended to his side a cavalry sabre and wore an army fatigue cap."[118] In March 1865 four thousand blacks gathered in Charleston, South Carolina, and paraded through the city in step with dancing musicians and "two marshals sitting high above the crowd on horseback, wearing red, white, and blue rosettes and blue sashes."[119] Peter Rutkoff and William Scott even assume that the parades with music, banners, and flags involving the unofficial election of the mayor of Bronzeville, Chicago, by local black residents in the 1930s may have been inspired by the Pinkster tradition.[120] Reidy also claims that in rural Mississippi in the 1860s, the Georgia Sea Islands and Rockford, Illinois, in the 1930s, and Harlem in the 1970s, African Americans elected leaders in the tradition of Pinkster.[121] Rather than being directly influenced by the New York Pinkster celebrations, however, these election ceremonies show the dissemination of and attachment to rituals with roots in the old brotherhood tradition.[122]

Minstrelsy

Pinkster traditions also survived outside of African American parade culture. The reference to Master Diamond's famous double-shuffle and heel-and-toe breakdown in Joel Munsell's recollections of the bygone Pinkster tradition in Albany shows how certain elements of the Pinkster festival also evolved into what came to be known in the 1840s as "minstrel shows." Munsell establishes a direct connection between the traditional Pinkster celebrations and these shows: "[Pinkster] festivals seldom failed to attract large crowds from the city, as well as from the rural districts, affording them a huge amount of unalloyed fun. Negro minstrelsy has held its own to the present day, it now being in full feather, and is likely to continue for years to come."[123] Around the same time, a similar claim was made by Joseph Felt in regard to the traditionally black festivities on "Negro Election Days" in New England. According to Felt, this traditionally black entertainment "was followed by a small proportion of whites until a recent period."[124]

In recent scholarship, Claire Sponsler and Dale Cockrell also claim that certain elements of Pinkster festivals lived on in minstrelsy.[125] Cockrell observes that minstrel characters such as George Washington Dixon's Zip Coon were

ZIP COON

ON THE GO-AHEAD PRINCIPLE.

I went down to Sandy hollar t'other arternoon,
I went down to Sandy hollar t'othe**w** arternoon,
I went down to Sandy hollar t'other arternoon,
An de first man I chanc'd to meet war ole Zip Coon,
 Ole Zip Coon he is a larn'd scholar,
 Ole Zip Coon he is a larn'd scholar,
 Ole Zip Coon he is a larn'd scholar,
For he plays upon de banjo, "Cooney in de hollar."
  Tudle tadle, tudle, tadle, tuadellel dump,
  O tuadellel, tuadellel, tuadellel dump,
  Ri tum tuadellel, tuadelleldec.

Cooney in de hollar an racoon up a stump,
 Cooney in de hollar, &c.
And all dose 'tickler tunes Zip use to jump.
 Oh de Buffo Dixon he beat Tom Rice,—*(repeat.)*
And he walk into Jim Crow a little too nice.

Ole Sukey Blueskin she is in love with me,
 Ole Sukey Blueskin, &c.
An I went to Suke's house all for to drink tea,
 An what do you think Sue and I had for supper,
 An what do you think, &c.
Why possum fat an hominy, without any butter.

My old missus she's mad wid me,
 My ole missus, &c.
Kase I wouldn't go wid her into Tennessee.
 Massa build him a barn to put in fodder,
 Massa build him, &c.
'Twas dis ting an dat ting, one thing or odder.

Did you eber see he wild goose sailing on a ocean,
 Did you eber, &c.
De wild goose motion is a mighty pretty notion,
 De wild goose wink and he beacon to de swallow,
 De wild goose wink, &c.
An de wild goose hollar google, google gollar.

I spose you heard ob de battle New Orleans,
 I spose you heard, &c.
Whar ole gineral Jackson gib de British beans;
 Dare the Yankee boys de de job so slick,
 Dare de Yankee, &c.
For dey cotch Pakenham, an row'd him up de creek.

Away down south dare close to the moon,
 Away down, &c.
Dare lives a nullifier what they call Calhoun,
 When gineral Jackson kills Calhoun,
 When gineral, &c.
Why de berry next President be ole Zip Coon.

He try to run ole Hickory down,
 He try to run, &c.
But he strike a snag an run aground,
 Dis snag by gum war a wapper,
 Dis snag by, &c.
And sent him into dock to get a new copper.

In Phil a del fie is old Biddle's Bank,
 In Phil a del fie, &c.
Ole Hickory zamin'd him an found him rather crank
 He tell Nick to go and not make a muss,
 He tell Nick to go, &c.
So hurrah for Jackson he's de boy for us.

Possum on a log play wid im toes,
 Possum on a log, &c.
Up comes a guinea hog and off he goes,
 Buffalo in cane break, ole owl in a bush,
 Buffalo in a canebreak, &c.
Laffin at de blacksnake trying to eat mush.

Nice corn's a growing, Sukey loves gin,
 Nice corn's a growing, &c.
Rooster's done crowing at ole niggars shin,
 Oh Coone's in de hollar and a Possum in de stubble,
 Oh Coone's in the hollar, &c.
And its walk chalk ginger blue, jump double trouble.

Oh a bullfrog sot an watch an alligator,
 Oh a bullfrog sot, &c.
An jump upon a stump an offer him a tater;
 De alligator grinned an tried for to blush,
 De alligator grinned, &c.
An de bullfrog laughed an cried oh hush.

Oh if I was president ob dese Nited States,
 Oh if I was, &c.
I'd lick lasses candy and swing upon de gates,
 An does I dina like why I strike em off de docket,
 An does I dina like, &c.
De way I ns'd em up was a sin to Davy Crocket.

L. DEMING, at the sign of the Barber's Pole, No. 62, Hanover Street, Boston; and at MIDDLEBURY, Vt. Sold wholesale and retail, by

Anonymous, *Zip Coon*, ca. 1832. This broadside, published by Leonard Deming (Boston), depicts George Washington Dixon's minstrelsy character Zip Coon with a sword and a broom, as a mixture of a Pinkster king and chimney sweep. Courtesy the American Antiquarian Society.

depicted with a sword and a broom, as a mixture of a Pinkster king and chimney sweep. Dixon, whom some believed to be a mulatto, was derided by his
enemies with terms reminiscent of black brotherhoods such as "Field Marshal,"
"Capting" (sic), and "King of Congo."[126] As Cockrell suggests, "Zip Coon was
around, at least sartorially, when the Pinkster King in New York wore a British
brigadier's jacket of scarlet, a tricornered cocked hat, and yellow buckskins."[127]

This connection corresponds to the assumption by Shane White that many
of the constituent elements of minstrel shows had their origins in white observations of northern black culture in places such as New York City's Mulberry
Bend, the Bowery, and Five Points, where poor whites and blacks lived side
by side.[128] It was in Five Points that Charles Dickens in 1842 observed a black
dancer, who performed the same type of dance passes Munsell mentioned in his
characterization of King Charles's performance in Albany: "Single shuffle, double shuffle, cut and cross-cut; snapping his fingers, rolling his eyes, turning in his
knees, presenting the backs of his legs in front, spinning about on his toes and
heels like nothing but the man's fingers on the tambourine."[129] As Eric Lott has
argued, early minstrel figures were known to resist with provocation the stifling
Protestant ethics of their time. It is, thus, not unlikely that some minstrel dancers had in their youth been among those in the white community who ignored
moral concerns against participation at slave celebrations such as Pinkster.[130]

African American Pinkster celebrations had always attracted the curiosity
of whites. No other tradition could have served as better evidence that African
American music and dance had the potential to reach nationwide popularity
among people of all ethnic backgrounds. The fame of Dutch-speaking African American dancers also survived in local folklore. The legend of Martense's
Lane in Brooklyn tells the story of a "Dutch Negro" who challenged the devil
to dance. According to the *Saratoga Sentinel*, "the Negro and the devil began a
breakdown, and the former danced with such energy and so long that the devil
was completely tired out, and angrily kicking the boulder so hard as to leave his
footprint there, he disappeared." The newspaper continues that "the old Dutch
Negroes, as they were called, were famous for their dancing. The veteran Long
Islanders are wont to tell stories of Negroes dancing for eels on a barn floor in
the olden times, and they say that modern minstrelsy is a tame imitation of the
fun given by these old Dutch servants."[131]

Since the beginning of the nineteenth century, certain elements of Pinkster
festivals had also become integrated in white popular theater. This is evident from
the *New York Evening Post* announcement of a "pantomime interlude . . . Pinxter
Monday or Harlequin's frolics" in May 1804.[132] Considering that early minstrelsy
was an interstitial art whereby minstrels performed between the acts of "respectable" theatrical productions, this "interlude" indicates that minstrelsy was a continuation of a tradition that had already been initiated in New York City in the

late eighteenth century.[133] In fact, the nation's earliest reference to a "Negro dance" in a stage entertainment, dating back to April 9, 1767, appeared precisely in the *New York Journal.*[134]

Open markets played an important role in the transition of Pinkster traditions to minstrelsy. In his *Annals and Occurrences of New York City and State in the Olden Days* (1846), John Watson writes that "the negroes used to dance in the markets, where they used tomtoms, horns, &c., for music."[135] In 1829 it was observed that "Negro Pinxter music" had become a popular whistling tune in New York City, which was illustrated with a saying from the Fly Market: "With hurried step and nodding knee, the Negroes keep their jubilee; While Cuffee, with protruding lip, bravuras to the darky's skip."[136] The Fly Market was held at the foot of Maiden Lane on Manhattan, facing the East River. It dated back to Dutch times, as revealed in the word *fly* derived from the Dutch *vallei*, meaning valley or creek.[137] The Fly Market had the reputation of being a rough area. One of New York City's black criminal gangs in the mid-nineteenth century was known as the Fly Boys.[138] It was there that the Irish American Johnny "Master" Diamond had started to dance for throw money in the late 1830s and acquired fame with his "Negro Camptown Hornpipe," "Ole Virginny Breakdown," "Double Shuffle," "Smokehouse Dance," "Five Mile Out of Town Dance," and other types of violin dances. Around 1840 the showman Phineas Taylor Barnum engaged Diamond to perform at the Vauxhall Gardens and later took him on a traveling minstrel show, where he toured as "King of Diamonds" or "Master Diamond" through the United States and Europe in the circus circuit.[139] In those early years of minstrelsy, professional dancers typically challenged locals to beat them. Diamond's main rival was the black minstrel William Henry Lane, known as "Master Juba," whose dances Sterling Stuckey believes to have been inspired by the Pinkster festival and whose name Roger Abrahams relates to the Kikongo verb *zuba*, to slap.[140]

The connection between Pinkster celebrations and the dances at the Fly Market is also notable in Henry Stiles's *History of the City of Brooklyn* (1867–70). According to Stiles, there was intense commercial traffic, especially by butchers, on the ferries that connected the old market in Brooklyn with Manhattan's Fly Market. These butchers were assisted by "Dutch Negroes," who used to celebrate "their annual Pinkster holiday" on the Brooklyn market.[141] One can assume that many of these "Dutch Negroes" spoke Dutch as their native language. In fact, markets in New York City preserved a Dutch character well into the nineteenth century. When the native Dutch Reverend Gerardus Bosch visited America in 1826, he wrote in his diary that on market days, when farmers from New Jersey and Long Island came over to New York City, one could still hear many people speaking Dutch.[142] The old Washington Market in downtown Manhattan, for instance, had an addition along Vesey Street, between Greenwich and

Washington, that was known as the Buttermilk Market. According to the *Daily Graphic*, this used to be "a great mart for the sale of butter, cheese, curd, eggs and buttermilk, which were brought over the river by the Jersey Dutch women."[143]

By the time the Dutch language was disappearing in America, there were still many people in New York and New Jersey who had grown up in a Dutch-speaking environment and who must have spoken a singular form of English, characterized by a Dutch accent.[144] While we do not know how their English sounded, there are strong indications that their accent was characterized by the replacement of the voiced dental fricative /ð/ with the alveolar stop /d/ or /t/. This transfer effect that typically occurs when native speakers of Dutch talk English was observed by Alexander Coventry, who notes in 1785 in his diary that "[t]he Low Dutch understood and could talk the English language, though generally pronounced the 'th' as if 'd.'"[145] This characteristic consistently shows up in reproductions of the English speech of African Americans who had grown up in a predominantly Dutch-speaking environment. For example, the *Troy Daily Whig* published in 1837 a story about an "old fashioned Dutch Negro," whose English speech was reproduced by the author as "dis coat," "dot's all" and "if dey got a chance."[146] We encounter the same characteristic in an article from January 29, 1852, in the *Oneida Morning Gerald* (Utica, New York), where the author reproduced the English spoken by an "old Dutch Negro" as "dat's my young missus," "my mudder," and "my fader." The article also pointed out the use of typically Dutch phrases with English words such as "How does you do now-a-tays mit yourself?," an almost literal translation of the Dutch *Hoe gaat het met jou?*[147]

The influence of Pinkster on early minstrelsy in New York raises the question of whether minstrels may have copied not only the way blacks danced but also the way they spoke, and whether it was through minstrelsy that some originally Low Dutch words and expressions acquired nationwide use. Among these words may have been the term "boss"—derived from the Dutch *baas*, meaning master. In his *Letters from America*, dating to 1818–20, James Flint observes that "Master is not a word in the vocabulary of hired people. *Boss*, a Dutch one of similar import, is substituted. The former is used by Negroes, and is by free people considered as synonymous with slave-keeper."[148] This is confirmed by John Bartlett, who in his *Dictionary of Americanisms* (1848) writes that the word "probably originated in New York, and is now used in many parts of the US. The blacks often employ it in addressing white men in the Northern States, as they do *massa* (master) in the Southern States."[149] Although less likely, another word that may have entered American English through Low Dutch is the n-word—possibly derived from the Dutch word *neger* that was commonly used to refer to a black person.[150] Although the n-word in American English is generally considered to be a phonetic spelling of the white Southern (mis)pronunciation of Negro, it should be pointed out that the first use of this word in a North American context occurred when English colonists in Virginia bought slaves from a Dutch slave trader in 1619: "About the last of August came in a dutch man of warre that sold us twenty *Negars*."[151] As Randall Kennedy has shown, the n-word did not originate as a slur in American English but only took on a derogatory connotation by the end of the first third of the nineteenth century, which coincides with the beginning of minstrelsy in New York City.[152]

A connection between Pinkster, "market dancing" and minstrelsy has also been provided by Thomas De Voe, who in his *Market Book* (1862) shows how Catherine Market in Manhattan was a place where slaves from Long Island, in search of pocket money in preparation for Pinkster, performed dances. According to De Voe, "they would be hired by some joking butcher or individual to engage in a jig or break-down, as that was one of their pastimes at home on the barn-floor, or in a frolic, and those that could and would dance soon raised a collection." Yet, some of them did more "in 'turning around and shying off' from the designated spot than keeping to the regular 'shake-down,' which caused them all to be confined to a 'board,' (or shingle, as they called it,) and not allowed off it." De Voe explains that "each had his particular 'shingle' brought with him as part of his stock in trade. This board was usually about five to six feet long, of large width, with its particular spring in it, and to keep it in its place while dancing on it, it was held down by one on each end." Their music was "usually given by one of their party, which was done by beating their hands on the sides of their legs and the noise of the heel."[153]

Catherine Market was located in the neighborhood where the famous minstrel Thomas Dartmouth Rice grew up, which makes it likely that he too was familiar with Pinkster celebrations. In 1837 James Gordon Bennett, the editor of the *New York Herald*, confirmed that Rice had carefully studied "the negro character in all its varieties. He eat [sic], drank and slept with them, went to their frolics, and made himself the best white black man in existence."[154] It was in that same neighborhood that Micah Hawkins wrote the earliest American blackface song: "Backside Albany." The song ridiculed the British during the War of 1812 and was to be sung "in the character of a Negro sailor."[155]

Charles Rockwell's *Recollections* (1880) also point to a connection between Pinkster and minstrelsy. According to Rockwell, "when the tune was that to which the song of the 'Bowery Gals' was sung and came to the chorus, all joined in singing it" and "old men whose heads began to show the white and appeared to show the infirmities of age as they walked along the streets would take a young girl for a partner and dance the Virginia reel equal to George Christy in his palmy days." Later, "they began to sing a song called *Jim Crow*" and "at the close of the chorus some one of the girls or boys would take the floor and throw off some of their best steps to a music called *Patting Juber*, which was clapping the hands and keeping time with the foot."[156] This scene reveals how minstrel dances such as Thomas Dartmouth Rice's "Jump Jim Crow" (1828), Cool White's "Buffalo Gals" (1844), and the "Juba Dance" that had been popularized in 1840s by William Lane had become part of Pinkster celebrations. This indicates that minstrel adaptations of African dances that had once been performed at Pinkster festivals were embraced by African Americans in the late 1840s, who thereupon reintroduced their own adaptations of these dances in mid-nineteenth-century Pinkster celebrations.[157]

This conclusion partly contradicts Frederick Douglass's critical interpretation of minstrelsy as the work of "the filthy scum of white society, who have stolen from us a complexion denied to them by nature, in which to make money, and pander to the corrupt taste of their white fellow citizens."[158] As Rockwell's memoires indicate, many African Americans in the 1840s were not at all disgusted by minstrelsy but rather copied these dances enthusiastically. While it is understandable that in his eagerness to debunk stereotypical images of blacks, Douglass distanced himself from Pinkster and even more so from white blackface adaptations of its songs and dances, there can be no doubt that minstrelsy was more than just a white caricature of blacks that only appealed to the "corrupt taste" of the "filthy scum of white society." Despite its tendency to parody and ridicule blacks (but also Germans, Irish, and Dutch), early minstrelsy did reflect a genuine interest in black performance culture.[159] W. T. Lhamon goes as far as to claim that early minstrelsy had an antiracist dimension that "saw blacks as people with an implicit intelligence evidenced by explicit talent, irony, and capacious resistance."[160] While certain verses in minstrel songs such as "Jim Crow" mocked blacks, Cockrell has shown that others were surprisingly anti-slavery, such as:

> Should dey get to fighting,
> Perhaps the blacks will rise,
> For deir wish for freedom,
> Is shining in deir eyes....
> I'm for freedom,
> And for Union altogether,
> Aldough I'm a black man,
> De white is call'd my broder.[161]

The content of early minstrel songs like "Jim Crow" corresponds to the same mixture of condescension and admiration one finds in Absalom Aimwell's *Pinkster Ode* (1803), which again indicates that what later came to be known as minstrelsy had its roots in an early-nineteenth-century tendency to introduce certain elements of African American performance culture into white mainstream popular culture. While this tendency was naturally influenced by the white racist stereotyping of that time, it also reflected curiosity and even fascination with black performance culture.

It is possible that this tendency did not limit itself to white popular music and dance but also applied to parade culture. In 1898 Orville Platt claimed that to the conventional wisdom of the era, festive parades organized by whites in New England had been inspired by black traditions.[162] Roger Abrahams confirms that by the late nineteenth century, many originally black celebrations were "taken over by working-class ethnic whites through parish organizations."[163] In their study *In Hope of Liberty* (1997), James and Lois Horton argue that there must have been a connection between the appearance of blackface parades in America and the ban on black participation on militia days. They suggest that the use of blackface in white parade culture directly relates to the decline of opportunities for whites to participate directly in familiar aspects of black celebration culture.[164] This assumption allows for a different explanation of the parallels between African American Pinkster processions and white parades known as "Callithumpians" and "Fantasticals." While they have traditionally been explained with reference to European carnival and charivari traditions, "Callithumpians" and "Fantasticals" may—like minstrelsy—also have originated out of a mixture of fascination with and parody of black performance traditions.[165]

James Fenimore Cooper

Pinkster also entered America's mainstream culture through literature, when James Fenimore Cooper devoted an extensive passage to the festival in *Satanstoe, or The Littlepage Manuscripts: A Tale of the Colony* (1845). In this novel, set in the mid-eighteenth century, Cooper describes the festival through the eyes of Cornelius—"Corny"—Littlepage, a New Yorker of mixed English-Dutch descent. During his visit to New York City on Pinkster day, Corny is accompanied by two friends, one of whom, Dirck Van Valkenburgh, is of Dutch descent, while Jason Newcome is an Anglo-American "Yankee" from Connecticut. Cooper's description of the Pinkster festival serves to highlight cultural differences between New Yorkers and New Englanders.

Jason's unfamiliarity with Pinkster is apparent in the "white wine" scene. First, Cooper shows how well Corny is acquainted with the Dutch custom of *pinkstermelken*, the traditional distribution of milk as a symbol of fertility during Pinkster. When arriving at Hanover Square, Corny sees a black man who cries "'White wine—white wine!'" and "I bought a delicious draught of the purest and best of a Communipaw vintage, eating a cake at the same time."[166] The "Yankee" Jason, however, fails to understand the vendor's ironic use of the word "wine" for the type of liquid he is selling because "when the cup was put into his hands, he shut his eyes determined to gulp its contents at a swallow, in the most approved 'bitters' style. . . . 'Buttermilk, by Jingo!' exclaimed the disappointed pedagogue, who expected some delicious combination of spices with rum."[167]

According to Corny, New Yorkers are different from New Englanders because "the English possessions were met, on its western boundary, by those of the Dutch, and were thus separated from the other colonies of purely Anglo-Saxon origin."[168] Corny claims that one of the most striking differences between the two relates to the distinctive way in dealing with people of color, because "there is something in the character of these Anglo-Saxons that predisposes them to laugh, and turn up their noses, at other races."[169] These differences are also notable in the friends' reactions to the Pinkster festival. While Dirck and Corney are acquainted with the African American dances in New York City Park, Jason was "confounded with the noises, dances, music, and games that were going on."[170]

Not only do the reactions of the characters serve Cooper's goal to highlight cultural differences between New York and New England, the narrator also points out a series of differences in the way slaves are treated in a Dutch compared to an English tradition. Omitting the fact that in places such as Suriname, Dutch slaveholders were considered among the cruelest in the world, he argues that "among the Dutch, in particular, the treatment of the negro was of the kindest character, a trusty field slave often having quite as much to say on the subject of the tillage and the crops, as the man who owned both the land he worked, and himself." As an example he mentions the Dutch custom "that when a child of the family reached the age of six, or eight, a young slave of the same age and sex, was given to him, or her, with some little formality, and from that moment the fortunes of the two were considered to be, within the limits of their respective pursuits and positions, as those of man and wife."[171] Cooper took this reference from Anne Grant, who in her childhood recollections *Memoirs of an American Lady* (1808) had painted the master-slave relationship in Albany in rosy terms.[172] Like Grant, Cooper had pleasant childhood recollections of the Dutch American community in Albany. Born in 1789 in Burlington, New Jersey, his parents moved to Otsego County, New York, one year later, where he spent his youth. Since Albany was the nearest large city in the region, there was significant interaction with the Dutch American community. In 1800–1801, Cooper spent a year of college preparation in Albany and later wrote about this city: "It was the only outlet we had, in my childhood, to the world."[173] Cooper also had a personal connection to Dutch culture. His wife Susan Augusta De Lancey had relatives in Fishkill who were of Dutch heritage. Cooper visited the Netherlands several times, in 1828, 1831, and 1832.[174]

In order to fully understand Cooper's questionable decision to portray slavery in the Dutch American community as a benevolent system, it is important to note that *Satanstoe* was conceived as a reaction to the "anti-rent war" of the 1840s, which involved influential Dutch American families.[175] This "war" began with the death of patroon Stephen van Rensselaer in 1839, whose tenants owed him $400,000. When Van Rensselaer's sons attempted to collect these debts, the tenants refused to pay. Eventually the Judiciary Committee of the New York State Assembly supported the landlords in an 1842 decision. In response, angry tenants formed the "Anti-Rent Movement," which violently resisted legal action favoring the landowners' position. The movement grew considerably in the next decade and gained political importance when anti-renters decided to back specific candidates who favored their positions.

Cooper, who was personally acquainted with some of the Dutch American land-owning families involved in the dispute, considered anti-rentism "the great New York question of the day."[176] He felt that the anti-renters' behavior represented an opportunistic distortion of republican principles, which he saw as a threat to the nation's future. In *Satanstoe*, as well as in his later novels *The Chainbearer* (1845) and *The Redskins* (1846), Cooper idealized the landlord class as humanitarian gentlemen. He also added an ethnic perspective to the anti-rent discussion by marking the difference between two types of America: one with an exclusively English background as opposed to one with a Dutch-English background, or, as he called it, "a 'melange' of Dutch quietude and English aristocracy."[177] This opposition was related to Cooper's view of two different notions of freedom and, in extrapolation, two different ideas of what American identity represented. Irritated by what he considered to be the selfish behavior of the anti-renters, Cooper focused on New York's Dutch heritage in order to distinguish between Yankees, who interpreted the notion of freedom as individual freedom in an Anglo-Saxon tradition, and New Yorkers, whose understanding of freedom he believed to have been shaped by the Dutch community-oriented mentality in a bourgeois tradition. It was this latter mentality that he had experienced as a child in Albany, a place which to him had always been "a town of excellent social feeling and friendly connexions [sic]."[178]

Accordingly, Cooper portrayed slavery in a Dutch American tradition as a friendly system in which slaves allegedly enjoyed respect because they were considered part of one and the same community by their masters. He deliberately contrasted this with slavery in exclusively Anglo-American areas, where an individualistic interpretation of freedom reigned and the world of the slaves had always remained segregated from that of the masters. This English refusal to consider slaves part of their own community reflected, in Cooper's eyes, a broader problem that was also at the heart of the "anti-rent war": the evolution of the United States into a nation where citizens do not perceive themselves as brothers and sisters of one community but rather act as selfish individuals who only look after their own interests.

With this questionable interpretation of Dutch identity, Cooper's *Satanstoe* stands at the beginning of a tendency in late-nineteenth-century American literature and historiography—from John Lothrop Motley's *The Rise of the Dutch Republic* (1856) and Mary Mapes Dodge's *Hans Brinker* (1865) to Douglas Campbell's *The Puritan in Holland, England, and America* (1892)—to idealize the Netherlands as a nation characterized by a strong spirit of community and to use this image as a mirror for readers in the United States. Due to New York's Dutch heritage, this semiotic strategy not only had a comparative value but served as a vision of what America could have been.

Inspired by these influential works, the image of the Dutch in America underwent a radical change in the late nineteenth century. During his visit to America in 1826, Gerardus Bosch had been shocked about the fact that whenever telling people that he was Dutch, they "automatically began to chuckle."[179] By the end of the nineteenth century, however, the image of the Dutch in America had changed completely. Once ridiculed as clumsy yokels in Washington Irving's *History of New York* (1809), the Dutch were now glorified as New York's visionary forefathers who on the island of Manhattan had built the foundations of what had made America the world's greatest nation. American values such as the love of liberty, religious tolerance, and freedom of conscience were suddenly claimed to have Dutch roots, and even the American Declaration of Independence was credited to have been inspired by the Netherlands' sixteenth-century Act of Abjuration. In this wave of "Holland mania," typical Dutch symbols such as carillons, tulip gardens, and windmills popped up everywhere in the country, American museums massively collected "Netherlandish" seventeenth-century art, and American travel authors promoted an image of the Netherlands as a pastoral Eden.[180]

The only blot on the otherwise immaculate image of the Dutch was slavery. In this respect, Cooper's biased interpretation of the Pinkster tradition as a reflection of the Dutch community spirit proved to be a useful argument in downplaying the practice of slavery among Dutch Americans. In *The Story of New Netherland* (1909), historian William Elliot Griffis goes so far as to claim that no surer proof existed of the fact that "slavery in New Netherland was very mild in form" and that "the black slave . . . scarcely felt his bonds" than the existence of Pinkster.[181] Late-nineteenth-century American authors and folklorists such as Edwin Lassetter Bynner, Ruth Hall, and Alice Morse Earle also projected upon New York's Pinkster festival the utopian vision of a harmonious society that Cooper wished to see in America.[182] While Pinkster at the beginning of the century had been portrayed as a deplorable excess, they interpreted it as a festival of racial and social harmony. This questionable interpretation of Pinkster got a political connotation when Theodore Roosevelt decided to play his Dutch heritage as a trump card in the 1882 New York state election campaign. For someone who glorified his Dutch ancestors as "the very first to establish free-dom as we now understand the word," the topic of slavery could only be an embarrassment.[183] Roosevelt thus had every interest in giving continuation to Cooper's laudatory interpretation of Pinkster, which he repeats almost literally in his book *New York*: "Pinkster . . . grew to be especially the negroes' day, all of the blacks of the city and neighboring country gathering to celebrate it. There was a great fair, with merry-making and games of all kinds on the Common, where the City Hall park now is; while the whites also assembled to look on, and sometimes to take part in the fun."[184]

The Reinvention of Pinkster

In the 1980s this bucolic image of Pinkster in the tradition of Cooper inspired people to revive, or rather reinvent, the tradition. A well-known example is that of Sleepy Hollow, where a local historical society recreated the annual Pente-cost celebration at the formerly Dutch Philipsburg Manor.[185] The goal of the organizers was "to advance the knowledge, understanding and appreciation of the Hudson River Valley's historic, scenic, and cultural resources as a national treasure."[186] In 2010 the revival of Pinkster even led to the decision by New York Governor David Paterson to officially repeal the 1811 ban on Pinkster issued by the Albany City Council.[187] In contrast to New Orleans' Mardi Gras, however, nothing has remained in Philipsburg of the indulgence and Dionysian revelry that once characterized African American Pinkster celebrations. Claire Spon-sler refers to the Philipsburg festival as a "sanitized version" of Pinkster.[188] Rather than relaunching a lost tradition, the family-friendly event inadvertently ended up focusing attention on one of the main reasons why Pinkster disappeared: its incompatibility with the Protestant norms and values that shaped American society in the aftermath of the Second Great Awakening. The exotic combina-tion of Dutch folkloristic traditions with workshops on African drum music in Philipsburg also conveys the impression that during Pinkster celebrations, masters and slaves felt happily united as a community. Such a reinvention of Pinkster as innocent multicultural folklore runs the risk of glossing over the deep inequalities that characterized the type of society in which the Pinkster tradition developed. In this respect, it continues a tendency that was initiated by Cooper: the (mis)use of Pinkster to create the utopian image of a racially and socially harmonious society.

Conclusion

What began as a book project on a festive tradition, Pinkster, has developed into a study that identified brotherhoods and mutual aid as key concepts in understanding the cultural and social behavior of slave communities in New York and New Jersey. While the importance of African American brotherhoods providing mutual aid in North America's post-slavery eras has long been acknowledged, this book's focus on the social capital of slaves traces concern for mutual aid back to seventeenth-century Manhattan and suggests a stronger impact of the charter generation's Afro-Iberian cultural and social concepts on the development of New York and New Jersey's Dutch-owned slave communities than has hitherto been assumed. By analyzing the New York and New Jersey slave societies in a broader Atlantic context, the book also offers many parallels to the development of slave societies elsewhere in the Americas. These parallels confirm the importance of Afro-Iberian syncretic cultural continuities in the American diaspora.

This conclusion calls for a new paradigm in the general analysis of slavery in North America. While the earliest historians working on slave culture in a North American context were mainly interested in an assumed process of assimilation according to European standards, later generations pointed out the need to look for indigenous African continuities as well as for the creation of syncretic cultures and innovations in the New World. The findings of this book suggest the need to complement the latter with an increased focus on the amount of contact Africans had with European—primarily Portuguese—culture *before* they were shipped as slaves to the Americas. Since the transatlantic trade made the entire western African coastal area part of an intercultural Atlantic zone, it is natural to conclude that enslaved Africans brought not only indigenous African traditions to the New World but also syncretic traditions such as those that had developed in the context of Afro-Iberian brotherhoods.

This appeal for a new paradigm also suggests more differentiation in the understanding of African resistance against European aggression in the context of transatlantic slavery. Since European cultural elements had entered African societies long before the first enslaved Africans arrived in North America, anti-slavery resistance should not be reduced to the attachment to indigenous traditions. While the adoption of European elements in African societies did not emerge from a situation devoid of conflict, it began at a time when Africans were still firmly in control of their continent and able to negotiate deals on their own terms. It would thus be wrong to assume that the adoption of European elements necessarily implied submission to European standards.

This acknowledgment requires a change in attitude regarding the role of Christianity in African and African American culture. Many of those who have studied American slave societies from a neo-Marxist perspective have displayed a tendency to spontaneously assume that all enslaved Africans in America were eager to hold on to indigenous African traditions only and have subsequently been inclined to interpret all signs of Christian devotion in slave communities as submission to the standards of a society that oppressed them or as puppetry to elude the Christian slaveholder. Although there are many examples of Africans in the American diaspora who did, in fact, use Christianity as a smoke-screen behind which they continued to practice indigenous religious traditions, this was not a general pattern. A substantial number of Africans—especially West-Central Africans—who entered the New World were already familiar with Christianity and proudly considered Christian elements to be part of their African identity. That this process of transculturation in West-Central Africa did not imply submission to European standards can be illustrated by the occurrences surrounding the 1760 Battle of Kitombo. Convinced that they had been victorious in that battle thanks to a miraculous intervention of St. Luke, the rulers of the Kongolese region of Soyo decided to establish a new national holiday dedicated to this Catholic saint. They did so after their army had administered a humiliating defeat to the Portuguese, members of the same nation that in 1491 had brought Christianity to Central Africa.[1]

The new paradigm suggested in this book also calls for a revaluation of archival and translation work, all the more since classic books on early European explorations along the African west coast have until now remained largely untranslated. The use of materials in languages other than English is crucial to the advancement of our understanding of slave societies in North America. In this respect, Sojourner Truth's legacy provides a meaningful example. In the 1840s, while she was living in Northampton, Massachusetts, the illiterate Truth dictated her *Narrative* to her friend and amanuensis Olive Gilbert. Speaking about her mother, named Elizabeth, Truth referred to her familiarly in Dutch as Mama Bet, which Gilbert transcribed as Mau-Mau Bett.[2] Ever since, Gilbert's transcription error has remained in virtually all studies—including academic studies—on Truth, leading to the general assumption that Truth's mother had the mysterious, African-sounding name Mau-Mau. This unfortunate mis-interpretation of Truth's legacy by later generations is a revealing example of the widespread ignorance of an important chapter in both black and white

Anonymous, *Portrait of Sojourner Truth*. Truth (ca. 1797–1883) was born in a hamlet near Kingston, NY, as the daughter of a slave woman owned by the Dutch American Hardenbergh family and grew up in an entirely Dutch-speaking environment. Her printed legacy has remained available in English only. Courtesy the Burton Historical Collection, Detroit Public Library.

American history, occasioned by the rapid and radical effacement of New York's and New Jersey's Dutch identity in the early nineteenth century.

Sojourner Truth, the person with whom this book began, has often been perceived as an exceptional figure in African American history.[3] While there can be no doubt that her speeches and social achievements are of exceptional importance, Truth's decision to reject Pinkster in 1827 and to embrace evangelical Christianity corresponds to a general pattern in her community. The traditional framework of negotiation between black and white in the context of brotherhoods had become outdated following the abolition of slavery in the state of New York, and she switched to a new, more promising one by opting for an evangelical church community.

However, Truth's strategy to demand justice and ultimately freedom for herself, for her son Peter, and for black people in general continued to be inspired by black brotherhood traditions. While her new framework no longer involved the election and celebration of a king, the metaphor of a wise king warranting justice remained part of her rhetoric. Significantly, when Truth spoke at a Women's Rights Convention at the Broadway Tabernacle in New York City in September 1853, she confronted the crowd with the story of King Ahasuerus, whose wise policy, she claimed, could serve as a model to "the King of the United States."[4] In this Old Testament story from the Book of Esther, Ahasuerus re-establishes harmony by condemning his closest confidant Haman to death, while the story's hero, Esther's stepfather Mordechai, is asked to parade on the king's horse, dressed in royal robes—as if he were a Pinkster king.

Notes

Introduction

1. Sojourner Truth, *Narrative of Sojourner Truth*, ed. Margaret Washington (1850; New York: Vintage, 1993), 48.

2. Edwin Olson, "Social Aspects of Slave Life in New York," *Journal of Negro History* 26, no. 1 (January 1941): 71.

3. Jeroen Dewulf, "Pinkster: An Atlantic Creole Festival in a Dutch-American Context," *Journal of American Folklore* 126, no. 501 (2013): 245–71.

4. Herbert Aptheker, *American Negro Slave Revolts* (1943; New York: International Publishers, 1978), 70.

5. Shane White, *Somewhat More Independent: The End of Slavery in New York City, 1770–1810* (Athens: University of Georgia Press, 1991), 95.

6. Dena J. Epstein, *Sinful Tunes and Spirituals: Black Folk Music to the Civil War* (Urbana: University of Illinois Press, 1977), 68.

7. Gabriel Furman, *Antiquities of Long Island* (New York: J.W. Bouton, 1874), 266–67.

8. Henry Reed Stiles, *A History of the City of Brooklyn* (Brooklyn: Pub. by subscription, 1867–70), 38.

9. Maud Wilder Goodwin, *Dutch and English on the Hudson: A Chronicle of Colonial New York* (New Haven, CT: Yale University Press, 1921), 115.

10. Shane White, "Afro-Dutch Syncretization in New York City and the Hudson Valley," *Journal of American Folklore* 102, no. 403 (1989): 72–74; Shane White, "'It Was a Proud Day': African Americans, Festivals, and Parades in the North, 1741–1834," *Journal of American History* 81, no. 1 (1994): 20.

11. Claire Sponsler, *Ritual Imports: Performing Medieval Drama in America* (Ithaca, NY: Cornell University Press, 2004), 50–55.

12. Graham Russell Hodges, *Slavery and Freedom in the Rural North: African Americans in Monmouth County, New Jersey, 1665–1865* (Madison, WI: Madison House, 1997), 31, 58, 153; Graham Russell Hodges, *Root and Branch: African Americans in New York and East Jersey 1613–1863* (Chapel Hill: University of North Carolina Press, 1999), 63, 87–88.

13. Shane White, "Pinkster in Albany, 1803: A Contemporary Description," *New York History* 70, no. 2 (1989): 195. For similar views, see David Steven Cohen, "In Search of Carolus Africanus Rex: Afro-Dutch Folklore in New York and New Jersey," *Journal of the Afro-American Historical and Genealogical Society* 5, no. 3–4 (1984): 163; Renee Newman, "Pinkster and Slavery in Dutch New York," *De Halve Maen* 66 (Spring 1993): 1–8; Leslie M. Harris, *In the Shadow of*

Slavery: African Americans in New York City, 1626–1863 (Chicago: University of Chicago Press, 2003), 69; Christopher Moore, "A World of Possibilities: Slavery and Freedom in Dutch New Amsterdam," *Slavery in New York*, ed. Ira Berlin and Leslie M. Harris (New York: New Press, 2005), 52; Andrea C. Mosterman, "Researching African and Dutch Exchanges in Early New York," *De Halve Maen* 86 (Fall 2013): 47–52.

14. White, *Somewhat More Independent*, 189–90; Thelma Wills Foote, *Black and White Manhattan: The History of Racial Formation in Colonial New York City* (Oxford and New York: Oxford University Press, 2004), 192.

15. Erlene Stetson and Linda David, *Glorying in Tribulation: The Lifework of Sojourner Truth* (East Lansing: Michigan State University Press, 1994), 40.

16. Truth, *Narrative of Sojourner Truth*, 48–49; Arthur Huff Fauset, *Sojourner Truth: God's Faithful Pilgrim* (Chapel Hill: University of North Carolina Press, 1938), 44.

17. Cohen, "In Search of Carolus Africanus Rex," 149–62.

18. Samuel Kinser, *Carnival, American Style: Mardi Gras at New Orleans and Mobile* (Chicago: University of Chicago Press, 1990), 214.

19. Sterling Stuckey, *Going through the Storm: The Influence of African American Art in History* (Oxford and New York: Oxford University Press, 1994), 53–80.

20. Albert James Williams-Myers, *Long Hammering: Essays on the Forging of an African American Presence in the Hudson Valley to the Early Twentieth Century* (Trenton, NJ: Africa World Press, 1994), 88; Willie F. Page, *The Dutch Triangle: The Netherlands and the Atlantic Slave Trade, 1621–1664* (New York/London: Garland, 1997), 218; Linda Pershing, "Representations of Racial Identity in a Contemporary Pinkster Celebration," *Mighty Change, Tall Within: Black Identity in the Hudson Valley*, ed. Myra B. Young Armstead (Albany: State University of New York Press, 2003), 195; Oscar Williams, "Slavery in Albany, New York, 1624–1827," *Afro-Americans in New York Life and History* 34, no. 2 (July 2010): 160.

21. Melville J. Herskovits, *The Myth of the Negro Past* (1941; Boston: Beacon Press, 1958), 2.

22. Ira Berlin, "From Creole to African: Atlantic Creoles and the Origins of African-American Society in Mainland North America," *William and Mary Quarterly* 53, no. 2 (1996): 251–88.

23. John K. Thornton, *Africa and Africans in the Making of the Atlantic World, 1400–1680* (Cambridge, UK: Cambridge University Press, 1992), 209–11; Henk den Heijer, "The West African Trade of the Dutch West India Company, 1674–1740," *Riches from Atlantic Commerce: Dutch Transatlantic Trade and Shipping, 1585–1817*, ed. Johannes Postma and Victor Enthoven (Leiden, NL: Brill, 2003), 151–56.

24. Kristin Mann and Edna Bay, *Rethinking the African Diaspora: The Making of a Black Atlantic World in the Bight of Benin and Brazil* (Portland, OR: Frank Cass, 2001), 10.

25. Linda M. Heywood and John Thornton, *Central Africans, Atlantic Creoles, and the Foundation of the Americas, 1585–1660* (Cambridge, UK: Cambridge University Press, 2007), 238.

26. Linda M. Heywood and John Thornton, "Intercultural Relations between Europeans and Blacks in New Netherland," *Four Centuries of Dutch-American Relations 1609–2009*, ed. Hans Krabbendam, Cornelis A. van Minnen, and Giles Scott-Smith (Albany: State University of New York Press, 2009), 199.

27. Jaap Jacobs, "'In Such a Far Distant Land, Separated from All the Friends': Why Were the Dutch in New Netherland?," *The Worlds of the Seventeenth-Century Hudson Valley*, ed. Jaap Jacobs and L. H. Roper (Albany: State University of New York Press, 2014), 159.

28. Jeroen Dewulf, "Emulating a Portuguese Model: The Slave Policy of the West India Company and the Dutch Reformed Church in Dutch Brazil (1630–1654) and New Netherland (1614–1664) in Comparative Perspective," *Journal of Early American History* 4 (2014): 3–36.

29. Sidney W. Mintz and Richard Price, *An Anthropological Approach to the Afro-American Past: A Caribbean Perspective* (Philadelphia: Institute for the Study of Human Issues, 1976), 25–26; Gwendolyn Midlo Hall, *Slavery and African Ethnicities in the Americas: Restoring the Links* (Chapel Hill: University of North Carolina Press, 2005), 169.

30. Paul Gilroy, *The Black Atlantic: Modernity and Double Consciousness* (New York: Verso, 1993), 15.

31. Thornton, *Africa and Africans in the Making of the Atlantic World*, 8.

32. Victor Witter Turner, *The Ritual Process: Structure and Anti-Structure* (Chicago: Aldine, 1969).

33. White, "Pinkster in Albany," 193; White, "Afro-Dutch Syncretization in New York City and the Hudson Valley," 70.

34. Terrence W. Epperson, "The Contested Commons: Archaeologies of Race, Repression, and Resistance in New York City," *Historical Archaeologies of Capitalism*, ed. Mark P. Leone and Parker B. Potter Jr. (New York: Plenum, 1999), 98.

35. Bradford Verter, "Interracial Festivity and Power in Antebellum New York: The Case of Pinkster," *Journal of Urban History* 28, no. 4 (2002): 400.

36. Joyce D. Goodfriend, "Slavery in Colonial New York City," *Urban History* 35, no. 3 (December 2008): 495; Pierre Bourdieu, "The Forms of Capital," *Handbook of Theory and Research for the Sociology of Education*, ed. J. Richardson (New York: Greenwood, 1986), 241–58.

37. Craig Steven Wilder, "Black Life in Freedom: Creating a Civic Culture," *Slavery in New York*, ed. Ira Berlin and Leslie M. Harris (New York: New Press, 2005), 218.

38. Ira Berlin, *Generations of Captivity: A History of African-American Slaves* (Cambridge, MA: Harvard University Press, 2003), 109.

39. Mitch Kachun, *Festivals of Freedom: Memory and Meaning in African American Emancipation Celebrations, 1808–1915* (Amherst: University of Massachusetts Press, 2003), 17.

40. Geneviève Fabre, "Pinkster Festival, 1776–1811: An African-American Celebration," *Feasts and Celebrations in North American Ethnic Communities*, ed. Ramón A. Gutiérrez and Geneviève Fabre (Albuquerque: University of New Mexico Press, 1995), 18.

41. Aptheker, *American Negro Slave Revolts*, 64.

42. Frederick Douglass, *Narrative of the Life of Frederick Douglass, an American Slave. Written by Himself*, ed. David W. Blight (1845; Boston: Bedford/St. Martin's, 1993), 80.

43. Sidney W. Mintz and Richard Price, *The Birth of African-American Culture: An Anthropological Perspective* (Boston: Beacon Press, 1992), 27.

44. Ira Berlin, *Many Thousands Gone: The First Two Centuries of Slavery in North America* (Cambridge, MA: Harvard University Press, 1998), 1.

45. Melvin Wade, "'Shining in Borrowed Plumage': Affirmation of Community in the Black Coronation Festivals of New England (c. 1750-c. 1850)," *Western Folklore* XL, no. 3 (1981): 228.

46. Eugene D. Genovese, *Roll, Jordan, Roll: The World the Slaves Made* (New York: Pantheon, 1974), 148.

47. Thornton, *Africa and Africans in the Making of the Atlantic World*, 301.

Chapter 1

1. Johannes ter Gouw, *De volksvermaken* (Haarlem, NL: Erven F. Bohn, 1871), 221–33; Hermina C. A. Grolman, *Nederlandsche volksgebruiken naar oorsprong en betekenis* (Zutphen, NL: Thieme, 1931), 152–60; Catharina van de Graft and Tjaard W. R. de Haan, *Nederlandse volksgebruiken bij hoogtijdagen* (Utrecht, NL: Het Spectrum, 1978), 89–105; Gerard Nijsten, *Volkscultuur in de late Middeleeuwen. Feesten, processies en (bij)geloof* (Utrecht, NL: Kosmos, 1994), 94; Bart Lauvrijs, *Een jaar vol feesten* (Delft, NL: Elmar, 2004), 191–206; Benjamin B. Roberts, *Sex and Drugs before Rock 'n' Roll: Youth Culture and Masculinity during Holland's Golden Age* (Amsterdam: Amsterdam University Press, 2012), 104–5.

2. G. D. J. Schotel, *Het maatschappelijk leven onzer vaderen in de zeventiende eeuw* (Amsterdam: J.G. Strengholt, 1905), 427–28; B. W. E. Veurman, "Kinderfolklore," *Folklore der Lage Landen*, ed. Tj. W. R. de Haan (Amsterdam: Elsevier, 1972), 106–9, 125; Van de Graft and De Haan, *Nederlandse volksgebruiken bij hoogtijdagen*, 99; Marc Wingens, "De pinksterkroon is weer in 't land, hoezee! Het Pinksterkroonfeest in Deventer," *Volkscultuur* 6, no. 2 (1989): 8.

3. Ter Gouw, *De volksvermaken*, 277–78; Adriaan Buter, "Boerendansreveil van toen," *Neerlands Volksleven* 30, nos. 1 and 2 (1980): 35–42; Nijsten, *Volkscultuur in de late Middeleeuwen*, 100–102.

4. White, "Afro-Dutch Syncretization in New York City and the Hudson Valley," 71.

5. Nijsten, *Volkscultuur in de late Middeleeuwen*, 51; Herman Pleij, *Het gevleugelde woord. Geschiedenis van de Nederlandse literatuur 1400–1560* (Amsterdam: Bert Bakker, 2007), 120–24, 139–46; Arjan van Dixhoorn, *Lustige geesten. Rederijkers in de Noordelijke Nederlanden 1480–1650* (Amsterdam: Amsterdam University Press, 2009), 194.

6. Ter Gouw, *De volksvermaken*, 229–30.

7. Ibid., 270; Guido Marnef, *Antwerpen in de tijd van de Reformatie* (Antwerp, BE: Kritak, 1996), 51; Hugo Soly and Wim Blockmans, ed., *Charles V, 1500–1558, and His Time* (Antwerp, BE: Mercatorfonds, 1999), 276.

8. Marc Boone and Maarten Prak, "Rulers, Patricians and Burghers: The Great and the Little Traditions of Urban Revolt in the Low Countries," *A Miracle Mirrored: The Dutch Republic in European Perspective*, ed. Karel Davids and Jan Lucassen (Cambridge, UK: Cambridge University Press, 1995), 99–134.

9. Arie T. van Deursen, *Plain Lives in a Golden Age: Popular Culture, Religion and Society in Seventeenth-Century Holland*, trans. Maarten Ultee (1978–81; Cambridge, UK: Cambridge University Press, 1991), 108–9; Willem Frijhoff and Marijke Spies, *Nederlandse cultuur in Europese context: 1650. Bevochten eendracht* (The Hague: Sdu Uitgevers, 1999), 351–432; Hans Kosterman, *Het aanzien van een millennium: De Unie van Utrecht* (Utrecht, NL: Spectrum, 1999), 61–63; Van Dixhoorn, *Lustige geesten*, 196.

10. Peter Burke, *Popular Culture in Early Modern Europe* (New York: New York University Press, 1978), 212.

11. Van Deursen, *Plain Lives in a Golden Age*, 86.

12. F. G. Naerebout, "Snoode exercitien. Het zeventiende-eeuwse Nederlandse protestantisme en de dans," *Volkskundig bulletin* 16 (1990): 125–55; Paul Vandenbroeck, *Over wilden en narren, boeren en bedelaars. Beeld van de andere, vertoog over het zelf* (Antwerp, BE: Koninklijk Museum voor Schone Kunsten, 1987), 63–116.

13. Simon Schama, *The Embarrassment of Riches: An Interpretation of Dutch Culture in the Golden Age* (1987; New York: Random House, 1997), 182.

14. Arie T. van Deursen, *Bavianen en slijkgeuzen. Kerk en kerkvolk ten tijde van Maurits en Oldenbarnevelt* (Assen, NL: Van Gorcum, 1974), 133–34; Willem Frijhoff, *Wegen van Evert Willemsz. Een Hollands weeskind op zoek naar zichzelf 1607-1647* (Nijmegen, NL: SUN, 1995), 75; Christine Kooi, *Calvinists and Catholics during Holland's Golden Age: Heretics and Idolaters* (Cambridge, UK: Cambridge University Press, 2012), 32.

15. Ter Gouw, *De volksvermaken*, 225; Wingens, "De Pinksterkroon is weer in 't land," 8; Van Deursen, *Plain Lives in a Golden Age*, 107; Frijhoff and Spies, *Nederlandse cultuur in Europese context*, 364; Frijhoff, *Wegen van Evert Willemsz.*, 100; Peter Jan Margry, *Teedere Quaesties: Religieuze rituelen in conflict* (Hilversum, NL: Verloren, 2000), 177, 289–94; Van Dixhoorn, *Lustige geesten*, 202, 224, 232; Kooi, *Calvinists and Catholics during Holland's Golden Age*, 36.

16. I would like to thank folklorist Cees Slegers for this information.

17. Andrea C. Mosterman, "Sharing Spaces in a New World Environment: African-Dutch Contributions to North American Culture, 1626–1826" (Ph.D. diss., Boston University, 2012), 186.

18. Ter Gouw, *De volksvermaken*, 231.

19. Oliver A. Rink, *Holland on the Hudson: An Economic and Social History of Dutch New York* (Ithaca, NY: Cornell University Press, 1986); Oliver A. Rink, "Before the English (1609–1664)," *The Empire State: A History of New York*, ed. Milton M. Klein (Ithaca, NY: Cornell University Press, 2001), 3–112; Jaap Jacobs, *New Netherland: A Dutch Colony in Seventeenth-Century America* (Leiden, NL: Brill, 2005); Charles T. Gehring, "New Netherland: The Formative Years, 1609–1632," *Four Centuries of Dutch-American Relations 1609–2009*, ed. Hans Krabbendam, Cornelis A. van Minnen, and Giles Scott-Smith (Albany: State University of New York Press, 2009), 74–84; Jaap Jacobs, "Migration, Population, and Government in New Netherland," *Four Centuries of Dutch-American Relations 1609–2009*, 85–96.

20. Janny Venema, *Kiliaen van Rensselaer (1586-1643): Designing a New World* (Hilversum, NL: Verloren, 2010), 241–67.

21. "Resolution" (5 December 1643; 18 May 1644; 26 May 1644; 2 April 1654), in Charles T. Gehring and J. A. Schiltkamp, ed., *Curaçao Papers 1640-1665: New Netherland Documents* (Interlaken, NY: Heart of the Lakes, 1987), 30, 36–38, 55; Arnold J. F. van Laer, *New York Historical Manuscripts: Dutch*, 4 vols. (Baltimore, MD: Genealogical Publishing, 1974), 2:264, 451, 455, 456, 467; 3:7; 4:333–34.

22. Jacobs, "Migration, Population, and Government in New Netherland," 86.

23. Anthony F. Buccini, "The Dialectal Origins of New Netherland Dutch," *The Berkeley Conference on Dutch Linguistics 1993: Dutch Linguistics in a Changing Europe*, ed. Thomas F. Shannon and Johan P. Snapper (Lanham, MD: University Press of America, 1995), 211–63.

24. Frijhoff and Spies, *Nederlandse cultuur in Europese context*, 160.

25. Hodges, *Root and Branch*, 6–7; Mark Meuwese, *Brothers in Arms, Partners in Trade: Dutch-Indigenous Alliances in the Atlantic World, 1595-1674* (Leiden, NL: Brill, 2012), 118–19.

26. "Deposition Concerning the Erection of Fort Amsterdam" (22 March 1639), in Edmund Bailey O'Callaghan, Berthold Fernow, and John Romeyn Brodhead, ed., *Documents Relative to the Colonial History of the State of New York*, 15 vols. (Albany, NY: Weed, Parsons and Company, 1853–87), 14:18.

27. "Council Minutes" (12 February 1652), in Charles T. Gehring, ed., *Council Minutes, 1652–1654. New York Historical Manuscripts*. Baltimore, MD: Genealogical Publishing, 1983), 11; "Ordinance establishing a new village at the Northern end of Manhattan Island" (4 March 1658), in Charles T. Gehring, ed., *Laws & Writs of Appeal 1647–1663* (Syracuse, NY: Syracuse University Press, 1991), 99.

28. "Council Minutes" (9 October 1654), in Gehring, *Council Minutes, 1652–1654*, 185; "Council Minutes" (3 February 1639; 25 July 1657; 12 April 1658; 15 April 1658; 13 July 1658), in Edmund Bailey O'Callaghan, ed., *Calendar of Historical Manuscripts in the Office of the Secretary of State, Albany, New York*, 2 vols. (Albany, NY: Weed, Parsons and Company, 1856–66), 1:66, 112, 194, 195, 198.

29. "Freedom and Exemptions for New Netherland" (19 July 1640), in O'Callaghan, Fernow and Brodhead, *Documents Relative to the Colonial History of the State of New York*, 1:123.

30. Janny Venema, *Beverwijck: A Dutch Village on the American Frontier, 1652–1664* (Albany, NY: State of New York University Press, 2003), 131–32; Jacobs, *New Netherland*, 291–95.

31. Van Deursen, *Bavianen en slijkgeuzen*, 13–21; Robert Alexander, "Religion in Rensselaerswijck," *A Beautiful and Fruitful Place: Selected Rensselaerswijck Seminar Papers*, ed. Nancy A.M. Zeller (New York: New Netherland Publishing, 1991), 309–15; Leendert Jan Joosse, *Geloof in de Nieuwe Wereld. Ontmoeting met Afrikanen en Indianen 1600–1700* (Kampen, NL: Kok, 2008), 127, 250.

32. David Pietersz de Vries, "Korte Historiael ende Journaels Aenteyckeninge, 1634–1644," *Narratives of New Netherland, 1609–1664*, ed. J. Franklin Jameson (1655; New York: Barnes & Noble, 1953), 203–4.

33. Joyce D. Goodfriend, "The Struggle over the Sabbath in Petrus Stuyvesant's New Amsterdam," *Power and the City in the Netherlandic World*, eds. Wayne te Brake and Wim Klooster (Leiden, NL: Brill, 2006), 205–24.

34. Jaap Jacobs, "Like Father, Like Son? The Early Years of Petrus Stuyvesant," *Revisiting New Netherland: Perspectives on Early Dutch America*, ed. Joyce D. Goodfriend (Leiden, NL: Brill, 2005), 205–44.

35. "Correspondence from America. Stuyvesant to the Classis in Amsterdam," in Hugh Hastings and Edward Tanjore Corwin, ed., *Ecclesiastical Records, State of New York*, 7 vols. (Albany, NY: The State Historian, 1901–16), 1:262; "Ordinance regulating taverns in New Amsterdam" (10 March 1648), in Van Laer, *New York Historical Manuscripts*, 4:496–97.

36. "Ordinances of New Amsterdam" (26 October 1656), in Berthold Fernow, ed., *The Records of New Amsterdam from 1653 to 1674*, 7 vols. (New York: The Knickerbocker Press, 1897), 1:24–26.

37. Venema, *Beverwijck*, 112–13.

38. Alice Morse Earle, *Colonial Days in Old New York* (1896; Port Washington, NY: Ira J. Friedman, 1962), 185–203; Peter G. Rose, *Food, Drink and Celebrations of the Hudson Valley Dutch* (Charleston, SC: The History Press, 2009): 101–6.

39. "Ordinance for the Regulation of Trade and Navigation" (10 March 1648), in Edmund Baily O'Callaghan, ed., *Laws and Ordinances of New Netherland, 1638–1674. Compiled and Translated from the Original Dutch Records in the Office of the Secretary of State, Albany, New York* (Albany, NY: Weed, Parsons and Company, 1868), 89.

40. James Riker, *Revised History of Harlem (City of New York): Its Origin and Early Annals, Prefaced by Home Scenes in the Fatherlands, or, Notices of its Founders before Emigration* (New York: New Harlem Publishing, 1904), 197–98; Dennis Sullivan, *The Punishment of Crime in Colonial New York: The Dutch Experience in Albany during the Seventeenth Century* (New York: Peter Lang, 1997), 56–57.

41. "Petition of the Consistory of Wildwyck" (12 February 1664), in O'Callaghan, *Laws and Ordinances of New Netherland*, 334.

42. "Council Minutes" (25 and 27 February 1654), in Gehring, *Council Minutes, 1652–1654*, 117–20; Bayard Tuckerman, *Peter Stuyvesant: Director-General for the West India Company in New Netherland* (New York: Dodd, Mead, 1893), 152.

43. "Court Minutes of New Amsterdam" (8 February 1655), in Fernow, *The Records of New Amsterdam from 1653 to 1674*, 1:286.

44. Jaap Jacobs, "'To Favor This New and Growing City of New Amsterdam with a Court of Justice': The Relations between Rulers and Ruled in New Amsterdam," *Amsterdam-New York: Transatlantic Relations and Urban Identities since 1653*, ed. George Harinck and Hans Krabbendam (Amsterdam: VU University Press, 2005), 17–29.

45. "Court Minutes of New Amsterdam" (26 February 1654), in Fernow, *The Records of New Amsterdam from 1653 to 1674*, 1:172.

46. "Court Minutes of New Amsterdam" (18 March 1664), in Ibid., 5:38–39.

47. "Letter of Reverend Jonas Michaëlius," in Hastings and Corwin, *Ecclesiastical Records, State of New York*, 1:62.

48. "Ordinance" (10 March 1648), in O'Callaghan, *Laws and Ordinances of New Netherland*, 89.

49. "Court Minutes" (9 May 1655), Charles T. Gehring, ed., *Fort Orange Minutes 1652–1660* (Syracuse, NY: Syracuse University Press, 1990), 192.

50. "Ordinance Prohibiting New Year and May Day Disruptions" (30 December 1655), in Gehring, *Laws & Writs of Appeal 1647–1663*, 52–53.

51. Esther Singleton, *Dutch New York* (New York: Dodd, Mead, 1909), 296.

52. Benjamin Bullivant, "A Glance at New York in 1697: The Travel Diary of Benjamin Bullivant," ed. Wayne Andrews, *New-York Historical Society Quarterly* vol. XL, nr. 1 (January 1956): 66.

53. Isaac Newton Phelps Stokes, *The Iconography of Manhattan Island, 1498–1909*, 6 vols. (New York: Robert H. Dodd, 1922), 4:242.

54. To Anna van Rensselaer" (10/20 June 1668), in Arnold J. F. van Laer, ed., *Correspondence of Jeremias van Rensselaer 1651–1674* (Albany: University of the State of New York, 1932), 403.

55. Ronald W. Howard, "The English Province (1664–1776)," *The Empire State: A History of New York*, ed. Milton M. Klein (Ithaca, NY: Cornell University Press, 2001), 113–28; Jacobs, *New Netherland*, 185–86; Christian J. Koot, *Empire at the Periphery: British Colonists, Anglo-Dutch Trade, and the Development of the British Atlantic, 1621–1713* (New York: New York University Press, 2011), 111–16.

56. Firth Haring Fabend, *A Dutch Family in the Middle Colonies, 1660–1800* (New Brunswick, NJ: Rutgers University Press, 1991), 12–13; Simon Middleton, "The Waning of Dutch New York," *Four Centuries of Dutch-American Relations 1609–2009*, ed. Hans Krabbendam,

Cornelis A. van Minnen, and Giles Scott-Smith (Albany: State University of New York Press, 2009), 108–19.

57. David G. Hackett, *The Rude Hand of Innovation: Religion and Social Order in Albany, New York, 1652–1836* (Oxford and New York: Oxford University Press, 1991), 28–31; Howard, "The English Province (1664–1776)," 126–88; Claudia Schnurmann, "Representative Atlantic Entrepreneur: Jacob Leisler, 1640–1691," *Riches from Atlantic Commerce: Dutch Transatlantic Trade and Shipping, 1585–1817*, ed. Johannes Postma and Victor Enthoven (Leiden, NL: Brill, 2003), 259–83; Simon Middleton, "A Class Struggle in New York?," *Class Matters: Early North America and the Atlantic World*, ed. Simon Middleton and Billy G. Smith (Philadelphia: University of Pennsylvania Press, 2008), 88–98.

58. Jerome R. Reich, *Leisler's Rebellion: A Study of Democracy in New York 1664–1720* (Chicago: University of Chicago Press, 1953), 129–30; Howard, "The English Province," 126–35; Middleton, "A Class Struggle in New York?," 98.

59. Randall H. Balmer, *A Perfect Babel of Confusion: Dutch Religion and English Culture in the Middle Colonies* (Oxford and New York: Oxford University Press, 1989), 49–50.

60. "Selijns, Van Varick and Dellius to the Classis of Amsterdam" (2 October 1692), Hastings and Corwin, *Ecclesiastical Records*, 2:1041–45.

61. "On the Re-Burial of Leisler under the Dutch Church" (14 October 1698), in Ibid., 2:1242.

62. Randall H. Balmer, "The Social Roots of Dutch Pietism in the Middle Colonies," *Church History* 53, no. 2 (1984): 192.

63. "Lord Cornbury to the Lords of Trade" (9 September 1703), in O'Callaghan, Fernow, and Brodhead, *Documents Relative to the Colonial History of the State of New York*, 4:1071.

64. David William Voorhees, "Family and Factions: The Dutch Roots of Colonial New York's Factional Politics," *Explorers, Fortunes & Love Letters: A Window on New Netherland*, ed. Martha Dickinson Shattuck (New York: Mount Ida Press, 2009), 129–47.

65. Robert Hunter, "Androboros: A Biographical Farce in Three Acts," *Satiric Comedies*, ed. Walter J. Meserve and William R. Reardon (1714; Bloomington: Indiana University Press, 1969), 24.

66. Quoted in Howard, "The English Province (1664–1776)," 170.

67. Joyce D. Goodfriend, "Archibald Laidlie (1727–1779): The Scot who Revitalized New York City's Dutch Reformed Church," *Transatlantic Pieties: Dutch Clergy in Colonial America*, ed. Leon van den Broeke, Hans Krabbendam, and Dirk Mouw (Grand Rapids, MI: Eerdmans, 2012), 239–57.

68. Gerald F. de Jong, *The Dutch in America, 1609–1974* (Boston: Twayne, 1975), 48–66; Brendan McConville, *These Daring Disturbers of the Public Peace: The Struggle for Property and Power in Early New Jersey* (Ithaca, NY: Cornell University Press, 1999), 58–64.

69. "Letter to the Lords of Trade" (28 November 1700), in O'Callaghan, Fernow, and Brodhead, *Documents Relative to the Colonial History of the State of New York*, 4:791.

70. Joyce D. Goodfriend, "The Social Life and Cultural Life of Dutch Settlers, 1664–1776," *Four Centuries of Dutch-American Relations 1609–2009*, 120–31; Joyce D. Goodfriend, "The Dutch Book Trade in Colonial New York City: The Transatlantic Connection," *Books between Europe and the Americas: Connections and Communities, 1620–1860*, ed. Leslie Howsam and James Raven (Basingstoke, UK: Palgrave Macmillan, 2011), 128–56.

71. Quoted in de Jong, *The Dutch in America*, 84.

72. Peter Kalm, *Travels into North America, 1748-1749*, ed. John Reinhold Forster (1753–61; Barre, MA: Imprint Society, 1972), 332.

73. Lucas Ligtenberg, *De nieuwe wereld van Peter Stuyvesant. Nederlandse voetsporen in de Verenigde Staten* (Amsterdam: Uitgeverij Balans, 1999), 74–85; Jan Noordegraaf, "Dutch Language and Literature in the United States," *Four Centuries of Dutch-American Relations 1609-2009*, 166–78; Nicoline van der Sijs, *Cookies, Coleslaw, and Stoops: The Influence of Dutch on the North American Languages* (The Hague: Nederlandse Taalunie, 2009), 27–37.

74. Frijhoff, *Wegen van Evert Willemsz.*, 354–61; Fred van Lieburg, "Interpreting the Dutch Great Awakening (1749-1755)," *Church History 77*, no. 2 (2008): 318–36.

75. Earl W. Kennedy, "Guiliam Bertholf (1656-1726): Irenic Dutch Pietist in New Jersey and New York," *Transatlantic Pieties: Dutch Clergy in Colonial America*, 197–216.

76. Joel R. Beeke, "Introduction," *Forerunner of the Great Awakening: Sermons by Theodorus Jacobus Frelinghuysen, 1691-1747*, ed. Joel R. Beeke (Grand Rapids, MI: Eerdmans, 2000), i–xliii; Jeroen Dewulf, "The Many Languages of American Literature: Interpreting Sojourner Truth's *Narrative* (1850) as Dutch-American Contact Literature," *Dutch Crossing 38*, no. 3 (2014): 231.

77. Beeke, "Introduction," xi–xv.

78. Cortlandt van Rensselaer, *The Presbyterian Magazine* (Philadelphia: W. H. Mitchell, 1851), 524.

79. James Tanis, *Dutch Calvinistic Pietism in the Middle Colonies* (The Hague: Martinus Nijhoff, 1967), 143; Fabend, *A Dutch Family in the Middle Colonies*, 138–40; Hastings and Corwin, *Ecclesiastical Records*, 1:657–58.

80. Henry P. Thompson, *History of the Reformed Church at Readington, NJ, 1719–1881* (New York: Board of Publication of the Reformed Church in America, 1882), 55–56.

81. Dina van Bergh, *The Diary of Dina Van Bergh, 1747-1748*, ed. Gerard Van Dyke and J. David Muyskens (New Brunswick, NJ: Historical Society of the Reformed Church in America, 1993), 71.

82. Alexander Coventry, "Memoirs of an Emigrant: The Journal of Alexander Coventry, M.D. in Scotland, the United States and Canada during the Period 1783-1831," Manuscripts Collection, New York State Library (1978), 108 (4 and 5 June 1786), 161 (27 and 28 May 1897).

83. John F. Watson, *Annals and Occurrences of New York City and State, in the Olden Time* (Philadelphia: Henry F. Anners, 1846), 204.

84. *Albany Centinel,* June 13, 1803.

85. Robert Lowell, *A Story or Two from an Old Dutch Town* (Boston: Roberts Brothers, 1878), 260. In a letter to J. H. Ward, dated November 14, 1878, Lowell admitted that his account was fictional but added that his description of Pinkster was well received by members of the town's Dutch community who thought it to be very authentic. Special Collection Library, University of Virginia, MSS 7843, R. Howell to J. H. Ward.

86. *Troy Daily Times*, September 19, 1872.

87. James Eights, "Pinkster Festivities in Albany Sixty Years Ago," *Collections on the History of Albany*, ed. Joel Munsell, 4 vols. (Albany NY: Munsell, 1865–71), 2:324.

88. *The Schenectady Cabinet, or, Freedom's Sentinel*, July 28, 1846.

89. Eights, "Pinkster Festivities in Albany Sixty Years Ago," 2:324.

90. Alice Morse Earle, "Pinkster Day," *New Outlook* 49 (1894): 743–44; John Russell Bartlett, *Dictionary of Americanisms: A Glossary of Words and Phrases Usually Regarded as Peculiar to the United States* (1848; Boston: Little, Brown, 1877), 468.

Chapter 2

1. "A Brief Report on the State that is Composed of the Four Conquered Captaincies" (14 January 1638), in Stuart B. Schwartz and Clive Willis, ed., *Early Brazil: A Documentary Collection to 1700* (Cambridge, UK: Cambridge University Press, 2010), 245.

2. C. R. Boxer, *The Dutch in Brazil, 1624–1654* (Oxford: Clarendon Press, 1957), 32–66; Ernst van den Boogaart and Pieter C. Emmer, "The Dutch Participation in the Atlantic Slave Trade, 1596–1650," *The Uncommon Market: Essays in the Economic History of the Atlantic Slave Trade*, ed. Henry A. Gemery and Jan S. Hogendorn (New York: Academic Press, 1979), 353–71; Johannes Menne Postma, *The Dutch in the Atlantic Slave Trade, 1600–1815* (Cambridge, UK: Cambridge University Press, 1990), 14–25; Thornton, *Africa and Africans in the Making of the Atlantic World*, 63–65; Robin Blackburn, *The Making of New World Slavery: From the Baroque to the Modern 1492–1800* (London and New York: Verso, 1997), 188–201; Klaas Ratelband, *Nederlanders in West-Afrika 1600–1650. Angola, Kongo en São Tomé*, ed. René Baesjou (Zutphen, NL: Walburg Pers, 2000), 91–283; Jelmer Vos, David Eltis, and David Richardson, "The Dutch in the Atlantic World: New Perspectives from the Slave Trade with Particular Reference to the African Origins of the Traffic," *Extending the Frontiers: Essays on the New Transatlantic Slave Trade Database*, ed. David Eltis and David Richardson (New Haven, CT: Yale University Press, 2008), 228–49; Meuwese, *Brothers in Arms, Partners in Trade*, 15–54.

3. "Carta de D. Garcia II Rei do Congo ao governador holandês no Brasil" (20 February 1643), in António Brásio, ed., *Monumenta missionária Africana*, 15 vols. (Lisbon: Agência Geral do Ultramar [vols. 1–11], 1952–71; Academia Portuguesa da História [vols. 12–15], 1988), 9:13–16; "Carta de Sousa Coutinho ao conde da Vidigueira" (10 October 1643), in Brásio, *Monumenta Missionária Africana*, 9:81; "Extrait d'une lettre de Hans Mols aux XIX" (19 September 1643), in Louis Jadin, ed., *L'Ancien Congo et l'Angola 1639–1655 d'après les archives romaines, portugaises, néerlandaises et espagnoles*, 3 vols. (Brussels and Rome: Institut Historique Belge de Rome, 1975), 1:482–83; Louis Jadin, "Rivalités luso-néerlandaises du Sohio, Congo, 1600–1675," *Bulletin de l'Institut Historique Belge de Rome* XXXVII (1966): 150–51; Cécile Fromont, *The Art of Conversion: Christian Visual Culture in the Kingdom of Kongo* (Chapel Hill: University of North Carolina Press, 2014), 114–23.

4. Jaap Jacobs, *New Netherland*, 261.

5. "Freedoms and Exemptions for the patroons" (7 June 1620), in Arnold J. F. van Laer, ed., *Van Rensselaer Bowier Manuscripts: Being the Letters of Kiliaen van Rensselaer, 1630–1643, and Other Documents Relating to the Colony of Rensselaerswyck* (Albany: University of the State of New York, 1908), 153; "New Project of Freedoms and Exemptions," in O'Callaghan, Fernow, and Brodhead, *Documents Relative to the Colonial History of the State of New York*, 1:9; Edmund Baily O'Callaghan, ed., *Voyages of the Slavers St. John and Arms of Amsterdam, 1659, 1663: Together with Additional Papers Illustrative of the Slave Trade under the Dutch* (Albany, NY: Munsell, 1867), xiii; Postma, *The Dutch in the Atlantic Slave Trade*, 19; Foote, *Black and White Manhattan*, 37.

6. "Letter of Reverend Jonas Michaëlius to Adrian Smoutius" (1 August 1628), in Hastings and Corwin, *Ecclesiastical Records, State of New York*, 1:62.

7. Jacobs, *New Netherland*, 77–83.

8. "Report of the Board of Accounts on New Netherland" (1644), in O'Callaghan, Fernow, and Brodhead, *Documents Relative to the Colonial History of the State of New York*, 1:152.

9. Ibid., 1:154.

10. Stokes, *The Iconography of Manhattan Island*, 4:106; O'Callaghan, *Voyages of the Slavers St. John and Arms of Amsterdam*, xvi–xvii.

11. "Instructie van de hoge raden voor de commiezen Walien Jorisz. en Laurens van Heusden" (30 December 1645), Dutch National Archives, The Hague, Oude West-Indische Compagnie (OWIC), item nr. 43; "Council Minutes" (17 June 1646), in Van Laer, *New York Historical Manuscripts*, 4:324; "Bill of Sale of the Ship Amandare," in Ibid., 2:401–2.

12. O'Callaghan, *Voyages of the Slavers St. John and Arms of Amsterdam*, xix–xx.

13. "Sundry Papers in Relation to the Case of Jan Gaillardo and his Negro Slaves" (26 April 1658), O'Callaghan, Fernow, and Brodhead, *Documents Relative to the Colonial History of the State of New York*, 23–47.

14. "Letter from the Directors in Amsterdam to P. Stuyvesant" and "Letter from the Directors in Amsterdam to the inhabitants of Manhattan" (4 April 1652), Charles T. Gehring, ed., *New Netherland Documents Series Volume XI: Correspondence 1647–1653* (Syracuse, NY: Syracuse University Press, 2000), 144–60.

15. "Resolution of the Chamber at Amsterdam" (9 November 1654), Charles T. Gehring, ed., *New Netherland Documents Series Volume XII: Correspondence 1654–1658* (Syracuse, NY: Syracuse University Press, 2003), 34.

16. "Ordinance Imposing a Duty on Exported Negroes" (6 August 1655), Charles T. Gehring, ed., *Council Minutes 1655–1656* (Syracuse, NY: Syracuse University Press, 1995), 70.

17. "Proposed Contract to Import Slaves into New Netherland" and "Remonstrance on the Preceding Proposed Contract" (3 May 1660), O'Callaghan, *Voyages of the Slavers St. John and Arms of Amsterdam*, 169–76.

18. Van den Boogaart and Emmer, "The Dutch Participation in the Atlantic Slave Trade," 371–75; Han Jordaan, "The Curaçao Slave Market: From *Asiento* Trade to Free Trade, 1700–1730," *Riches from Atlantic Commerce: Dutch Transatlantic Trade and Shipping, 1585–1817*, ed. Johannes Postma and Victor Enthoven (Leiden, NL: Brill, 2003), 219–34; Joyce D. Goodfriend, "Burghers and Blacks: The Evolution of a Slave Society at New Amsterdam," *New York History* LIX, no. 2 (April 1978): 135–38; Postma, *The Dutch in the Atlantic Slave Trade*, 26–55; Vos, Eltis, and Richardson, "The Dutch in the Atlantic World," 235.

19. Jordaan, "The Curaçao Slave Market," 237; "Letter Matthias Beck to Petrus Stuyvesant" (23 August 1659), in Gehring and Schiltkamp, *Curaçao Papers*, 124–27; "Resoluties WIC Kamer van Amsterdam" (13 June 1669), in J. H. J. Hamelberg, ed., *Documenten behoorende bij "De Nederlanders op de West-Indische eilanden"* (1901–1903; Amsterdam: Emmering, 1979), 83.

20. "Extract from a Letter from Stuyvesant to the Directors in Holland" (26 December 1659), in O'Callaghan, Fernow, and Brodhead, *Documents Relative to the Colonial History of the State of New York*, 14:454–55.

21. "Vice-Director Beck to Director Stuyvesant" (23 August 1659), "Jan Pietersen van Dockum" (24 August 1659), "Jan Jansen Eyckenboom" (8 May 1660), and "Dirck Jansen van

Oldenburch" (31 August 1660 and 21 July 1661), in Gehring and Schiltkamp, *Curaçao Papers*, 125, 141, 168, 174, 177; "Letter from Director Stuyvesant to the Directors in Holland" (25 June 1660), in O'Callaghan, Fernow, and Brodhead, *Documents Relative to the Colonial History of the State of New York*, 14:477; "Director Stuyvesant to the Directors at Amsterdam" (25 June 1660), "Director Stuyvesant to Vice-Director Beck" (5 July 1660), "Director Stuyvesant to the Directors at Amsterdam (10 June 1664), and "Director Stuyvesant to Vice-Director Beck" (30 July 1664), in O'Callaghan, *Voyages of the Slavers St. John and Arms of Amsterdam*, 178–80, 205–6, 216–21.

22. "Letter from the Directors to Stuyvesant" (9 March 1660), in O'Callaghan, Fernow, and Brodhead, *Documents Relative to the Colonial History of the State of New York*, 14:458–59; "Directors at Amsterdam to Director Stuyvesant" (11 April 1661), in O'Callaghan, *Voyages of the Slavers St. John and Arms of Amsterdam*, 183–86; Elizabeth Donnan, ed., *Documents Illustrative of the History of the Slave Trade,* 4 vols. (Washington: Carnegie Institute, 1930–35), 3:406.

23. "Journal of the Slaver *The Arms of Amsterdam* and her Capture" (13 October 1663), in O'Callaghan, *Voyages of the Slavers St. John and Arms of Amsterdam,* 89–95.

24. "Vice-Director Beck to Lords in Amsterdam" (21 July 1664), in Gehring and Schiltkamp, *Curaçao Papers*, 186–87; "Contract for a Cargo of Slaves for New Netherland," "Directors at Amsterdam to Director Stuyvesant" (20 January 1664), "Bill of Lading for Three Hundred Negroes Sent to the Manhattans" (21 July 1664), "Director Stuyvesant to Vice-Director Beck" (30 July 1664), "The Council of New Netherland to the Directors at Amsterdam" (17 August 1664), and "Receipt for the above Negroes" (30 August 1664), in O'Callaghan, *Voyages of the Slavers St. John and Arms of Amsterdam,* 194–200, 214–25.

25. "Report on the Surrender of New Netherland" (1666), in O'Callaghan, Fernow, and Brodhead, *Documents Relative to the Colonial History of the State of New York*, 2:430.

26. Heywood and Thornton, *Central Africans, Atlantic Creoles,* ix; Joseph C. Miller, "Central Africans during the Era of the Slave Trade, c. 1490s–1850s," *Central Africans and Cultural Transformation in America*, ed. Linda M. Heywood (Cambridge, UK: Cambridge University Press, 2002), 21–69.

27. Fromont, *The Art of Conversion*, 16.

28. Samuel S. Purple, ed., *Marriages from 1639 to 1801 in the Reformed Dutch Church, New Amsterdam, New York City. Collections of the New York Genealogical and Biographical Society*, vol. 9 (1890; New York: Genealogical and Biographical Society, 1940), 10–30; Thomas Grier Evans, ed., *Records of the Reformed Dutch Church in New Amsterdam and New York: Baptisms from 25 December, 1639, to 27 December 1730*. Collections of the New York Genealogical and Biographical Society, II (New York: Clearfield, 1901), 10–38; "Council Minutes" (23 November 1640 and 17–24 January 1641), in Van Laer, *New York Historical Manuscripts*, 4:96–100.

29. Heywood and Thornton, "Intercultural Relations between Europeans and Blacks in New Netherland," 199.

30. Joyce D. Goodfriend, "Merging the Two Streams of Migration to New Netherland," *The Worlds of the Seventeenth-Century Hudson Valley*, ed. Jaap Jacobs and L. H. Roper (Albany: State University of New York Press, 2014), 246.

31. Purple, *Marriages from 1639 to 1801 in the Reformed Dutch Church*, 11.

32. "Court Minutes of New Amsterdam" (13 February 1666), in Fernow, *The Records of New Amsterdam from 1653 to 1674*, 5:337, 340. For more cases, see Peter R. Christoph, "The Freedmen

of New Amsterdam," *A Beautiful and Fruitful Place: Selected Rensselaerswijck Seminar Papers*, ed. Nancy A. M. Zeller (New York: New Netherland Publishing, 1991), 162.

33. Rink, "Before the English (1609–1664)," 52; Foote, *Black and White Manhattan*, 37. On the Portuguese roots of Papiamentu, see Linda M. Rupert, *Creolization and Contraband: Curaçao and the Early Modern Atlantic World* (Athens: University of Georgia Press, 2012), 214–21; on Saramaccan, see John McWhorter and Jeff Good, *A Grammar of Saramaccan Creole* (Berlin: De Gruyter, 2012).

34. Peter Kolbe, *The Present State of the Cape*, 2 vols. (1719; London: Johnson Reprint, 1968), 2:363.

35. "Court Minutes of New Amsterdam" (28 February and 28 March 1662), Fernow, *The Records of New Amsterdam from 1653 to 1674*, 4:41–42, 56–57; "Order Increasing the Salary of Resolved Waldron" (10 June 1657), New Netherland Documents, Doc. 8:595b (New York State Museum, Albany); "Sundry Papers in Relation to the Case of Jan Gaillardo and his Negro Slaves; Appendix 5" (26 April 1658), O'Callaghan, Fernow, and Brodhead, *Documents Relative to the Colonial History of the State of New York*, 31; Evans, *Records of the Reformed Dutch Church in New Amsterdam and New York*, 38; Purple, *Marriages from 1639 to 1801 in the Reformed Dutch Church*, 29; "New York Colonial Manuscripts" XXOOO: 275 (New York State Archives); Jasper Dankers and Peter Sluyter, *Journal of a Voyage to New York and a Tour in Several of the American Colonies in 1679–80*, ed. Henry C. Murphy (1680; Brooklyn: Long Island Historical Society, 1867), 137.

36. "Contract of sale between Adam Roelantsen and Ulderick Klein" (8 August 1642), in Van Laer, *New York Historical Manuscripts*, 2:59–60; Stokes, *The Iconography of Manhattan Island*, 2:207, 297, and 4:88, 193; Goodfriend, "Burghers and Blacks," 125–44; Hodges, *Root and Branch*, 10.

37. "Court Minutes of New Amsterdam" (8 April 1664), in Fernow, *The Records of New Amsterdam from 1653 to 1674*, 5:45; Edmund Bailey O'Callaghan, ed., *History of New Netherland*, 2 vols. (New York: D. Appleton, 1846–48), 2:348–49; Stokes, *The Iconography of Manhattan Island*, 4:218.

38. O'Callaghan, *History of New Netherland*, 1:441; Dirk Mouw, Gijs Boink, and Tom Weterings, ed., *The Memorandum Book of Anthony de Hooges* (Albany: New Netherland Research Center and New Netherland Institute, 2012), 59.

39. "Letter from the Directors at Amsterdam to the Director General and Council" (19 December 1656), in Gehring, *Correspondence 1654–1658*, 111.

40. "Instructions for the Director and Council in New Netherland" (26 May 1657) and "Letter from the Directors in Holland to Stuyvesant" (20 September 1660), in O'Callaghan, Fernow, and Brodhead, *Documents Relative to the Colonial History of the State of New York*, 14:392, 482.

41. Goodfriend, "Burghers and Blacks," 132–42; Susanah Shaw Romney, *New Netherland Connections: Intimate Networks and Atlantic Ties in Seventeenth-Century America* (Chapel Hill: University of North Carolina Press, 2014), 206–7.

42. Foote, *Black and White Manhattan*, 36; Jacobs, *New Netherland*, 380–88; Jacobs, "Migration, Population, and Government in New Netherland," 86.

43. "To Jan Baptist van Rensselaer" (20 August 1659), in Van Laer, ed., *Correspondence of Jeremias van Rensselaer 1651–1674*, 167.

44. Jacobs, *New Netherland*, 387; Moore, "A World of Possibilities," 39; Heywood and Thornton, "Intercultural Relations between Europeans and Blacks in New Netherland," 192–203.

45. O'Callaghan, *Calendar of Historical Manuscripts in the Office of the Secretary of State, Albany, New York*, 1:259.

46. "Council Minutes" (25 June 1646), in Van Laer, *New York Historical Manuscripts*, 4:326–28. See also Cynthia J. Van Zandt, *Brothers among Nations: The Pursuit of Intercultural Alliances in Early America, 1580–1660* (Oxford and New York: Oxford University Press, 2008), 159–62.

47. Joosse, *Geloof in de Nieuwe Wereld*, 425–26; Evan Haefeli, *New Netherland and the Dutch Origins of American Religious Liberty* (Philadelphia: University of Pennsylvania Press, 2012), 100.

48. Van Deursen, *Bavianen en slijkgeuzen*, 139.

49. Ibid., 137.

50. "Ordinance" (15 April 1638), in O'Callaghan, *Laws and Ordinances of New Netherland, 1638–1674*, 12.

51. Evans, *Records of the Reformed Dutch Church in New Amsterdam and New York*, 23; Purple, *Marriages from 1639 to 1801 in the Reformed Dutch Church*, 16; David Steven Cohen, *The Ramapo Mountain People* (New Brunswick, NJ: Rutgers University Press, 1974), 26–31; Moore, "A World of Possibilities," 47–48. For interracial marriages in Dutch Brazil, see Joosse, *Geloof in de Nieuwe Wereld*, 508–9.

52. Frijhoff, *Wegen van Evert Willemsz.*, 529; Joosse, *Geloof in de Nieuwe Wereld*, 166.

53. Frijhoff, *Wegen van Evert Willemsz.*, 530–31.

54. "Classicale Acta van Brazilië" (3 March 1637), in Historisch Genootschap, *Kroniek van het Historisch Genootschap* 29, vol. 6, no. 4 (Utrecht: Kemink en zoon, 1874), 314; Frans Leonard Schalkwijk, *The Reformed Church in Dutch Brazil, 1630–1654* (Zoetermeer, NL: Boekencentrum, 1998), 151; Joosse, *Geloof in de Nieuwe Wereld*, 507–8; Evan Haefeli, "Breaking the Christian Atlantic: The Legacy of Dutch Tolerance in Brazil," *The Legacy of Dutch Brazil*, ed. Michiel van Groesen (Cambridge, UK: Cambridge University Press, 2014), 124–45. For Angola, see Joosse, *Geloof in de Nieuwe Wereld*, 169. For the Dutch Cape Colony, see Robert C.-H. Shell, *Children of Bondage: A Social History of the Slave Society at the Cape of Good Hope, 1652–1838* (Hanover, CT, and London: Wesleyan University Press, 1994), 337; Ad Biewenga, *De Kaap de Goede Hoop: Een Nederlandse vestigingskolonie, 1680–1730* (Amsterdam: Prometheus-Bert Bakker, 1999), 184–88. For Dutch colonies in Southeast Asia, see G. J. Schutte, "De kerk onder de Compagnie," *Het Indisch Sion. De Gereformeerde Kerk onder Verenigde Oost-Indische Compagnie*, ed. G. J. Schutte (Hilversum, NL: Verloren, 2002), 60–62.

55. "Acta Deputatorum ad res Exteras" (19 November 1641), Hastings and Corwin, *Ecclesiastical Records*, I:142; Evans, *Records of the Reformed Dutch Church in New Amsterdam and New York*, 10–38; Jacobs, *New Netherland*, 312–18; Foote, *Black and White Manhattan*, 48; Hodges, *Root and Branch*, 16; Romney, *New Netherland Connections*, 214.

56. "Rapport de Pieter Moortamer au Conseil du Brésil" (14 October 1642), in Jadin, *L'Ancien Congo et l'Angola 1639–1655*, 1:348.

57. Olfert Dapper, *Naukeurige beschrijvinge der Afrikaensche gewesten* (Amsterdam: Jacob van Meurs, 1668), 588.

58. "A Brief Report on the State That is Composed of the Four Conquered Captaincies, Pernambuco, Itamaracá, Paraíba, and Rio Grande, Situated in the North of Brazil" (14 January 1638), in Schwartz and Willis, *Early Brazil*, 239.

59. "To the Directors of the Zeeland Chamber of the West India Company" (8 June 1636), in B. N. Teensma and Niels Erik Hyldgaard Nielsen, ed., *Seventeen Letters by Vincent Joachim Soler, Protestant Minister in the Service of the West Indies Company, Written in Recife, Brazil, Between 1636 and 1643* (Rio de Janeiro: Index, 1999), 11–12.

60. "Letters of Wouter van Twiller and the Director General and Council of New Netherland to the Amsterdam Chamber of the Dutch West India Company" (14 August 1636), in Arnold J. F. van Laer, ed., *Quarterly Journal of the New York State Historical Association* 1 (October 1919): 48. See also Jacobs, *New Netherland*, 313.

61. Joosse, *Geloof in the Nieuwe Wereld*, 242.

62. L. Knappert, "De eerste honderd jaren der Protestantische gemeente op Curaçao," *Gedenkboek Nederland-Curaçao 1634–1934* (Amsterdam: J.H. de Bussy, 1934), 34–56; Rupert, *Creolization and Contraband*, 85–90.

63. "Classis of Amsterdam. Act of the Deputies" (25 October 1660), in Hastings and Corwin, *Ecclesiastical Records,* 1:493.

64. "Classis of Amsterdam. Act of the Deputies. Letter to Rev. Van Beaumont" (9 July 1661), in Ibid., 1:508.

65. "Beaumont to the Amsterdam Classis" (5 December 1662), Archief Classis Amsterdam, Stadsarchief Amsterdam, inv. nr. 224, fol. 17–21; Daniel Noorlander, "Serving God and Mammon: The Reformed Church and the Dutch West India Company in the Atlantic World, 1621–1674" (Ph.D. diss., Georgetown University, 2011), 277; Joosse, *Geloof in de Nieuwe Wereld,* 344–45.

66. "Rev. Henry Selyns, Minister at Brooklyn, L.I., to the Classis of Amsterdam" (4 October 1660), Hastings and Corwin, *Ecclesiastical Records,* 1:479.

67. "Vice Director Beck to Petrus Stuyvesant, Curaçao" (15 November 1664), in Gehring and Schiltkamp, *Curaçao Papers*, 451.

68. *Acta Synodi Nationalis* (Dordrecht, NL: Typis Isaaci Ioannidis Caninii, 1620), quoted in Shell, *Children of Bondage,* 335.

69. Godefridus Udemans, *'t geestelyk roer van 't coopmansschip* (Dordrecht, NL: Francois Boels, 1640), 183.

70. Joosse, *Geloof in de Nieuwe Wereld,* 506; Mosterman, "Sharing Spaces in a New World Environment," 162–64.

71. "Act of the Director and Council of New Netherland emancipating certain Negro Slaves therein mentioned" (25 February 1644), in O'Callaghan, *Laws and Ordinances of New Netherland,* 36–37.

72. "Short Digest of the Excesses and Highly Injurious Neglect" (27 January 1650), in O'Callaghan, Fernow, and Brodhead, *Documents Relative to the Colonial History of the State of New York,* 1:335.

73. "Answer of the West India Company to the Remonstrance of New Netherland" (31 January 1650), in Ibid., 1:343.

74. "Act of the Director and Council of New Netherland manumitting a Negro slave" (27 September 1646), in O'Callaghan, *Laws and Ordinances of New Netherland,* 60.

75. "Manumission of Manuel the Spaniard by Philip Jansz Ringo" (15 February 1649) and "Will of Jan Jansen Damen" (12 December 1649), in Van Laer, *New York Historical Manuscripts,* 3:82–83, 208–10.

76. Charles T. Gehring, ed., *New York Historical Manuscripts: Dutch, Volumes GG, HH & II; Land Papers* (Baltimore, MD: Genealogical Publishing, 1980), 24, 34, 36, 48.

77. "Minutes of Executive Boards" (8 May 1663), in Berthold Fernow, ed., *The Minutes of the Orphanmasters of New Amsterdam, 1655 to 1663*, 2 vols. (New York: F.P. Harper, 1902–07), 2:46.

78. Jacobs, *New Netherland*, 388; Joyce D. Goodfriend, "Black Families in New Netherland," *A Beautiful and Fruitful Place: Selected Rensselaerswijck Seminar Papers*, ed. Nancy A. M. Zeller (New York: New Netherland Publishing, 1991), 152.

79. "New York Colonial Manuscripts" X/3: 329–32 and "Land Patents," II: 102–15 (New York State Archives); Gehring, *Land Papers*, 24, 34, 36, 48, 55–56, 58; Cohen, *The Ramapo Mountain People*, 25–42; Christoph, "The Freedmen of New Amsterdam," 163–65.

80. Romney, *New Netherland Connections*, 227.

81. Stokes, *The Iconography of Manhattan Island*, 4:265–66; Hodges, *Root and Branch*, 13–15; Foote, *Black and White Manhattan*, 40.

82. Stokes, *The Iconography of Manhattan Island*, 1:76, 4:97, 6:73–76, 123–24.

83. Dankers and Sluyter, *Journal of a Voyage to New York and a Tour in Several of the American Colonies in 1679–80*, 136.

84. "Register" (14 January 1662), in Edmund Bailey O'Callaghan, ed., *Register of Salomon Lachaire: Notary Public of New Amsterdam, 1661–1662* (Baltimore, MD: Genealogical Publishing, 1978), 99–100.

85. Goodfriend, "The Struggle over the Sabbath in Petrus Stuyvesant's New Amsterdam," 217–18; Hodges, *Root and Branch*, 15–16.

86. William Stuart, "Negro Slavery in New Jersey and New York," *Americana* XVI, no. 4 (October 1922): 354.

87. Page, *The Dutch Triangle*, 218.

88. Giles R. Wright, *Afro-Americans in New Jersey: A Short History* (Trenton: New Jersey Historical Commission, 1988), 22; James Oliver Horton and Lois E. Horton, *In Hope of Liberty: Culture, Community, and Protest Among Northern Free Blacks, 1700–1860* (Oxford and New York: Oxford University Press, 1997), 12; Hodges, *Root and Branch*, 40–43, 74–82; Jill Lepore, "The Tightening Vise: Slavery and Freedom in British New York," *Slavery in New York*, ed. Ira Berlin and Leslie M. Harris (New York: New Press, 2005), 57–90; Philip Misevich, "In Pursuit of Human Cargo: Philip Livingston and the Voyage of the Sloop *Rhode Island*," *New York History* 86, no. 3 (Summer 2005): 185–87.

89. White, *Somewhat More Independent*, 18–20; David Steven Cohen, *The Dutch-American Farm* (New York: New York University Press, 1992), 145; David N. Gellman, *Emancipating New York: The Politics of Slavery and Freedom 1777–1827* (Baton Rouge: Louisiana State University Press, 2006), 19.

90. Peter O. Wacker, *Land and People. A Cultural Geography of Preindustrial New Jersey: Origins and Settlement Patterns* (New Brunswick, NJ: Rutgers University Press, 1975), 203; Cohen, *The Ramapo Mountain People*, 25–42; Moore, "A World of Possibilities," 47; Christoph, "The Freedmen of New Amsterdam," 165; Hodges, *Root and Branch*, 35, 70; Harris, *In the Shadow of Slavery*, 39; Foote, *Black and White Manhattan*, 149–50; Berlin, *Generations of Captivity*, 85.

91. William Strickland, *Journal of a Tour in the United States of America, 1794–1795*, ed. J. E. Strickland (1795; New York: New York Historical Society, 1971), 41, 163.

92. Quoted in Henry P. Johnston, *The Campaign of 1776 around New York and Brooklyn* (Brooklyn: Long Island Historical Society, 1878), 97.

93. Coventry, "Memoirs of an Emigrant," 142 (2 February 1787); François Alexandre Frédéric, Duc de La Rochefoucauld Liancourt, *Travels through the United States of North America, the Country of the Iroquois, and Upper Canada in the Years 1795, 1796, and 1797*, 2 vols. (London: T. Gillet for R. Phillips, 1800), 2:233.

94. La Rochefoucauld-Liancourt, *Travels through the United States of North America*, 2:305, 458.

95. Roderic H. Blackburn and Ruth Piwonka, *Remembrance of Patria: Dutch Arts and Culture in Colonial America 1609–1776* (Albany, NY: Albany Institute of History and Art, 1988), 196, 231.

96. Alice P. Kenney, *The Gansevoorts of Albany: Dutch Patricians in the Upper Hudson Valley* (Syracuse, NY: Syracuse University Press, 1969), 139.

97. Anne Grant, *Memoirs of an American Lady with Sketches of Manners and Scenes in America as they Existed Previous to the Revolution* (1808; New York: Dodd, Mead, 1909), 81.

98. I would like to thank Cynthia McLeod for this information.

99. Grant, *Memoirs of an American Lady*, 86.

100. "Baptisms in the Reformed Protestant Dutch Church," in Joel Munsell, ed., *Annals of Albany*, 10 vols. (Albany, NY: Joel Munsell, 1871), III: 326.

101. Quoted in Hodges, *Root and Branch*, 79.

102. White, *Somewhat More Independent*, 190; Cohen, *The Dutch-American Farm*, 145; Goodfriend, "The Social Life and Cultural Life of Dutch Settlers," 123.

103. Graham Russell Hodges and Alan Edward Brown, ed., *Pretends to Be Free: Runaway Slave Advertisements from Colonial and Revolutionary New York and New Jersey* (New York: Garland, 1994), 11, 12, 111.

104. Ibid., 87, 97, 112.

105. Alexander Hamilton, *Gentlemen's Progress: The Itinerarium of Dr. Alexander Hamilton, 1744*, ed. Carl Bridenbaugh (Pittsburgh, PA: University of Pittsburgh Press, 1948), 40–41.

106. Nina Moore Tiffany and Francis Tiffany, eds., *Harm Jan Huidekoper* (Cambridge, MA: Riverside Press, 1904), 30.

107. Truth, *Narrative of Sojourner Truth*, 15.

108. H. Hendricks, "Sojourner Truth," *National Magazine: A Monthly Journal of American History* 16, no. 6 (October 1802): 671.

109. Gertrude Lefferts Vanderbilt, *The Social History of Flatbush and Manners and Customs of the Dutch Settlers in Kings County* (New York: D. Appleton, 1882), 252.

110. *Troy Daily Times*, August 31, 1885.

111. John Jea, "The Life, History, and Unparalleled Sufferings of John Jea, the African Preacher (1811)," *Black Itinerants of the Gospel: The Narratives of John Jea and George White*, ed. Graham Russell Hodges (Madison, WI: Madison House, 1993), 113.

112. K. Leroy Irvis, "Negro Tales from Eastern New York," *New York Folklore Quarterly* XI, no. 3 (1955): 165.

113. Alexander Graydon, *Memoirs of a Life Chiefly Passed in Pennsylvania, Within the Last Sixty Years* (Edinburgh, UK: W. Blackwood, 1822), 259.

114. Grant, *Memoirs of an American Lady*, 80–81.

115. Coventry, "Memoirs of an Emigrant," 145 (14 February 1787).

116. James Flint, *Letters from America: Containing Observations on the Climate and Agriculture of the Western States, the Manners of the People, the Prospects of Emigrants &c.*, ed. Reuben Gold Thwaites (1822; Cleveland, OH: Arthur Clark, 1904), 37.

117. Ibid., 40.

118. *Troy Daily Times*, August 31, 1885.

119. Norman C. Wittwer, *The Faithful and the Bold: The Story of the First Service of the Zion Evangelical Lutheran Church, Oldwick, New Jersey* (Oldwick, NJ: Zion Evangelical Lutheran Church, 1984), 7.

120. Louis Duermyer, ed., *Records of the Reformed Dutch Church of Albany, New York, 1689–1809: Marriages, Baptisms, Members, etc. Excerpted from Year Books of the Holland Society of New York* (Baltimore, MD: Genealogical Publishing, 1978), 52, 55–57, 58, 71, 110; Gerald F. de Jong, "The Dutch Reformed Church and Negro Slavery in Colonial America," *Church History* 12, no. 4 (1971): 423–36; Gerald F. de Jong, *The Dutch Reformed Church in the American Colonies* (Grand Rapids, MI: Eerdmans, 1978), 138, 167; White, *Somewhat More Independent*, 79–113; Harris, *In the Shadow of Slavery*, 35, 52; Hodges, *Root and Branch*, 62, 181; Dennis J. Maika, "Encounters: Slavery and the Philipse Family, 1680–1751," *Dutch New York: The Roots of Hudson Valley Culture*, ed. Roger Panetta (Bronx, NY: Fordham University Press, 2009), 46–48; Goodfriend, "The Social Life and Cultural Life of Dutch Settlers," 123–24; Anne-Claire Merlin-Faucquez, "De la Nouvelle-Néerlande à New York: la naissance d'une société esclavagiste (1624–1712)" (Ph.D. diss., Université Paris VIII, 2011), 459; Mosterman, "Sharing Spaces in a New World Environment," 150–81.

121. Roswell Randall Hoes, ed., *Baptismal and Marriage Registers of the Old Dutch Church of Kingston, Ulster County, New York* (New York: De Vinne Press, 1891), 70.

122. "Elias Neau to Secretary of S.P.G.," (30 April 1706), quoted in Hodges, *Slavery, Freedom and Culture among Early American Workers* (Armond, NY: M.E. Sharpe, 1998), 37. See also Hodges, *Root and Branch*, 63.

123. John Sharpe, "Proposals for Erecting a School, Library and Chapel at New York (1713)," *Collections of the New-York Historical Society for the Year 1880* (New York: Trow & Smith, 1880), 353.

124. Berlin, *Generations of Captivity*, 86.

125. Ukawsaw Gronniosaw, "A Narrative of the Most Remarkable Particulars in the Life of James Albert Ukawsaw Gronniosaw, an African Prince, Written by Himself," *Black Atlantic Writers of the Eighteenth Century: Living the New Exodus in England and the Americas*, ed. Adam Potkay and Sandra Burr (ca. 1770; New York: St. Martin's Press, 1995), 27–63.

126. Gronniosaw, "Narrative," 35–36, 40–46; Dewulf, "The Many Languages of American Literature," 227–32.

127. Truth, *Narrative of Sojourner Truth*, 7.

128. Quoted in Firth Haring Fabend, *Zion on the Hudson: Dutch New York and New Jersey in the Age of Revivals* (New Brunswick, NJ: Rutgers University Press, 2000), 180.

129. "Court Minutes" (7 March 1671), Fernow, *The Records of New Amsterdam from 1653 to 1674*, 6:286.

130. "Minutes of the Common Council" (4, 5, 6 October 1682; 8 August 1692), in Herbert I. Osgood, Charles Alexander Nelson, and Austin Baxter Keep, ed., *Minutes of the Common Council of the City of New York, 1675–1776*, 8 vols. (New York: Dodd, Mead, 1905), 1:92, 276–77.

131. Edgar J. McManus, *A History of Negro Slavery in New York* (Syracuse, NY: Syracuse University Press, 1966), 87; Hodges, *Root and Branch*, 48, 50, 115; Harris, *In the Shadow of Slavery*, 43; Gellman, *Emancipating New York*, 20; Dennis Sullivan, *The Punishment of Crime in Colonial New York: The Dutch Experience in Albany during the Seventeenth Century* (New York: Peter Lang, 1997), 229.

132. Quoted in Joyce D. Goodfriend, *Before the Melting Pot: Society and Culture in Colonial New York City, 1664–1730* (Princeton, NJ: Princeton University Press, 1992), 121.

133. Oscar Williams, *African Americans and Colonial Legislation in the Middle Colonies* (New York: Garland, 1998), 76; Hodges, *Root and Branch*, 48–51; Lepore, "The Tightening Vise," 76.

134. See Harris, *In the Shadow of Slavery*, 37.

135. Quoted in Hodges, *Root and Branch*, 50.

136. Quoted in Verter, "Interracial Festivity and Power in Antebellum New York," 408.

137. Quoted in Foote, *Black and White Manhattan*, 203.

138. Ibid., 138.

139. Ibid., 167.

140. McManus, *A History of Negro Slavery in New York*, 86, 140; Hodges, *Root and Branch*, 67; Harris, *In the Shadow of Slavery*, 40–47; Lepore, "The Tightening Vise," 76.

141. White, *Somewhat More Independent*, 108–12, 150–53; Harris, *In the Shadow of Slavery*, 40.

142. Percy van Epps, *Contributions to the History of Glenville* (Glenville, NY: Glenville Town Board, 1932), 101–2.

143. *New-York Tribune*, February 23, 1902.

144. Walter Auclair, "Simeon Button (1757–1836), Pittstown Farmer and Rensselaer County Justice of the Peace," *Pittstown Historical Society Newsletter* XV (Spring 2009): 5.

145. *Albany Chronicle*, July 8, 1803.

146. Grant, *Memoirs of an American Lady*, 92.

147. Coventry, "Memoirs of an Emigrant," 108 (4 and 5 June 1786), 211 (11 April 1789), 215 (1 June 1789).

148. Quoted in Watson, *Annals and Occurrences of New York City and State*, 177–78.

149. William Dunlap, *Diary of William Dunlap (1766–1839): The Memoirs of a Dramatist, Theatrical Manager, Painter, Critic, Novelist, and Historian*, 3 vols. (New York: New York Historical Society, 1930), 1:65.

150. *Albany Centinel*, June 13, 1803.

151. Hall, *Slavery and African Ethnicities in the Americas*, 80–81.

152. Grant, *Memoirs of an American Lady*, 80.

153. "A Glimpse of an Old Dutch Town: Pinkster Festival in Albany Two Centuries Ago," *Harper's New Monthly Magazine* 62 (March 1881): 525–26.

154. Volkert P. Douw was the son of Petrus Douw, who had married Anna, daughter of Hendrick van Rensselaer and Catrina van Brugh, who was a granddaughter of Anneke Jans. *Troy Daily Times*, December 18, 1890; *Harper's New Monthly Magazine* 62 (March 1881): 525–26; www.nysm.nysed.gov/albany/bios/d/vopdouw2234.html.

155. The mansion at Wolvenhoeck was built in 1724 by Volkert's father Petrus Douw and later became known as Douws' Point, Riverside Avenue. *Troy Daily Times*, December 18, 1890.

156. People claimed that Charles was 125 years old when he passed away. Joel Munsell, "Theatrical Reminiscences," *Collections on the History of Albany*, ed. Joel Munsell, 4 vols. (Albany, NY: J. Munsell, 1865–71), 2:56.

157. Eights, "Pinkster Festivities in Albany Sixty Years Ago," 2:323–27.

158. In 1819, the city directory identified Adam Blake as a "free person of color." Following the death of patroon Van Rensselaer, Blake lived with his family on Third Street in Arbor Hill and became a regular participant in services at the North Dutch church. www.nysm.nysed.gov/albany/bios/b/adblake.html.

159. The Dutch Kwakkenbos family, whose name was later anglicized into Quackenbush, came to the Hudson Valley around 1662. Hendrick was a middle son of Rensselaerswyck residents Peter W. Quackenbush and his wife Anna Oothout. Austin A. Yates, *Schenectady County, New York: Its History to the Close of the Nineteenth Century* (New York: New York History Company, 1902), 236; www.nysm.nysed.gov/albany/bios/q/heq2111.html.

160. Other publications by an author using the pseudonym Absalom Aimwell were written by Andrew Adgate (1762–1793), a musician and music director from Philadelphia. Since Adgate passed away ten years before the *Pinkster Ode* was published, it is unlikely that he is the author. Harmon Dean Cummings, "Andrew Adgate: Philadelphia Psalmodist and Music Educator" (Ph.D. diss., University of Rochester, 1975).

161. Absalom Aimwell Esq., "A Pinkster Ode for the Year 1803," ed. Geraldine R. Pleat and Agnes N. Underwood, *New York Folklore Quarterly* 8 (1952): 35.

162. "Pinxter Customs in the By-Gone," *Manhattan and de la Salle Monthly* (May 1875): 272–73.

163. "Albany Fifty Years Ago," *Harper's New Monthly Magazine* (April 1857): 453.

164. "A Glimpse of an Old Dutch Town," 526.

165. Ibid., 536; *Troy Daily Times*, December 18, 1890.

166. *Family Magazine or Monthly Abstract of General Knowledge* (1836): 363–64.

167. *Schenectady Cabinet, or, Freedom's Sentinel*, July 28, 1846.

168. *Schenectady Daily Evening Star and Times*, May 21, 1866.

169. Munsell, "Theatrical Reminiscences," 2:56.

170. *Schenectady Daily Evening Star and Times*, May 21, 1866.

171. *Chittenango Herald*, January 5, 1836.

172. Arthur J. Weise, *History of the City of Troy: From the Expulsion of the Mohegan Indians to the Present Centennial Year of the Independence of the United States of America* (Troy, NY: W.H. Young, 1876), 63–64.

173. *Troy Daily Times*, September 19, 1872.

174. *Kingston Daily Freeman*, August 19, 1881.

175. *Balance and Columbian Repository*, May 29, 1804.

176. Windmill Hill is the old name of Prospect Hill, which later became Academy Hill. The name relates to a wind gristmill built on the hill by Joseph Barnard in 1789. Anna R. Bradbury, *History of the City of Hudson, New York: with Biographical Sketches of Henry Hudson and Robert Fulton* (Hudson, NY: Record Printing and Publishing, 1908), 30.

177. *Albany Evening Journal*, September 1, 1859.

178. David Murdoch, *The Dutch Dominie of the Catskills; The Times of the "Bloody Brandt"* (New York: Derby & Jackson, 1861), 279–80, 311, 364.

179. Jacqueline Bernard, *Journey toward Freedom: The Story of Sojourner Truth*, ed. Nell Irvin Painter (1967; New York: Feminist Press at City University of New York, 1990), 43.

180. Grace Greylock Niles, *The Hoosac Valley, its Legends and its History* (New York: G.P. Putnam's Sons, 1912), 415, 488.

181. Stuckey, *Going through the Storm*, 77.

182. *New-York Times*, May 28, 1882.

183. *Evening Post*, May 1, 1850.

184. Rachel Van Dyke, *To Read My Heart: The Journal of Rachel van Dyke, 1810–1811*, ed. Lucia McMahon and Deborah Schriver (Philadelphia: University of Pennsylvania Press, 2000), 44.

185. Nelson Greene, *The Story of Old Fort Plain and the Middle Mohawk Valley: A Review of Mohawk Valley History from 1609 to the Time of the Writing of this Book, 1912–1914* (Fort Plain, NY: O'Connor Brothers, 1915), 302.

186. Earle, *Colonial Days in Old New York*, 196.

187. Charles F. Rockwell, *Recollections of Men, Customs and Events in Milford Pennsylvania and Vicinity* (Milford, PA: s.p., 1889), 45–47. I would like to thank the Pike County Historical Society for providing a copy of this source.

188. James Fenimore Cooper, *The Legends and Traditions of a Northern County* (New York: G.P. Putnam's Sons, 1920), 99, 202.

189. James Fenimore Cooper, *Satanstoe, or The Littlepage Manuscripts: A Tale of the Colony (1845)*, ed. Kay Seymour House and Constance Ayers Denne (New York: State University of New York Press, 1990), 61–65.

190. For the history of the Burial Ground, see Andrea E. Frohne: *The African Burial Ground in New York City: Memory, Spirituality, and Space* (Syracuse, NY: Syracuse University Press, 2015).

191. Sharpe, "Proposals for Erecting a School," 355.

192. David T. Valentine, *Manual of the Common Council of New York* (New York: D.T. Valentine, 1865), 567.

193. White, "Afro-Dutch Syncretization in New York City and the Hudson Valley," 72.

194. Kay Seymour House, "Historical Introduction," in James Fenimore Cooper, *Satanstoe*, xvii.

195. James H. Pickering, "Fenimore Cooper and Pinkster," *New York Folklore Quarterly* XXII, no. 1 (1966): 17.

196. Stuckey, *Going through the Storm*, 73, 77.

197. Epperson, "The Contested Commons," 81–110; Leslie M. Alexander, *African or American? Black Identity and Political Activism in New York City, 1784–1861* (Urbana: University of Illinois Press, 2008), 6.

198. Watson, *Annals and Occurrences of New York City and State*, 204; Stiles, *A History of the City of Brooklyn*, 38–40.

1989. Furman, *Antiquities of Long Island*, 265; *The Corrector*, March 18, 1882.

200. Thomas F. De Voe, *The Market Book (1862)*, 2 vols. (New York: August M. Kelley, 1970), 1:344.

201. *Public Advertiser*, May 23, 1809.

202. *The Sun*, April 30, 1876; *New-York Times*, June 11, 1878; *New York Evening Express*, May 16, 1880.

Chapter 3

1. White, "Pinkster in Albany," 195. For similar views, see Cohen, *The Dutch-American Farm*, 163; Newman, "Pinkster and Slavery in Dutch New York," 1–8; Pershing, "Representations of Racial Identity in a Contemporary Pinkster Celebration," 52; Merlin-Faucquez, "De la Nouvelle-Néerlande à New York," 513–16.

2. Mosterman, "Sharing Spaces in a New World Environment," 183, 216.

3. Ibid., 189–90.

4. *Schenectady Cabinet, or, Freedom's Sentinel*, July 28, 1846.

5. Furman, *Antiquities of Long Island*, 266–67.

6. Henry Onderdonk Jr., *History of the First Reformed Dutch Church of Jamaica* (Jamaica, NY: The Consistory, 1884), 27.

7. Henry C. Castellanos, *New Orleans as it was* (New Orleans: L. Graham & Son, 1895), 158.

8. Aimwell, "A Pinkster Ode for the Year 1803," 37–39. Aimwell's orthographic mistakes when trying to quote foreign languages—German "peer" instead of "Bier"; Dutch "yaw" and "nayn" instead of "ja" and "neen"; French "Carmanole" instead of "Carmagnole" and "sac cra je" instead of "sacredieu"—and his familiarity with British cultural and religious affairs indicates that he had an Anglo-American background.

9. Jeptha Root Simms, *History of Schoharie County and Border Wars of New York* (Albany, NY: Munsell & Tanner, 1845), 163; "Pinxter Customs in the By-Gone," *Manhattan and de la Salle Monthly* (May 1875): 272–73; Niles, *The Hoosac Valley, its Legends and its History*, 415.

10. Schuyler van Rensselaer, *History of the City of New York in the Seventeenth Century*, 2 vols. (New York: Macmillan, 1909), 1:462; Donna Merwick, *Possessing Albany, 1630–1710: The Dutch and English Experiences* (Cambridge, UK: Cambridge University Press, 1990), 75; Sponsler, *Ritual Imports*, 48.

11. Frijhoff, *Wegen van Evert Willemsz.*, 775.

12. Fred van Lieburg, "The Dutch and their Religion," *Four Centuries of Dutch-American Relations 1609–2009*, 157.

13. Jacobs, *New Netherland*, 312. See also Venema, *Beverwijck*, 103–4; Haefeli, *New Netherland and the Dutch Origins of American Religious Liberty*, 280.

14. Hodges, *Slavery and Freedom in the Rural North*, 31, 58, 87, 153. See also Armstead, *Mighty Change, Tall Within*, 6; Harris, *In the Shadow of Slavery*, 41.

15. White, *Somewhat More Independent*, 99.

16. Roger D. Abrahams, "The Shaping of Folklore Traditions in the British West Indies," *Journal of Inter-American Studies* 9 (1967): 462.

17. Herman Pleij, *Het gilde van de Blauwe Schuit. Literatuur, volksfeest en burgermoraal in de late middeleeuwen* (Amsterdam: Meulenhoff, 1979), 33; Armand Sermon, *Carnaval. Geschiedenis van het carnaval van Keizer Karel tot Eedje Anseele* (Ghent, BE: SMK, 2001), 42–45; Van Dixhoorn, *Lustige geesten*, 60.

18. "Resolution to Suppress Shrovetide Activities" (26 January 1654), Charles T. Gehring and Janny Venema, ed., *Fort Orange Records, 1654–1679* (Syracuse, NY: Syracuse University Press, 2009), 56.

19. Frans De Potter, "Schets eener geschiedenis der gemeentefeesten in Vlaanderen," *Annales de la Société des Beaux-Arts et de littérature de Gand* 12 (1870): 26, 144; Lod. Torfs and

C.-J. Hansen, "Nederlandsche Krijgs- en Partijnamen," *Annales de l'Académie d'Archéologie de Belgique XXX*, vol. 10, no. 2 (Antwerp, BE: J-E Buschmann, 1874), 432–34; Ludovic Pinchin, *Dissertations receuillis. Le Roy des Ribauds* (Paris: Claudin, 1878), 171; Willy L. Braekman, *Spel en kwel in vroeger tijd. Verkenningen van charivari, exorcisme, toverij, spot en spel in Vlaanderen* (Ghent, BE: Stiching Mens en Kultuur, 1992), 294; Pieter Spierenburg, *The Spectacle of Suffering: Executions and the Evolution of Repression: from a Preindustrial Metropolis to the European Experience* (Cambridge, UK: Cambridge University Press, 1984), 21; Sermon, *Carnaval*, 47–48.

20. Herman Pleij, *De sneeuwpoppen van 1511. Literatuur en stadscultuur tussen middeleeuwen en moderne tijd* (Amsterdam: Meulenhoff, 1988), 148–49; Frijhoff and Spies, *Nederlandse cultuur in Europese context: 1650*, 212.

21. Kevin Dawson, "The Cultural Geography of Enslaved Ship Pilots," *The Black Urban Atlantic in the Age of the Slave Trade*, ed. Jorge Cañizares-Esguerra, Matt D. Childs, and James Sidbury (Philadelphia: University of Pennsylvania Press, 2013), 175.

22. Jori Zijlmans, *Leidens Ontzet: vrijheidsstrijd & volksfeest* (Leiden, NL: Primavera Pers, 2011), 116.

23. Van Dixhoorn, *Lustige geesten*, 224.

24. *New-England Palladium*, June 4, 1814.

25. "Court Minutes" (9 May 1655), Gehring, *Fort Orange Minutes 1652–1660*, 192.

26. Edward George Geoffrey Smith Stanley, Earl of Derby, *Journal of a Tour in America, 1824–1825* (London: private printing, 1930), 252–58.

27. Alcée Fortier, "Customs and Superstitions in Louisiana," *Journal of American Folklore* 1, no. 2 (1888): 138.

28. John Fanning Watson, *Annals of Philadelphia, and Pennsylvania, in the Olden Time*, 3 vols. (1830; Philadelphia: E.S. Stuart, 1899), 2:23.

29. Henry B. Whipple, *Bishop Whipple's Southern Diary, 1843–1844* (Minneapolis: University of Minnesota Press, 1937), 51.

30. Dankers and Sluyter, *Journal of a Voyage to New York and a Tour in Several of the American Colonies in 1679–80*, 345.

31. Susan G. Davis, *Parades and Power: Street Theatre in Nineteenth-Century Philadelphia* (Philadelphia: Temple University Press, 1986), 40; White, "'It Was a Proud Day,'" 18; Kenneth E. Marshall, *Manhood Enslaved: Bondmen in Eighteenth- and Early Nineteenth-Century New Jersey* (Rochester, NY: University of Rochester Press, 2011), 119–23.

32. Andrew D. Mellick Jr., *Lesser Crossroads: Edited by Hubert G. Schmidt from the Story of an Old Farm* (1889; New Brunswick, NJ: Rutgers University Press, 1948), 355–56, 376.

33. C. W. Larison, *Silvia Dubois: A Biography of the Slav Who Whipt her Mistres and Gand her Freedom (1883)*, ed. Jared C. Lobdell (New York and Oxford: Oxford University Press, 1988), 67.

34. Kenney, *The Gansevoorts of Albany*, 128.

35. *Balance and State Journal*, June 4, 1811.

36. *Evening Post: New York*, May 1, 1850.

37. Marius Schoonmaker, *The History of Kingston, New York, from Its Early Settlement to the Year 1820* (New York: Burr Printing House, 1888), 433–34.

38. Susan G. Davis, "The Career of Colonel Pluck: Folk Drama and Popular Protest in Early Nineteenth-Century Philadelphia," *Pennsylvania Magazine of History and Biography* 109, no. 2 (April 1985): 179–202.

39. Davis, *Parades and Power*, 73–112; Dale Cockrell, *Demons of Disorder: Early Blackface Minstrels and Their World* (Cambridge, UK: Cambridge University Press, 1997), 32–33.

40. Horton and Horton, *In Hope of Liberty*, 35–42.

41. Paul A. Gilje and Howard B. Rock, "'Sweep O! Sweep O!': African-American Chimney Sweeps and Citizenship in the New Nation," *William and Mary Quarterly* 51, no. 3 (July 1994): 507–38; Harris, *In the Shadow of Slavery*, 77–80.

42. Edmund K. Chambers, *The Mediaevel Stage*, 2 vols. (Oxford: Oxford University Press, 1903), 1:173–79, 199; George L. Phillips, "May-Day is Sweeps' Day," *Folklore* 60, no. 1 (March 1949): 217–18; Benita Cullingford, *British Chimney Sweeps: Five Centuries of Chimney Sweeping* (Sussex: Book Guild, 2008), 190.

43. William Hone, *The Every-Day Book, or, a Guide to the Year: Describing the Popular Amusements, Sports, Ceremonies, Manners, Customs, and Events, Incident to the Three Hundred and Sixty-Five Days, in Past and Present Times*, 2 vols. (London: Ward, 1888–89), 1:292.

44. Stuckey, *Going through the Storm*, 73.

45. Orville Platt, "Negro Governors," *New Haven Colony Historical Society Papers* vol. 6 (1900): 325; Joseph P. Reidy, "'Negro Election Day' & Black Community Life in New England, 1750–1860," *Marxist Perspectives* 1, no. 3 (Fall 1978): 103; Wade, "'Shining in Borrowed Plumage,'" 212.

46. Benjamin Lynde, *The Diaries of Benjamin Lynde and of Benjamin Lynde Jr.* (Boston, MA: privately published, 1880), 109. As Reidy confirms, slaveholders would traditionally give their slaves some pocket money at the occasion of "Election Day." Reidy, "Negro Election Day," 104.

47. Quoted in Platt, "Negro Governors," 323–24.

48. William Bentley, *The Diary of William Bentley, D.D., Pastor of the East Church, Salem, Massachusetts*, 4 vols. (Gloucester, MA: P. Smith, 1962), 4:457.

49. Reidy, "Negro Election Day," 104; White, "'It Was a Proud Day,'" 13.

50. Eights, "Pinkster Festivities in Albany Sixty Years Ago," 2:325; Reidy, "Negro Election Day," 103; William D. Piersen, *Black Yankees: The Development of an Afro-American Subculture in Eighteenth-Century New England* (Amherst: University of Massachusetts Press, 1988), 131.

51. *Albany Argus*, July 26, 1816.

52. W. Jeffrey Bolster, *Black Jacks: African American Seamen in the Age of Sail* (Cambridge, MA: Harvard University Press, 1997), 108–10, 127.

53. Joseph Valpey, *Journal of Joseph Valpey, Jr., of Salem, November 1813-April 1815, With Other Papers Relating to his Experience in Dartmoor Prison* (Detroit: Michigan Society of Colonial Wars, 1922), 19; Nathaniel Hawthorne, ed., *The Yarn of a Yankee Privateer* (New York: Funk and Wagnalls, 1926), 183, 196.

54. George Hugh Crichton, "Old Boston and its Once Familiar Faces: Sketches of Some Odd Characters who have Flourished in Boston during the Past Fifty Years" (unpub. Mss., Boston, 1881), Boston Athenaeum, Boston, MA. See also Bolster, *Black Jacks*, 111; Horton and Horton, *In Hope of Liberty*, 184.

55. Platt, "Negro Governors," 322–23; White, "'It Was a Proud Day,'" 17.

56. Sol Smith, *Theatrical Management in the West and South for Thirty Years (1868)* (New York: B. Blom, 1968), 12.

57. Platt, "Negro Governors," 324; Wade, "Shining in Borrowed Plumage," 216.

58. William Chauncey Fowler, *History of Durham, Connecticut, from the First Grant of Land in 1662 to 1866* (Hartford, CT: Press of Wiley, 1866), 162.

59. Frances Manwaring Caulkins, *History of Norwich, Connecticut: From its Possession by the Indians to the Year 1866* (Hartford, CT: Caulkins, 1866), 330–31.

60. Platt, "Negro Governors," 318–20.

61. Piersen, *Black Yankees*, 130.

62. Joseph Barlow Felt, *Annals of Salem*, 2 vols. (Salem, MA: W. & S. B. Ives, 1845–49), 2:419.

63. Wilkins Updike, *History of the Episcopal Church in Narragansett, Rhode Island* (New York: Henry M. Onderdonk, 1847), 178.

64. I. W. Stuart, *Sketches of Hartford in Olden Times* (Hartford, CT: Stuart, 1853), 40; Wade, "Shining in Borrowed Plumage," 226–27.

65. Reidy, "Negro Election Day," 105; Wade, "Shining in Borrowed Plumage," 225; Horton and Horton, *In Hope of Liberty*, 23–24.

66. Platt, "Negro Governors," 323–24.

67. Piersen, *Black Yankees*, 134.

68. Ibid., 132–33.

69. Henry Reed Stiles, *The History of Ancient Windsor, Connecticut, Including East Windsor, South Windsor, and Ellington* (New York: C.B. Norton, 1859), 492.

70. James Newhall, *History of Lynn, Essex County, Massachusetts Including Lynnfield, Saugus, Swampscott, and Nahant*, 2 vols. (Lynn, MA: Nichols Press, 1897), 2:236.

71. White, "Afro-Dutch Syncretization in New York City and the Hudson Valley," 70; White, *Somewhat More Independent*, 99. For similar conclusions, see Piersen, *Black Yankees*, 117; Eric Lott, *Love and Theft: Blackface Minstrelsy and the American Working Class* (New York: Oxford University Press, 1993), 47.

72. Felt, *Annals of Salem*, 2:420.

73. Platt, "Negro Governors," 319–20.

74. Constance Rourke, *American Humor: A Study of the National Character* (1931; Tallahassee: Florida State University Press, 1986), 88.

75. Timothy Flint, *Recollections of the Last Ten Years in the Valley of the Mississippi (1826)*, ed. George R. Brooks (Carbondale and Edwardsville: Southern Illinois University Press, 1968), 103.

76. Kinser, *Carnival, American Style*, 57.

77. Quoted in Lucien Peytraud, *L'Esclavage aux Antilles Françaises avant 1789 d'après des documents inédits des archives coloniales* (Paris: Hachette, 1897), 182–83.

78. James M. Phillippo, *Jamaica: Its Past and Present State* (Philadelphia: J.M. Campbell, 1843), 93.

79. Henry H. Breen, *St. Lucia: Historical, Statistical, and Descriptive* (London: Longman, Brown, Green, and Longmans, 1844), 192.

80. Thurlow Weed, *Letters from Europe and the West Indies, 1843–1862* (Albany, NY: Weed, Parsons, 1866), 345.

81. James Rodway, *History of British Guiana*, 2 vols. (Georgetown: J. Thomson, 1893), 2:295–97.

82. Marie Bertrand de Cothonay, *Trinidad: journal d'un missionnaire dominicain des Antilles anglaises* (Paris: V. Retaux et fils, 1893), 62–63.

83. Victor Schoelcher, *Colonies étrangères et Haiti*, 2 vols. (Paris: Pagnerre, 1843), 2:299–30.

84. Errol Hill, *The Trinidad Carnival: Mandate for a National Theatre* (Austin: University of Texas Press, 1972), 19; Emmanuel C. Paul, *Panorama du Folklore Haïtien. Présence Africaine en Haïti* (Port-au-Prince: Les Éditions Fardin, 1978), 147–49.

85. Bernal Díaz del Castillo, *Historia verdadera de la conquista de la Nueva España*, ed. Joaquín Ramírez Cabañas, 3 vols. (1632; Mexico City: Editorial Pedro Robredo, 1944), 3:180–82.

86. Guy Le Gentil de la Barbinais, *Nouveau voyage auteur du monde*, 3 vols. (Amsterdam: Pierre Mortier, 1728), 1:114–15.

87. John G. Wurdemann, *Notes on Cuba* (Boston: James Munroe, 1844), 83, 113–14.

88. Walter Goodman, *The Pearl of the Antilles, or An Artist in Cuba* (London: Henry S. King, 1873), 137.

89. Lydia Cabrera, *Reglas de Congo, palo monte, mayombe* (Miami: Peninsular, 1979), 15–16.

90. Daniel E. Walker, *No More, No More: Slavery and Cultural Resistance in Havana and New Orleans* (Minneapolis: University of Minnesota Press, 2004), 103. See also Fernando Ortiz Fernández, "Los cabildos afrocubanos," *Revista Bimestre Cubana* XVI (January-February 1921): 5–39; Arthur Ramos, *As culturas negras no Novo Mundo* (Rio de Janeiro: Civilização Brasileira, 1937), 161–65.

91. Marina de Mello e Souza, *Reis negros no Brasil escravista. História da festa de coroação de Rei Congo* (Belo Horizonte, BR: UFMG, 2002), 38.

92. For Argentina, see Patricia Fogelman and Marta Goldberg, "'El rey de los congos': The Clandestine Coronation of Pedro Duarte in Buenos Aires, 1787," *Afro-Latino Voices: Narratives from the Early Modern Ibero-Atlantic World, 1550–1812*, ed. Kathryn Joy McKnight and Leo J. Garofalo (Indianapolis: Hackett, 2009), 155–74.

93. Walker, *No More, No More*, 3.

94. Cohen, "In Search of Carolus Africanus Rex," 149–62.

95. Piersen, *Black Yankees*, 124.

96. Betty M. Kuyk, "The African Derivation of Black Fraternal Orders in the United States," *Comparative Studies in Society and History* 25, no. 4 (1983): 559–92; Margaret Washington Creel, *A Peculiar People: Slave Religion and Community-Culture among the Gullahs* (New York: New York University Press, 1988), 45–54, 181–82; Michael A. Gomez, *Exchanging our Country Marks: The Transformation of African Identities in the Colonial and Antebellum South* (Chapel Hill: University of North Carolina Press, 1998), 99–102; James H. Sweet, *Recreating Africa: Culture, Kinship, and Religion in the African-Portuguese World, 1441–1770* (Chapel Hill: University of North Carolina Press, 2003), 207; Barbara S. Glass, *African American Dance: An Illustrated History* (Jefferson, NC: McFarland, 2007), 77; Ras Michael Brown, *African-Atlantic Cultures and the South Carolina Lowcountry* (Cambridge, UK: Cambridge University Press, 2012), 198–250.

97. Quoted in George R. Howell and Jonathan Tenny, *History of the County of Albany, from 1609 to 1886* (Albany, NY: Munsell, 1886), 725.

98. Giovanna Fiume, "St. Benedict the Moor: From Sicily to the New World," *Saints and Their Cults in the Atlantic World*, ed. Margaret Cormack (Columbia: University of South Carolina Press, 2007), 16–51.

99. Ortiz Fernández, "Los cabildos afrocubanos," 5–39.

100. Roger Bastide, *As religiões africanas no Brasil: Contribuição a uma sociologia das Interpretações de civilizações*, ed. Maria Eloisa Capellato and Olívia Krähenbühl, 2 vols. (1960; São Paulo: Pioneira Editora, 1971), 1:173.

101. Souza, *Reis negros no Brasil escravista*, 210.

102. Linda M. Heywood, ed., *Central Africans and Cultural Transformations in the American Diaspora* (Cambridge, UK: Cambridge University Press, 2002), 2, 12.

103. Carlos Hernández Soto and Edis Sánchez, "Los Congos de Villa Mella, República Dominicana," *Revista de música latinoamericana* 18, no. 2 (1997): 298.

104. Ibib., 300–301.

105. Frijhoff, *Wegen van Evert Willemsz.*, 774.

Chapter 4

1. Arquivo Histórico da Câmara Municipal, Lisbon, Câmara Municipal de Lisboa (1957–1964), Livro 3, Doc. 27, 203. For Spain, see Maureen Flynn, *Sacred Charity: Confraternities and Social Welfare in Spain 1400–1700* (Ithaca, NY: Cornell University Press, 1989); Isidoro Moreno, *La Antigua Hermandad de Los Negros de Sevilla. Etnicidad, poder y sociedad en 600 años de historia* (Sevilla: Universidad de Sevilla, 1997); Debra Blumenthal, "'La Casa dels Negres': Black African Solidarity in Late Medieval Valencia," *Black Africans in Renaissance Europe*, ed. T. F. Earle and K. J. P. Lowe (Cambridge, UK: Cambridge University Press, 2005), 225–46; Jeremy Lawrance, "Black Africans in Renaissance Spanish Literature," *Black Africans in Renaissance Europe*, 70–93.

2. Anne Winston, "Tracing the Origins of the Rosary: German Vernacular Texts," *Speculum: A Journal of Medieval Studies* 68 (July 1993): 634; Miri Rubin, *Mother of God: A History of the Virgin Mary* (New Haven, CT: Yale University Press, 2009), 332–38.

3. Didier Lahon, *O negro no coração do império: uma memória a resgatar—séculos XV–XIX* (Lisbon: Secretariado Coordenador dos Programas de Educação Multicultural, 1999), 58–76; Didier Lahon, "Vivência religiosa," *Os negros em Portugal—sécs. XV a XIX*, ed. Ana Maria Rodrigues (Lisbon: Comissão Nacional para as Comemorações dos Descobrimentos Portugueses, 1999), 127–64; Didier Lahon, "Esclavage, confréries noires, sainteté noire et pureté de sang au Portugal (XVIe et XVIIIe siècles)," *Lusitana Sacra* vol. 2, no. XIII–XIV (2001–2002): 119–62; Didier Lahon, "Black African Slaves and Freedmen in Portugal during the Renaissance: Creating a New Pattern of Reality," *Black Africans in Renaissance Europe*, 265–68; José Ramos Tinhorão, *As festas no Brasil colonial* (São Paulo: Editora 34, 2000), 87; Elizabeth W. Kiddy, *Blacks of the Rosary: Memory and History in Minas Gerais, Brazil* (University Park: Pennsylvania State University Press, 2005), 22–31; Fiume, "St. Benedict the Moor," 16–51; James H. Sweet, "The Hidden Histories of African Lisbon," *The Black Urban Atlantic in the Age of the Slave Trade*, 233–47; Francisco van der Poel, *Dicionário da religiosidade popular. Cultura e religião no Brasil* (Curitiba, BR: Nossa Cultura, 2013), 528.

4. A. C. de C. M. Saunders, *A Social History of Black Slaves and Freedmen in Portugal 1441–1555* (Cambridge, UK: Cambridge University Press, 1982), 105–7, 150–65; Mariza de Carvalho Soares, *Devotos da cor: Identidade étnica, religiosidade e escravidão no Rio de Janeiro, século XVIII* (Rio de Janeiro: Civilização brasileira, 2000), 155, 204; Souza, *Reis negros no Brasil escravista*, 172–79; Célia Maia Borges, *Escravos e libertos nas Irmandades do Rosário: Devoção e solidariedade em Minas Gerais—Séculos XVIII e XIX* (Juíz de Fora, BR: Editora UFJF, 2005), 83, 182–83, 190, 193–95.

5. José Ramos Tinhorão, *Os negros em Portugal. Uma presença silenciosa* (Lisbon: Caminho, 1988), 191; Souza, *Reis negros no Brasil escravista*, 209; Sílvia Hunold Lara, "Significados cruzados. Um reinado de Congos na Bahia setecentista," *Carnavais e outras f(r)estas. Ensaios de história social da cultura*, ed. Maria Clementina Pereira Cunha (Campinas, BR: Editora Unicamp, 2002), 85.

6. Bourdieu, "The Forms of Capital," 252–53.

7. Caio César Boschi, *Os leigos e o poder: Irmandades leigos e política colonizadora em Minas Gerais* (São Paulo: Editora Ática, 1986), 138–39.

8. Bastide, *As religiões africanas no Brasil*, 1:167; Mary C. Karasch, *Slave Life in Rio de Janeiro 1808–1850* (Princeton, NJ: Princeton University Press, 1987), 86; Richard Gray, *Black Christians and White Missionaries* (New Haven, CT: Yale University Press, 1990), 13; Soares, *Devotos da cor*, 13; Souza, *Reis negros no Brasil escravista*, 189, 209.

9. Lahon, "Black African Slaves and Freedmen in Portugal during the Renaissance," 272.

10. Souza, *Reis negros no Brasil escravista*, 163.

11. Kiddy, *Blacks of the Rosary*, 77.

12. Gray, *Black Christians and White Missionaries*, 11–27; Blackburn, *The Making of New World Slavery*, 330.

13. Moreno, *La Antigua Hermandad de Los Negros de Sevilla*, 132; Borges, *Escravos e libertos nas Irmandades do Rosário*, 89–98.

14. Luís Chaves, *Folclore religioso* (Porto, PT: Portucalense, 1945), 94; Cabrera, *Reglas de Congo*, 103; Enrique Martínez López, *Tablero de Ajedrez: Imágenes del negro heroico en la comedia Española y en la literature e iconografia sacra del Brasil esclavista* (Paris: Gulbenkian, 1998), 61–74; Karasch, *Slave Life in Rio de Janeiro*, 272; Anderson José Machado de Oliveira, *Devoção negra: santos pretos e catequese no Brasil colonial* (Rio de Janeiro: Quartet, 2008), 99–100.

15. Lahon, "Esclavage, confréries noires, sainteté noire et pureté de sang au Portugal," 140, 148–62; Fiume, "St. Benedict the Moor," 26, 30–41.

16. *Jornalero del año de 1633 y 1634, por um frade capuchino*. British Library, Department of Manuscripts. Additional Mss. Sloane, Mss. 1572. Fl. 61–62.

17. Fiume, "St. Benedict the Moor," 25.

18. António de Oliveira de Cadornega, *Descrição de Vila Viçosa*, ed. Heitor Gomes Teixeira (1683; Lisbon: IN-CM, 1982), 28–29.

19. Miri Rubin, *Corpus Christi: The Eucharist in Late Medieval Culture* (Cambridge, UK: Cambridge University Press, 1991), 164–76; Flynn, *Sacred Charity*, 136.

20. Violet Alford, "Midsummer and Morris in Portugal," *Folklore* 44, no. 2 (June 1933): 218–35; Rodney Gallop, *Portugal: A Book of Folk-Ways* (Cambridge, UK: Cambridge University Press, 1936), 117, 163–68; Francis George Very, *The Spanish Corpus Christi Procession: A Literary and Folkloric Study* (Valencia, ES: Moderna, 1962); Affonso Ávila, *Resíduos Seiscentistas em Minas. Textos do século de ouro e as projeções do mundo barroco*, 2 vols. (Belo Horizonte, BR: Centro de Estudos Mineiros, 1967), I:3–128; Tinhorão, *As festas no Brasil colonial*, 76–77; Max Harris, *Carnival and Other Christian Festivals: Folk Theology and Folk Performance* (Austin: University of Texas Press, 2003), 12–14, 85–86.

21. Chaves, *Folclore religioso*, 138.

22. Tinhorão, *Os negros em Portugal*, 141–58; Ortiz Fernández, *Los cabildos y la fiesta afrocubanos del Día de Reyes*, 6; Moreno, *La Antigua Hermandad de Los Negros de Sevilla*, 32–33, 54; Souza, *Reis negros no Brasil escravista*, 261–62.

23. Karasch, *Slave Life in Rio de Janeiro*, 130; Moreno, *La Antigua Hermandad de Los Negros de Sevilla*, 51; Philip A. Howard, *Changing History: Afro-Cuban Cabildos and Societies of Color in the Nineteenth Century* (Baton Rouge: Louisiana State University Press, 1998), 44; Soares, *Devotos da cor*, 156; Matt D. Childs, *The 1812 Aponte Rebellion in Cuba and the Struggle against Atlantic Slavery* (Chapel Hill: University of North Carolina Press, 2006), 117.

24. Chaves, *Folclore religioso*, 98–103; Souza, *Reis negros no Brasil escravista*, 84, 226; Lara, "Significados cruzados," 87–88; Mary C. Karasch, "Central Africans in Central Brazil, 1780–1835," *Central Africans and Cultural Transformation in the American Diaspora*, ed. Linda M. Heywood (Cambridge, UK: Cambridge University Press, 2002), 149–51.

25. Carlos Francisco Moura, *Teatro a bordo de naus portuguesas nos séculos XV, XVI, XVII e XVIII* (Rio de Janeiro: Instituto Luso-Brasileiro de História, 2000), 97–109.

26. Isabel dos Guimarães Sá, "Ecclesiastical Structures and Religious Action," *Portuguese Oceanic Expansion, 1400–1800*, ed. Francisco Bethencourt and Diogo Ramada Curto (Cambridge, UK: Cambridge University Press, 2007), 267–68.

27. Toby Green, *The Rise of the Trans-Atlantic Slave Trade in Western Africa, 1300–1589* (Cambridge, UK: Cambridge University Press, 2012), 105.

28. "Carta do ouvidor geral, João Vieira de Andrade, ao rei D. José" (26 July 1762), in Daniel A. Pereira, *Estudos da história de Cabo Verde* (Praia, CV: Alfo-Comunicações, 2005), 338.

29. Christiano José de Senna Barcellos, *Subsídios para a história de Cabo Verde e Guiné* (Lisboa: Academia das Ciências de Lisboa, 1900), 244–45.

30. Pedro Monteiro Cardoso, *Folclore Caboverdeano* (Porto, PT: Maranus, 1933), 39, 43; Pereira, *Estudos da história de Cabo Verde*, 352; José Maria Semedo and Maria R. Turano, *Cabo Verde: O cíclo ritual das festividades da tabanca* (Praia, CV: Speel-Edições, 1997), 59–90.

31. John K. Thornton, "The Portuguese in Africa," *Portuguese Oceanic Expansion, 1400–1800*, 148–49.

32. Francis Moore, *Travels into the Inland Parts of Africa: Containing a Description of the Several Nations for the Space of Six Hundred Miles up the River Gambia* (London: Edward Cave, 1738), 29.

33. Green, *The Rise of the Trans-Atlantic Slave Trade in Western Africa*, 12.

34. Gerhard Seibert, "Creolization and Creole Communities in the Portuguese Atlantic: São Tomé, Cape Verde, the Rivers of Guinea and Central Africa in Comparison," *Brokers of Change: Atlantic Commerce and Cultures in Precolonial Western Africa*, ed. Toby Green (Oxford and New York: Oxford University Press, 2012), 49.

35. George E. Brooks, *Eurafricans in Western Africa: Commerce, Social Status, Gender, and Religious Observance from the Sixteenth to the Eighteenth Century* (Athens: Ohio University Press, 2003), 216.

36. Thornton, "The Portuguese in Africa," 155; Nuno da Silva Gonçalves, *Os Jesuítas e a missão de Cabo Verde, 1604–1642* (Lisbon: Brotéria, 1996), 127–44.

37. Walter Hawthorne, *From Africa to Brazil: Culture, Identity, and an Atlantic Slave Trade, 1600–1830* (Cambridge, UK: Cambridge University Press, 2010), 211, 224–33.

38. "Carta de El-Rei D. João III" (9 July 1526), in Brásio, *Monumenta missionária Africana*, 1:472–74.

39. Raimundo J. da Cunha Matos, *Compêndio histórico das possessões de Portugal na África* (1836; Rio de Janeiro: Ministério de Justiça e Negócios Interiores, 1963), 148.

40. Luiz Felipe de Alencastro, *O trato dos viventes. Formação do Brasil no Atlântico Sul, séculos XVI e XVII* (São Paulo: Companhia das Letras, 2000), 63–70.

41. Valentim Fernandes, *Códice Valentim Fernandes*, ed. José Pereira da Costa (1506–7; Lisbon: Academia Portuguesa da História, 1997), 163; Manuel do Rosário Pinto, *Relação do descobrimento da ilha de São Tomé*, ed. Arlindo Manuel Caldeira (1734; Lisbon: Centro de História de Além-Mar, 2006), 55.

42. Robert Garfield, *A History of São Tomé Island 1470–1655: The Key to Guinea* (San Francisco: Mellen Research University Press, 1992), 16. For a similar pattern in Portugal, see Lahon, "Esclavage, confréries noires, sainteté noire et pureté de sang au Portugal," 130; Didier Lahon, "Da escravidão à liberdade," *Os negros em Portugal—sécs. XV a XIX*, ed. Anna Maria Rodrigues (Lisbon: Comissão Nacional para a Comemoração dos Descobrimentos Portugueses, 1999), 81–85.

43. Green, *The Rise of the Trans-Atlantic Slave Trade in Western Africa*, 113–14.

44. "Instruction du Comte de Nassau et du Conseil Sécret du Brésil" (28 May 1641), in Jadin, *L'Ancien Congo et l'Angola 1639–1655 d'après les archives romaines, portugaises, néerlandaises et espagnoles*, 1:38.

45. Alonso de Sandoval, *Treatise on Slavery: Selections from De instaurada aethiopum salute (1627)*, ed. Nicole von Germeten (Indianapolis: Hackett, 2008), 14, 38; Alan Ryder, "Missionary Activity in the Kingdom of Warri to the Early Nineteenth Century," *Journal of the Historical Society of Nigeria* 2 (1960): 1–26; John Thornton, "On the Trail of Voodoo: African Christianity in Africa and the Americas," *The Americas* 44, no. 3 (January 1988): 265; Adrian Hastings, *The Church in Africa 1450–1950* (Oxford: Clarendon Press, 1994), 118–20; Robin Law, "Ouidah as a Multiethnic Community," *The Black Urban Atlantic in the Age of the Slave Trade*, 57–58.

46. Sandoval, *Treatise on Slavery*, 47.

47. Leopoldo da Rocha, *As confrarias de Goa (séculos XVI–XX). Conspecto histórico-jurídico* (Lisbon: Centro de Estudos Históricos Ultramarinos, 1973), 12, 35, 157, 167.

48. Girma Beshah and Merid Wolde Aregay, *The Question of the Union of the Churches in Luso-Ethiopian Relations, 1500–1632* (Lisbon: Centro de Estudos Históricos Ultramarinos, 1964), 21–104.

49. Hodges, *Root and Branch*, 40.

50. António Brásio, *História e missiologia. Inéditos e esparsos* (Luanda: Instituto de Investigação Científica de Angola, 1973), 547–62; Borges, *Escravos e libertos nas Irmandades do Rosário*, 50; Hastings, *The Church in Africa*, 120–23; Thornton, "The Portuguese in Africa," 155–56; Sá, "Ecclesiastical Structures and Religious Action," 259.

51. "Carta do Rei do Congo aos senhores do reino" (1512), in Brásio, *Monumenta missionária Africana*, 1:256–59; Filippo Pigafetta, *A Report of the Kingdom of Congo and the Surrounding Countries; Drawn out of the Writings and Discourses of the Portuguese Duarte Lopez*, ed. Margarite Hutchinson (1591; New York: Negro Universities Press, 1969), 70–89; António Brásio, ed., *História do Reino do Congo. Ms. 8080 da Biblioteca Nacional de Lisboa* (Lisbon: Centro de Estudos Históricos Ultramarinos, 1969), 77–80.

52. Jean Cuvelier, *L'ancien royaume de Congo* (Brussels: De Brouwer, 1946), 104–12; Georges Balandier, *Daily Life in the Kingdom of the Kongo from the Sixteenth to the Eighteenth Century* (New York: Pantheon, 1968), 42–58; John K. Thornton, *The Kingdom of Kongo: Civil War and Transition 1641–1718* (Madison: University of Wisconsin Press, 1983), 65; Anne Hilton, *The Kingdom of the Kongo* (Oxford: Clarendon Press, 1985), 62–64; Wyatt MacGaffey, *Religion and Society in Central Africa: The BaKongo of Lower Zaire* (Chicago: University of Chicago Press,

1986), 198–203; Thornton, *Africa and Africans in the Making of the Atlantic World*, 257–59; Ilídio do Amaral, *O Reino do Congo, os Mbundu (ou Ambundos), o Reino dos 'Ngola' (ou de Angola) e a presença portuguesa, de finais do século XV a meados do século XVI* (Lisbon: Ministério da Ciência e da Technologia, 1996), 21–32; Jason R. Young, *Rituals of Resistance: African Atlantic Religion in Kongo and the Lowcountry South in the Era of Slavery* (Baton Rouge: Louisiana State University Press, 2007), 49; Fromont, *The Art of Conversion*, 26–33.

53. António Custódio Gonçalves, "As influências do Cristianismo na organização política do Reino do Congo," *Congresso Internacional Bartolomeu Dias e a sua época. Actas*, 5 vols. (Porto, PT: Universidade do Porto, 1989), V:523–39; Hastings, *The Church in Africa*, 73–77; John K. Thornton, "Religious and Ceremonial Life in the Kongo and Mbundu Areas 1500–1700," *Central Africans and Cultural Transformation in the American Diaspora*, 86; Heywood and Thornton, *Central Africans*, 135–43; Sá, "Ecclesiastical Structures and Religious Action," 270–71; Fromont, *The Art of Conversion*, 47–59, 71, 130.

54. Fromont, *The Art of Conversion*, 1–20.

55. Heywood and Thornton, *Central Africans*, 65.

56. "Érection du diocese de San Salvador" (1595), in J. Cuvelier and L. Jadin, ed., *L'Ancien Congo d'après les archives romaines, 1518–1640* (Brussels: Académie Royale des Sciences Coloniales, 1954), 187; Laurent de Lucques [Lorenzo da Lucca], *Relations sur le Congo du Père Laurent de Lucques (1700–1718)*, ed. J. Cuvelier (Brussels: Institut Royal Colonial Belge, 1953), 202. See also P. Hildebrand, *Le martyr Georges de Geel et les débuts de la mission au Congo, 1645–1652* (Antwerp, BE: Archives des Capucins, 1940), 253–54; Kiddy, *Blacks of the Rosary*, 32; Richard Gray, "A Kongo Princess and the Papacy," *Christianity and the African Imagination: Essays in Honor of Adrian Hastings*, ed. David Maxwell and Ingrid Lawrie (Leiden, NL: Brill, 2002), 30–31; Fromont, *The Art of Conversion*, 202–6.

57. Raphaël Batsîkama ba Mampuya ma Ndâwla, *L'ancien royaume du Congo et les Bakongo. Séquences d'histoire populaire* (Paris: L'Harmattan, 1999), 5, 15.

58. Linda Heywood and John Thornton, "The Kongo Kingdom and European Diplomacy," *Kongo Across the Waters*, ed. Susan Cooksey, Robin Poynor, and Hein Vanhee (Gainesville: University Press of Florida, 2013), 52–57.

59. "Supplique des ambassadeurs du roi du Congo" (9 May 1648), in Jadin, *L'Ancien Congo et l'Angola*, 2:987; Hastings, *The Church in Africa*, 79–94; John K. Thornton, "The Development of an African Catholic Church in the Kingdom of Kongo, 1491–1750," *Journal of African History* 25, no. 2 (1984): 147–67; Fromont, *The Art of Conversion*, 26–33.

60. David Birmingham, *Trade and Conflict in Angola: The Mbundu and Their Neighbours under the Influence of the Portuguese 1483–1790* (Oxford: Clarendon Press, 1966), 42–161; Hilton, *The Kingdom of the Kongo*, 104–12; Thornton, "The Portuguese in Africa," 150–53.

61. António de Oliveira de Cadornega, *História Geral das Guerras Angolanas*, ed. José Matias Delgado, 3 vols. (1680; Lisboa: Agência-Geral do Ultramar, 1972), 3:14, 28; Heywood and Thornton, *Central Africans*, 188; Souza, "Virgem Imperial," 48; Roquinaldo Ferreira, *Cross-Cultural Exchange in the Atlantic World: Angola and Brazil during the Era of the Slave Trade* (Cambridge, UK: Cambridge University Press, 2012), 91–92.

62. "Cofradia da Nossa Senhora do Rosário aos Cardinais da Propaganda" (29 June 1658), in Brásio, *Monumenta missionária Africana*, 12:164–65; "Resposta do governador de Angola à carta régia de 10 de Março de 1692 sobre missões (24 April 1693), in Levy Maria Jordão,

ed., *História do Congo. Obra posthuma do Visconde de Paiva Manso* (Lisbon: Typographia da Academia, 1877), 335–36.

63. Elias Alexandre da Silva Corrêa, *História de Angola*, 2 vols. (Lisbon: Atica, 1937), 1:74.

64. Herbert Klein, "The Atlantic Slave Trade to 1650," *Tropical Babylons: Sugar and the Making of the Atlantic World, 1450–1680*, ed. Stuart B. Schwartz (Chapel Hill: University of North Carolina Press, 2004), 211–12.

65. "Décision de la Propaganda" (7 May 1675), in Jadin, "Rivalités luso-néerlandaises du Sohio," 312–14; Hastings, *The Church in Africa*, 94–102.

66. S. J. António Franco, *Synopsis Annalium Societatis Jesu in Lusitania ab 1540 usque ad annum 1725* (Augsburg, DE: Sumptibus Philippi, Martini, & Joannis Veith, Haeredum, 1726), 250, 253; MacGaffey, *Religion and Society in Central Africa*, 203–8; Thornton, "The Development of an African Catholic Church in the Kingdom of Kongo," 163–64; Hilton, *The Kingdom of the Kongo*, 97; Gray, *Black Christians and White Missionaries*, 34–56; Rubin, *Mother of God*, 394; Fromont, *The Art of Conversion*, 202–6.

67. Hildebrand, *Le martyr Georges de Geel et les débuts de la mission au Congo*, 251.

68. Antonio de Gaeta, *La maravigliosa conversione alla fede di Cristi della Regina Signa e dell suo Regno di Matamba* (Naples, IT: Per Giacinto Passaro, 1669), 387.

69. John K. Thornton, *The Kongolese Saint Anthony: Dona Beatriz Kimpa Vita and the Antonian Movement, 1684–1706* (Cambridge, UK: Cambridge University Press, 1998), 27; Thornton, "Religious and Ceremonial Life in the Kongo and Mbundu Areas," 71–90; John K. Thornton, *A Cultural History of the Atlantic World, 1250–1820* (Cambridge, UK: Cambridge University Press, 2012), 417; Fromont, *The Art of Conversion*, 5–12, 143–52. Unlike what has been suggested by Hodges, Loango is not a synonym for Luanda; Hodges, *Root and Branch*, 24.

70. Fromont, *The Art of Conversion*, 103.

71. Thornton, "The Development of an African Catholic Church in the Kingdom of Kongo," 154.

72. Fromont, *The Art of Conversion*, 78–79, 202–6.

73. Heywood and Thornton, *Central Africans*, 64.

74. Hilton, *The Kingdom of the Kongo*, 94–98; Kiddy, *Blacks of the Rosary*, 56; Luc de Heusch, *Le roi de Kongo et les monstres sacrés. Mythes et rites bantous III* (Paris: Gallimard, 2000), 83; Thornton, *A Cultural History of the Atlantic World*, 416. For more on *minkisi*, see John M. Janzen and Wyatt MacGaffey, *An Anthology of Kongo Religion: Primary Texts from Lower Zaïre* (Lawrence: University of Kansas Publications in Anthropology, 1974), 34–38; Robert Farris Thompson and Joseph Cornet, *The Four Moments of the Sun: Kongo Art in Two Worlds* (Washington: National Gallery of Art, 1981), 37–39; MacGaffey, *Religion and Society in Central Africa*, 137–68; Wyatt MacGaffey, *Kongo Political Culture: The Conceptual Challenge of the Particular* (Bloomington: Indiana University Press, 2000), 79–96; Ras Michael Brown, *African-Atlantic Cultures and the South Carolina Lowcountry* (Cambridge, UK: Cambridge University Press, 2012), 90–138.

75. Joseph van Wing, *Études Bakongo. Sociologie, religion et magie* (1921; Bruges, BE: Desclée de Brouwer, 1959), 78; MacGaffey, *Religion and Society in Central Africa*, 203–11; Adriano Vasco Rodrigues, "Aculturação artística e social no Reino do Congo resultante da evangelização após a chegada dos Portugueses," *Congresso Internacional Bartolomeu Dias e a sua época. Actas*, 5 vols. (Porto, PT: Universidade do Porto, 1989), 5:541–53; Thornton, *The Kingdom of*

Kongo, 62–64; Hilton, *The Kingdom of the Kongo*, 206–7; Maureen Warner-Lewis, *Central Africa in the Caribbean: Transcending Time, Transforming Cultures* (Barbados, Jamaica, and Trinidad and Tobago: University of the West Indies Press, 2003), 188–90; John M. Janzen, "Renewal and Reinterpretation in Kongo Religion," *Kongo Across the Waters*, ed. Susan Cooksey, Robin Poynor, and Hein Vanhee (Gainesville: University Press of Florida, 2013), 132–42; Fromont, *The Art of Conversion*, 206–12.

76. Girolamo da Sorrento Merolla, *Breve, e succinta relatione del viaggio nel Regno di Congo* (Naples, IT: Francesco Mollo, 1692), 105.

77. De Lucques, *Relations sur le Congo*, 109.

78. Gallop, *Portugal: A Book of Folk-Ways*, 66, 133–34, Chaves, *Folclore religioso*, 141–49.

79. George E. Brooks, "The Observance of All Souls' Day in the Guinea-Bissau Region: A Christian Holy Day, an African Harvest Festival, an African New Year's Celebration, or All of the Above (?)," *History of Africa* 11 (1984): 11. See also Hastings, *The Church in Africa*, 74.

80. Semedo and Turano, *Cabo Verde*, 40.

81. Gallop, *Portugal: A Book of Folk-Ways*, 49–83.

82. Maria Benedita Araújo, *Superstições populares Portuguesas. Contribuições para um estudo* (Lisbon: Colibri, 1997), 78–79; Thornton, *A Cultural History of the Atlantic World*, 417–18.

83. Carlos Alberto Garcia, "A acção dos portugueses no antigo reino do Congo (1482–1543)," *Boletim Geral do Ultramar* vol. 513 (March 1968): 3–30; vol. 515 (May 1968): 11–36; vol. 516 (June 1968): 77–90.

84. Malyn Newitt, ed., *The Portuguese in West Africa, 1415–1670: A Documentary History* (Cambridge, UK: Cambridge University Press, 2010), 13; Teobaldo Filesi, *San Salvador: Cronache dei Re del Congo* (Bologna, IT: E.M.I., 1974), 25–28.

85. Garcia de Resende, *Crónica de D. João II e miscelânea*, ed. Joaquim Veríssimo Serrão (Lisbon: Imprensa Nacional-Cada da Moeda, 1973), 222.

86. Rui de Pina, *Relação do Reino do Congo. Manuscrito inédito do Códice Riccardiano 1910*, ed. Carmen M. Radulet (1492; Lisbon: Imprensa Nacional-Casa da Moeda, 1992), 105.

87. Brásio, *História do Reino do Congo*, 82.

88. "Rol de objectos a enviar para o Congo" (1512), in Brásio, *Monumenta missionária Africana*, 1:247–53.

89. Heywood and Thornton, *Central Africans*, 213; Thornton, *A Cultural History of the Atlantic World*, 389.

90. "Letter P. Mortamer" (31 October 1642), Dutch National Archives, The Hague, Koninklijk Huisarchief, J. Maurits papers. Copy in the University of California, Berkeley Bancroft Library, Engel Sluiter Historical Documents Collection, 98/79z, ctn. 61, Dutch (WIC) in W. Africa, May-December 1643.

91. Sandoval, *Treatise on Slavery*, 41.

92. "Relação da Perdição da Nao Belem da qual era Capitão Joseph Cabreira, Mestre Miguel Jorge grego e piloto Mathias Figueira," Manuscript Collection, Biblioteca da Ajuda, Lisbon, s.d., fl. 25v.

93. "Rapport de la visite *ad limina* pour le diocèse de São Salvador, présente au Pape et à la congrégation du concile par l'évêque Francisco de Soveral," (1 April 1631), in Jadin, "Relations sur le Congo et l'Angola tirées des archives de la Compagnie de Jésus 1621–1631," 429–40; Jadin, "Rivalités luso-néerlandaises du Sohio," 290.

94. "Relação dos Carmelitas descalços" (1584), in Brásio, *Monumenta missionária Africana*, 4:393–415.

95. Andrea da Pavia, "Voyages apostoliques aux missions d'Afrique du P. Andrea da Pavia, Prédicateur Capucin 1685–1702," ed. Louis Jadin, *Bulletin de L'Institut Historique Belge de Rome* XLI (1970) : 446–48.

96. Ibid., 444.

97. Ibid., 449–51.

98. "Giuseppe-Maria da Busseto au procureur général," (18 April 1674), in Jadin, "Rivalités luso-néerlandaises du Sohio," 288–93; Jean-François de Rome [Giovanni Francesco Romano], *Brève relation de la fondation de la mission des Frères Mineurs Capucins du Séraphique Père Saint François au Royaume de Congo (1648)*, ed. François Bontinck (Louvain, BE: Nauwelaerts, 1964), 129.

99. Fra Luca da Caltanisetta, *Diaire Congolais (1690–1701)*, ed. François Bontinck (Louvain, BE: Nauwelaerts, 1970), 5–6; Marcellino d'Atri, *L'anarchia Congolese nel sec. XVII. La relazione inedita di Marcellino d'Atri (1702)*, ed. Carlo Toso (Genova, IT: Bozzi Editore, 1984), 68; Balandier, *Daily Life in the Kingdom of the Kongo*, 119–20; Thornton, *The Kongolese Saint Anthony*, 30–35; Fromont, *The Art of Conversion*, 21–64.

100. Heywood and Thornton, *Central Africans*, 212–13; Thornton, *A Cultural History of the Atlantic World*, 394.

101. "Relação das festas que a residençia de Angolla fez na Beatificação do Beato Padre Francisco de Xavier" (1620), in Alfredo de Albuquerque Felner, ed., *Angola: Apontamentos sobre a ocupação e inínicio do estabelecimento dos Portugueses no Congo, Angola e Benguela extraídos de documentos históricos* (Coimbra, PT: Imprensa da Universidade, 1933), 531–43.

102. Hein Vanhee and Jelmer Vos, "Kongo in the Age of Empire," *Kongo Across the Waters*, 78–89; Fromont, *The Art of Conversion*, 215–62.

103. James Hingston Tuckey, *Narrative of an expedition to explore the river Zaire, usually called the Congo, in South Africa, in 1816, under the direction of Captain J.K. Tuckey, R.N.* (New York, W.B. Gilley, 1818), 80.

104. José Almeida Santos, *Apenas um punhado de bravos!* (Luanda, Angola Câmara Municipal de Luanda, 1971), 200.

105. Joachim John Monteiro, *Angola and the River Congo* (New York: Macmillan, 1876), 120.

106. Alfredo de Sarmento, *Os sertões d'Africa. Apontamentos de viagem* (Lisbon: Francisco Arthur da Silva, 1880), 89–91.

107. José Redinha, *Relatório Anual do Museu do Dundo* (Dundo, Angola: DIAMANG, 1943), 172–73.

108. Frederick P. Bowser, *The African Slave in Colonial Peru 1524–1650* (Stanford, CA: Stanford University Press, 1974), 247; Klein, "The Atlantic Slave Trade to 1650," 206.

109. Ortiz Fernández, *Los cabildos y la fiesta afrocubanos del Día de Reyes*, 46.

110. Odulfo van der Vat, *Princípios da Igreja no Brasil* (Petrópolis, BR: Vozes, 1952), 104; Serafim Leite, *História da Companhia de Jesus no Brasil*, 10 vols. (Rio de Janeiro: Civilização Brasileira, 1938–50), 3:340–41; Leonardo Arroyo, *Igrejas de São Paulo* (Rio de Janeiro: José Olympio, 1954), 261; Borges, *Escravos e libertos nas Irmandades do Rosário*, 51; Nicole von Germeten, *Black Blood Brothers: Confraternities and Social Mobility for Afro-Mexicans* (Gainesville: University Press of Florida, 2006), 2–3, 13–14; Matt D. Childs, "Re-creating African Ethnic Identities in Cuba," *The Black Urban Atlantic in the Age of the Slave Trade*, 86, 90.

111. Girolamo Benzoni, *History of the New World, by Girolamo Benzoni, of Milan. Shewing his Travels in America from A.D. 1541 to 1556*, ed. W. H. Smyth (London: Hakluyt Society, 1857), 94.

112. Sandoval, *Treatise on Slavery*, 71. See also Nicole von Germeten, "Introduction," in Alonso de Sandoval, *Treatise on Slavery: Selections from De instaurada aethiopum salute*, ed. Nicole von Germeten (Indianapolis: Hackett , 2008), xii–xiii.

113. Sandoval, *Treatise on Slavery*, 134.

114. Quoted in Thornton, *Africa and Africans in the Making of the Atlantic World*, 202.

115. Thornton, *The Kongolese Saint Anthony*, 29–30.

116. Dionigio de Carli, "A Curious and Exact Account of a Voyage to Congo, in the Years 1666 and 1667 by the R.R.F.F. Michael Angelo of Gattina and Denis de Carli of Piacenza," *A General Collection of the Best and Most Interesting Voyages and Travels in All Parts of the World*, ed. John Pinkerton (London: Hurst, 1814), 152.

117. Cabrera, *Reglas de Congo*, 58, 108–9.

118. Caspar van Baerle, *The History of Brazil under the Governorship of Count Johan Maurits of Nassau, 1636–1644*, ed. Blanche T. van Berckel-Ebeling Koning (Gainesville: University Press of Florida, 2011), 236; Bastide, *As religiões africanas no Brasil*, 1:121–35; R. K. Kent, "Palmares: An African State in Brazil," *Journal of African History* VI, no 2 (1965): 166–68; Eugene D. Genovese, *From Rebellion to Revolution: Afro-American Slave Revolts in the making of the Modern World* (Baton Rouge: Louisiana State University Press, 1979), 62; Thornton, *Africa and Africans in the Making of the Atlantic World*, 269; Thornton, *A Cultural History of the Atlantic World*, 336–37; Flávio Gomes, *Mocambos de Palmares. História e fontes Séc. XVI–XIX* (Rio de Janeiro: 7Letras, 2010), 170, 222.

119. José Alípio Goulart, *Da fuga ao suicídio: aspectos de rebeldia dos escravos no Brasil* (Rio de Janeiro: Conquista, 1972), 213–16.

120. Gerald Cardoso, *Negro Slavery in the Sugar Plantations of Veracruz and Pernambuco, 1550–1680* (Washington: University Press of America, 1983), 54–58; Thornton, *Africa and Africans in the Making of the Atlantic World*, 269.

121. Quoted in Jane Landers, "The African Landscape of Seventeenth-Century Cartagena and Its Hinterland," *The Black Urban Atlantic in the Age of the Slave Trade*, 155–56.

122. Marina de Mello e Souza, "Reis do Congo no Brasil. Séculos XVIII e XIX," *Revista de História* 152, no. 1 (2005): 83.

123. Renaldo Vainfas, ed., *Dicionário do Brasil colonial: 1500–1808* (Rio de Janeiro: Objetiva, 2000), 67–68.

124. Sandoval, *Treatise on Slavery*, 128.

125. Tulio Aristizábal and Anna Maria Splendiani, ed., *Proceso de beatificación y canonización de San Pedro Claver* (Bogotá: CEJA, 2000), 112–13.

126. Thornton, *The Kongolese Saint Anthony*, 272–73.

127. Sweet, *Recreating Africa*, 208; Thornton, *Africa and Africans in the Making of the Atlantic World*, 461.

128. Urbain Souchu de Rennefort, *Histoire des Indes Orientales (1688)*, ed. Dominique Huet (Saint-Clotilde, Réunion: ARS Terres Créoles, 1988), 225.

129. "Classicale Acta van Brazilië" (17 October 1641), 402.

130. Luís da Camara Cascudo, *Dicionário do folclore brasileiro* (São Paulo: Melhoramentos, 1979), 88; Cardoso, *Negro Slavery in the Sugar Plantations of Veracruz and Pernambuco*, 134.

131. Henry Koster, *Travels in Brazil* (London: Longman, Hurst Rees, Orme and Brown, 1816), 243–44.

132. Martha Abreu, *O Império do Divino. Festas religiosas e cultura popular no Rio de Janeiro, 1830–1900* (Rio de Janeiro: Editora Nova Fronteira, 1999), 47–64; Fiume, "St. Benedict the Moor," 26–28.

133. Cascudo, *Dicionário do folclore brasileiro*, 242–45, 294; Borges, *Escravos e libertos nas Irmandades do Rosário*, 85; Souza, *Reis negros no Brasil escravista*, 113; Van der Poel, *Dicionário da religiosidade popular*, 241–45.

134. Marlyse Meyer, *De Carlos Magno e outras histórias. Cristãos e Mouros no Brasil* (Natal, BR: Universidade Federal do Rio Grande do Norte, 1995), 55.

135. Cécile Fromont, "Dancing for the King of Congo from Early Modern Central Africa to Slavery-Era Brazil," *Colonial Latin American Review* 22, no. 2 (2013): 199; Fromont, *The Art of Conversion*, 60–62.

136. Marina de Mello e Souza, "Kongo King Festivals in Brazil: From Kings of Nations to Kings of Kongo," *African Studies Quarterly* 15, no. 3 (June 2015): 43.

137. Richard Francis Burton, *Explorations of the Highlands of the Brazil*, 2 vols. (London: Tinsley Brothers, 1869), 1:237–38. For his trip to West-Central Africa, see Richard Francis Burton, *Two Trips to Gorilla Land and the Cataracts of the Congo*, 2 vols. (London: Sampson Low, Marston, Low, and Stearle, 1876).

138. Cabrera, *Reglas de Congo*, 78.

139. Elizabeth W. Kiddy, "Who is the King of Congo? A New Look at African and Afro-Brazilian Kings in Brazil," *Central Africans and Cultural Transformation in the American Diaspora*, 159, 171. See also Oliveira, *Devoção negra*, 278–81.

140. Patricia Mulvey, "Black Brothers and Sisters: Membership in the Black Lay Brotherhoods of Colonial Brazil," *Luso-Brazilian Review* 17 (1982): 261.

141. Epstein, *Sinful Tunes and Spirituals*, 79; Robert Chaudenson, *Creolization of Language and Culture. Revised in Collaboration with Salikoko S. Mufwene* (London: Routledge, 2001), 74, 92.

142. Jeroen Dewulf, "Black Brotherhoods in North America: Afro-Iberian and West-Central African Influences," *African Studies Quarterly* 15, no. 3 (June 2015): 19–38.

143. Green, *The Rise of the Trans-Atlantic Slave Trade in Western Africa*, 189, 194, 208.

144. Heywood and Thornton, *Central Africans*, ix.

145. Miller, "Central Africans during the Era of the Slave Trade, c. 1490s–1850s," 61.

146. Linda M. Heywood, "The Angolan-Afro-Brazilian Cultural Connections," *Slavery & Abolition: A Journal of Slave and Post-Slave Studies* 20, no. 1 (1999): 21.

147. Nicole von Germeten, "Black Brotherhoods in Mexico City," *The Black Urban Atlantic in the Age of the Slave Trade*, 252.

148. Heywood and Thornton, *Central Africans*, 238.

149. Miller, "Central Africans during the Era of the Slave Trade," 61.

150. Berlin, "From Creole to African," 275–76.

151. Ibid.

152. Cañizares-Esguerra, Childs, and Sidbury, *The Black Urban Atlantic in the Age of the Slave Trade*, 9.

153. Antoine Biet, "Father Antoine Biet's visit to Barbados in 1654," ed. Jerome S. Handler, *Journal of the Barbados Museum and Historical Society* 32 (1967): 61, 67, 71.

154. "Jean Mongin à une personne de condition du Languedoc" (St. Christophe, May 1682), in Marcel Chantillon, ed., "L'évangelisation des esclaves au XVIIe siècle. Lettres du R.P. Jean Mongin," *Bulletin de la Société d'histoire de la Guadeloupe* 60, no. 1 (1984): 86.

155. Jean-Baptiste Labat, *Voyages aux Isles de l'Amérique (Antilles), 1693–1705*, ed. Daniël Radford (Paris: Éditions Duchartre, 1979), 42; Médéric L. E. Moreau de Saint-Méry, *Description topographique physique, civile, politique et historique de la partie Française de l'isle Saint-Domingue*, ed. Blanche Maurel and Étienne Taillemite, 3 vols. (1797; Paris: Société de l'histoire des Colonies Françaises, 1958), 1:53.

156. Gabriel Debien, "Les origines des esclaves des Antilles," *Bulletin de l'Institut Fondamental de l'Afrique Noire*, série B, no. 26 (1964): 178–82.

157. Michael Mullin, *Africa in America: Slave Acculturation and Resistance in the American South and the British Caribbean, 1736–1831* (Urbana: University of Illinois Press, 1992), 26.

158. John Storm Roberts, *Black Music of Two Worlds: African, Caribbean, Latin, and African-American Traditions* (New York: Schirmer, 1998), 34.

159. Marie Bertrand de Cothonay, *Trinidad: journal d'un missionnaire dominicain des Antilles anglaises* (Paris: V. Retaux et fils, 1893), 303–4.

160. Warner-Lewis, *Central Africa in the Caribbean*, 177–78, 188.

161. Kenneth Bilby and Kia Bunseki Fu-Kiau, *Kumina: A Kongo-Based Tradition in the New World* (Brussels: ASDOC-Studies, 1983), 59.

162. Christian Georg Andrea Oldendorp, *History of the Mission of the Evangelical Brethren on the Caribbean Islands of St. Thomas, St. Croix, and St. John (1770)*, ed. Arnold R. Highfield and Vladimir Barac (Ann Arbor, MI: Karoma, 1987), 263.

163. Warner-Lewis, *Central Africa in the Caribbean*, 186.

164. Thurlow Weed, *Letters from Europe and the West Indies, 1843–1862* (Albany, NY: Weed, Parsons, 1866), 345–48; Neville A. T. Hall, *Slave Society in the Danish West Indies: St. Thomas, St. John and St. Croix*, ed. B. W. Higman (Baltimore, MA: Johns Hopkins University Press, 1992), 200.

165. Moreau de Saint-Méry, *Description topographique physique, civile, politique et historique de la partie Française de l'isle Saint-Domingue*, 1:111.

166. Quoted in David Geggus, "The Slaves and Free People of Color of Cap Français," *The Black Urban Atlantic in the Age of the Slave Trade*, 118.

167. Thomas Madiou, *Histoire d'Haïti*, 3 vols. (Port-au-Prince: J. Courtois, 1904), 1:181; John K. Thornton, "I am the Subject of the King of Kongo: African Political Ideology and the Haitian Revolution," *Journal of World History* 4, no. 2 (1993): 181–85, 204.

168. Carolyn E. Fick, *The Making of Haiti: The Saint-Domingue Revolution from Below* (Knoxville: University of Tennessee Press, 1990), 127; Terry Rey, "The Virgin Mary and Revolution in Saint-Domingue: The Charisma of Romaine-la-Prophétesse," *Journal of Historical Sociology* 11, no. 3 (1998): 341–69.

169. "San Domingo Disturbances," *General Advertiser*, October 11, 1791.

170. Laurent Dubois, *Haiti: The Aftershocks of History* (New York: Metropolitan Books, 2012), 62.

171. Childs, *The 1812 Aponte Rebellion in Cuba*, 124, 161–63.

172. Eights, "Pinkster Festivities in Albany Sixty Years Ago," 2:323–27.

173. Hall, *Slave Society in the Danish West Indies*, 74; Paul Brenneker: *Zjozjoli: Gegevens over de volkskunde van Curaçao, Aruba en Bonaire* (Curaçao: Publisidat Antiano, 1986), 251.

174. John Alden Mason, "Porto-Rican Folklore," *Journal of American Folklore* 31, No. 21 (July-September 1918): 289–450; Max Harris, "Masking the Site: The Fiestas de Santiago Apóstol in Loíza, Puerto Rico," *Journal of American Folklore* 114 (2001): 358–69.

175. Henry Rowe Schoolcraft, ed., *Information Respecting the History, Condition and Prospects of the Indian Tribes of the United States*, 6 vols. (Philadelphia: Lippincott, 1853), 2:309.

176. Moreau de Saint-Méry, *Description topographique physique, civile, politique et historique de la partie Française de l'isle Saint-Domingue*, 1:67.

177. Louis M. C. A. Drouin de Bercy, *De Saint-Domingue* (Paris: Chez Hocquet, 1814), 176–78.

178. Alasdair Pettinger, "'Eh, eh! Bomba, hen! hen!': Making Sense of a Vodou Chant," *Obeah and Other Powers: The Politics of Caribbean Religion and Healing*, ed. Diana Paton and Maarit Forde (Durham, NC: Duke University Press, 2012), 80–101.

179. Thornton, "I am the Subject of the King of Kongo," 261–78. See also Warner-Lewis, *Central Africa in the Caribbean*, 157.

180. Hein Vanhee, "Central African Popular Christianity and the Making of Haitian Vodou Religion," *Central Africans and Cultural Transformation in the American Diaspora*, 243–64; Terry Rey, "Kongolese Catholic Influences on Haitian Popular Catholicism: A Sociohistorical Exploration," *Central Africans and Cultural Transformation in the American Diaspora*, 265–85.

181. Alfred Métraux, *Le Vaudou Haïtien* (Paris: Gallimar, 1958), 287.

182. Harold Courlander, *Haiti Singing* (1939; New York: Cooper Square, 1973), 26, 40.

183. Milo Rigaud, *La tradition Voudoo et le Voudoo Haïtien: Son temple, ses mystères, sa magie* (Paris: Éditions Niclaus, 1953), 257; De Heusch, *Le roi de Kongo et les monstres sacrés*, 343–49; Elizabeth McAlister, *Rara! Vodou, Power, and Performance in Haiti and Its Diaspora* (Berkeley: University of California Press, 2004), 4. For linguistic parallels, see Batsîkama, *L'ancien royaume du Congo et les Bakongo*, 33–38.

184. Courlander, *Haiti Singing*, 169.

185. David Geggus, "Haitian Voodoo in the Eighteenth Century: Language, Culture, Resistance," *Jahrbuch für Geschichte Lateinamerikas* 28, no. 1 (January 1991): 46.

186. Geggus, "The Slaves and Free People of Color of Cap Français," 118–19.

187. Félix Carteau, *Soirées Bermudiennes, ou Entretiens sur les évènemens qui ont opéré la ruine de la partie française de l'île Saint-Domingue, ouvrage où l'on expose les causes de ces évènemens, les moyens employés pour renverser cette colonie* (Bordeaux, FR: Pellier-Lawalle, 1802), 81.

188. Brown, *African-Atlantic Cultures and the South Carolina Lowcountry*, 49–51.

189. Francis Le Jau, "Slave Conversion on the Carolina Frontier (1706–17)," *African American Religious History: A Documentary Witness*, ed. Milton C. Sernett (Durham, NC: Duke University Press, 1999), 27–30.

190. Quoted in Mark M. Smith, ed., *Stono: Documenting and Interpreting a Southern Slave Revolt* (Columbia: University of South Carolina Press, 2005), 13–15.

191. Ibid., 108–23.

192. Thomas Wenthworth Higginson: "Slave Songs and Spirituals," in *African American Religious History*, 115.

193. Thomas Turpin, "Missionary Sketch," *Christian Advocate and Journal*, January 31, 1834.

194. Nick Lindsay, ed., *An Oral History of Edisto Island: Sam Gadsden Tells the Story* (Goshen College, IN: Pinchpenny Press, 1975), 72.

195. According to the *Trans-Atlantic Slave Trade Database*, 332,000 of the 2,545,000 slaves who were shipped to the British Caribbean until 1800 were of West-Central African origin. www.slavevoyages.org/tast/database/search.faces.

196. Quoted in Hodges, *Root and Branch*, 124.

197. *New-York Gazette*, August 27, 1733.

198. Correa Arlindo, *Informazione sul regno del Congo di Fra Raimondo da Dicomano (1798)*, Lisbon, Arquivo Histórico Ultramarino, Diversos, caixa 823, sala 12; Alfredo de Sarmento, *Os sertões d'Africa. Apontamentos de viagem* (Lisbon: Francisco Arthur da Silva, 1880), 49; Heywood and Thornton, *Central Africans, Atlantic Creoles*, 135–43; Fromont, *The Art of Conversion*, 47–59, 71, 130.

199. White, *Somewhat More Independent*, 155; Hodges, *Root and Branch*, 40–41, 78–79, 104; Foote, *Black and White Manhattan*, 146.

200. "Governor Hunter to the Lords of Trade" (23 June 1712), in O'Callaghan, Fernow, and Brodhead, *Documents Relative to the Colonial History of the State of New York*, 5:342.

201. Eliga H. Gould, "Entangled Histories, Entangled Worlds: The English-Speaking Atlantic as a Spanish Periphery," *American Historical Review* 112, no. 3 (June 2007): 764.

202. Hebe Mattos, "'Black Troops' and Hierarchies of Color in the Portuguese Atlantic World: The Case of Henrique Dias and His Black Regiment," *Luso-Brazilian Review* 45, no. 1 (2008): 6–29.

203. Hodges and Brown, *Pretends to Be Free*, 134.

204. White, "Pinkster in Albany," 193; White, "Afro-Dutch Syncretization in New York City and the Hudson Valley," 71, 74.

205. Verter, "Interracial Festivity and Power in Antebellum New York," 400, 419.

206. Hodges, *Root and Branch*, 223.

207. Eduardo Silva, *Prince of the People: Life and Times of a Brazilian Free Man of Colour* (London: Verso, 1993).

Chapter 5

1. Berlin, "From Creole to African," 268–72.

2. Hodges, *Root and Branch*, 28.

3. Berlin, *Generations of Captivity*, 36; Van Zandt, *Brothers among Nations*, 137; Romney, *New Netherland Connections*, 217.

4. Stokes, *The Iconography of Manhattan Island*, 4:82.

5. Unlike what Hodges has suggested, "de reus," Dutch for "the giant," was not Manuel's nickname. In actual fact, the name "de Reus" is derived from the French name De Reux. Hodges, *Root and Branch*, 16; Christoph, "The Freedmen of New Amsterdam," 167.

6. "Council Minutes" (17 January 1641), in van Laer, *New York Historical Manuscripts*, 4:97–100; Purple, *Marriages from 1639 to 1801 in the Reformed Dutch Church*, 11; "Act of the Director and Council of New Netherland emancipating certain Negro Slaves therein mentioned" (25

February 1644), in O'Callaghan, *Laws and Ordinances of New Netherland, 1638–1674*, 36–37. See also Van Zandt, *Brothers among Nations*, 149–59; Romney, *New Netherland Connections*, 222.

7. "Council Minutes" (23 November 1640), in Van Laer, *New York Historical Manuscripts*, 4:96; Evans, *Records of the Reformed Dutch Church in New Amsterdam and New York*, 17–19; Gehring, *Land Papers*, 56; Christoph, "The Freedmen of New Amsterdam," 159; Frijhoff, *Wegen van Evert Willemsz.*, 769; Heywood and Thornton, *Central Africans*, 264; Romney, *New Netherland Connections*, 215–17.

8. Evans, *Records of the Reformed Dutch Church in New Amsterdam and New York*, 21, 23; Hodges, *Root and Branch*, 11–12; Moore, "A World of Possibilities," 47–48.

9. José António Gonsalves de Mello, *Henrique Dias, governador dos crioulos, negros e mulatos do Brasil* (Recife, BR: Editora Massangana, 1988), 50; Mattos, "Black Troops and Hierarchies of Color in the Portuguese Atlantic World," 6–29.

10. Johann Gregor Aldenburgk, "Reise nach Brasilien 1623–1626," *Reisebeschreibungen von deutschen Beamten und Kriegsleuten im Dienst der niederländischen West- und Ost-Indischen Kompagnien 1602–1797*, ed. S. P. L'Honoré Naber, 10 vols. (1627; The Hague: Martinus Nijhoff, 1930), 1:32.

11. Ambrosius Richshoffer, "Reise nach Brasilien 1629–1632," *Ibid.*, 1:59.

12. José António Gonsalves de Mello, *Nederlanders in Brazilië, 1624–1654* (1947; Zutphen, NL: Walburg Pers, 2001), 184, 197; van Baerle, *The History of Brazil under the Governorship of Count Johan Maurits of Nassau*, 51; Joosse, *Geloof in de Nieuwe Wereld*, 505.

13. "Dagelijkse Notulen, Recife" (25 May 1637), quoted in de Mello, *Nederlanders in Brazilië*, 198.

14. Van Zandt, *Brothers among Nations*, 221.

15. "The Commonality of New Netherland" (29 August 1641), in O'Callaghan, Fernow, and Brodhead, *Documents Relative to the Colonial History of the State of New York*, 1:415.

16. "Act of the Director and Council of New Netherland emancipating certain Negro Slaves therein mentioned" (25 February 1644), in O'Callaghan, *Laws and Ordinances of New Netherland, 1638–1674*, 36–37.

17. "Protest by Director & Council against the Fiscal for Neglect of Duty" (5 January 1644), in O'Callaghan, Fernow, and Brodhead, *Documents Relative to the Colonial History of the State of New York*, 14:52.

18. "Kiliaen van Rensselaer to Adriaen van der Donck" (9 March 1643), in van Laer, *Van Rensselaer Bowier Manuscripts*, 642. See also Moore, "A World of Possibilities," 41.

19. "De Deckere to Stuyvesant and Councilors Concerning Local Matters" (26 May 1656), Gehring and Venema, *Fort Orange Records*, 90.

20. "Council Minutes" (8 April 1654), in Gehring, *Council Minutes, 1652–1654*, 129–30.

21. "Extract from a letter of Director Stuyvesant to the Vice-Director at Curaçao" (17 February 1660), in O'Callaghan, Fernow, and Brodhead, *Documents Relative to the Colonial History of the State of New York*, 13:142–43.

22. "Letter from Petrus Stuyvesant to Secretary van Ruyven" (18 March 1660), Ibid., 13:152.

23. "Letter from Captain Cregier to Director Stuyvesant" (5 July 1663), Ibid., 13:273; "Journal of the Esopus War, by Captain Martin Cregier," Ibid., 13:328, 330, 338; "Issues Debtor to Powder Delivered between the 7th January and the 29th December 1663" (29 December 1663), Ibid., 2:467.

24. Dewulf, "Emulating a Portuguese Model," 3–36.

25. "New York Colonial Manuscripts" X/2: 429, X/3:317 and X/3:327 (New York State Archives); Christoph, "The Freedmen of New Amsterdam," 164.

26. Klooster, "The Dutch in the Atlantic," *Four Centuries of Dutch-American Relations 1609–2009*, 64.

27. Nigel Worden, *Slavery in Dutch South Africa* (Cambridge, UK: Cambridge University Press, 1985), 166–67; Christoph, "The Freedmen of New Amsterdam," 157–70; Postma, *The Dutch in the Atlantic Slave Trade*, 17; Thornton, *Africa and Africans in the Making of the Atlantic World*, 156; Rink, "Before the English (1609–1664)," 56; Kees Zandvliet, *The Dutch Encounter with Asia, 1600–1950* (Amsterdam: Rijksmuseum, 2002), 99; Meuwese, *Brothers in Arms, Partners in Trade*, 158–61.

28. Hodges, *Root and Branch*, 26.

29. De Mello, *Nederlanders in Brazilië*, 190; Pedro Puntoni, *A miséria sorte. A escravidão Africana no Brasil Holandês e as guerras do tráfico no Atlântico Sul, 1621–1648* (São Paulo: Editora Hucitec, 1999), 163.

30. "Letter from the Director to Stuyvesant" (7 April 1657), in Gehring, *New Netherland Documents Series Volume XII: Correspondence 1654–1658*, 127. Appeals had, indeed, been made in Dutch Brazil to European craftsmen to "teach their craft to one or more blacks." Some of these black craftsmen were later sent to Luanda to assist the Dutch in building a new fortress. See "Brief van de Raad der Heren XIX aan de Graaf van Nassau en de Hoge Raad" (24 October 1643) and "Brief van de Raad der Heren XIX aan de Hoge Raad" (17 September 1644), in de Mello, *Nederlanders in Brazilië*, 195–96.

31. Goodfriend, "Black Families in New Netherland," 152; Thornton, *A Cultural History of the Atlantic World*, 460.

32. Samuel Brun, *Schiffarten in etliche newe Länder und Insulen*, ed. Walter Hirschberg (1624; Graz, AT: Akademische Druck- und Verlagsanstalt, 1969), 22–23.

33. "Annexe-Relation de Pieter Moortamer à la Chambre de Zélande" (29 June 1643) and "Les directeurs C. Nieulant et Hans Mols aux XIX" (10 June 1643), in Jadin, *L'Ancien Congo et l'Angola 1639–1655*, 1:355, 429–31.

34. Heywood and Thornton, *Central Africans*, 272.

35. Purple, *Marriages from 1639 to 1801 in the Reformed Dutch Church*, 14; Evans, *Records of the Reformed Dutch Church in New Amsterdam and New York: Baptisms from 25 December, 1639, to 27 December 1730*, 17, 18, 19, 23, 95, 100, 104, 111; Henricus Selyns, "List of Members of the Dutch Reformed Church in New York in 1686," *Yearbook of the Holland Society of New York* ([1686] 1916), 31–34; Frijhoff, *Wegen van Evert Willemsz.*, 772; Heywood and Thornton, *Central Africans, Atlantic Creoles*, 264; Christoph, "The Freedmen of New Amsterdam," 164.

36. Frijhoff, *Wegen van Evert Willemsz.*, 779.

37. "Henricus Selijns. Second Letter," (9 June 1664), in A. P. G. J. van der Linde, ed., *Old First Dutch Reformed Church of Brooklyn, New York: First Book of Records, 1660–1752. New York Historical Manuscripts: Dutch* (Baltimore, MD: Genealogical Publishing, 1983), 230–31.

38. Evans, *Records of the Reformed Dutch Church in New Amsterdam and New York*, 26.

39. Cardoso, *Negro Slavery in the Sugar Plantations of Veracruz and Pernambuco*, 140–41.

40. Mark Meuwese, "Dutch Calvinism and Native Americans: A Comparative Study of the Motivations for Protestant Conversion among the Tupis in Northeastern Brazil (1630–1654)

and the Mohawks in Central New York (1690–1710)," *The Spiritual Conversion of the Americas*, ed. James Muldoon (Gainesville: University of Florida Press, 2004), 118–41.

41. Hodges, *Root and Branch*, 17–18.

42. J. van Goor, *De Nederlandse koloniën. Geschiedenis van de Nederlandse expansie, 1600–1975* (The Hague: Uitgeverij Koninginnengracht, 1994), 111–12; G. J. Schutte, "Een hutje in den wijngaard," *Het Indisch Sion. De Gereformeerde Kerk onder Verenigde Oost-Indische Compagnie*, ed. G. J. Schutte (Hilversum, NL: Verloren, 2002), 182–83.

43. Cotton Mather, *Diary of Cotton Mather, 1663–1728*, ed. Worthington Chauncey Ford, 2 vols. (Boston: Massachusetts Historical Society, 1911–12), 1:176.

44. Janny Venema, ed., *Deacons' Accounts 1652–1674 Beverwijck/Albany* (Rockport, ME: Picton Press, 1998), 223–24.

45. "Court Minutes of New Amsterdam" (18 February and 7 March 1662), in Fernow, *The Records of New Amsterdam from 1653 to 1674*, 4:41–42, 45–46.

46. Moore, "A World of Possibilities," 52.

47. A. M. van der Woude, "Het gebruik van de familienaam in de 17ᵉ eeuw," *Holland* 5 (1973): 109–31.

48. Kenney, *The Gansevoorts of Albany*, 262.

49. Heywood and Thornton, *Central Africans*, 208.

50. Ibid., 278.

51. Goodfriend, "Black Families in New Netherland," 153; Cuvelier, *L'ancien royaume de Congo*, 280–81.

52. Frijhoff, *Wegen van Evert Willemsz.*, 774.

53. Mintz and Price, *An Anthropological Approach to the Afro-American Past*, 25–26; Hall, *Slavery and African Ethnicities in the Americas*, 169; Heywood and Thornton, *Central Africans*, 262.

54. Heywood and Thornton, *Central Africans*, 238; Frijhoff, *Wegen van Evert Willemsz.*, 777.

55. *New-York Weekly Journal*, June 12, 1738.

56. *New-York Weekly Journal*, March 7 and 21, 1736; Hodges, *Slavery and Freedom in the Rural North*, 56–67; Hodges, *Root and Branch*, 88.

57. Roger D. Abrahams and John F. Szwed, *After Africa: Extracts from British Travel Accounts and Journals of the Seventeenth, Eighteenth, and Nineteenth Centuries concerning the Slaves, their Manners, and Customs in the British West Indies* (New Haven, CT: Yale University Press, 1983), 39–47; Martha Warren Beckwith, *Black Roadways: A Study of Jamaican Folk Life* (Chapel Hill: University of North Carolina Press, 1929), 104.

58. Thornton, *A Cultural History of the Atlantic World*, 394.

59. Murdoch, *The Dutch Dominie of the Catskills*, 279–80, 311, 364.

60. Theophilus Conneau, *A Slaver's Log Book, or Twenty Years' Residence in Africa* (1853; Englewood Cliffs, NJ: Prentice-Hall, 1976).

61. John H. Weeks, *Among the Primitive Bakongo* (London: Seely, Service, 1914), 131–32.

62. Daniel Horsmanden, *The New York Conspiracy*, ed. Thomas J. Davis (1744; Boston: Beacon Press, 1971), 386.

63. De Voe, *The Market Book*, 1:264–65; Horton and Horton, *In Hope of Liberty*, 44; Craig Steven Wilder, *In the Company of Black Men: The African Influence on African American Culture in New York City* (New York: New York University Press, 2001), 25–29; Foote, *Black and White Manhattan*, 25–29.

64. *New-York Gazette,* February 5, 1738.

65. *New-York Weekly Journal,* January 24, 1738.

66. *New York Gazette,* February 14, 1738.

67. Horsmanden, *The New York Conspiracy,* 67, 419, 451.

68. Ibid., 158.

69. Ibid., 283.

70. Ibid., 143–44.

71. Ibid., 81, 191, 196.

72. Ibid., 345–46

73. Ibid., 130.

74. Jill Lepore, *New York Burning: Liberty, Slavery, and Conspiracy in Eighteenth-Century Manhattan* (New York: Alfred A. Knopf, 2005), 159.

75. Ibid., 182.

76. Hodges, *Root and Branch,* 93–98; Peter Linebaugh and Marcus Rediker, *The Many-Headed Hydra: Sailors, Salves, Commoners, and the Hidden History of the Revolutionary Atlantic* (Boston: Beacon Press, 2000), 186–90; Lepore, *New York Burning,* 181. For the "Spanish Negroes," see also Horsmanden, *The New York Conspiracy,* 139, and the "List of Negroes committed on account of the conspiracy" at the end of Horsmanden's book.

77. Horsmanden, *The New York Conspiracy,* 149.

78. Ibid., 378.

79. *New-York Weekly Journal,* August 17, 1741.

80. Horsmanden, *The New York Conspiracy,* 211.

81. Linebaugh and Rediker, *The Many-Headed Hydra,* 205.

82. Thornton, *The Kongolese Saint Anthony,* 211; John K. Thornton, "African Dimensions," *Stono: Documenting and Interpreting a Southern Slave Revolt,* ed. Mark M. Smith (Columbia: University of South Carolina, 2005), 76.

83. Quoted in Childs, *The 1812 Aponte Rebellion in Cuba,* 43.

84. Quoted in David Barry Gaspar, *Bondmen and Rebels: A Study of Master-Slave Relations in Antigua* (Baltimore, MD: Johns Hopkins University Press, 1985), 23–24.

85. Peter H. Wood, *Black Majority: Negroes in Colonial South Carolina from 1670 through the Stono Rebellion* (New York: W.W. Norton, 1974), 312–14; Mullin, *Africa in America,* 23–24; Jane Landers, "The Central African Presence in Spanish Maroon Communities," *Central Africans and Cultural Transformation in the American Diaspora,* 227–43; Berlin, *Generations of Captivity,* 44–47.

86. Horsmanden, *The New York Conspiracy,* 349, 418.

87. Peter Charles Hoffer, *The Great New York Conspiracy of 1741: Slavery, Crime, and Colonial Law* (Lawrence: University Press of Kansas, 2003), 138–51.

88. Ibid., 346.

89. Juan de Torquemada, *Monarquía indiana,* 3 vols. (1615; México City: S. Chávez Hayhoe, 1943–44), 1, bk. 5, cpt. 76.

90. Quoted in Thornton, *Africa and Africans in the Making of the Atlantic World,* 203, 302.

91. Quoted in Gaspar, *Bondmen and Rebels,* 212.

92. Mullin, *Africa in America,* 223–25.

93. Quoted in Mullin, *Africa in America,* 223.

94. Rodway, *History of British Guiana,* 2:295–97.

95. Quoted in Warner-Lewis, *Central Africa in the Caribbean*, 65.

96. Genovese, *From Rebellion to Revolution*, xiv.

97. Mullin, *Africa in America*, 236.

98. "Letter from John Sharpe to the Secretary" (23 June 1712), in Foote, *Black and White Manhattan*, 133; Kenneth Scott, "The Slave Insurrection in New York in 1712," *New-York Historical Society Quarterly* XLV, no. 1 (January 1961): 43–74.

99. Horsmanden, *The New York Conspiracy*, 265–66.

100. Quoted in Gaspar, *Bondmen and Rebels*, 227, 236–37.

101. John K. Thornton, "The Coromantees: An African Cultural Group in Colonial North America and the Caribbean," *Journal of Caribbean History* 32, nos. 1 and 2 (1998): 170.

102. Quoted in Gaspar, *Bondmen and Rebels*, 243.

103. Lucilene Reginaldo, *Os Rosários dos Angolas. Irmandades de africanos e crioulos na Bahia Setecentista* (São Paulo: Alameda, 2011), 151–63; João José Reis, "African Nations in Nineteenth-Century Salvador, Brazil," *The Black Urban Atlantic in the Age of the Slave Trade*, 71, 82; Genovese, *From Rebellion to Revolution*, 99; Michael Craton, *Testing the Chains: Resistance to Slavery in the British West Indies* (Ithaca, NY: Cornell University Press, 1982), 113–16.

104. Lepore, *New York Burning*, 147, 157.

105. Horsmanden, *The New York Conspiracy*, 327.

106. Quoted in James Duncan Phillips, *Salem in the Eighteenth Century* (Boston: Houghton Mifflin, 1937), 272.

107. Truth, *Narrative of Sojourner Truth*, 16.

108. Margaret Washington, *Sojourner Truth's America* (Urbana: University of Illinois Press, 2009), 10.

109. Considering the Iberian roots of Truth's name, it should be written as "Isabel." The Italianized form "Isabella" was a Dutch adaptation of her name; the Portuguese princess Isabel de Portugal (1503–39) became known in the Netherlands as "Isabella van Portugal." Following a Dutch pattern, the abbreviation of Truth's name was "Bella," "Belle," or "Bel," but not "Bell." Truth, *Narrative of Sojourner Truth*, 5.

110. Suzanne P. Fitch and Roseann M. Mandziuk, *Sojourner Truth as Orator: Wit, Story and Song* (Westport, CT: Greenwood Press, 1997), 77, 107, 125, 141, 218; Truth, *Narrative of Sojourner Truth*, 7, 53.

111. White, *Somewhat More Independent*, 107–12, 150–53; Hodges, *Slavery and Freedom in the Rural North*, 128–29; Harris, *In the Shadow of Slavery*, 40; Michael E. Groth, "Laboring for Freedom in Dutchess County," *Mighty Change, Tall Within*, 64–65.

112. Gellman, *Emancipating New York*, 8.

113. Fitch and Mandziuk, *Sojourner Truth as Orator*, 11.

114. Truth, *Narrative of Sojourner Truth*, 16.

115. David Maldwyn Ellis, *Landlords and Farmers in the Hudson-Mohawk Region 1790–1850* (Ithaca, NY: Cornell University Press, 1946), 7–8; Kenney, *The Gansevoorts of Albany*, 129; Sung Bok Kim, *Landlord and Tenant in Colonial New York: Manorial Society, 1664–1775* (Chapel Hill: University of North Carolina Press, 1978), 162–234; Middleton, "The Waning of Dutch New York," 115.

116. Ellis, *Landlords and Farmers*, 12.

117. "A Glimpse of an Old Dutch Town," 525–26.

118. Ellis, *Landlords and Farmers*, 1–15; Albert James Williams-Myers, *On the Morning Tide: African Americans, History and Methodology in the Historical Ebb and Flow of the Hudson River Society* (Trenton, NJ: Africa World Press, 2003), 8.

119. Hackett, *The Rude Hand of Innovation*, 29.

120. C. M. Woolsey, *History of the Town of Marlborough, Ulster County, New York, from its Earliest Discovery* (Albany, NY: J.B. Lyon, 1908), 234.

121. Ibid., 231.

122. *Laws of the State of New-York passed at the Seventy Second Session of the Legislature, begun the second day of January, and ended the eleventh day of April, 1849, at the city of Albany* (Troy, NY: Albert W. Scribner and Albert West, 1849), 9.

123. "A Glimpse of an Old Dutch Town," 525–26.

Chapter 6

1. Hackett, *The Rude Hand of Innovation*, 57.

2. Michael Kammen, *Colonial New York: A History* (New York: Charles Scribner's Sons, 1975), 294; Alice P. Kenney, *Stubborn for Liberty: The Dutch in New York* (Syracuse, NY: Syracuse University Press, 1975), 211–33; Timothy J. Shannon, "Avenue of Empire: The Hudson Valley in an Atlantic Context," *The World of the Seventeenth-Century Hudson Valley*, eds. Jaap Jacobs and L. H. Roper (Albany: State University of New York Press, 2014), 67–84.

3. Kenney, *The Gansevoorts of Albany*, 42; Rink, "Before the English (1609–1664)," 105.

4. Grant, *Memoirs of an American Lady*, 293–99; de Jong, *The Dutch Reformed Church in the American Colonies*, 143.

5. William Kennedy, *O Albany! Improbable City of Political Wizards, Fearless Ethnics, Spectacular Aristocrats, Splendid Nobodies, and Underrated Scoundrels* (New York: Viking, 1983), 79. See also Ellis, *Landlords and Farmers in the Hudson-Mohawk Region 1790–1850*, 21; Gellman, *Emancipating New York*, 115.

6. Carel de Vos van Steenwijk, *Een grand tour naar de nieuwe republiek: journaal van een reis door Amerika, 1783–1784*, ed. Wayne te Brake (Hilversum, NL: Verloren, 1999), 77, 87, 166, 171.

7. Strickland, *Journal of a Tour in the United States of America*, 102.

8. *New-York Tribune*, May 18, 1880.

9. Verter, "Interracial Festivity and Power in Antebellum New York," 410.

10. Despite official objections, some blacks did also serve in military roles for the Patriots during the war. Hodges, *Root and Branch*, 141.

11. V. H. Paltsits, ed., *Minutes of the Commissioners for Detecting and Defeating Conspiracies in the State of New York*, 3 vols. (Albany: State of New York, 1909–10), 1:304.

12. McManus, *A History of Negro Slavery in New York*, 158–59; Hodges, *Root and Branch*, 139–61; Harris, *In the Shadow of Slavery*, 55; Stefan Bielinski, "Albany County," *The Other New York: The American Revolution beyond New York City, 1763–1787*, ed. Joseph Tiedemann and Eugene R. Fingerhut (Albany: State of New York University Press, 2005), 165; Gellman, *Emancipating New York*, 39.

13. David Northrup, "Identity among Liberated Africans in Sierra Leone," *The Black Urban Atlantic in the Age of the Slave Trade*, 32–33.

14. *New-York Gazetteer*, February 4, 1785; *New-York Journal*, February 15, 1785.

15. Dunlap, *Diary of William Dunlap*, 1:119.

16. Harris, *In the Shadow of Slavery*, 61.

17. Kachun, *Festivals of Freedom*, 25.

18. Ryan Fox Dixon, "The Negro Vote in Old New York," *Political Science Quarterly* 32, no. 2 (June 1917): 256.

19. Ibid.

20. Patrick Rael, "The Long Death of Slavery," *Slavery in New York*, 134; McManus, *A History of Negro Slavery in New York*, 186–87.

21. Dorothy Porter, ed., *Early Negro Writing, 1760–1837* (Baltimore, MD: Black Classic Press, 1995), 361.

22. Herman D. Bloch, "The New York Negro's Battle for Political Rights, 1777–1865," *International Review of Social History* IX (1964): 65–80; Rhoda Golden Freeman, *The Free Negro in New York City in the Era before the Civil War* (New York: Garland, 1994), 91; Hodges, *Root and Branch*, 193; Verter, "Interracial Festivity and Power in Antebellum New York," 407.

23. McManus, *A History of Negro Slavery in New York*, 182; Harris, *In the Shadow of Slavery*, 61.

24. de Jong, *The Dutch in America, 1609–1974*, 219.

25. Aptheker, *American Negro Slave Revolts*, 150.

26. Gellman, *Emancipating New York*, 70; Joyce D. Goodfriend, "Why New Netherland Matters," *Explorers, Fortunes & Love Letters: A Window on New Netherland*, ed. Martha Dickinson Shattuck (New York: Mount Ida Press, 2009), 153; Goodfriend, "The Social Life and Cultural Life of Dutch Settlers," 123.

27. White, *Somewhat More Independent*, xx.

28. John Jay, *The Correspondence and Public Papers of John Jay*, ed. Henry P. Johnston, 4 vols. (New York: G.P. Putnam's Sons, 1890–93), 3:413–15.

29. Jabez D. Hammond, *History of Political Parties in the State of New York*, 2 vols. (Albany, NY: Van Benthuysen, 1842), 1:581. The original is "bij donder en bliksem" (lit. "by thunder and lightning").

30. Kenney, *The Gansevoorts of Albany*, 135–36; Verter, "Interracial Festivity and Power in Antebellum New York," 409.

31. Joel Munsell, *Collections on the History of Albany*, 4 vols. (Albany, NY: J. Munsell, 1865–71), 2:378.

32. Aimwell, "A Pinkster Ode for the Year 1803," 33.

33. Ibid., 34–35.

34. Ibid., 36–37.

35. Hammond, *History of Political Parties in the State of New York*, 1:194, 323–339; Richard Hildreth, *The History of the United States of America*, 6 vols. (New York: Harpers and Brothers, 1880), 5:477.

36. Aimwell, "A Pinkster Ode for the Year 1803," 40–41.

37. Ibid., 42–45.

38. Horton and Horton, *In Hope of Liberty*, 56–57.

39. McManus, *A History of Negro Slavery in New York*, 127–88; Harris, *In the Shadow of Slavery*, 102; Rael, "The Long Death of Slavery," 134; Gellman, *Emancipating New York*, 85–101.

40. *Balance and Columbian Repository*, May 29, 1804.

41. Robert W. Smith, "McKean, Thomas (1734–1817)," *The Louisiana Purchase: A Historical and Geographical Encyclopedia*, ed. Junius P. Rodriguez (Santa Barbara, CA: ABC CLIO, 2002), 221.

42. *Albany Centinel*, June 4, 1805.

43. Ibid.

44. Middleton, "The Waning of Dutch New York," 115.

45. *Albany Centinel*, June 13, 1803.

46. Verter, "Interracial Festivity and Power in Antebellum New York," 406.

47. *Albany Centinel*, June 13, 1803.

48. *Daily Advertiser*, June 29, 1803.

49. *Albany Centinel*, July 13, 1804.

50. Bartlett, *Dictionary of Americanisms*, 468.

51. S.A.R.A. City Records, "Common Council 1765–1840," Albany County Hall of Records, Box 1, 88–02947, nr. 131.

52. Cuyler Reynolds, ed., *Albany Chronicles of the City. Arranged Chronologically from the Earliest Settlement to the Present Time* (Albany, NY: J.B. Lyon Company, 1906), 409.

53. Verter, "Interracial Festivity and Power in Antebellum New York," 400.

54. White, "'It Was a Proud Day,'" 30.

55. Hackett, *The Rude Hand of Innovation*, 88–90.

56. Samuel McKee, *Labor in Colonial New York, 1664–1776* (New York: Columbia University Press, 1935), 166; Kenney, *The Gansevoorts of Albany*, 140.

57. Eights, "Pinkster Festivities in Albany Sixty Years Ago," 2:323.

58. Verter, "Interracial Festivity and Power in Antebellum New York," 402.

59. Eights, "Pinkster Festivities in Albany Sixty Years Ago," 2:323.

60. "A Glimpse of an Old Dutch Town," 525–26.

61. Henry S. Bannister, "From the Collector's Library: Joel Munsell, Printer and Antiquarian in Albany, New York," *The Courier* 11, no. 2 (1974): 11–13.

62. This court case was published in the *Troy Daily Whig* in 1844. The poor image quality of the newspaper facsimile did not allow identifying the precise date of publication. The case related to the killing of a German immigrant in Sand Lake, near Albany, for which William Miller, also German, was hung in Troy's new jail on January 28, 1845.

63. Furman, *Antiquities of Long Island*, 265.

64. White, "'It Was a Proud Day,'" 31.

65. Sponsler, *Ritual Imports*, 63.

66. Kyle T. Bulthuis, *Four Steeples over the City Streets: Religion and Society in New York's Early Republic Congregations* (New York: New York University Press, 2014), 125.

67. Kennedy, *O Albany!*, 252–66.

68. Hodges, *Slavery and Freedom in the Rural North*, 68.

69. Kennedy, *O Albany!*, 257.

70. Epstein, *Sinful Tunes and Spirituals*, 209.

71. Rockwell, *Recollections of Men*, 46.

72. *Albany Daily Evening Times*, July 30, 1872.

73. Jea, "The Life, History, and Unparalleled Sufferings of John Jea," 89–164. While it is generally assumed the "Triehuen" family where Jea served was Dutch, the names Oliver and Angelika Triehuen point at German rather than Dutch origin.

74. Ibid., 137.

75. Ibid., 119.

76. Thornton, *Africa and Africans in the Making of the Atlantic World*, 270.

77. Gomez, *Exchanging our Country Marks*, 250.

78. Hodges, *Slavery and Freedom in the Rural North*, 77–79, 138.

79. *Rivington's New-York Gazetteer*, June 8, 1775.

80. *New-York Gazette and the Weekly Mercury*, November 10, 1783.

81. *New Jersey Gazette*, August 7, 1786.

82. Billy G. Smith and Richard Wojtowicz, ed., *Blacks who Stole Themselves: Advertisements for Runaways in the Pennsylvania Gazette, 1728–1790* (Philadelphia: University of Pennsylvania Press, 1989), 110, 152.

83. *Owego Gazette*, July 27, 1911.

84. Hodges, *Root and Branch*, 183; Harris, *In the Shadow of Slavery*, 83–84; Leslie M. Alexander, *African or American? Black Identity and Political Activism in New York City, 1784–1861* (Urbana: University of Illinois Press, 2008), 9.

85. Hodges, *Slavery and Freedom in the Rural North*, 187–88.

86. Harris, *In the Shadow of Slavery*, 82.

87. Rael, "The Long Death of Slavery," 135; Hodges, *Root and Branch*, 187–88.

88. Wilder, "Black Life in Freedom," 218; Ned Sublette, *The World that Made New Orleans: From Spanish Silver to Congo Square* (Chicago: Lawrence Hill, 2008), 114–15.

89. Howard, *Changing History*, 122–47.

90. A. F. and D. Wells: *Friendly Societies in the West Indies* (London: Her Majesty's Stationary Office, 1953), 11–12.

91. Howard Johnson, "Friendly Societies in the Bahamas 1834–1910," *Slavery and Abolition* 12, no. 3 (December 1991): 184–87.

92. Rosanne Marion Adderley, *"New Negroes from Africa": Slave Trade, Abolition and Free African Settlement in the Nineteenth-Century Caribbean* (Bloomington: Indiana University Press, 2006), 203–6.

93. Kachun, *Festivals of Freedom*, 36.

94. Kennedy, *O Albany!*, 257.

95. Gilje and Rock, "'Sweep O! Sweep O!,'" 521–22.

96. In 1866 Adam Blake became proprietor of the Congress Hall Hotel on Capitol Hill, the former Pinkster Hill. When he died, he left an estate valued between $100,000 and $500,000. Reynolds, *Albany Chronicles*, 629; Kennedy, *O Albany!*, 254–55; Williams-Myers, *Long Hammering*, 136.

97. Alessandra Lorini, "Public Rituals and the Cultural Making of the New York African-American Community," *Feasts and Celebrations in North American Ethnic Communities*, 29–45.

98. James McCune Smith, *Introduction to a Memorial Discourse, by Rev. Henry Highland Garnet* (Philadelphia: Joseph M. Wilson, 1865), 21–22; *Albany Argus and City Gazette*, July 5, 1827.

99. Bernhard, Duke of Saxe-Weimar Eisenach, *Travels in North America* (Philadelphia: Carey, Lea & Carey, 1828), 127.

100. Kachun, *Festivals of Freedom*, 42.

101. Smith, *Introduction to a Memorial Discourse*, 24–25.

102. Hodges, *Root and Branch*, 225.

103. Piersen, *Black Yankees*, 159; Kachun, *Festivals of Freedom*, 26–27; Alexander, *African or American?*, 53–57.

104. Shane White and Graham White, *Stylin': African American Expressive Culture from Its Beginnings to the Zoot Suit* (Ithaca, NY: Cornell University Press, 1998), 108–24.

105. Alexis de Tocqueville, *Democracy in America*, ed. Henry Reeve, 2 vols. (1835–40; New York: Colonial Press, 1899), 1:365.

106. White, "'It Was a Proud Day,'" 33.

107. Kachun, *Festivals of Freedom*, 75.

108. Harris, *In the Shadow of Slavery*, 96–133; Alexander, *African or American?*, 57–67.

109. Kachun, *Festivals of Freedom*, 5, 20.

110. *Freedom's Journal*, July 18, 1828.

111. White and White, *Stylin'*, 137.

112. Quoted in Howard, *Changing History*, 167.

113. Karen Richman, "The Vodou State and the Protestant Nation: Haiti in the Long Twentieth Century," *Obeah and Other Powers: The Politics of Caribbean Religion and Healing*, ed. Diana Paton and Maarit Forde (Durham, NC: Duke University Press, 2012), 272.

114. Reidy, "'Negro Election Day,'" 113.

115. *Freedom's Journal*, June 22 and July 13, 1827.

116. Kachun, *Festivals of Freedom*, 54.

117. *Colored American*, August 15, 1840.

118. *New York Herald*, February 11, 1863.

119. Vennie Deas-Moore, "I've Got Something to Celebrate," *Jubilation! African American Celebrations in the Southeast*, ed. William H. Wiggins Jr. and Douglas DeNatale (Columbia: University of South Carolina Press, 1993), 29.

120. Peter M. Rutkoff and William B. Scott, *Fly Away: The Great African American Cultural Migrations* (Baltimore, MD: Johns Hopkins University Press, 2010), 205–43.

121. Reidy, "'Negro Election Day' & Black Community Life in New England," 102–17.

122. White and White, *Stylin'*, 139.

123. Munsell, "Theatrical Reminiscences," 2:56.

124. Joseph Barlow Felt, *Annals of Salem*, 2 vols. (Salem, MA: W. & S. B. Ives, 1845–49), 2:420.

125. Sponsler, *Ritual Imports*, 63; Cockrell, *Demons of Disorder*, 74.

126. Cockrell, *Demons of Disorder*, 106.

127. Ibid., 54.

128. White, "'It Was a Proud Day,'" 25.

129. Charles Dickens, *American Notes for General Calculation* (New York: Harper & Bros., 1842), 36.

130. Lott, *Love and Theft*, 40–50.

131. *Saratoga Sentinel* (ca. 1881–82; exact date illegible).

132. *New York Evening Post*, May 21, 1804. More examples can be found later in history. In 1893 a play by George C. Staley called *Antony the Trumpeter*—probably based on the character with the same name in Washington Irving's *History of New York* (1809)—included a "Pans Pinxter Dance." *New York Dramatic Mirror*, September 16, 1893.

133. Lott, *Love and Theft*, 112.

134. *New-York Journal or the General Advertiser*, April 9, 1767.

135. Watson, *Annals and Occurrences of New York City and State*, 204.

136. *Vermont Gazette*, July 14, 1829.

137. van der Sijs, *Cookies, Coleslaw, and Stoops*, 207.

138. De Voe, *The Market Book*, 1:264–65.

139. Mark Knowles, *Tap Roots: The Early History of Tap Dancing* (Jefferson, NC: McFarland, 2002), 86; Frank Cullen, *Vaudeville, Old and New: An Encyclopedia of Variety Performers in America* (New York: Routledge, 2007), 310.

140. Stuckey, *Going through the Storm*, 73; Roger D. Abrahams et al., *Blues for New Orleans: Mardi Gras and America's Creole Soul* (Philadelphia: University of Pennsylvania Press, 2006), 46.

141. Stiles, *A History of the City of Brooklyn*, 38.

142. Gerardus Balthazar Bosch, *Vaderlandsche letteroefeningen* (Amsterdam: G.S. Leeneman van der Kroe en J.W. IJntema, 1827), 176–77.

143. *Daily Graphic*, August 3, 1883.

144. Jeroen Dewulf, "'A Strong Barbaric Accent': America's Dutch-Speaking Black Community from Seventeenth-Century New Netherland to Nineteenth-Century New York and New Jersey," *American Speech: A Quarterly of Linguistic Usage* 90, no. 2 (May 2015): 131–53.

145. Coventry, "Memoirs of an Emigrant," 69 (12 September 1785).

146. *Troy Daily Whig*, April 26, 1837.

147. *Oneida Morning Gerald*, January 29, 1852.

148. Flint, *Letters from America*, 33.

149. Bartlett, *Dictionary of Americanisms*, 60.

150. John Dyneley Prince, "The Jersey Dutch Dialect," *Dialect Notes* 3 (1910): 477.

151. Edward Arber, ed., *Travels and Works of Captain John Smith: President of Virginia, and Admiral of New England, 1580–1631*, 2 vols. (1631; Edinburgh: John Grant, 1910), 541–42.

152. Randall Kennedy, *Nigger: The Strange Career of a Troublesome Word* (New York: Pantheon, 2002), 4.

153. De Voe, *The Market Book*, 1:344–45.

154. *New York Herald*, April 27, 1837.

155. W. T. Lhamon Jr., *Raising Cain: Blackface Performance from Jim Crow to Hip Hop* (Cambridge, MA: Harvard University Press, 1998), 8.

156. Rockwell, *Recollections of Men*, 45–47.

157. For a similar conclusion, see Lott, *Love and Theft*, 59; Cockrell, *Demons of Disorder*, 86.

158. *North Star*, October 27, 1848.

159. Eric, *Love and Theft*, 16.

160. Lhamon, *Raising Cain*, 43.

161. Quoted in Cockrell, *Demons of Disorder*, 89.

162. Platt, "Negro Governors," 319–20.

163. Abrahams, *Blues for New Orleans*, 37.

164. Horton and Horton, *In Hope of Liberty*, 165.

165. For a similar opinion, see Wade, "'Shining in Borrowed Plumage,'" 224.

166. Cooper, *Satanstoe*, 61.

167. Ibid., 63.

168. Ibid.

169. Ibid.

170. Ibid., 64.

171. Ibid., 69–70.

172. Grant, *Memoirs of an American Lady*, 80–81.

173. James Fenimore Cooper, *The Letters and Journals of James Fenimore Cooper*, ed. James Franklin Beard, 5 vols. (Cambridge, MA: Harvard University Press, 1860–68), 2:155.

174. Wayne Franklin, "Cooper in the Netherlands," *James Fenimore Cooper Society Miscellaneous Papers* 26 (2009): 3–8; House, "Historical Introduction," xvii.

175. Ellis, *Landlords and Farmers in the Hudson-Mohawk Region*, 288–96.

176. Cooper, *The Letters and Journals of James Fenimore Cooper*, 5:52.

177. James Fenimore Cooper, *Notions of the Americans: Picked up by a Travelling Bachelor*, 2 vols. (Philadelphia: Lea & Blanchard, 1840), 1:90.

178. Cooper, *The Letters and Journals of James Fenimore Cooper*, 2:155.

179. Bosch, *Vaderlandsche letteroefeningen*, 273.

180. Annette Stott, *Holland Mania: The Unknown Dutch Period in American Art and Culture* (New York: Overlook Press, 1998), 78–100.

181. William Elliot Griffis, *The Story of New Netherland: The Dutch in America* (Boston: Houghton Mifflin, 1909), 60.

182. Edwin Lassetter Bynner, *The Begum's Daughter* (Boston: Little, Brown, 1890), 362–66; Ruth Hall, *The Black Gown* (Boston: Houghton, Mifflin, 1900), 91–92; Earle, "Pinkster Day," 743–44.

183; Marie Joseph Brusse, *With Roosevelt through Holland* (Rotterdam, NL: W. L. & J. Brusse, 1911), 42.

184. Theodore Roosevelt, *New York* (New York: Longmans, 1891), 95–96.

185. Lynne Ames, "Pinkster Revisited," *New York Times*, May 26, 1985, 2.

186. Pershing, "Representations of Racial Identity in a Contemporary Pinkster Celebration," 195.

187. Jasmin K. Williams, "Governor Paterson Ends Ban of African Pinkster Celebration," *New York Amsterdam News*, June 3, 2010, 28.

188. Sponsler, *Ritual Imports*, 66; Pershing, "Representations of Racial Identity in a Contemporary Pinkster Celebration," 198.

Conclusion

1. Gray, *Black Christians and White Missionaries*, 43; Fromont, *The Art of Conversion*, 183–84.

2. Truth, *Narrative of Sojourner Truth*, 5.

3. Washington, *Sojourner Truth's America*, 1–3; Bulthuis, *Four Steeples over The City Streets*, 183.

4. "Women's Rights Convention, Broadway Tabernacle, New York" (7 September 1853), in Fitch and Mandziuk, *Sojourner Truth as Orator*, 112.

Bibliography

I. Primary Sources

A. Manuscripts

Albany County Hall of Records, NY

State Archives and Records Administration, City Records, Common Council 1765–1840

Arquivo Histórico da Câmara Municipal, Lisbon, Portugal

Câmara Municipal de Lisboa (CML)

Arquivo Histórica Ultramarino, Lisbon, Portugal

Diversos, Arlindo, Correa, Informazione sul regno del Congo di Fra Raimondo da Dicomano (1798)

Biblioteca da Ajuda, Lisbon, Portugal

Manuscript Collection, Relação da Perdição da Nao Belem da qual era Capitão Joseph Cabreira, Mestre Miguel Jorge grego e piloto Mathias Figueira (s.d.)

Boston Athenaeum, MA

Manuscript Collection, Crichton, George Hugh, Old Boston and its Once Familiar Faces: Sketches of Some Odd Characters who have flourished in Boston during the Past Fifty Years (1881)

British Library, London, Great Britain

Department of Manuscripts. Additional Mss. Sloane, Jornalero del año de 1633 y 1634, por um frade capuchino

Nationaal Archief, The Hague, the Netherlands

Archives of the Old West-India Company

http://en.nationaalarchief.nl/newsroom/news/archives-of-the-old-west-india-company -online

New York City Municipal Archives

Records of New Amsterdam, Ordinances 1647–1661

http://www.archives.nyc

New York State Library/Archives/Museum, Albany, NY

New Netherland Documents

New York Colonial Manuscripts

Land Patents

Coventry, Alexander. 1789. Memoirs of an Emigrant: The Journal of Alexander Coventry, M.D. in Scotland, the United States and Canada during the Period 1783–1831, The Albany Institute of History and Art and the New York State Library.
The People of Colonial Albany Materials
www.nysm.nysed.gov/albany/index.html
Stadsarchief Amsterdam, Netherlands
    Archief Classis Amsterdam
University of California, Berkeley. Bancroft Library
    The Engel Sluiter Historical Documents Collections
University of Virginia Library, VA
    Albert and Shirley Small Special Collections Library, Letters R. Howell to J. H. Ward

B. Newspapers and Periodicals

Albany Argus (Albany, NY, 1828–56)
Albany Argus and City Gazette (Albany, NY, 1825–27)
Albany Centinel (Albany, NY, 1797–1806)
Albany Chronicle (Albany, NY, 1803–28)
Albany Daily Evening Times (Albany, NY, 1869–81)
Albany Evening Journal (Albany, NY, 1830–1925)
Balance and Columbian Repository (Hudson, NY, 1801–7)
Balance and State Journal (Albany, NY, 1811)
Chittenango Herald (Chittenango, NY, 1831–36)
Colored American (New York, 1836–42)
The Corrector (Sag Harbor, NY, 1822–1911)
Daily Advertiser (New York, 1787–1806)
Daily Graphic (New York, 1873–89)
Evening Post (New York, 1832–1920)
Family Magazine or Monthly Abstract of General Knowledge (New York, 1834–41)
Freedom's Journal (New York, 1827–29)
General Advertiser (Philadelphia, 1791–94)
Harper's New Monthly Magazine (New York, 1855–99)
Kingston Daily Freeman (Kingston, NY, 1878–1969)
Lockport Journal (Lockport, NY, 1901–5)
Manhattan and de la Salle Monthly (New York, 1875)
New-England Palladium (Boston, 1803–14)
New Jersey Gazette (Burlington, NJ, 1777–86)
New York Dramatic Mirror (New York, 1879–1922)
New York Evening Express (New York, 1839–81)
New York Evening Post (New York, 1801–32)
New York Herald (New York, 1835–1924)
New-York Gazette (New York, 1725–44)
New-York Gazette and the Weekly Mercury (New York, 1768–83)
New-York Gazetteer (New York, 1784–85)

New-York Journal & Patriotic Register (New York, 1790–93)

New-York Journal or the General Advertiser (New York, 1766–77)

New-York Journal, or, the Weekly Register (New York, 1785–87)

New York Times (New York, since 1851)

New-York Tribune (New York, 1866–1924)

New-York Weekly Journal (New York, 1733–51)

North Star (New York, 1847–51)

Oneida Morning Gerald (Utica, NY, 1847–53)

Owego Gazette (Owego Village, NY, 1814–1967)

Public Advertiser (New York, 1807–13)

Rivington's New-York Gazetteer (New York, 1773–75)

Saratoga Sentinel (Saratoga Springs, NY, 1868–85)

Schenectady Cabinet, or, Freedom's Sentinel (Schenectady, NY, 1839–49)

Schenectady Daily Evening Star and Times (Schenectady, NY, 1863–68)

The Sun (New York, 1833–1916)

Troy Daily Times (Troy, NY, 1851–1903)

Troy Daily Whig (Troy, NY, 1834–73)

Vermont Gazette (Bennington, VT, 1816–29)

C. Printed Materials

Abrahams, Roger D. 1967. The Shaping of Folklore Traditions in the British West Indies. *Journal of Inter-American Studies* 9 (1967): 456–80.

Abrahams, Roger D., and John F. Szwed. 1983. *After Africa: Extracts from British Travel Accounts and Journals of the Seventeenth, Eighteenth, and Nineteenth Centuries concerning the Slaves, their Manners, and Customs in the British West Indies.* New Haven, CT: Yale University Press.

Abrahams, Roger D. et al. 2006. *Blues for New Orleans: Mardi Gras and America's Creole Soul.* Philadelphia: University of Pennsylvania Press.

Abreu, Martha. 1999. *O Império do Divino. Festas religiosas e cultura popular no Rio de Janeiro, 1830–1900.* Rio de Janeiro: Editora Nova Fronteira.

Adderley, Rosanne Marion. 2006. *"New Negroes from Africa": Slave Trade, Abolition and Free African Settlement in the Nineteenth-Century Caribbean.* Bloomington: Indiana University Press.

Aimwell, Absalom Esq. [1803] 1952. A Pinkster Ode for the Year 1803, ed. Geraldine R. Pleat and Agnes N. Underwood. *New York Folklore Quarterly* 8 (1952): 31–45.

Albany City Council. 1849. *Laws of the State of New-York passed at the Seventy Second Session of the Legislature, begun the second day of January, and ended the eleventh day of April, 1849, at the city of Albany.* Troy, NY: Albert W. Scribner and Albert West.

Aldenburgk, Johann Gregor. [1627] 1930. Reise nach Brasilien 1623–1626, *Reisebeschreibungen von deutschen Beamten und Kriegsleuten im Dienst der niederländischen West- und Ost-Indischen Kompagnien 1602–1797*, ed. S. P. L'Honoré Naber. Vol. 1, 1–98. The Hague: Martinus Nijhoff.

Alexander, Leslie M. 2008. *African or American? Black Identity and Political Activism in New York City, 1784–1861.* Urbana: University of Illinois Press.

Alexander, Robert. 1991. Religion in Rensselaerswijck. *A Beautiful and Fruitful Place: Selected Rensselaerswijck Seminar Papers*, ed. Nancy A. M. Zeller, 309–15. New York: New Netherland.

Alford, Violet. 1933. Midsummer and Morris in Portugal. *Folklore* 44, no. 2 (June 1993): 218–35.

Amaral, Ilídio do. 1996. *O Reino do Congo, os Mbundu (ou Ambundos), o Reino dos 'Ngola' (ou de Angola) e a presença portuguesa, de finais do século XV a meados do século XVI*. Lisbon: Ministério da Ciência e da Tecnologia.

Ames, Lynne. 1985. Pinkster Revisited. *New York Times,* May 26, 1985, 2.

Aptheker, Herbert. [1943] 1978. *American Negro Slave Revolts*. New York: International Publishers.

Araújo, Maria Benedita. 1997. *Superstições populares Portuguesas. Contribuições para um estudo*. Lisbon: Colibri.

Arber, Edward, ed. [1631] 1910. *Travels and Works of Captain John Smith: President of Virginia, and Admiral of New England, 1580–1631,* 2 vols. Edinburgh: John Grant.

Aristizábal, Tulio, and Anna Maria Splendiani, ed. 2000. *Processo de beatificación y canonización de San Pedro Claver*. Bogotá, CO: CEJA.

Armstead, Myra B. Young, ed. 2003. *Mighty Change, Tall Within: Black Identity in the Hudson Valley*. Albany: State University of New York Press.

Arroyo, Leonardo. 1954. *Igrejas de São Paulo*. Rio de Janeiro: José Olympio.

Auclair, Walter. 2009. Simeon Button (1757–1836), Pittstown Farmer and Rensselaer County Justice of the Peace. *Pittstown Historical Society Newsletter* XV (Spring 2009): 1–17.

Ávila, Affonso. 1967. *Resíduos Seiscentistas em Minas. Textos do século de ouro e as projeções do mundo barroco,* 2 vols. Belo Horizonte, BR: Centro de Estudos Mineiros.

Balandier, Georges. 1968. *Daily Life in the Kingdom of the Kongo from the Sixteenth to the Eighteenth Century*. New York: Pantheon.

Balmer, Randall H. 1984. The Social Roots of Dutch Pietism in the Middle Colonies. *Church History* 53, no. 2 (1984): 187–99.

———. 1989. *A Perfect Babel of Confusion: Dutch Religion and English Culture in the Middle Colonies*. Oxford and New York: Oxford University Press.

Bannister, Henry S. 1974. From the Collector's Library: Joel Munsell, Printer and Antiquarian in Albany, New York. *The Courier* 11, no. 2 (1974): 11–22.

Bartlett, John Russell. [1848] 1877. *Dictionary of Americanisms: A Glossary of Words and Phrases Usually Regarded as Peculiar to the United States*. Boston: Little, Brown.

Bastide, Roger. [1960] 1971. *As religiões africanas no Brasil: Contribuição a uma sociologia das Interpretações de civilizações,* ed. Maria Eloisa Capellato and Olívia Krähenbühl, 2 vols. São Paulo: Pioneira Editora.

Batsîkama, Raphaël ba Mampuya ma Ndâwla. 1999. *L'ancien royaume du Congo et les Bakongo. Séquences d'histoire populaire*. Paris: L'Harmattan.

Beckwith, Martha Warren. 1929. *Black Roadways: A Study of Jamaican Folk Life*. Chapel Hill: University of North Carolina Press.

Beeke, Joel R. 2000. Introduction. *Forerunner of the Great Awakening: Sermons by Theodorus Jacobus Frelinghuysen (1691–1747),* ed. Joel R. Beeke, I-XLIII. Grand Rapids, MI: Wm. B. Eerdmans.

Bentley, William, D.D. 1962. *The Diary of William Bentley, D.D., Pastor of the East Church, Salem, Massachusetts*. Gloucester, MA: P. Smith.

Benzoni, Girolamo. [1556] 1857. *History of the New World, by Girolamo Benzoni, of Milan. Shewing his Travels in America from A.D. 1541 to 1556*, ed. W. H. Smyth. London: Hakluyt Society.

Berlin, Ira. 1996. From Creole to African: Atlantic Creoles and the Origins of African American Society in Mainland North America. *William and Mary Quarterly* 53, no. 2 (1996): 251–88.

———. 1998. *Many Thousands Gone: The First Two Centuries of Slavery in North America*. Cambridge, MA: Harvard University Press.

———. 2003. *Generations of Captivity: A History of African American Slaves*. Cambridge, MA: Harvard University Press.

Bernard, Jacqueline. [1967] 1990. *Journey Toward Freedom: The Story of Sojourner Truth*, ed. Nell Irvin Painter. New York: Feminist Press at City University of New York.

Bernhard, Duke of Saxe-Weimar Eisenach. 1828. *Travels in North America*. Philadelphia: Carey, Lea & Carey.

Beshah, Girma, and Merid Wolde Aregay. *The Question of the Union of the Churches in Luso-Ethiopian Relations, 1500–1632*. Lisbon: Centro de Estudos Históricos Ultramarinos.

Bielinski, Stefan. 2005. Albany County. *The Other New York: The American Revolution beyond New York City, 1763–1787*, ed. Joseph Tiedemann and Eugene R. Fingerhut, 155–73. Albany: State of New York University Press.

Biet, Antoine. [1654] 1967. Father Antoine Biet's visit to Barbados in 1654, ed. Jerome S. Handler. *Journal of the Barbados Museum and Historical Society* 32 (1967): 56–76.

Biewenga, Ad. 1999. *De Kaap de Goede Hoop: Een Nederlandse vestigingskolonie, 1680–1730*. Amsterdam: Prometheus-Bert Bakker.

Bilby, Kenneth, and Kia Bunseki Fu-Kiau. 1983. *Kumina: A Kongo-Based Tradition in the New World*. Brussels: ASDOC-Studies.

Birmingham, David. 1966. *Trade and Conflict in Angola: The Mbundu and Their Neighbours under the Influence of the Portuguese 1483–1790*. Oxford, UK: Clarendon Press.

Blackburn, Robin. 1997. *The Making of New World Slavery: From the Baroque to the Modern 1492–1800*. London and New York: Verso.

Blackburn, Roderic H., and Ruth Piwonka. 1988. *Remembrance of Patria: Dutch Arts and Culture in Colonial America 1609–1776*. Albany, NY: Albany Institute of History and Art.

Bloch, Herman D. 1964. The New York Negro's Battle for Political Rights, 1777–1865. *International Review of Social History* IX (1964): 65–80.

Blumenthal, Debra. 2005. "La Casa dels Negres": Black African Solidarity in Late Medieval Valencia. *Black Africans in Renaissance Europe*, ed. T. F. Earle and K. J. P. Lowe, 225–46. Cambridge, UK: Cambridge University Press.

Bolster, W. Jeffrey. 1997. *Black Jacks: African American Seamen in the Age of Sail*. Cambridge, MA: Harvard University Press.

Boone, Marc, and Maarten Prak. 1995. Rulers, Patricians and Burghers: The Great and the Little Traditions of Urban Revolt in the Low Countries. *A Miracle Mirrored: The Dutch Republic in European Perspective*, ed. Karel Davids and Jan Lucassen, 99–134. Cambridge, UK: Cambridge University Press.

Borges, Célia Maia. 2005. *Escravos e libertos nas Irmandades do Rosário: Devoção e solidariedade em Minas Gerais—Séculos XVIII e XIX*. Juíz de Fora, BR: Editora UFJF.

Bosch, Gerard Balthazar. 1827. *Vaderlandsche letteroefeningen*. Amsterdam: G.S. Leeneman van der Kroe en J.W. IJntema.

Boschi, Caio César. 1986. *Os leigos e o poder: Irmandades leigos e política colonizadora em Minas Gerais*. São Paulo: Editora Ática.

Bourdieu, Pierre. 1986. The Forms of Capital. *Handbook of Theory and Research for the Sociology of Education*, ed. J. Richardson, 241–58. New York: Greenwood.

Bowser, Frederick P. 1974. *The African Slave in Colonial Peru 1524–1650*. Stanford, CA: Stanford University Press.

Boxer, C. R. 1957. *The Dutch in Brazil, 1624–1654*. Oxford: Clarendon Press.

Bradbury, Anna R. 1908. *History of the City of Hudson, New York: with Biographical Sketches of Henry Hudson and Robert Fulton*. Hudson, NY: Record Printing and Publishing.

Braekman, Willy L. 1992. *Spel en kwel in vroeger tijd. Verkenningen van charivari, exorcisme, toverij, spot en spel in Vlaanderen*. Ghent, BE: Stiching Mens en Kultuur.

Brásio, António, ed. 1952–1988. *Monumenta missionária Africana*, 15 vols. Lisbon: Agência Geral do Ultramar (vols. 1–11); Academia Portuguesa da História (vols. 12–15).

———, ed. 1969. *História do Reino do Congo. Ms. 8080 da Biblioteca Nacional de Lisboa*. Lisbon: Centro de Estudos Históricos Ultramarinos.

———, ed. 1973. *História e missiologia. Inéditos e esparsos*. Luanda: Instituto de Investigação Científica de Angola.

Breen, Henry H. 1844. *St. Lucia: Historical, Statistical, and Descriptive*. London: Longman, Brown, Green, and Longmans.

Brenneker, Paul. 1986. *Zjozjoli: Gegevens over de volkskunde van Curaçao, Aruba en Bonaire*. Curaçao: Publisidat Antiano.

Brooks, George E. 1984. The Observance of All Souls' Day in the Guinea-Bissau Region: A Christian Holy Day, an African Harvest Festival, an African New Year's Celebration, or All of the Above (?). *History of Africa* 11 (1984): 1–34.

———. 2003. *Eurafricans in Western Africa: Commerce, Social Status, Gender, and Religious Observance from the Sixteenth to the Eighteenth Century*. Athens: Ohio University Press.

Brown, Ras Michael. 2012. *African-Atlantic Cultures and the South Carolina Lowcountry*. Cambridge: Cambridge University Press.

Brun, Samuel. [1624] 1969. *Schiffarten in etliche newe Länder und Insulen*, ed. Walter Hirschberg. Graz, AT: Akademische Druck- und Verlagsanstalt.

Brusse, Marie Joseph. 1911. *With Roosevelt through Holland*. Rotterdam, NL: W.L. & J. Brusse.

Buccini, Anthony F. 1995. The Dialectal Origins of New Netherland Dutch. *The Berkeley Conference on Dutch Linguistics 1993: Dutch Linguistics in a Changing Europe*, ed. Thomas F. Shannon and Johan P. Snapper, 211–63. Lanham, MD: University Press of America.

Bullivant, Benjamin. [1697] 1956. "A Glance at New York in 1697: The Travel Diary of Benjamin Bullivant," ed. Wayne Andrews. *New-York Historical Society Quarterly* XL, nr. 1 (January 1956): 55–73.

Bulthuis, Kyle T. 2014. *Four Steeples over The City Streets: Religion and Society in New York's Early Republic Congregations*. New York: New York University Press.

Burke, Peter. 1978. *Popular Culture in Early Modern Europe*. New York: New York University Press.

Burton, Richard Francis. 1869. *Explorations of the Highlands of the Brazil*, 2 vols. London: Tinsley Brothers.

———. 1876. *Two Trips to Gorilla Land and the Cataracts of the Congo*, 2 vols. London: Sampson Low, Marston, Low, and Stearle.

Buter, Adriaan. 1980. Boerendansreveil van toen. *Neerlands Volksleven* 30, no. 1/2 (1980): 35–42.

Bynner, Edwin Lassetter. 1890. *The Begum's Daughter*. Boston: Little, Brown.

Cabrera, Lydia. 1979. *Reglas de Congo, palo monte, mayombe*. Miami: Peninsular.

Cadornega, António de Oliveira de. [1680] 1972. *História Geral das Guerras Angolanas*, ed. José Matias Delgado. 3 vols. Lisboa: Agência-Geral do Ultramar.

———. [1683] 1982. *Descrição de Vila Viçosa*, ed. Heitor Gomes Teixeira. Lisbon: IN-CM.

Campbell, Douglas. 1892. *The Puritan in Holland, England, and America: An Introduction to American History*. New York: Harper & Brothers.

Cañizares-Esguerra, Jorge, Matt D. Childs, and James Sidbury, ed. 2013. *The Black Urban Atlantic in the Age of the Slave Trade*. Philadelphia: University of Pennsylvania Press.

Cardoso, Gerald. 1983. *Negro Slavery in the Sugar Plantations of Veracruz and Pernambuco, 1550–1680*. Washington: University Press of America.

Cardoso, Pedro Monteiro. 1933. *Folclore Caboverdeano*. Porto, PT: Maranus.

Carteau, Félix. 1802. *Soirées Bermudiennes, ou Entretiens sur les évènemens qui ont opéré la ruine de la partie française de l'île Saint-Domingue, ouvrage où l'on expose les causes de ces évènemens, les moyens employés pour renverser cette colonie*. Bordeaux, FR: Pellier-Lawalle.

Cascudo, Luís da Camara. 1979. *Dicionário do folclore brasileiro*. São Paulo: Melhoramentos.

Castellanos, Henry C. 1895. *New Orleans as it Was*. New Orleans: L. Graham & Son.

Caulkins, Frances Manwaring. 1866. *History of Norwich, Connecticut: From its Possession by the Indians to the Year 1866*. Hartford, CT: Caulkins.

Chambers, Edmund K. 1903. *The Mediaevel Stage*, 2 vols. Oxford: Oxford University Press.

Chantillon, Marcel, ed. 1984. L'évangelisation des esclaves au XVIIe siècle. Lettres du R. P. Jean Mongin. *Bulletin du Société d'Histoire de la Guadeloupe* 60 (1984): 1–136.

Chaudenson, Robert. 2001. *Creolization of Language and Culture. Revised in Collaboration with Salikoko S. Mufwene*. London: Routledge.

Chaves, Luís. 1945. *Folclore religioso*. Porto, PT: Portucalense Editora.

Childs, Matt D. 2006. *The 1812 Aponte Rebellion in Cuba and the Struggle against Atlantic Slavery*. Chapel Hill: University of North Carolina Press.

———. 2013. Re-creating African Ethnic Identities in Cuba. *The Black Urban Atlantic in the Age of the Slave Trade*, ed. Jorge Cañizares-Esguerra, Matt D. Childs, and James Sidbury, 85–100. Philadelphia: University of Pennsylvania Press.

Christoph, Peter R. 1991. The Freedmen of New Amsterdam. *A Beautiful and Fruitful Place: Selected Rensselaerswijck Seminar Papers*, ed. Nancy A. M. Zeller, 157–70. New York: New Netherland.

Cockrell, Dale. 1997. *Demons of Disorder: Early Blackface Minstrels and Their World*. Cambridge, UK: Cambridge University Press.

Cohen, David Steven. 1974. *The Ramapo Mountain People*. New Brunswick, NJ: Rutgers University Press.

———. 1984. In Search of Carolus Africanus Rex: Afro-Dutch Folklore in New York and New Jersey. *Journal of the Afro-American Historical and Genealogical Society* 5, no. 3–4 (1984): 149–62.

———. 1992. *The Dutch-American Farm*. New York: New York University Press.

Conneau, Theophilus. [1853] 1976. *A Slaver's Log Book, or Twenty Years' Residence in Africa*. Englewood Cliffs, NJ: Prentice-Hall.

Cooper, James Fenimore. [1845] 1990. *Satanstoe, or The Littlepage Manuscripts: A Tale of the Colony*, ed. Kay Seymour House and Constance Ayers Denne. New York: State University of New York Press.

———. 1840. *Notions of the Americans: Picked up by a Travelling Bachelor*, 2 vols. Philadelphia: Lea & Blanchard.

———. 1860–68. *The Letters and Journals of James Fenimore Cooper*, ed. James Franklin Beard, 4 vols. Cambridge, MA: Harvard University Press.

———. 1920. *The Legends and Traditions of a Northern County*. New York: G.P. Putnam's Sons.

Corrêa, Elias Alexandre da Silva. 1937. *História de Angola*, 2 vols. Lisbon: Atica.

Corwin, Edward T. 1902. *A Manual of the Reformed Church in America*. New York: Board of Publication of the Reformed Church in America.

Courlander, Harold. [1939] 1973. *Haiti Singing*. New York: Cooper Square.

———. 1960. *The Drum and the Hoe: Life and Lore of the Haitian People*. Berkeley: University of California Press.

Craton, Michael. 1982. *Testing the Chains: Resistance to Slavery in the British West Indies*. Ithaca, NY: Cornell University Press.

Creel, Margaret Washington. 1988. *A Peculiar People: Slave Religion and Community Culture among the Gullahs*. New York: New York University Press.

Cullen, Frank. 2007. *Vaudeville, Old and New: An Encyclopedia of Variety Performers in America*. New York: Routledge.

Cullingford, Benita. 2008. *British Chimney Sweeps: Five Centuries of Chimney Sweeping*. Sussex, UK: Book Guild.

Cummings, Harmon Dean. 1975. Andrew Adgate: Philadelphia Psalmodist and Music Educator. Ph.D. diss., University of Rochester.

Cuvelier, Jean. 1946. *L'ancien royaume de Congo*. Brussels: De Brouwer.

Cuvelier, Jean, and Louis Jadin. 1954. *L'Ancien Congo d'après les archives romaines, 1518–1640*. Brussels: Académie Royale des Sciences Coloniales.

Da Caltanisetta, Fra Luca. [1701] 1970. *Diaire Congolais (1690–1701)*, ed. François Bontinck. Louvain, BE: Éditions Nauwelaerts.

Dankers, Jasper, and Peter Sluyter. [1680] 1867. *Journal of a Voyage to New York and a Tour in Several of the American Colonies in 1679–80*, ed. Henry C. Murphy. Brooklyn: Long Island Historical Society.

Da Pavia, Andrea. [1702] 1970. Voyages apostoliques aux missions d'Afrique du P. Andrea da Pavia, Prédicateur Capucin 1685–1702, ed. Louis Jadin. *Bulletin de L'Institut Historique Belge de Rome* XLI (1970): 375–592.

Dapper, Olfert. 1668. *Naukeurige beschrijvinge der Afrikaensche gewesten*. Amsterdam: Jacob van Meurs.

Da Rocha, Leopoldo. 1973. *As confrarias de Goa (séculos XVI–XX). Conspecto histórico-jurídico*. Lisbon: Centro de Estudos Históricos Ultramarinos.

D'Atri, Marcellino. [1702] 1984. *L'anarchia Congolese nel sec. XVII. La relazione inedita di Marcellino d'Atri*, ed. Carlo Toso. Genova, IT: Bozzi Editore.

Davis, Susan G. 1985. The Career of Colonel Pluck: Folk Drama and Popular Protest in Early Nineteenth-Century Philadelphia. *Pennsylvania Magazine of History and Biography* 109, no. 2 (Apr. 1985): 179–202.

———. 1986. *Parades and Power: Street Theatre in Nineteenth-Century Philadelphia.* Philadelphia: Temple University Press.

Dawson, Kevin. 2013. The Cultural Geography of Enslaved Ship Pilots. *The Black Urban Atlantic in the Age of the Slave Trade,* ed. Jorge Cañizares-Esguerra, Matt D. Childs, and James Sidbury, 163–84. Philadelphia: University of Pennsylvania Press.

De Alencastro, Luiz Felipe. 2000. *O trato dos viventes. Formação do Brasil no Atlântico Sul, séculos XVI e XVII.* São Paulo: Companhia das Letras.

Deas-Moore, Vennie. 1993. I've Got Something to Celebrate. *Jubilation! African American Celebrations in the Southeast,* ed. William H. Wiggins Jr. and Douglas DeNatale, 23–33. Columbia: University of South Carolina Press.

Debien, Gabriel. 1964. Les origines des esclaves des Antilles. *Bulletin de l'Institute Fondamentale de l'Afrique Noire* vol. B, no. 26 (1964): 178–82.

De Carli, Dionigio. [1674] 1814. A Curious and Exact Account of a Voyage to Congo, in the Years 1666 and 1667 by the R.R.F.F. Michael Angelo of Gattina and Denis de Carli of Piacenza, Capuchins and Apostolic Missioners in the said Kingdom of Congo. *A General Collection of the Best and Most Interesting Voyages and Travels in All Parts of the World,* ed. John Pinkerton, 148–94. London: Hurst.

De Cothonay, Marie Bertrand. 1893. *Trinidad: journal d'un missionnaire dominicain des Antilles anglaises.* Paris: V. Retaux et fils.

De Heusch, Luc. 2000. *Le roi de Kongo et les monstres sacrés. Mythes et rites bantous III.* Paris: Gallimard.

De Jong, Gerald F. 1971. The Dutch Reformed Church and Negro Slavery in Colonial America. *Church History* 12, no. 4 (1971): 423–36.

———. 1975. *The Dutch in America, 1609–1974.* Boston: Twayne.

———. 1978. *The Dutch Reformed Church in the American Colonies.* Grand Rapids, MI: Eerdmans.

De Lucques, Laurent [Lorenzo da Lucca]. [1717] 1953. *Relations sur le Congo du Père Laurent de Lucques (1700–1718),* ed. J. Cuvelier. Brussels: Institut Royal Colonial Belge.

De Mello, José António Gonsalves. [1947] 2001. *Nederlanders in Brazilië (1624–1654).* Zutphen, NL: Walburg.

———. 1988. *Henrique Dias, governador dos crioulos, negros e mulatos do Brasil.* Recife, BR: Editora Massangana.

Den Heijer, Henk. 2003. The West African Trade of the Dutch West India Company, 1674–1740. *Riches from Atlantic Commerce: Dutch Transatlantic Trade and Shipping, 1585–1817,* ed. Johannes Postma and Victor Enthoven, 139–69. Leiden, NL: Brill, 2003.

De Potter, Frans. 1870. Schets eener geschiedenis der gemeentefeesten in Vlaanderen. *Annales de la Société des Beaux-Arts et de littérature de Gand* 12 (1870): 41–188.

Derby, Edward George Geoffrey Smith Stanley, Earl of. [1825] 1930. *Journal of a Tour in America, 1824–1825.* London: Priv. print.

De Resende, Garcia. 1973. *Crónica de D. João II e miscelânea,* ed. Joaquim Veríssimo Serrão. Lisbon: Imprensa Nacional-Cada da Moeda.

De Rome, Jean-François [Giovanni Francesco Romano]. [1648] 1964. *Brève relation de la fondation de la mission des frères mineurs Capucins du Séraphique Père Saint François au Royaume de Congo*, ed. François Bontinck. Louvain, NL: Nauwelaerts.

De Tocqueville, Alexis. [1835 and 1840] 1899. *Democracy in America*, ed. Henry Reeve, 2 vols. New York: Colonial Press.

De Torquemada, Juan. [1615] 1943–44. *Monarquía indiana*, 3 vols. México City: S. Chávez Hayhoe.

De Voe, Thomas F. [1862] 1970. *The Market Book*, 2 vols. New York: August M. Kelley.

De Vos van Steenwijk, Carel. [1784] 1999. *Een grand tour naar de nieuwe republiek: journaal van een reis door Amerika, 1783–1784*, ed. Wayne te Brake. Hilversum, NL: Verloren.

De Vries, David Pietersz. [1655] 1953. Korte Historiael ende Journaels Aenteyckeninge, 1633–1643. *Narratives of New Netherland, 1609–1664*, ed. J. Franklin Jameson, 181–234. New York: Barnes & Noble.Dewulf, Jeroen. 2013. Pinkster: An Atlantic Creole Festival in a Dutch-American Context. *Journal of American Folklore* 126, no. 501 (Summer 2013): 245–71.

———. 2014. "Black Brotherhoods in North America: Afro-Iberian and West-Central African Influences." *African Studies Quarterly* 15, no. 3 (June 2015): 19–38.

———. 2014. Emulating a Portuguese Model: The Slave Policy of the West India Company and the Dutch Reformed Church in Dutch Brazil (1630–1654) and New Netherland (1614–1664) in Comparative Perspective. *Journal of Early American History* 4 (2014): 3–36.

———. 2014. The Many Languages of American Literature: Interpreting Sojourner Truth's *Narrative* (1850) as Dutch-American Contact Literature. *Dutch Crossing* 38, no. 3 (2014): 220–34.

———. 2015. "A Strong Barbaric Accent": America's Dutch-Speaking Black Community from Seventeenth-Century New Netherland to Nineteenth-Century New York and New Jersey. *American Speech: A Quarterly of Linguistic Usage* 90, no. 2 (May 2015): 131–53.

Díaz del Castillo, Bernal. [1632] 1944. *Historia verdadera de la conquista de la Nueva España*, ed. Jaoquín Ramírez Cabañas, 3 vols. Mexico City: Editorial Pedro Robredo.

Dickens, Charles. 1842. *American Notes for General Calculation*. New York: Harper & Bros.

Dixon, Ryan Fox. 1917. The Negro Vote in Old New York. *Political Science Quarterly* 32, No. 2 (June 1917): 252–75.

Dodge, Mary Mapes. 1865. *Hans Brinker: Or, the Silver Skates, a Story of Life in Holland*. New York: James O'Kane.

Donnan, Elizabeth, ed. 1930–35. *Documents Illustrative of the History of the Slave Trade*, 4 vols. Washington: Carnegie Institute.

Douglass, Frederick. [1845] 1993. *Narrative of the Life of Frederick Douglass, an American Slave. Written by Himself*, ed. David W. Blight. Boston: Bedford Books of St. Martin's Press.

Drouin de Bercy, Louis M. C. A. 1814. *De Saint-Domingue*. Paris: Chez Hocquet.

Dubois, Laurent. 2012. *Haiti: The Aftershocks of History*. New York: Metropolitan.

Duermyer, Louis, ed. 1978. *Records of the Reformed Dutch Church of Albany, New York, 1689–1809: Marriages, Baptisms, Members, etc. Excerpted from Year Books of the Holland Society of New York*. Baltimore, MD: Genealogical Publishing.

Dunlap, William. [1839] 1930. *Diary of William Dunlap (1766–1839): The Memoirs of a Dramatist, Theatrical Manager, Painter, Critic, Novelist, and Historian*, 3 vols. New York: New York Historical Society.

Earle, Alice Morse. [1896] 1962. *Colonial Days in Old New York*. Port Washington, NY: Ira J. Friedman.

———. 1894. Pinkster Day. *New Outlook* 49 (1894): 743–44.

Eights, James. 1867. Pinkster Festivities in Albany Sixty Years Ago. *Collections on the History of Albany*, ed. Joel Munsell, vol. 2, 323–27. Albany, NY: Munsell.

Ellis, David Maldwyn. 1946. *Landlords and Farmers in the Hudson-Mohawk Region 1790–1850.* Ithaca, NY: Cornell University Press.

Epperson, Terrence W. 1999. The Contested Commons: Archaeologies of Race, Repression, and Resistance in New York City. *Historical Archaeologies of Capitalism*, ed. Mark P. Leone and Parker B. Potter Jr., 81–110. New York: Plenum.

Epstein, Dena J. 1977. *Sinful Tunes and Spirituals: Black Folk Music to the Civil War.* Urbana: University of Illinois Press.

Evans, Thomas Grier, ed. 1901. *Records of the Reformed Dutch Church in New Amsterdam and New York: Baptisms from 25 December, 1639, to 27 December 1730.* Collections of the New York Genealogical and Biographical Society, II. New York: Clearfield.

Fabend, Firth Haring. 1991. *A Dutch Family in the Middle Colonies, 1660–1800.* New Brunswick, NJ: Rutgers University Press.

———. 2000. *Zion on the Hudson: Dutch New York and New Jersey in the Age of Revivals.* New Brunswick, NJ: Rutgers University Press.

Fabre, Geneviève. 1995. Pinkster Festival, 1776–1811: An African American Celebration. *Feasts and Celebrations in North American Ethnic Communities*, ed. Ramón A. Gutiérrez and Geneviève Fabre, 13–28. Albuquerque: University of New Mexico Press.

Fauset, Arthur Huff. 1938. *Sojourner Truth: God's Faithful Pilgrim.* Chapel Hill: University of North Carolina Press.

Felner, Alfredo de Albuquerque, ed. 1933. *Angola: Apontamentos sobre a ocupação e início do estabelecimento dos Portugueses no Congo, Angola e Benguela extraídos de documentos históricos.* Coimbra, PT: Imprensa da Universidade.

Felt, Joseph Barlow. 1845–1849. *Annals of Salem*, 2 vols. Salem, MA: W. & S. B. Ives.

Fernandes, Valentim. [1506–1507] 1997. *Códice Valentim Fernandes*, ed. José Pereira da Costa. Lisbon: Academia Portuguesa da História.

Fernow, Berthold, ed. 1897. *The Records of New Amsterdam from 1653 to 1674*, 7 vols. New York: Knickerbocker Press.

———, ed. 1902–1907. *The Minutes of the Orphanmasters of New Amsterdam, 1655 to 1663*, 2 vols. New York: F.P. Harper.

Ferreira, Roquinaldo. 2012. *Cross-Cultural Exchange in the Atlantic World: Angola and Brazil during the Era of the Slave Trade.* Cambridge, UK: Cambridge University Press.

Fick, Carolyn E. 1990. *The Making of Haiti: The Saint-Domingue Revolution from Below.* Knoxville: University of Tennessee Press.

Filesi, Teobaldo. 1974. *San Salvador: Cronache dei Re del Congo.* Bologna, IT: E.M.I.

Fitch, Suzanne P., and Roseann M. Mandziuk. 1997. *Sojourner Truth as Orator: Wit, Story and Song.* Westport, CT: Greenwood.

Fiume, Giovanna. 2007. St. Benedict the Moor: From Sicily to the New World. *Saints and Their Cults in the Atlantic World*, ed. Margaret Cormack, 16–51. Columbia: University of South Carolina Press.

Flint, James. [1822] 1904. *Letters from America: Containing Observations on the Climate and Agriculture of the Western States, the Manners of the People, the Prospects of Emigrants &c.*, ed. Reuben Gold Thwaites. Cleveland, OH: Arthur Clark, 1904.

Flint, Timothy. [1826] 1968. *Recollections of the Last Ten Years in the Valley of the Mississippi*, ed. George R. Brooks. Carbondale and Edwardsville: Southern Illinois University Press.

Flynn, Maureen. 1989. *Sacred Charity: Confraternities and Social Welfare in Spain 1400–1700*. Ithaca, NY: Cornell University Press.

Fogelman, Patricia, and Marta Goldberg. 2009. "El rey de los congos": The Clandestine Coronation of Pedro Duarte in Buenos Aires, 1787. *Afro-Latino Voices: Narratives from the Early Modern Ibero-Atlantic World, 1550–1812*, ed. Kathryn Joy McKnight and Leo J. Garofalo, 155–74. Indianapolis: Hackett.

Foote, Thelma Wills. 2004. *Black and White Manhattan: The History of Racial Formation in Colonial New York City*. Oxford and New York: Oxford University Press.

Fortier, Alcée. 1888. Customs and Superstitions in Louisiana. *Journal of American Folklore* 1, no. 2 (1888): 136–40.

Fowler, William Chauncey. 1866. *History of Durham, Connecticut, from the First Grant of Land in 1662 to 1866*. Hartford, CT: Press of Wiley.

Franco, António, S. J. 1726. *Synopsis Annalium Societatis Jesu in Lusitania ab 1540 usque ad annum 1725*. Augsburg, DE: Sumptibus Philippi, Martini, & Joannis Veith, Haeredum.

Franklin, Wayne. 2009. Cooper in the Netherlands. *James Fenimore Cooper Society Miscellaneous Papers* 26 (2009): 3–8.

Freeman, Rhoda Golden. 1994. *The Free Negro in New York City in the Era before the Civil War*. New York: Garland.

Frelinghuysen, Theodorus Jacobus. [1691–1747] 2000. *Forerunner of the Great Awakening: Sermons by Theodorus Jacobus Frelinghuysen (1691–1747)*, ed. Joel R. Beeke. Grand Rapids, MI: Eerdmans.

Frijhoff, Willem. 1995. *Wegen van Evert Willemsz. Een Hollands weeskind op zoek naar zichzelf 1607–1647*. Nijmegen, NL: SUN.

Frijhoff, Willem, and Marijke Spies. 1999. *Nederlandse cultuur in Europese context: 1650. Bevochten eendracht*. The Hague: Sdu Uitgevers.

Frohne, Andrea E. 2015. *The African Burial Ground in New York City: Memory, Spirituality, and Space*. Syracuse, NY: Syracuse University Press.

Fromont, Cécile. 2013. Dancing for the King of Congo from Early Modern Central Africa to Slavery-Era Brazil. *Colonial Latin American Review* 22, no. 2 (2013): 184–208.

———. 2014. *The Art of Conversation: Christian Visual Culture in the Kingdom of Kongo*. Chapel Hill: University of North Carolina Press.

Furman, Gabriel. 1874. *Antiquities of Long Island*. New York: J.W. Bouton.

Gaeta, Antonio de. 1669. *La maravigliosa conversione alla fede di Cristi della Regina Signa e dell suo Regno di Matamba*. Naples, IT: Per Giacinto Passaro.

Gallop, Rodney. 1936. *Portugal: A Book of Folk-Ways*. Cambridge, UK: Cambridge University Press.

Garcia, Carlos Alberto. 1968. A acção dos portugueses no antigo reino do Congo (1482–1543). *Boletim Geral do Ultramar* 513 (March 1968): 3–30; 515 (May 1968): 11–36; 516 (June 1968): 77–90.

Garfield, Robert. 1992. *A History of São Tomé Island 1470–1655: The Key to Guinea*. San Francisco: Mellen Research University Press.

Gaspar, David Barry. 1985. *Bondmen and Rebels: A Study of Master-Slave Relations in Antigua*. Baltimore, MD: Johns Hopkins University Press.

Geggus, David. 1991. Haitian Voodoo in the Eighteenth Century: Language, Culture, Resistance. *Jahrbuch Für Geschichte Lateinamerikas* 28, no. 1 (January 1991): 21–51.

———. 2013. The Slaves and Free People of Color of Cap Français. *The Black Urban Atlantic in the Age of the Slave Trade*, ed. Jorge Cañizares-Esguerra, Matt D. Childs, and James Sidbury, 101–21. Philadelphia: University of Pennsylvania Press.

Gehring, Charles T. 2009. New Netherland: The Formative Years, 1609–1632. *Four Centuries of Dutch-American Relations 1609–2009*, ed. Hans Krabbendam, Cornelis A. van Minnen, and Giles Scott-Smith, 74–84. Albany: State University of New York Press.

———, ed. 2003. *New Netherland Documents Series Volume XII: Correspondence 1654–1658*. Syracuse, NY: Syracuse University Press.

———, ed. 1980. *New York Historical Manuscripts: Dutch, Volumes GG, HH & II; Land Papers*. Baltimore, MD: Genealogical Publishing.

———, ed. 1981. *New York Historical Manuscripts: Dutch, Volumes XVIII-XIX; Delaware Papers (Dutch Period)*. Baltimore, MD: Genealogical Publishing.

———, ed. 1983. *Council Minutes, 1652–1654. New York Historical Manuscripts*. Baltimore, MD: Genealogical Publishing.

———, ed. 1990. *Fort Orange Court Minutes 1652–1660*. Syracuse, NY: Syracuse University Press.

———, ed. 1995. *Council Minutes 1655–1656*. Syracuse, NY: Syracuse University Press.

———, ed. 2000. *New Netherland Documents Series Volume XI: Correspondence 1647–1653*. Syracuse, NY: Syracuse University Press.

———, ed. 1991. *Laws & Writs of Appeal 1647–1663*. Syracuse, NY: Syracuse University Press.

Gehring, Charles T., and J. A. Schiltkamp, ed. 1987. *Curaçao Papers 1640–1665. New Netherlands Documents*. Vol. XVII. Interlaken, NY: Heart of the Lakes.

Gehring, Charles T., and Janny Venema, ed. 2009. *Fort Orange Records, 1654–1679*. Syracuse, NY: Syracuse University Press.

Gellman, David N. 2006. *Emancipating New York: The Politics of Slavery and Freedom 1777–1827*. Baton Rouge: Louisiana State University Press.

Genovese, Eugene D. 1974. *Roll, Jordan, Roll: The World the Slaves Made*. New York: Pantheon.

———. 1979. *From Rebellion to Revolution: Afro-American Slave Revolts in the making of the Modern World*. Baton Rouge: Louisiana State University Press.

Gilje, Paul A., and Howard B. Rock. 1994. "Sweep O! Sweep O!": African American Chimney Sweeps and Citizenship in the New Nation. *William and Mary Quarterly* 51, no. 3 (July 1994): 507–38.

Gilroy, Paul. 1993. *The Black Atlantic: Modernity and Double Consciousness*. London and New York: Verso.

Glass, Barbara S. 2007. *African American Dance: An Illustrated History*. Jefferson, NC: McFarland.

Gomes, Flávio. 2010. *Mocambos de Palmares. História e fontes Séc. XVI–XIX*. Rio de Janeiro: 7Letras.

Gomez, Michael A. 1998. *Exchanging Our Country Marks: The Transformation of African Identities in the Colonial and Antebellum South*. Chapel Hill: University of North Carolina Press.

Gonçalves, António Custódio. 1989. As influências do Cristianismo na organização política do Reino do Congo. *Congresso Internacional Bartolomeu Dias e a sua época. Actas,* 5 vols., 523–39. Porto, PT: Universidade do Porto.

Gonçalves, Nuno da Silva. 1996. *Os Jesuítas e a missão de Cabo Verde, 1604–1642.* Lisbon: Brotéria.

Goodfriend, Joyce D. 1978. Burghers and Blacks: The Evolution of a Slave Society at New Amsterdam. *New York History* LIX, no. 2 (April 1978): 125–44.

———. 1991. Black Families in New Netherland. *A Beautiful and Fruitful Place: Selected Rensselaerswijck Seminar Papers,* ed. Nancy A. M. Zeller, 147–56. New York: New Netherland.

———. 1992. *Before the Melting Pot: Society and Culture in Colonial New York City, 1664–1730.* Princeton, NJ: Princeton University Press.

———. 2006. The Struggle over the Sabbath in Petrus Stuyvesant's New Amsterdam. *Power and the City in the Netherlandic World,* ed. Wayne te Brake and Wim Klooster, 205–24. Leiden, NL: Brill.

———. 2008. Slavery in Colonial New York City. *Urban History* 35, no. 3 (December 2008): 485–96.

———. 2009. The Social Life and Cultural Life of Dutch Settlers, 1664–1776. *Four Centuries of Dutch-American Relations 1609–2009,* ed. Hans Krabbendam, Cornelis A. van Minnen, and Giles Scott-Smith, 120–31. Albany: State University of New York Press.

———. 2009. Why New Netherland Matters. *Explorers, Fortunes and Love Letters: A Window on New Netherland,* ed. Martha Dickinson Shattuck, 148–61. New York: Mount Ida Press.

———. 2011. The Dutch Book Trade in Colonial New York City: The Transatlantic Connection. *Books between Europe and the Americas: Connections and Communities, 1620–1860,* ed. Leslie Howsam and James Raven, 128–56. Basingstoke: Palgrave Macmillan.

———. 2012. Archibald Laidlie (1727–1779): The Scot who Revitalized New York City's Dutch Reformed Church. *Transatlantic Pieties: Dutch Clergy in Colonial America,* ed. Leon van den Broeke, Hans Krabbendam, and Dirk Mouw, 239–57. Grand Rapids, MI: Eerdmans.

———. 2014. Merging the Two Streams of Migration to New Netherland. *The Worlds of the Seventeenth-Century Hudson Valley,* ed. Jaap Jacobs and L. H. Roper, 237–52. Albany: State University of New York Press.

Goodman, Walter. 1873. *The Pearl of the Antilles, or An Artist in Cuba.* London: Henry S. King.

Goodwin, Maud Wilder. 1921. *Dutch and English on the Hudson: A Chronicle of Colonial New York.* New Haven, CT: Yale University Press.

Goulart, José Alípio. 1972. *Da fuga ao suicídio: aspectos de rebeldia dos escravos no Brasil.* Rio de Janeiro: Conquista.

Gould, Eliga H. 2007. Entangled Histories, Entangled Worlds: The English-Speaking Atlantic as a Spanish Periphery. *American Historical Review* 112, no. 3 (June 2007): 764–86.

Grant, Anne. [1808] 1909. *Memoirs of an American Lady with Sketches of Manners and Scenes in America as they existed Previous to the Revolution.* New York: Dodd, Mead.

Gray, Richard. 1990. *Black Christians and White Missionaries.* New Haven, CT: Yale University Press.

———. 2002. A Kongo Princess and the Papacy. *Christianity and the African Imagination: Essays in Honor of Adrian Hastings,* ed. David Maxwell and Ingrid Lawrie, 25–40. Leiden, NL: Brill.

Graydon, Alexander. 1822. *Memoirs of a Life Chiefly Passed in Pennsylvania, Within the Last Sixty Years*. Edinburgh, UK: W. Blackwood.

Green, Toby. 2012. *The Rise of the Trans-Atlantic Slave Trade in Western Africa, 1300–1589*. Cambridge, UK: Cambridge University Press.

Greene, Nelson. 1915. *The Story of Old Fort Plain and the Middle Mohawk Valley: A Review of Mohawk Valley History from 1609 to the Time of the Writing of this Book (1912–1914)*. Fort Plain, NY: O'Connor Brothers.

Griffis, William Elliot. 1909. *The Story of New Netherland: The Dutch in America*. Boston: Houghton Mifflin.

Grolman, Hermina C. A. 1931. *Nederlandsche volksgebruiken naar oorsprong en betekenis*. Zutphen, NL: Thieme.

Gronniosaw, Ukawsaw. [ca. 1770] 1995. A Narrative of the Most Remarkable Particulars in the Life of James Albert Ukawsaw Gronniosaw, an African Prince, Written by Himself. *Black Atlantic Writers of the Eighteenth Century: Living the New Exodus in England and the Americas*, ed. Adam Potkay and Sandra Burr, 27–63. New York: St. Martin's Press.

Groth, Michael E. 2003. Laboring for Freedom in Dutchess County. *Mighty Change, Tall Within: Black Identity in the Hudson Valley*, ed. Myra B. Young Armstead, 58–79. Albany: State University of New York Press.

Hackett, David G. 1991. *The Rude Hand of Innovation: Religion and Social Order in Albany, New York, 1652–1836*. Oxford and New York: Oxford University Press.

Haefeli, Evan. 2012. *New Netherland and the Dutch Origins of American Religious Liberty*. Philadelphia: University of Pennsylvania Press.

———. 2014. Breaking the Christian Atlantic: The Legacy of Dutch Tolerance in Brazil. *The Legacy of Dutch Brazil*, ed. Michiel van Groesen, 124–45. Cambridge, UK: Cambridge University Press.

Hall, Gwendolyn Midlo. 2005. *Slavery and African Ethnicities in the Americas: Restoring the Links*. Chapel Hill: University of North Carolina Press.

Hall, Neville A. T. 1992. *Slave Society in the Danish West Indies: St. Thomas, St. John and St. Croix*, ed. B. W. Higman. Baltimore, MA: Johns Hopkins University Press.

Hall, Ruth. 1900. *The Black Gown*. Boston: Houghton, Mifflin.

Hamelberg, J. H. J., ed. [1901–1903] 1979. *Documenten behoorende bij "De Nederlanders op de West-Indische eilanden."* Amsterdam: Emmering.

Hamilton, Alexander. [1744] 1948. *Gentlemen's Progress: The Itinerarium of Dr. Alexander Hamilton, 1744*, ed. Carl Bridenbaugh. Pittsburgh, PA: University of Pittsburgh Press.

Hammond, Jabez D. 1842. *History of Political Parties in the State of New York*, 2 vols. Albany, NY: Van Benthuysen.

Handler, Jerome S., and Frederick W. Lange. 1978. *Plantation Slavery in Barbados: An Archaelogical and Historical Investigation*. Cambridge, MA: Harvard University Press.

Harris, Leslie M. 2003. *In the Shadow of Slavery: African Americans in New York City, 1626–1863*. Chicago: University of Chicago Press.

Harris, Max. 2001. Masking the Site: The Fiestas de Santiago Apóstol in Loíza, Puerto Rico. *Journal of American Folklore* 114 (2001): 358–69.

———. 2003. *Carnival and Other Christian Festivals: Folk Theology and Folk Performance*. Austin: University of Texas Press.

Hastings, Adrian. 1994. *The Church in Africa 1450–1950*. Oxford: Clarendon.

Hastings, Hugh, and Edward Tanjore Corwin, ed. 1901–1916. *Ecclesiastical Records, State of New York*, 7 vols. Albany, NY: State Historian.

Hawthorne, Nathaniel, ed. 1926. *The Yarn of a Yankee Privateer*. New York: Funk and Wagnalls.

Hawthorne, Walter. 2010. *From Africa to Brazil: Culture, Identity, and an Atlantic Slave Trade, 1600–1830*. Cambridge, UK: Cambridge University Press.

Hendricks, H. 1892. Sojourner Truth. *National Magazine: A Monthly Journal of American History* 16, no. 6 (October 1892): 665–71.

Hernández Soto, Carlos, and Edis Sánchez. 1997. Los Congos de Villa Mella, República Dominicana. *Revista de música latinoamericana* 18, no. 2 (1997): 297–316.

Herskovits, Melville J. [1941] 1958. *The Myth of the Negro Past*. Boston: Beacon Press.

Heywood, Linda M. 1999. The Angolan-Afro-Brazilian Cultural Connections. *Slavery & Abolition: A Journal of Slave and Post-Slave Studies* 20, no. 1 (1999): 9–23.

———, ed. 2002. *Central Africans and Cultural Transformations in the American Diaspora*. Cambridge, UK: Cambridge University Press.

Heywood, Linda M., and John Thornton. 2007. *Central Africans, Atlantic Creoles, and the Foundation of the Americas, 1585–1660*. Cambridge, UK: Cambridge University Press.

———. 2009. Intercultural Relations between Europeans and Blacks in New Netherland. *Four Centuries of Dutch-American Relations 1609–2009*, ed. Hans Krabbendam, Cornelis A. van Minnen, and Giles Scott-Smith, 192–203. Albany: State University of New York Press.

———. 2013. The Kongo Kingdom and European Diplomacy. *Kongo Across the Waters*, ed. Susan Cooksey, Robin Poynor, and Hein Vanhee, 52–57. Gainesville: University Press of Florida.

Higginson, Thomas Wentworth. [1867] 1999. Slave Songs and Spirituals. *African American Religious History: A Documentary Witness*, ed. Milton C. Sernett, 112–35. Durham, NC: Duke University Press.

Hildebrand, P. 1940. *Le martyr Georges de Geel et les débuts de la mission au Congo (1645–1652)*. Antwerp, BE: Archives des Capucins.

Hildreth, Richard. 1880. *The History of the United States of America*, 6 vols. New York: Harper and Brothers.

Hill, Errol. 1972. *The Trinidad Carnival: Mandate for a National Theatre*. Austin: University of Texas Press.

Hilton, Anne. 1985. *The Kingdom of the Kongo*. Oxford, UK: Clarendon.

Historisch Genootschap (Utrecht). 1874. Classicale Acta van Brazilië, *Kroniek van het Historisch Genootschap* 29, vol. 6, no. 4. Utrecht, NL: Kemink en zoon.

Hodges, Graham Russell. 1997. *Slavery and Freedom in the Rural North: African Americans in Monmouth County, New Jersey, 1665–1865*. Madison, WI: Madison House.

———. 1998. *Slavery, Freedom and Culture among Early American Workers*. Armond, NY: M.E. Sharpe.

———. 1999. *Root and Branch: African Americans in New York and East Jersey 1613–1863*. Chapel Hill: University of North Carolina Press.

Hodges, Graham Russell, and Alan Edward Brown, ed. 1994. *Pretends to Be Free: Runaway Slave Advertisements from Colonial and Revolutionary New York and New Jersey*. New York: Garland.

Hoes, Roswell Randall, ed. 1891. *Baptismal and Marriage Registers of the Old Dutch Church of Kingston, Ulster County, New York*. New York: De Vinne Press.

Hoffer, Peter Charles. 2003. *The Great New York Conspiracy of 1741: Slavery, Crime, and Colonial Law*. Lawrence: University Press of Kansas.

Hone, William. 1888–89. *The Every-Day Book, or, a Guide to the Year: Describing the Popular Amusements, Sports, Ceremonies, Manners, Customs, and Events, Incident to the Three Hundred and Sixty-Five Days, in Past and Present Times*, 2 vols. London: Ward.

Horsmanden, Daniel. [1744] 1971. *The New York Conspiracy*, ed. Thomas J. Davis. Boston: Beacon Press.

Horton, James Oliver, and Lois E. Horton. 1997. *In Hope of Liberty: Culture, Community, and Protest among Northern Free Blacks, 1700–1860*. Oxford and New York: Oxford University Press.

House, Kay Seymour. 1990. Historical Introduction. James Fenimore Cooper, *Satanstoe, or the Littlepage Manuscripts: A Tale of the Colony*, ed. Kay Seymour House and Constance Ayers Denne, xiii–xxxviii. New York: State University of New York Press.

Howard, Philip A. 1998. *Changing History: Afro-Cuban Cabildos and Societies of Color in the Nineteenth Century*. Baton Rouge: Louisiana State University Press.

Howard, Ronald W. 2001. The English Province (1664–1776). *The Empire State: A History of New York*, ed. Milton M. Klein, 113–228. Ithaca, NY: Cornell University Press.

Howell, George R., and Jonathan Tenny. 1886. *History of the County of Albany, from 1609 to 1886*. Albany, NY: W.W. Munsell.

Hunter, Robert. [1714] 1969. Androboros: A Biographical Farce in Three Acts. *Satiric Comedies*, ed. Walter J. Meserve and William R. Reardon, 1–40. Bloomington: Indiana University Press.

Irving, Washington. 1809. *A History of New York, from the Beginning of the World to the End of the Dutch Dynasty. By Diedrich Knickerbocker*. New York: Inskeep & Bradford.

Irvis, K. Leroy. 1955. Negro Tales from Eastern New York. *New York Folklore Quarterly* XI, no. 3 (1955): 165–76.

Jacobs, Jaap. 2005. "To Favor This New and Growing City of New Amsterdam with a Court of Justice": The Relations between Rulers and Ruled in New Amsterdam. *Amsterdam-New York: Transatlantic Relations and Urban Identities since 1653*, ed. George Harinck and Hans Krabbendam, 17–29. Amsterdam: VU University Press.

———. 2005. Like Father, Like Son? The Early Years of Petrus Stuyvesant. *Revisiting New Netherland: Perspectives on Early Dutch America*, ed. Joyce D. Goodfriend, 205–44. Leiden, NL: Brill.

———. 2005. *New Netherland: A Dutch Colony in Seventeenth-Century America*. Leiden, NL: Brill.

———. 2009. Migration, Population, and Government in New Netherland. *Four Centuries of Dutch-American Relations 1609–2009*, ed. Hans Krabbendam, Cornelis A. van Minnen, and Giles Scott-Smith, 85–96. Albany: State University of New York Press.

———. 2014. "In Such a Far Distant Land, Separated from All the Friends": Why Were the Dutch in New Netherland? *The Worlds of the Seventeenth-Century Hudson Valley*, ed. Jaap Jacobs and L. H. Roper, 147–68. Albany: State University of New York Press.

Jadin, Louis. 1966. Rivalités luso-néerlandaises du Sohio, Congo, 1600–1675. *Bulletin de l'Institut Historique Belge de Rome* XXXVII (1966): 137–360.

——, ed. 1968. Relations sur le Congo et l'Angola tirées des archives de la Compagnie de Jésus 1621–1631. *Bulletin de L'Institut Historique Belge de Rome* XXXIX (1968): 333–454.

——, ed. 1975. *L'Ancien Congo et l'Angola 1639–1655 d'après les archives romaines, portugaises, néerlandaises et espagnoles*, 3 vols. Brussels and Rome: Institut Historique Belge de Rome.

Janzen, John M. 2013. Renewal and Reinterpretation in Kongo Religion. *Kongo Across the Waters*, ed. Susan Cooksey, Robin Poynor, and Hein Vanhee, 132–42. Gainesville: University Press of Florida.

Janzen, John M., and Wyatt MacGaffey. 1974. *An Anthology of Kongo Religion: Primary Texts from Lower Zaïre*. Lawrence: University of Kansas Publications in Anthropology.

Jay, John. 1890–1893. *The Correspondence and Public Papers of John Jay*, ed. Henry P. Johnston, 4 vols. New York: G.P. Putnam's Sons.

Jea, John. [1811] 1993. The Life, History, and Unparalleled Sufferings of John Jea, the African Preacher. *Black Itinerants of the Gospel: The Narratives of John Jea and George White*, ed. Graham Russell Hodges, 89–164. Madison, WI: Madison House.

Johnson, Howard. 1991. Friendly Societies in the Bahamas 1834–1910. *Slavery and Abolition* 12, no. 3 (December 1991): 183–99.

Johnston, Henry P. 1878. *The Campaign of 1776 around New York and Brooklyn*. Brooklyn: Long Island Historical Society.

Joosse, Leendert Jan. 2008. *Geloof in de Nieuwe Wereld. Ontmoeting met Afrikanen en Indianen 1600–1700*. Kampen, NL: Kok.

Jordaan, Han. 2003. The Curaçao Slave Market: From *Asiento* Trade to Free Trade, 1700–1730. *Riches from Atlantic Commerce: Dutch Transatlantic Trade and Shipping, 1585–1817*, ed. Johannes Postma and Victor Enthoven, 219–57. Leiden, NL: Brill.

Jordão, Levy Maria. 1877. *História do Congo. Obra posthuma do Visconde de Paiva Manso*. Lisbon: Typographia da Academia.

Kachun, Mitch. 2003. *Festivals of Freedom: Memory and Meaning in African American Emancipation Celebrations, 1808–1915*. Amherst: University of Massachusetts Press.

Kalm, Peter (Pehr). [1753–1761] 1972. *Travels into North America, 1748–1749*, ed. John Reinhold Forster. Barre, MA: Imprint Society.

Kammen, Michael. 1975. *Colonial New York: A History*. New York: Charles Scribner's Sons.

Karasch, Mary C. 1987. *Slave Life in Rio de Janeiro 1808–1850*. Princeton, NJ: Princeton University Press.

——. 2002. Central Africans in Central Brazil, 1780–1835. *Central Africans and Cultural Transformation in the American Diaspora*, ed. Linda M. Heywood, 117–52. Cambridge, UK: Cambridge University Press.

Kennedy, Earl W. 2012. Guiliam Bertholf (1656–1726): Irenic Dutch Pietist in New Jersey and New York. *Transatlantic Pieties: Dutch Clergy in Colonial America*, ed. Leon van den Broeke, Hans Krabbendam, and Dirk Mouw, 197–216. Grand Rapids, MI: Eerdmans.

Kennedy, Randall. 2002. *Nigger: The Strange Career of a Troublesome Word*. New York: Pantheon.

Kennedy, William. 1983. *O Albany! Improbable City of Political Wizards, Fearless Ethnics, Spectacular Aristocrats, Splendid Nobodies, and Underrated Scoundrels*. New York: Viking.

Kenney, Alice P. 1969. *The Gansevoorts of Albany: Dutch Patricians in the Upper Hudson Valley*. Syracuse, NY: Syracuse University Press.

———. 1975. *Stubborn for Liberty: The Dutch in New York*. Syracuse, NY: Syracuse University Press.

Kent, R. K. 1965. Palmares: An African State in Brazil. *Journal of African History* VI, no. 2 (1965): 161–75.

Kiddy, Elizabeth W. 2002. Who Is the King of Congo? A New Look at African and Afro-Brazilian Kings in Brazil. *Central Africans and Cultural Transformation in the American Diaspora*, ed. Linda M. Heywood, 153–82. Cambridge, UK: Cambridge University Press.

———. 2005. *Blacks of the Rosary: Memory and History in Minas Gerais, Brazil*. University Park: Pennsylvania State University Press.

Kim, Sung Bok. 1978. *Landlord and Tenant in Colonial New York: Manorial Society, 1664–1775*. Chapel Hill: University of North Carolina Press.

Kinser, Samuel. 1990. *Carnival, American Style: Mardi Gras at New Orleans and Mobile*. Chicago: University of Chicago Press.

Klein, Herbert. 2004. The Atlantic Slave Trade to 1650. *Tropical Babylons: Sugar and the Making of the Atlantic World, 1450–1680*, ed. Stuart B. Schwartz, 201–36. Chapel Hill: University of North Carolina Press.

Klooster, Wim. 2009. The Dutch in the Atlantic. *Four Centuries of Dutch-American Relations 1609–2009*, ed. Hans Krabbendam, Cornelis A. van Minnen, and Giles Scott-Smith, 63–73. Albany: State University of New York Press.

Knappert, L. 1934. De eerste honderd jaren der Protestantische gemeente op Curaçao. *Gedenkboek Nederland-Curaçao 1634–1934*, 34–56. Amsterdam: J.H. de Bussy.

Knowles, Mark. 2002. *Tap Roots: The Early History of Tap Dancing*. Jefferson, NC: McFarland.

Kolbe, Peter. [1719] 1968. *The Present State of the Cape*, 2 vols. London: Johnson Reprint.

Kooi, Christine. 2012. *Calvinists and Catholics during Holland's Golden Age: Heretics and Idolaters*. Cambridge, UK: Cambridge University Press.

Koot, Christian J. 2011. *Empire at the Periphery: British Colonists, Anglo-Dutch Trade, and the Development of the British Atlantic, 1621–1713*. New York: New York University Press.

Koster, Henry. 1816. *Travels in Brazil*. London: Longman, Hurst Rees, Orme and Brown.

Kosterman, Hans. 1999. *Het aanzien van een millennium: De Unie van Utrecht*. Utrecht, NL: Spectrum.

Kuyk, Betty M. 1983. The African Derivation of Black Fraternal Orders in the United States. *Comparative Studies in Society and History* 25, no. 4 (1983): 559–92.

Labat, Jean-Baptiste. [1722] 1979. *Voyages aux Isles de l'Amérique (Antilles), 1693–1705*, ed. Daniël Radford. Paris: Éditions Duchartre.

Lahon, Didier. 1999. Da escravidão à liberdade, *Os negros em Portugal—sécs. XV a XIX*, ed. Anna Maria Rodrigues, 81–98. Lisbon: Comissão Nacional para a Comemoração dos Descobrimentos Portugueses.

———. 1999. *O negro no coração do império: uma memória a resgatar—séculos XV-XIX*. Lisbon: Secretariado Coordenador dos Programas de Educação Multicultural.

———. 1999. Vivência religiosa. *Os negros em Portugal—sécs. XV a XIX*, ed. Anna Maria Rodrigues, 127–64. Lisbon: Comissão Nacional para a Comemoração dos Descobrimentos Portugueses.

———. 2002. Esclavage, confréries noires, sainteté noire et pureté de sang au Portugal (XVIe et XVIIIe siècles). *Lusitana Sacra* 2, no. XIII–XIV (2001–2): 119–62.

——. 2005. Black African Slaves and Freedmen in Portugal during the Renaissance: Creating a New Pattern of Reality. *Black Africans in Renaissance Europe*, ed. T. F. Earle and K. J. P. Lowe, 261–79. Cambridge, UK: Cambridge University Press.

Landers, Jane. 2002. The Central African Presence in Spanish Maroon Communities. *Central Africans and Cultural Transformation in the American Diaspora*, ed. Linda M. Heywood, 227–42. Cambridge, UK: Cambridge University Press.

——. 2013. The African Landscape of Seventeenth-Century Cartagena and Its Hinterland. *The Black Urban Atlantic in the Age of the Slave Trade*, ed. Jorge Cañizares-Esguerra, Matt D. Childs, and James Sidbury, 147–62. Philadelphia: University of Pennsylvania Press.

Lara, Silvia Hunold. 2002. Significados cruzados. Um reinado de Congos na Bahia setecentista. *Carnavais e outras f(r)estas. Ensaios de história social da cultura*, ed. Maria Clementina Pereira Cunha, 71–100. Campinas, BR: Editora Unicamp.

Larison, C. W. [1883] 1988. *Silvia Dubois: A Biografy of the Slav Who Whipt her Mistres and Gand her Freedom*, ed. Jared C. Lobdell. New York: Oxford University Press.

La Rochefoucauld Liancourt, François Alexandre Frédéric, duc de. [1799] 1800. *Travels through the United States of North America, the Country of the Iroquois, and Upper Canada in the Years 1795, 1796, and 1797*, 2 vols. London: T. Gillet for R. Phillips.

Lauvrijs, Bart. 2004. *Een jaar vol feesten*. Delft, NL: Elmar.

Law, Robin. 2013. Ouidah as a Multiethnic Community. *The Black Urban Atlantic in the Age of the Slave Trade*, ed. Jorge Cañizares-Esguerra, Matt D. Childs, and James Sidbury, 42–62. Philadelphia: University of Pennsylvania Press.

Lawrance, Jeremy. 2005. Black Africans in Renaissance Spanish Literature. *Black Africans in Renaissance Europe*, ed. T. F. Earle and K. J. P. Lowe, 70–93. Cambridge, UK: Cambridge University Press.

Le Gentil de la Barbinais, Guy. 1728. *Nouveau voyage auteur du monde*, Vol. I–III. Amsterdam: Pierre Mortier.

Leite, Serafim. 1938–50. *História da Companhia de Jesus no Brasil*, 10 vols. Rio de Janeiro: Civilização Brasileira.

Le Jau, Francis. [1706–17] 1999. Slave Conversion on the Carolina Frontier. *African American Religious History: A Documentary Witness*, ed. Milton C. Sernett, 25–33. Durham, NC: Duke University Press.

Lepore, Jill. 2005. *New York Burning: Liberty, Slavery, and Conspiracy in Eighteenth-Century Manhattan*. New York: Alfred A. Knopf.

——. 2005. The Tightening Vise: Slavery and Freedom in British New York. *Slavery in New York*, ed. Ira Berlin and Leslie M. Harris, 57–90. New York: New Press.

Lhamon, W. T., Jr. 1998. *Raising Cain: Blackface Performance from Jim Crow to Hip Hop*. Cambridge, MA: Harvard University Press.

Ligtenberg, Lucas. 1999. *De nieuwe wereld van Peter Stuyvesant. Nederlandse voetsporen in de Verenigde Staten*. Amsterdam: Uitgeverij Balans.

Lindsay, Nick, ed. 1975. *An Oral History of Edisto Island: Sam Gadsden Tells the Story*. Goshen College, IN: Pinchpenny Press.

Linebaugh, Peter, and Marcus Rediker. 2000. *The Many-Headed Hydra: Sailors, Salves, Commoners, and the Hidden History of the Revolutionary Atlantic*. Boston: Beacon Press.

Lorini, Alessandra. 1995. Public Rituals and the Cultural Making of the New York African American Community. *Feasts and Celebrations in North American Ethnic Communities*, ed. Ramón A. Gutiérrez and Geneviève Fabre, 29–46. Albuquerque: University of New Mexico Press.

Lott, Eric. 1993. *Love and Theft: Blackface Minstrelsy and the American Working Class*. New York: Oxford University Press.

Lowell, Robert. 1878. *A Story or Two from an Old Dutch Town*. Boston: Roberts Brothers.

Lynde, Benjamin. 1880. *The Diaries of Benjamin Lynde and of Benjamin Lynde Jr*. Boston: Priv. print.

MacGaffey, Wyatt. 1986. *Religion and Society in Central Africa: The BaKongo of Lower Zaire*. Chicago: University of Chicago Press.

———. 2000. *Kongo Political Culture: The Conceptual Challenge of the Particular*. Bloomington: Indiana University Press.

Madiou, Thomas. 1904. *Histoire d'Haïti*, 3 vols. Port-au-Prince: J. Courtois.

Maika, Dennis J. 2009. Encounters: Slavery and the Philipse Family, 1680–1751. *Dutch New York: The Roots of Hudson Valley Culture*, ed. Roger Panetta, 35–72. Bronx, NY: Fordham University Press.

Mann, Kristin, and Edna Bay. 2001. *Rethinking the African Diaspora: The Making of a Black Atlantic World in the Bight of Benin and Brazil*. Portland, OR: Frank Cass.

Margry, Peter Jan. 2000. *Teedere Quaesties: Religieuze rituelen in conflict*. Hilversum, NL: Verloren.

Marnef, Guido. 1996. *Antwerpen in de tijd van de Reformatie*. Antwerp, BE: Kritak.

Marshall, Kenneth E. 2011. *Manhood Enslaved: Bondmen in Eighteenth- and Early Nineteenth-Century New Jersey*. Rochester, NY: University of Rochester Press.

Martínez López, Enrique. 1998. *Tablero de Ajedrez: Imágenes del Negro heroico en la comedia Española y en la literature e iconografia sacra del Brasil esclavista*. Paris: Gulbenkian.

Mason, John Alden. 1918. Porto-Rican Folklore. *Journal of American Folklore* 31, no. 21 (July–September 1918): 289–450.

Mather, Cotton. 1911–1912. *Diary of Cotton Mather, 1663–1728*, ed. Worthington Chauncey Ford, 2 vols. Boston: Massachusetts Historical Society.

Matos, Raimundo J. da Cunha. [1836] 1963. *Compêndio histórico das possessões de Portugal na África*. Rio de Janeiro: Ministério de Justiça e Negócios Interiores.

Mattos, Hebe. 2008. "Black Troops" and Hierarchies of Color in the Portuguese Atlantic World: The Case of Henrique Dias and His Black Regiment. *Luso-Brazilian Review* 45, no. 1 (2008): 6–29.

McAlister, Elizabeth. 2004. *Rara! Vodou, Power, and Performance in Haiti and Its Diaspora*. Berkeley: University of California Press.

McConville, Brendan. 1999. *These Daring Disturbers of the Public Peace: The Struggle for Property and Power in Early New Jersey*. Ithaca, NY: Cornell University Press.

McKee, Samuel. 1935. *Labor in Colonial New York, 1664–1776*. New York: Columbia University Press.

McManus, Edgar J. 1966. *A History of Negro Slavery in New York*. Syracuse, NY: Syracuse University Press.

McWhorter, John, and Jeff Good. 2012. *A Grammar of Saramaccan Creole*. Berlin: De Gruyter.

Mellick, Andrew D., Jr. [1889] 1948. *Lesser Crossroads: Edited by Hubert G. Schmidt from the Story of an Old Farm*. New Brunswick, NJ: Rutgers University Press.

Merlin-Faucquez, Anne-Claire. 2011. De la Nouvelle-Néerlande à New York: la naissance d'une société esclavagiste (1624–1712). Ph.D. diss., Université Paris VIII.

Merolla, Girolamo da Sorrento. 1692. *Breve, e succinta relatione del viaggio nel Regno di Congo.* Naples, IT: Francesco Mollo.

Merwick, Donna. 1990. *Possessing Albany, 1630–1710: The Dutch and English Experiences.* Cambridge, UK: Cambridge University Press.

Métraux, Alfred. 1958. *Le Vaudou Haïtien.* Paris: Gallimar.

Meuwese, Mark. 2004. Dutch Calvinism and Native Americans: A Comparative Study of the Motivations for Protestant Conversion among the Tupis in Northeastern Brazil (1630–1654) and the Mohawks in Central New York (1690–1710). *The Spiritual Conversion of the Americas,* ed. James Muldoon, 118–41. Gainesville: University of Florida Press.

———. 2012 *Brothers in Arms, Partners in Trade: Dutch–Indigenous Alliances in the Atlantic World, 1595–1674.* Leiden, NL: Brill.

Meyer, Marlyse. 1995. *De Carlos Magno e outras histórias. Cristãos e Mouros no Brasil.* Natal, BR: UFRN.

Middleton, Simon. 2008. A Class Struggle in New York? *Class Matters: Early North America and the Atlantic World,* ed. Simon Middleton and Billy G. Smith, 88–98. Philadelphia: University of Pennsylvania Press.

———. 2009. The Waning of Dutch New York. *Four Centuries of Dutch-American Relations 1609–2009,* ed. Hans Krabbendam, Cornelis A. van Minnen, and Giles Scott-Smith, 108–19. Albany: State University of New York Press.

Miller, Joseph C. 2002. Central Africans during the Era of the Slave Trade, c. 1490s–1850s. *Central Africans and Cultural Transformation in America,* ed. Linda M. Heywood, 21–69. Cambridge, UK: Cambridge University Press.

Mintz, Sidney W., and Richard Price. 1976. *An Anthropological Approach to the Afro-American Past: A Caribbean Perspective.* Philadelphia: Institute for the Study of Human Issues.

———. 1992. *The Birth of African American Culture: An Anthropological Perspective.* Boston: Beacon Press.

Misevich, Philip. 2005. In Pursuit of Human Cargo: Philip Livingston and the Voyage of the Sloop *Rhode Island. New York History* 86, no. 3 (Summer 2005): 185–204.

Monteiro, Joachim John. 1876. *Angola and the River Congo.* New York: Macmillan.

Moore, Christopher. 2005. A World of Possibilities: Slavery and Freedom in Dutch New Amsterdam. *Slavery in New York,* ed. Ira Berlin and Leslie M. Harris, 29–56. New York: New Press.

Moore, Francis. 1738. *Travels into the Inland Parts of Africa: Containing a Description of the Several Nations for the Space of Six Hundred Miles up the River Gambia.* London: Edward Cave.

Moreau de Saint-Méry, Médéric L. E. [1797] 1958. *Description topographique physique, civile, politique et historique de la partie Française de l'isle Saint-Domingue,* ed. Blanche Maurel and Étienne Taillemite. Paris: Société de l'Histoire des Colonies Françaises.

Moreno, Isidoro. 1997. *La Antigua Hermandad de Los Negros de Sevilla. Etnicidad, poder y sociedad en 600 años de historia.* Sevilla, ES: Universidad de Sevilla.

Mosterman, Andrea C. 2012. Sharing Spaces in a New World Environment: African-Dutch Contributions to North American Culture, 1626–1826. Ph.D. diss., Boston University.

———. 2013. Researching African and Dutch Exchanges in Early New York. *De Halve Maen* 86 (Fall 2013): 47–52.

Motley, John Lothrop. 1856. *The Rise of the Dutch Republic.* New York: Harper & Brothers.

Moura, Carlos Francisco. 2000. *Teatro a bordo de naus portuguesas nos séculos XV, XVI, XVII e XVIII*. Rio de Janeiro: Instituto Luso-Brasileiro de História.

Mouw, Dirk, Gijs Boink, and Tom Weterings, ed. 2012. *The Memorandum Book of Anthony de Hooges*. Albany, NY: New Netherland Research Center/New Netherland Institute. www.newnetherlandinstitute.org/files/5413/5543/9455/DeHoogesTranscriptionFinal.pdf.

Mullin, Michael. 1992. *Africa in America: Slave Acculturation and Resistance in the American South and the British Caribbean, 1736–1831*. Urbana and Chicago: University of Illinois Press.

Mulvey, Patricia. 1982. Black Brothers and Sisters: Membership in the Black Lay Brotherhoods of Colonial Brazil. *Luso-Brazilian Review* 17 (1982): 253–79.

Munsell, Joel, ed. 1865–1871. *Collections on the History of Albany*, 4 vols. Albany, NY: J. Munsell.

———, ed. 1871. *Annals of Albany*, 10 vols., 2nd ed. Albany, NY: Joel Munsell.

Murdoch, David. 1861. *The Dutch Dominie of the Catskills; The Times of the "Bloody Brandt."* New York: Derby & Jackson.

Naerebout, F. G. 1990. Snoode exercitien. Het zeventiende-eeuwse Nederlandse protestantisme en de dans. *Volkskundig bulletin* 16 (1990): 125–55.

New York Historical Society. 1914. *Collections of the New-York Historical Society for the Year 1913: The John Watts De Peyster Publication Fund*. New York: New-York Historical Society.

Newhall, James. 1897. *History of Lynn, Essex County, Massachusetts Including Lynnfield, Saugus, Swampscott, and Nahant*, 2 vols. Lynn, MA: Nichols Press.

Newitt, Malyn, ed. 2010. *The Portuguese in West Africa, 1415–1670: A Documentary History*. Cambridge, UK: Cambridge University Press.

Newman, Renee. 1993. Pinkster and Slavery in Dutch New York. *De Halve Maen* 66 (Spring 1993): 1–8.

Nijsten, Gerard. 1994. *Volkscultuur in de late Middeleeuwen. Feesten, processies en (bij)geloof*. Utrecht, NL: Kosmos.

Niles, Grace Greylock. 1912. *The Hoosac Valley, its Legends and its History*. New York: G.P. Putnam's Sons.

Noordegraaf, Jan. 2009. Dutch Language and Literature in the United States. *Four Centuries of Dutch-American Relations 1609–2009*, ed. Hans Krabbendam, Cornelis A. van Minnen, and Giles Scott-Smith, 166–78. Albany: State University of New York Press.

Noorlander, Daniel. 2011. Serving God and Mammon: The Reformed Church and the Dutch West India Company in the Atlantic World, 1621–1674. Ph.D. diss., Georgetown University.

Northrup, David. 2013. Identity among Liberated Africans in Sierra Leone. *The Black Urban Atlantic in the Age of the Slave Trade*, ed. Jorge Cañizares-Esguerra, Matt D. Childs, and James Sidbury, 21–41. Philadelphia: University of Pennsylvania Press.

O'Callaghan, Edmund Bailey, ed. 1846–48. *History of New Netherland*, 2 vols. New York: D. Appleton.

———, ed. 1850–51. *The Documentary History of the State of New York*, 4 vols. Albany, NY: Charles van Benthuysen.

———, ed. 1865–66. *Calendar of Historical Manuscripts in the Office of the Secretary of State, Albany, New York*. 2 vols. Albany, NY: Weed, Parsons.

———, ed. 1867. *Voyages of the Slavers St. John and Arms of Amsterdam, 1659, 1663: Together with Additional Papers Illustrative of the Slave Trade under the Dutch*. Albany, NY: Munsell.

———, ed. 1868. *Laws and Ordinances of New Netherland, 1638–1674. Compiled and Translated from the Original Dutch Records in the Office of the Secretary of State, Albany, New York.* Albany, NY: Weed, Parsons.

———, ed. 1978. *Register of Salomon Lachaire: Notary Public of New Amsterdam, 1661-1662.* Baltimore, MD: Genealogical Publishing.

O'Callaghan, Edmund Bailey, Berthold Fernow, and John Romeyn Brodhead, ed. 1853–87. *Documents Relative to the Colonial History of the State of New York*, 15 vols. Albany, NY: Weed, Parsons.

Oldendorp, Christian Georg Andrea. [1770] 1987. *History of the Mission of the Evangelical Brethren on the Caribbean Islands of St. Thomas, St. Croix, and St. John*, ed. Arnold R. High-field and Vladimir Barac. Ann Arbor, MI: Karoma.

Oliveira, Anderson José Machado de. 2008. *Devoção negra: santos pretos e catequese no Brasil colonial.* Rio de Janeiro: Quartet.

Olson, Edwin. 1941. Social Aspects of Slave Life in New York. *Journal of Negro History* 26, no. 1 (January 1941): 66–77.

Onderdonk, Henry, Jr. 1884. *History of the First Reformed Dutch Church of Jamaica.* Jamaica, NY: The Consistory.

Ortiz Fernández, Fernando. 1921. Los cabildos afrocubanos. *Revista Bimestre Cubana* XVI (January-February 1921): 5–39.

———. 1992. *Los cabildos y la fiesta afrocubanos del Día de Reyes.* La Habana: Editorial de Ciencias Sociales.

Osborn, John Hosey. 1967. *Life in the Old Dutch Homesteads.* Paramus, NJ: Highway Printing.

Osgood, Herbert I., Charles Alexander Nelson, and Austin Baxter Keep, ed. 1905. *Minutes of the Common Council of the City of New York, 1675-1776*, 8 vols. New York: Dodd, Mead.

Page, Willie F. 1997. *The Dutch Triangle: The Netherlands and the Atlantic Slave Trade, 1621-1664.* New York and London: Garland.

Paltsits, V. H., ed. 1909–1910. *Minutes of the Commissioners for Detecting and Defeating Conspiracies in the State of New York*, 3 vols. Albany: State of New York.

Paul, Emmanuel C. 1978. *Panorama du Folklore Haïtien (Présence Africaine en Haïti).* Port-au-Prince: Les Éditions Fardin.

Pereira, Daniel A. 2005. *Estudos da história de Cabo Verde.* Praia, CV: Alfo-Comunicações.

Pershing, Linda. 2003. Representations of Racial Identity in a Contemporary Pinkster Celebration. *Mighty Change, Tall Within: Black Identity in the Hudson Valley*, ed. Myra B. Young Armstead, 190–209. Albany: State University of New York Press.

Pettinger, Alasdair. 2012. "Eh, eh! Bomba, hen! hen!": Making Sense of a Vodou Chant. *Obeah and Other Powers: The Politics of Caribbean Religion and Healing*, ed. Diana Paton and Maarit Forde, 80–101. Durham, NC: Duke University Press.

Peytraud, Lucien. 1897. *L'Esclavage aux Antilles Françaises avant 1789 d'après des documents inédits des archives coloniales.* Paris: Hachette.

Phillippo, James M. 1843. *Jamaica: Its Past and Present State.* Philadelphia: J.M. Campbell.

Phillips, George L. 1949. May-Day Is Sweeps' Day. *Folklore* 60, no. 1 (March 1949): 217–27.

Phillips, James Duncan. 1937. *Salem in the Eighteenth Century.* Boston: Houghton Mifflin.

Pickering, James H. 1966. Fenimore Cooper and Pinkster. *New York Folklore Quarterly* XXII, no. 1 (1966): 15–19.

Piersen, William D. 1988. *Black Yankees: The Development of an Afro-American Subculture in Eighteenth-Century New England*. Amherst: University of Massachusetts Press.

Pigafetta, Filippo. [1591] 1969. *A Report of the Kingdom of Congo and the Surrounding Countries; Drawn out of the Writings and Discourses of the Portuguese Duarte Lopez*, ed. Margarite Hutchinson. New York: Negro Universities Press.

Pina, Rui de. [1492] 1992. *Relação do Reino do Congo. Manuscrito inédito do Códice Riccardiano 1910*, ed. Carmen M. Radulet. Lisbon: Imprensa Nacional—Casa da Moeda.

Pinchin, Ludovic. 1878. *Dissertations receuillis. Le roy des Ribauds*. Paris: Claudin.

Pinto, Manuel do Rosário. [1734] 2006. *Relação do descobrimento da ilha de São Tomé*, ed. Arlindo Manuel Caldeira. Lisbon: Centro de História de Além-Mar.

Platt, Orville. 1900. Negro Governors. *New Haven Colony Historical Society Papers* 6 (1900): 315–35.

Pleij, Herman. 1979. *Het gilde van de Blauwe Schuit. Literatuur, volksfeest en burgermoraal in de late middeleeuwen*. Amsterdam: Meulenhoff.

———. 1988. *De sneeuwpoppen van 1511. Literatuur en stadscultuur tussen middeleeuwen en moderne tijd*. Amsterdam: Meulenhoff.

———. 2007. *Het gevleugelde woord. Geschiedenis van de Nederlandse literatuur 1400–1560*. Amsterdam: Bert Bakker.

Porter, Dorothy, ed. 1995. *Early Negro Writing, 1760–1837*. Baltimore, MD: Black Classic Press.

Postma, Johannes Menne. 1990. *The Dutch in the Atlantic Slave Trade, 1600–1815*. Cambridge, UK: Cambridge University Press.

Prince, John Dyneley. 1910. The Jersey Dutch Dialect. *Dialect Notes* 3 (1910): 459–84.

Puntoni, Pedro. 1999. *A miséria sorte. A escravidão Africana no Brasil Holandês e as guerras do tráfico no Atlântico Sul, 1621–1648*. São Paulo: Editora Hucitec.

Purple, Samuel S., ed. [1890] 1940. *Marriages from 1639 to 1801 in the Reformed Dutch Church, New Amsterdam, New York City. Collections of the New York Genealogical and Biographical Society*, vol. 9. New York: Genealogical and Biographical Society.

Rael, Patrick. 2005. The Long Death of Slavery. *Slavery in New York*, ed. Ira Berlin and Leslie M. Harris, 111–46. New York: New Press.

Ramos, Arthur. 1937. *As culturas negras no Novo Mundo*. Rio de Janeiro: Civilização Brasileira.

Ratelband, Klaas. 2000. *Nederlanders in West-Afrika 1600–1650. Angola, Kongo en São Tomé*, ed. René Baesjou. Zutphen, NL: Walburg Pers.

Redinha, José. 1943. *Relatório Anual do Museu do Dundo*. Dundo, Angola: DIAMANG.

Reginaldo, Lucilene. 2011. *Os Rosários dos Angolas. Irmandades de africanos e crioulos na Bahia Setecentista*. São Paulo: Alameda.

Reich, Jerome R. 1953. *Leisler's Rebellion: A Study of Democracy in New York 1664–1720*. Chicago: University of Chicago Press.

Reidy, Joseph P. 1978. "Negro Election Day" and Black Community Life in New England, 1750–1860. *Marxist Perspectives* 1, no. 3 (Fall 1978): 102–17.

Reis, João José. 2013. African Nations in Nineteenth-Century Salvador, Brazil. *The Black Urban Atlantic in the Age of the Slave Trade*, ed. Jorge Cañizares-Esguerra, Matt D. Childs, and James Sidbury, 63–82. Philadelphia: University of Pennsylvania Press.

Rey, Terry. 1998. The Virgin Mary and Revolution in Saint-Domingue: The Charisma of Romaine-la-Prophétesse. *Journal of Historical Sociology* 11, no. 3 (1998): 341–69.

——. 2002. Kongolese Catholic Influences on Haitian Popular Catholicism: A Sociohistorical Exploration. *Central Africans and Cultural Transformation in the American Diaspora*, ed. Linda M. Heywood, 265–85. Cambridge, UK: Cambridge University Press.

Reynolds, Cuyler. 1906. *Albany Chronicles: A History of the City Arranged Chronologically from the Earliest Settlement to the Present Time*. Albany, NY: J.B. Lyon.

Richman, Karen. 2012. The Vodou State and the Protestant Nation: Haiti in the Long Twentieth Century. *Obeah and Other Powers: The Politics of Caribbean Religion and Healing*, ed. Diana Paton and Maarit Forde, 268–87. Durham, NC: Duke University Press.

Richshoffer, Ambrosius. [1677] 1930. Reise nach Brasilien 1629–1632. *Reisebeschreibungen von deutschen Beamten und Kriegsleuten im Dienst der niederländischen West- und Ost-Indischen Kompagnien 1602–1797*, ed. S. P. L'Honoré Naber, vol. 1, 1–141. The Hague: Martinus Nijhoff.

Rigaud, Milo. 1953. *La tradition Voudoo et le Voudoo Haïtien: Son temple, ses mystères, sa magie*. Paris: Éditions Niclaus.

Riker, James. 1904. *Revised History of Harlem (City of New York): Its Origin and Early Annals, Prefaced by Home Scenes in the Fatherlands, or, Notices of its Founders before Emigration*. New York: New Harlem.

Rink, Oliver A. 1986. *Holland on the Hudson: An Economic and Social History of Dutch New York*. Ithaca, NY: Cornell University Press.

——. 2001. Before the English (1609–1664). *The Empire State: A History of New York*, ed. Milton M. Klein, 3–112. Ithaca, NY: Cornell University Press.

Roberts, Benjamin B. 2012. *Sex and Drugs before Rock 'n' Roll: Youth Culture and Masculinity during Holland's Golden Age*. Amsterdam: Amsterdam University Press.

Roberts, John Storm. 1998. *Black Music of Two Worlds: African, Caribbean, Latin, and African American Traditions*. New York: Schirmer.

Rockwell, Charles F. 1889. *Recollections of Men, Customs and Events in Milford Pennsylvania and Vicinity*. Milford, PA: s.n.

Rodrigues, Adriano Vasco. 1989. Aculturação artística e social no Reino do Congo resultante da evangelização após a chegada dos Portugueses. *Congresso Internacional Bartolomeu Dias e a sua época. Actas*, 5 vols., 541–53. Porto, PT: Universidade do Porto.

Rodway, James. 1893. *History of British Guiana*, 2 vols. Georgetown, GY: J. Thomson.

Romney, Susanah Shaw. 2014. *New Netherland Connections: Intimate Networks and Atlantic Ties in Seventeenth-Century America*. Chapel Hill: University of North Carolina Press.

Roosevelt, Theodore. 1891. *New York*. New York: Longmans.

Rose, Peter G. 2009. *Food, Drink and Celebrations of the Hudson Valley Dutch*. Charleston, SC: History Press.

Rourke, Constance. [1931] 1986. *American Humor: A Study of the National Character*. Tallahassee: Florida State University Press.

Rubin, Miri. 1991. *Corpus Christi: The Eucharist in Late Medieval Culture*. Cambridge, UK: Cambridge University Press.

——. 2009. *Mother of God: A History of the Virgin Mary*. New Haven, CT: Yale University Press.

Rupert, Linda M. 2012. *Creolization and Contraband: Curaçao and the Early Modern Atlantic World*. Athens: University of Georgia Press.

Rutkoff, Peter M., and William B. Scott. 2010. *Fly Away: The Great African American Cultural Migrations.* Baltimore, MD: Johns Hopkins University Press.

Ryder, Alan. 1960. Missionary Activity in the Kingdom of Warri to the Early Nineteenth Century. *Journal of the Historical Society of Nigeria* 2 (1960): 1–26.

Sá, Isabel dos Guimarães. 2007. Ecclesiastical Structures and Religious Action. *Portuguese Oceanic Expansion, 1400–1800,* ed. Francisco Bethencourt and Diogo Ramada Curto, 255–82. Cambridge, UK: Cambridge University Press.

Sandoval, Alonso de. [1627] 2008. *Treatise on Slavery: Selections from De instaurada aethiopum salute,* ed. Nicole von Germeten. Indianapolis: Hackett.

Santos, José Almeida. 1971. *Apenas um punhado de bravos!* Luanda, Angola: Câmara Municipal de Luanda.

Sarmento, Alfredo de. 1880. *Os sertões d'Africa. Apontamentos de viagem.* Lisbon: Francisco Arthur da Silva.

Saunders, A. C. de C. M. 1982. *A Social History of Black Slaves and Freedmen in Portugal 1441–1555.* Cambridge, UK: Cambridge University Press.

Schalkwijk, Frans Leonard. 1998. *The Reformed Church in Dutch Brazil, 1630–1654.* Zoetermeer: Boekencentrum.

Schama, Simon. [1987] 1997. *The Embarrassment of Riches: An Interpretation of Dutch Culture in the Golden Age.* New York: Random House.

Schnurmann, Claudia. 2003. Representative Atlantic Entrepreneur: Jacob Leisler, 1640–1691. *Riches from Atlantic Commerce: Dutch Transatlantic Trade and Shipping, 1585–1817,* ed. Johannes Postma and Victor Enthoven, 259–83. Leiden, NL: Brill.

Schoelcher, Victor. 1843. *Colonies étrangères et Haiti,* 2 vols. Paris: Pagnerre.

Schoolcraft, Henry Rowe, ed. 1853. *Information Respecting the History, Condition and Prospects of the Indian Tribes of the United States,* 6 vols. Philadelphia: Lippincott.

Schoonmaker, Marius. 1888. *The History of Kingston, New York, from Its Early Settlement to the Year 1820.* New York: Burr Printing House.

Schotel, G. D. J. 1905. *Het maatschappelijk leven onzer vaderen in de zeventiende eeuw.* Amsterdam: J.G. Strengholt.

Schutte, G. J. 2002. De kerk onder de Compagnie. *Het Indisch Sion. De Gereformeerde Kerk onder Verenigde Oost-Indische Compagnie,* ed. G. J. Schutte, 43–64. Hilversum, NL: Verloren.

———. 2002. Een hutje in den wijngaard. *Het Indisch Sion. De Gereformeerde Kerk onder Verenigde Oost-Indische Compagnie,* ed. G. J. Schutte, 177–88. Hilversum, NL: Verloren.

Schwartz, Stuart B., and Clive Willis, ed. 2010. *Early Brazil: A Documentary Collection to 1700.* Cambridge, UK: Cambridge University Press.

Scott, Kenneth. 1961. The Slave Insurrection in New York in 1712. *New-York Historical Society Quarterly* XLV, no. 1 (January 1961): 43–74.

Seibert, Gerhard. 2012. Creolization and Creole Communities in the Portuguese Atlantic: São Tomé, Cape Verde, the Rivers of Guinea and Central Africa in Comparison. *Brokers of Change: Atlantic Commerce and Cultures in Precolonial Western Africa,* ed. Toby Green, 29–51. Oxford and New York: Oxford University Press.

Selyns, Henricus. [1686] 1916. Dominie Selyns' Church Records. *Yearbook of the Holland Society of New York,* 21–35.

Semedo, José Maria, and Maria R. Turano. 1997. *Cabo Verde: O cíclo ritual das festividades da tabanca*. Praia, CV: Speel-Edições.

Sermon, Armand. 2001. *Carnaval. Geschiedenis van het carnaval van Keizer Karel tot Eedje Anseele*. Ghent, BE: Stichting Mens en Kultuur.

Shannon, Timothy J. 2014. Avenue of Empire: The Hudson Valley in an Atlantic Context. *The World of the Seventeenth-Century Hudson Valley*, ed. Jaap Jacobs and L. H. Roper, 67–84. Albany: State University of New York Press.

Sharpe, John. [1713] 1880. Proposals for Erecting a School, Library and Chapel at New York. *Collections of the New-York Historical Society for the Year 1880*, 341–63. New York: Trow & Smith.

Shell, Robert C.-H. 1994. *Children of Bondage: A Social History of the Slave Society at the Cape of Good Hope, 1652–1838*. Hanover and London: Wesleyan University Press.

Silva, Eduardo. 1993. *Prince of the People: Life and Times of a Brazilian Free Man of Colour*. London and New York: Verso.

Simms, Jeptha Root. 1845. *History of Schoharie County and Border Wars of New York*. Albany, NY: Munsell & Tanner.

Singleton, Esther. 1909. *Dutch New York*. New York: Dodd, Mead.

Smith, Billy G., and Richard Wojtowicz, ed. 1989. *Blacks Who Stole Themselves: Advertisements for Runaways in the Pennsylvania Gazette, 1728–1790*. Philadelphia: University of Pennsylvania Press.

Smith, James McCune. 1865. *Introduction to a Memorial Discourse, by Rev. Henry Highland Garnet*. Philadelphia: Joseph M. Wilson.

Smith, Mark M., ed. 2005. *Stono: Documenting and Interpreting a Southern Slave Revolt*. Columbia: University of South Carolina Press.

Smith, Robert W. 2002. McKean, Thomas (1734–1817). *The Louisiana Purchase: A Historical and Geographical Encyclopedia*, ed. Junius P. Rodriguez, 221. Santa Barbara, CA: ABC CLIO.

Smith, Sol. [1868] 1968. *Theatrical Management in the West and South for Thirty Years*. New York: B. Blom.

Soares, Mariza de Carvalho. 2000. *Devotos da cor: Identidade étnica, religiosidade e escravidão no Rio de Janeiro, século XVIII*. Rio de Janeiro: Civilização brasileira.

Soler, Vincent Joachim. [1636–43] 1999. *Dutch Brazil: Vincent Joachim Soler's Seventeen Letters 1636–1643*, ed. B. N. Teensma, trans. Niels Erik Hyldgaard Nielsen. Rio de Janeiro: Editora Index.

Soly, Hugo, and Wim Blockmans, ed. 1999. *Charles V, 1500–1558, and His Time*. Antwerp, BE: Mercatorfonds.

Souchu de Rennefort, Urbain. [1688] 1988. *Histoire des Indes Orientales*, ed. Dominique Huet. Saint-Clotilde, Réunion: Ars Terres Créoles.

Souto Maior, Pedro. 1912. A Religião Reformada no Brasil no século XVII. Actas dos sínodos e classes do Brasil, no século XVII, durante o domínio holandês. *Revista do Instituto Histórico e Geográfico Brasileiro* 1, no. 1 (1912): 707–80.

Souza, Marina de Mello e. 2002. *Reis negros no Brasil escravista. História da festa de coroação de Rei Congo*. Belo Horizonte, BR: UFMG.

———. 2005. Reis do Congo no Brasil. Séculos XVIII e XIX. *Revista de História* 152, no. 1 (2005): 79–98.

———. 2015. Kongo King Festivals in Brazil: From Kings of Nations to Kings of Kongo. *African Studies Quarterly* 15, no. 3 (June 2015): 39–45.

Spierenburg, Pieter. 1984. *The Spectacle of Suffering: Executions and the Evolution of Repression: From a Preindustrial Metropolis to the European Experience.* Cambridge, UK: Cambridge University Press.

Sponsler, Claire. 2004. *Ritual Imports: Performing Medieval Drama in America.* Ithaca, NY: Cornell University Press.

Stetson, Erlene, and Linda David. 1994. *Glorying in Tribulation: The Lifework of Sojourner Truth.* East Lansing: Michigan State University Press.

Stiles, Henry Reed. 1859. *The History of Ancient Windsor, Connecticut, Including East Windsor, South Windsor, and Ellington.* New York: C.B. Norton.

———. 1867–70. *A History of the City of Brooklyn.* Brooklyn: Pub. by subscription.

Stokes, Isaac Newton Phelps. 1922. *The Iconography of Manhattan Island, 1498–1909,* 6 vols. New York: Robert H. Dodd.

Stott, Annette. 1998. *Holland Mania: The Unknown Dutch Period in American Art and Culture.* New York: Overlook Press.

Strickland, William. [1801] 1971. *Journal of a Tour in the United States of America, 1794–1795,* ed. J. E. Strickland. New York: New York Historical Society.

Stuart, I. W. 1853. *Sketches of Hartford in Olden Times.* Hartford, CT: Stuart.

Stuart, William. 1922. Negro Slavery in New Jersey and New York. *Americana* XVI, no. 4 (October 1992): 347–67.

Stuckey, Sterling. 1994. *Going through the Storm: The Influence of African American Art in History.* Oxford and New York: Oxford University Press.

Sublette, Ned. 2008. *The World that Made New Orleans: From Spanish Silver to Congo Square.* Chicago: Lawrence Hill.

Sullivan, Dennis. 1997. *The Punishment of Crime in Colonial New York: The Dutch Experience in Albany during the Seventeenth Century.* New York: Peter Lang.

Sweet, James H. 2003. *Recreating Africa: Culture, Kinship, and Religion in the African-Portuguese World, 1441–1770.* Chapel Hill: University of North Carolina Press.

———. 2013. The Hidden Histories of African Lisbon. *The Black Urban Atlantic in the Age of the Slave Trade,* ed. Jorge Cañizares-Esguerra, Matt D. Childs, and James Sidbury, 233–47. Philadelphia: University of Pennsylvania Press.

Tanis, James. 1967. *Dutch Calvinistic Pietism in the Middle Colonies.* The Hague: Martinus Nijhoff.

Ter Gouw, Johannes. 1871. *De volksvermaken.* Haarlem, NL: Erven F. Bohn.

Thompson, Henry P. 1882. *History of the Reformed Church at Readington, NJ, 1719–1881.* New York: Board of Publication of the Reformed Church in America.

Thompson, Robert Farris, and Joseph Cornet. 1981. *The Four Moments of the Sun: Kongo Art in Two Worlds.* Washington: National Gallery of Art.

Thornton, John K. 1983. *The Kingdom of Kongo: Civil War and Transition 1641–1718.* Madison: University of Wisconsin Press.

———. 1984. The Development of an African Catholic Church in the Kingdom of Kongo, 1491–1750. *Journal of African History* 25, no. 2 (1984): 147–67.

———. 1988. On the Trail of Voodoo: African Christianity in Africa and the Americas. *The Americas* 44, no. 3 (January 1988): 261–78.

———. 1992. *Africa and Africans in the Making of the Atlantic World, 1400–1680.* Cambridge, UK: Cambridge University Press.

———. 1993. I am the Subject of the King of Kongo: African Political Ideology and the Haitian Revolution. *Journal of World History* 4, no. 2 (1993): 181–214.

———. 1998. The Coromantees: An African Cultural Group in Colonial North America and the Caribbean. *Journal of Caribbean History* 32, no. 1 and 2 (1998): 161–78.

———. 1998. *The Kongolese Saint Anthony: Dona Beatriz Kimpa Vita and the Antonian Movement, 1684–1706.* Cambridge, UK: Cambridge University Press.

———. 2002. Religious and Ceremonial Life in the Kongo and Mbundu Areas 1500–1700. *Central Africans and Cultural Transformation in the American Diaspora*, ed. Linda M. Heywood, 71–90. Cambridge, UK: Cambridge University Press.

———. 2005. African Dimensions. *Stono: Documenting and Interpreting a Southern Slave Revolt*, ed. Mark M. Smith, 73–86. Columbia: University of South Carolina Press.

———. 2007. The Portuguese in Africa. *Portuguese Oceanic Expansion, 1400–1800*, ed. Francisco Bethencourt and Diogo Ramada Curto, 138–60. Cambridge, UK: Cambridge University Press.

———. 2012. *A Cultural History of the Atlantic World, 1250–1820.* Cambridge, UK: Cambridge University Press.

Tiffany, Nina Moore, and Francis Tiffany, ed. 1904. *Harm Jan Huidekoper.* Cambridge, MA: Riverside Press.

Tinhorão, José Ramos. 1988. *Os negros em Portugal. Uma presença silenciosa.* Lisbon: Caminho.

———. 2000. *As festas no Brasil colonial.* São Paulo: Editora 34.

Torfs, Lod, and C.-J. Hansen. 1874. Nederlandsche Krijgs- en Partijnamen. *Annales de l'Académie d'Archéologie de Belgique* XXX, serial number 2, vol. 10: 396–447.

Truth, Sojourner. [1850] 1993. *Narrative of Sojourner Truth*, ed. Margaret Washington. New York: Vintage.

Tuckerman, Bayard. 1893. *Peter Stuyvesant: Director-General for the West India Company in New Netherland.* New York: Dodd, Mead.

Tuckey, James Hingston. 1818. *Narrative of an expedition to explore the river Zaire, usually called the Congo, in South Africa, in 1816, under the direction of Captain J.K. Tuckey, R.N.* New York: W.B. Gilley.

Turner, Victor Witter. 1969. *The Ritual Process: Structure and Anti-Structure.* Chicago: Aldine.

Turpin, Thomas. 1834. Missionary Sketch. *Christian Advocate and Journal*, January 31, 1834.

Udemans, Godefridus. 1640. *'t geestelyk roer van 't coopmansschip.* Dordrecht, NL: Francois Boels.

Updike, Wilkins. 1847. *History of the Episcopal Church in Narragansett, Rhode Island.* New York: Henry M. Onderdonk.

Vainfas, Renaldo, ed. 2000. *Dicionário do Brasil colonial: 1500–1808.* Rio de Janeiro: Objetiva.

Valentine, David T. 1865. *Manual of the Common Council of New York.* New York: D.T. Valentine.

Valpey, Joseph. 1922. *Journal of Joseph Valpey, Jr., of Salem, November 1813-April 1815, With Other Papers Relating to his Experience in Dartmoor Prison.* Detroit: Michigan Society of Colonial Wars.

Van Baerle, Caspar [Caspar Barlaeus]. [1647] 2011. *The History of Brazil under the Governorship of Count Johan Maurits of Nassau, 1636–1644*, ed. Blanche T. van Berckel-Ebeling Koning. Gainesville: University Press of Florida.

Van Bergh, Dina. [1747–48] 1993. *The Diary of Dina Van Bergh*, ed. Gerard Van Dyke and J. David Muyskens. New Brunswick, NJ: Historical Society of the Reformed Church in America.

Van de Graft, Catharina, and Tjaard W. R. de Haan. 1978. *Nederlandse volksgebruiken bij hoogtijdagen.* Utrecht, NL: Het Spectrum.

Van den Boogaart, Ernst, and Pieter C. Emmer. 1979. The Dutch Participation in the Atlantic Slave Trade, 1596–1650. *The Uncommon Market: Essays in the Economic History of the Atlantic Slave Trade*, ed. Henry A. Gemery and Jan S. Hogendorn, 353–75. New York: Academic Press.

Van der Linde, A. P. G. J., ed. 1983. *Old First Dutch Reformed Church of Brooklyn, New York: First Book of Records, 1660–1752. New York Historical Manuscripts: Dutch.* Baltimore, MD: Genealogical Publishing.

Van der Poel, Francisco. 2013. *Dicionário da religiosidade popular. Cultura e religião no Brasil.* Curitiba, BR: Nossa Cultura.

Van der Sijs, Nicoline. 2009. *Cookies, Coleslaw, and Stoops: The Influence of Dutch on the North American Languages.* The Hague: Nederlandse Taalunie.

Van der Vat, Odulfo. 1952. *Princípios da Igreja no Brasil.* Petrópolis, BR: Vozes.

Van der Woude, A. M. 1973. Het gebruik van de familienaam in de 17e eeuw. *Holland* 5 (1973): 109–31.

Van Deursen, Arie T. [1978–81] 1991. *Plain Lives in a Golden Age: Popular Culture, Religion and Society in Seventeenth-Century Holland*, trans. Maarten Ultee. Cambridge, UK: Cambridge University Press.

———. 1974. *Bavianen en slijkgeuzen. Kerk en kerkvolk ten tijde van Maurits en Oldenbarnevelt.* Assen, NL: Van Gorcum.

Van Dixhoorn, Arjan. 2009. *Lustige geesten. Rederijkers in de Noordelijke Nederlanden (1480–1650).* Amsterdam: Amsterdam University Press.

Van Dyke, Rachel. 2000. *To Read My Heart: The Journal of Rachel van Dyke, 1810–1811*, ed. Lucia McMahon and Deborah Schriver. Philadelphia: University of Pennsylvania Press.

Van Epps, Percy M. 1932. *Contributions to the History of Glenville.* Glenville, NY: Glenville Town Board.

Van Goor, J. 1994. *De Nederlandse koloniën. Geschiedenis van de Nederlandse expansie, 1600–1975.* The Hague: Uitgeverij Koninginnengracht.

Van Laer, Arnold J. F., ed. 1932. *Correspondence of Jeremias van Rensselaer 1651–1674.* Albany: University of the State of New York.

———, ed. 1908. *Van Rensselaer Bowier Manuscripts: Being the Letters of Kiliaen van Rensselaer, 1630–1643, and Other Documents Relating to the Colony of Rensselaerswyck.* Albany: University of the State of New York.

———, ed. 1919. Letters of Wouter van Twiller and the Director General and Council of New Netherland to the Amsterdam Chamber of the Dutch West India Company, August 14, 1636. *Quarterly Journal of the New York State Historical Association* 1 (October 1919): 44–50.

———, ed. 1920. *Minutes of the Court of Fort Orange and Beverwyck, 1652–1656*, 2 vols. Albany: University of the State of New York.

———, ed. 1974. *New York Historical Manuscripts: Dutch*, 4 vols. Baltimore, MD: Genealogical Publishing.

Van Lieburg, Fred. 2008. Interpreting the Dutch Great Awakening (1749–1755). *Church History* 77, no. 2 (2008): 318–36.

———. 2009. The Dutch and their Religion. *Four Centuries of Dutch-American Relations 1609–2009*, ed. Hans Krabbendam, Cornelis A. van Minnen, and Giles Scott-Smith, 154–65. Albany: State University of New York Press.

Van Rensselaer, Cortlandt. 1851. *The Presbyterian Magazine*. Philadelphia: Wm. H. Mitchell.

Van Rensselaer, Mrs. Schuyler. 1909. *History of the City of New York in the Seventeenth Century*, 2 vols. New York: Macmillan.

Van Zandt, Cynthia J. 2008. *Brothers among Nations: The Pursuit of Intercultural Alliances in Early America, 1580–1660*. Oxford and New York: Oxford University Press.

Vandenbroeck, Paul. 1987. *Over wilden en narren, boeren en bedelaars. Beeld van de andere, vertoog over het zelf*. Antwerp, BE: Koninklijk Museum voor Schone Kunsten.

Vanderbilt, Gertrude Lefferts. 1882. *The Social History of Flatbush and Manners and Customs of the Dutch Settlers in Kings County*. New York: D. Appleton and Company.

Vanhee, Hein. 2002. Central African Popular Christianity and the Making of Haitian Vodou Religion. *Central Africans and Cultural Transformation in the American Diaspora*, ed. Linda M. Heywood, 243–64. Cambridge, UK: Cambridge University Press.

Vanhee, Hein, and Jelmer Vos. 2013. Kongo in the Age of Empire. *Kongo Across the Waters*, ed. Susan Cooksey, Robin Poyner, and Hein Vanhee, 78–89. Gainesville: University Press of Florida.

Van Wing, Joseph. [1921] 1959. Études Bakongo. Sociologie, religion et magie. Bruges, BE: Desclée de Brouwer.

Venema, Janny, ed. 1998. *Deacons' Accounts 1652–1674 Beverwijck/Albany*. Rockport, ME: Picton Press.

———. 2003. *Beverwijck: A Dutch Village on the American Frontier, 1652–1664*. Albany: State University of New York Press.

Verter, Bradford. 2002. Interracial Festivity and Power in Antebellum New York: The Case of Pinkster. *Journal of Urban History* 28, no. 4 (2002): 398–428.

Very, Francis George. 1962. *The Spanish Corpus Christi Procession: A Literary and Folkloric Study*. Valencia, ES: Tipografía Moderna.

Veurman, B. W. E. 1972. Kinderfolklore. *Folklore der Lage Landen*, ed. TJ. W. R. de Haan, 95–163. Amsterdam: Elsevier.

Von Germeten, Nicole. 2006. *Black Blood Brothers: Confraternities and Social Mobility for Afro-Mexicans*. Gainesville: University Press of Florida.

———. 2008. Introduction. Alonso de Sandoval, *Treatise on Slavery: Selections from De instaurada aethiopum salute*, ed. Nicole von Germeten, I–XXXI. Indianapolis: Hackett.

———. 2013. Black Brotherhoods in Mexico City. *The Black Urban Atlantic in the Age of the Slave Trade*, ed. Jorge Cañizares-Esguerra, Matt D. Childs, and James Sidbury, 248–68. Philadelphia: University of Pennsylvania Press.

Voorhees, David William. 2009. Family and Factions: The Dutch Roots of Colonial New York's Factional Politics. *Explorers, Fortunes & Love Letters: A Window on New Netherland*, ed. Martha Dickinson Shattuck, 129–47. New York: Mount Ida Press.

Vos, Jelmer, David Eltis, and David Richardson. 2008. The Dutch in the Atlantic World: New Perspectives from the Slave Trade with Particular Reference to the African Origins of the

Traffic. *Extending the Frontiers: Essays on the New Transatlantic Slave Trade Database*, ed. David Eltis and David Richardson, 228–49. New Haven, CT: Yale University Press.

Wacker, Peter O. 1975. *Land and People: A Cultural Geography of Preindustrial New Jersey: Origins and Settlement Patterns*. New Brunswick, NJ: Rutgers University Press.

Wade, Melvin. 1981. "Shining in Borrowed Plumage": Affirmation of Community in the Black Coronation Festivals of New England (c. 1750–c. 1850). *Western Folklore* XL, no. 3 (1981): 211–31.

Walker, Daniel E. 2004. *No More, No More: Slavery and Cultural Resistance in Havana and New Orleans*. Minneapolis: University of Minnesota Press.

Warner-Lewis, Maureen. 2003. *Central Africa in the Caribbean: Transcending Time, Transforming Cultures*. Barbados, Jamaica, and Trinidad and Tobago: University of the West Indies Press.

Washington, Margaret. 2009. *Sojourner Truth's America*. Urbana: University of Illinois Press.

Watson, John Fanning. [1830] 1899. *Annals of Philadelphia, and Pennsylvania, in the Olden Time*, 3 vols. Philadelphia: E.S. Stuart.

———. 1846. *Annals and Occurrences of New York City and State, in the Olden Time*. Philadelphia: Henry F. Anners.

Weed, Thurlow. 1866. *Letters from Europe and the West Indies, 1843–1862*. Albany, NY: Weed, Parsons.

Weeks, John H. 1914. *Among the Primitive Bakongo*. London: Seely, Service.

Weise, Arthur J. 1876. *History of the City of Troy: from the Expulsion of the Mohegan Indians to the Present Centennial Year of the Independence of the United States of America*. Troy, NY: W.H. Young.

Wells, A. F., and D. Wells. 1953. *Friendly Societies in the West Indies*. London: Her Majesty's Stationary Office.

Whipple, Henry B. 1937. *Bishop Whipple's Southern Diary, 1843–1844*. Minneapolis: University of Minnesota Press.

White, Shane. 1989. Afro-Dutch Syncretization in New York City and the Hudson Valley. *Journal of American Folklore* 102, no. 403 (1989): 68–75.

———. 1989. Pinkster in Albany, 1803: A Contemporary Description. *New York History* 70, No. 2 (1989): 191–99.

———. 1991. *Somewhat More Independent: The End of Slavery in New York City, 1770–1810*. Athens: University of Georgia Press.

———. 1994. "It Was a Proud Day": African Americans, Festivals, and Parades in the North, 1741–1834. *Journal of American History* 81, no. 1 (1994): 13–50.

White, Shane, and Graham White. 1998. *Stylin': African American Expressive Culture from Its Beginnings to the Zoot Suit*. Ithaca, NY: Cornell University Press.

Wilder, Craig Steven. 2001. *In the Company of Black Men: The African Influence on African American Culture in New York City*. New York: New York University Press.

———. 2005. Black Life in Freedom: Creating a Civic Culture. *Slavery in New York*, ed. Ira Berlin and Leslie M. Harris, 215–38. New York: New Press.

Williams, Jasmin K. 2010. Governor Paterson Ends Ban of African Pinkster Celebration. *New York Amsterdam News*, June 3, 2010, 28.

Williams, Oscar. 1998. *African Americans and Colonial Legislation in the Middle Colonies*. New York: Garland.

———. 2010. Slavery in Albany, New York, 1624–1827. *Afro-Americans in New York Life and History* 34, no. 2 (July 2010):154–68.

Williams-Myers, Albert James. 1994. *Long Hammering: Essays on the Forging of an African American Presence in the Hudson Valley to the Early Twentieth Century.* Trenton, NJ: Africa World Press.

———. 2003. *On the Morning Tide: African Americans, History and Methodology in the Historical Ebb and Flow of the Hudson River Society.* Trenton, NJ: Africa World Press.

Wingens, Marc. 1989. De Pinksterkroon is weer in 't land, hoezee! Het Pinksterkroonfeest in Deventer. *Volkscultuur* 6, no. 2 (1989):7–30.

Winston, Anne. 1993. Tracing the Origins of the Rosary: German Vernacular Texts. *Speculum: A Journal of Medieval Studies* 68 (July 1993): 619–36.

Wittwer, Norman C. 1984. *The Faithful and the Bold: The Story of the First Service of the Zion Evangelical Lutheran Church, Oldwick, New Jersey.* Oldwick, NJ: Zion Evangelical Lutheran Church.

Wood, Peter H. 1974. *Black Majority: Negroes in Colonial South Carolina from 1670 through the Stono Rebellion.* New York: W.W. Norton.

Woolsey, C. M. 1908. *History of the Town of Marlborough, Ulster County, New York, from its Earliest Discovery.* Albany, NY: J.B. Lyon.

Worden, Nigel. 1985. *Slavery in Dutch South Africa.* Cambridge, UK: Cambridge University Press.

Wright, Giles R. 1988. *Afro-Americans in New Jersey: A Short History.* Trenton, NJ: New Jersey Historical Commission.

Wurdemann, John G. 1844. *Notes on Cuba.* Boston: James Munroe.

Yates, Austin A. 1902. *Schenectady County, New York: Its History to the Close of the Nineteenth Century.* New York: New York History.

Young, Jason R. 2007. *Rituals of Resistance: African Atlantic Religion in Kongo and the Lowcountry South in the Era of Slavery.* Baton Rouge: Louisiana State University Press.

Zandvliet, Kees. 2002. *The Dutch Encounter with Asia, 1600–1950.* Amsterdam: Rijksmuseum.

Zijlmans, Jori. 2011. *Leidens Ontzet: vrijheidsstrijd & volksfeest.* Leiden, NL: Primavera Pers.

Index

www.ingramcontent.com/pod-product-compliance
Lightning Source LLC
Chambersburg PA
CBHW031413270326
41929CB00010BA/1434